COMMON DESTINY

This book offers a genuinely comparative analysis of the dictatorships that launched the Second World War: their origins, nature, dynamics, and common ruin. It seeks to understand their similarities and differences historically, without recourse to failed generic concepts such as "fascism." The result is an unconventional and compelling analytical overview from territorial unification in the 1860s to national catastrophe in 1943/45 that places Fascism and Nazism firmly in the tradition of revolutionary mass politics inaugurated in the French Revolution. Set within that overview are three chapters that interpret and explain Mussolini's poorly understood foreign policy and the character and performance of the military instruments upon which Fascist and Nazi success chiefly depended – the Italian and German armies. The chapter on the German army and the conclusion – which dissects the causes of the notable disparities between the two dictatorships in expansionist appetite, fighting power, and staying power – argue that a unique synthesis of Prusso-German military tradition and Nazi revolution propelled Germany's fight to the last cartridge in 1944-45.

MacGregor Knox is Stevenson Professor of International History at the London School of Economics and Political Science, and is writing a comparative history of the Italian and German dictatorships. His other works on Fascist and National Socialist foreign and military policies include *Mussolini Unleashed, 1939-1941: Politics and Strategy in Fascist Italy's Last War.*

COMMON DESTINY

Dictatorship, Foreign Policy, and War in Fascist Italy and Nazi Germany

MacGregor Knox

The London School of Economics and Political Science

PUBLISHED BY THE PRESS SYNDICATE OF THE UNIVERSITY OF CAMBRIDGE
The Pitt Building, Trumpington Street, Cambridge, United Kingdom

CAMBRIDGE UNIVERSITY PRESS
The Edinburgh Building, Cambridge CB2 2RU, UK http://www.cup.cam.ac.uk
40 West 20th Street, New York, NY 10011-4211, USA http://www.cup.org
10 Stamford Road, Oakleigh, Melbourne 3166, Australia
Ruiz de Alarcón 13, 28014 Madrid, Spain

First published 2000

Printed in the United States of America

Typeface Janson 10.5/12.5 pt. *System* QuarkXPress [CTK]

A catalog record for this book is available from the British Library.

Library of Congress Cataloging in Publication data
Knox, MacGregor.
Common destiny: dictatorship, foreign policy, and war in
Fascist Italy and Nazi Germany / MacGregor Knox.
p. cm.
Includes bibliographical references and index.
ISBN 0 521 58208 3
1. Fascism – Italy – History. 2. Italy – Foreign relations – 1922–1946.
3. Italy – Politics and government – 1922–1945. 4. National socialism –
History. 5. Germany – Foreign relations – 1933–1945. 6. Germany – Politics
and government – 1933–1945. I. Title.
DG571.K63 2000
943.08–dc21   99-16896
                                                                        CIP

ISBN 0 521 58208 3 hardback

for Tina

CONTENTS

ACKNOWLEDGMENTS

The essays in this book are explicitly or implicitly comparative. All are the result, either direct or indirect, of a quixotic project conceived fifteen years ago of writing a comparative history of the Western "great dictatorships" of the interwar era, Fascist Italy and National Socialist Germany. My interest in these regimes ultimately derives from the deep impression made upon me by the vivid recollections of my father, Bernard M. W. Knox, of his infantry service in Spain (XI International Brigade, 1936–37), France, and Italy (U.S. Army/Jedburgh/OSS, 1944–45). A childhood year in Florence, amid walls still scarred by German and American machine-gun fire and sporting only partially obliterated Mussolinian exhortations to "live one day as a lion rather than a hundred years as a sheep," further reinforced that impression.

Upon my own return from a far later war, Henry Ashby Turner, Jr.'s brilliantly organized and analytically merciless graduate seminar on "fascism" as a generic phenomenon at Yale University (fall 1970) inspired me to explore the nature and dynamics of the Italian regime. Study of German history and foreign policy under the guidance of my *Doktorvater*, the late and much-missed Hans W. Gatzke, helped to give a comparative dimension to my work on Mussolini's war, which was eventually published in 1982 as *Mussolini Unleashed, 1939–1941: Politics and Strategy in Fascist Italy's Last War* and in Italy somewhat later as *La guerra di Mussolini*. The idea of writing a large-scale comparative work came to me in the early 1980s, and has been with me – along with accumulating piles of notes and manuscript – ever since. There have been times when I thought that no single individual could possibly master even the necessary secondary material, much less conduct the archival soundings that such a project, properly conceived, entails. There have been times, especially during the last five years (four of which were spent doing battle as departmental chairman or its London School of Economics equivalent, "convener," and one of which was largely consumed by a transatlantic family move), when I thought I would never survive to finish the project. But on good days I think I may yet, granted life and health, see "War and Revolution: Origins and Dynamics of the Fascist and Nazi Dictatorships" into print.

Some of the essays that follow are entirely new, and I have extensively revised or recast all previously published work in the hope of welding the collection into a whole greater than the sum of its parts. I wrote Chapters 1 and 5 for this volume. The original version of Chapter 2 appeared in *The Journal of Modern History* 56:1 (1984). Chapter 3 is a much-revised and updated English text of "Il fascismo e la politica estera italiana," pp. 287–330 in Richard J. B. Bosworth and Sergio Romano, eds., *La politica estera italiana, 1860–1985* (Bologna: Il Mulino, 1991), which has not appeared in English. Chapter 4 is a distant descendant, with the addition of a great deal of new material and analysis, of the ground combat portions of "The Italian Armed Forces, 1940–1943," in Allen R. Millett and Williamson Murray, eds., *Military Effectiveness*, vol. 3 (Boston: Allen & Unwin, 1988). And a more detailed version of the conclusion appeared in Richard Bessel, ed., *Fascist Italy and Nazi Germany: Comparisons and Contrasts* (Cambridge University Press, 1996). I am grateful to the Società editrice Il Mulino of Bologna, Cambridge University Press, the University of Chicago Press, and Allen R. Millett and Williamson Murray for permission to reprint or adapt earlier work.

My thanks also to the John Simon Guggenheim Foundation, the Woodrow Wilson International Center for Scholars, the Institute for Advanced Study, and the German Marshall Fund of the United States for their early support of the comparative research from which these essays wholly or partially derive. I thank colleagues and friends, dead and living, old and new, Yale, Rochester, and the London School of Economics, for their long-standing support and encouragement: Sanford Elwitt, Hans Gatzke, and Christopher Lasch; Richard Kaeuper, William McGrath, and Perez and Honoré Zagorin; Paul Preston, Mia Rodríguez Salgado, David Stevenson, and Truman Anderson; Richard Bessel, Andrea Curami, Jürgen Förster, Michael Geyer, Adrian Lyttelton, Denis Mack Smith, Manfred Messerschmidt, Williamson Murray, Giorgio Rochat, and Richard A. Webster. The editor of my first book and of this one, Frank Smith, has been patient and steadfast. Herr Meentz of the Bundesarchiv-Zentralnachweisstelle, Aachen-Kornelimünster, and the Schriftleitung of the Militärgeschichtliches Forschungsamt, Potsdam, gave valuable and timely assistance to my research for Chapter 5. Lucio Ceva, Isabel Hull, and Brian R. Sullivan offered indispensable counsel on the new essays in this volume. Finally, I owe an immense and continuing debt to my parents, Bernard M. W. Knox and Bianca VanOrden, and a growing one to my children, Alice and Andrew Knox.

Above all, I am immeasurably beholden to my wife, Tina Isaacs, to whom, in love and gratitude, I dedicate this book. The faults of commission and omission it undoubtedly contains are nevertheless my responsibility alone.

MacGregor Knox
London, July 1999

ABBREVIATIONS

AAR: after-action report

ACS: Archivio Centrale dello Stato, Rome

ADAP: *Akten zur deutschen auswärtigen Politik* (Baden-Baden, Frankfurt, Göttingen, 1950–) (cited as series/volume/document)

Africa: Mario Montanari, *Le operazioni in Africa settentrionale*, 4 vols. (Rome, 1984–93)

Aloisi: Pompeo Aloisi, *Journal* (Paris, 1957)

AP: *Atti parlamentari* (Rome, various dates) (cited by chamber, year, volume, page, and date)

AdR: *Akten der Reichskanzlei* (Munich, 1968–), cited by chancellor and volume

AHR: *American Historical Review*

BA-MA: Bundesarchiv-Militärarchiv, Freiburg im Breisgau

BA-ZNS: Bundesarchiv-Zentralnachweisstelle, Aachen-Kornelimünster

Bottai: Giuseppe Bottai, *Diario 1935–1944*, ed. Giordano Bruno Guerri (Milan, 1982)

Ciano: Galeazzo Ciano, *Diario 1937–1943* (Milan, 1980)

DBFP: *Documents on British Foreign Policy* (London, 1947–) (cited as series/volume/document)

DDF: *Documents diplomatiques français* (Paris, 1963–) (cited as series/volume/document)

DDI: *I documenti diplomatici italiani* (Rome 1952–) (cited as series/volume/document)

DRZW: *Das Deutsche Reich und der Zweite Weltkrieg* (Stuttgart, 1979–)

GFM: U.S. National Archives microcopy T-120 (German Foreign Ministry files) (cited as serial/frame)

GNR: German Naval Records (NARA T-1022)

Halder diary: Franz Halder, *Kriegstagebuch: Tägliche Aufzeichnungen des Chefs des Generalstabes des Heeres 1939–1942*. 3 vols. (Stuttgart, 1962–64)

HDMG: Militärgeschichtliches Forschungsamt, *Handbuch zur deutschen Militärgeschichte* (Frankfurt am Main, Munich, 1964–81)

HPA: Heerespersonalamt (German Army Officer Personnel Office)

HRSA: Adolf Hitler, *Reden, Schriften, Anordnungen: Februar 1925 bis Januar 1933* (Munich, 1992–)

HSA: Adolf Hitler, *Sämtliche Aufzeichnungen 1905–1924*, ed. Eberhard Jäckel and Axel Kuhn (Stuttgart, 1980)

HVBl: *Heeres-Verordnungsblatt* (Berlin, 1918–)

IWM: Imperial War Museum, Department of Documents, London

MGM: *Militärgeschichtliche Mitteilungen*

MK: Adolf Hitler, *Mein Kampf*, tr. Ralph Manheim (New York, 1971)

MVSN: *Milizia Volontaria per la Sicurezza Nazionale* (Fascist paramilitary and military formations, 1922–43)

NARA: National Archives and Records Administration, Washington, D.C. (cited as microcopy number/roll/frame or record group/box)

NSDAP: *Nationalsozialistische Deutsche Arbeiterpartei* (National Socialist German Workers' Party)

OO: Benito Mussolini, *Opera omnia* (Florence and Rome, 1951–1978)

OKH: Oberkommando des Heeres (German Army High Command)

OKW: Oberkommando der Wehrmacht (Wehrmacht High Command)

PNF: *Partito Nazionale Fascista* (National Fascist Party)

SA: *Sturmabteilungen* (mass paramilitary formations of the NSDAP)

Schmundt diary: Dermot Bradley and Richard Schulze-Kossens, eds., *Tätigkeitsbericht des Chefs des Heerespersonalamtes General der Infanterie Rudolf Schmundt* (Osnabrück, 1984).

SPD: *Sozialdemokratische Partei Deutschlands* (Social Democratic Party of Germany)

SS: *Schutzstaffel* (elite paramilitary formations of the NSDAP, with police and military functions after 1933)

VfZG: *Vierteljahrshefte für Zeitgeschichte*

Introduction

WAR AND REVOLUTION IN EUROPE, 1789–1945

> A war is about to ignite, a war indispensable for consummating
> the Revolution.
>
> – *Maximin Isnard, of the Girondins, 5 January 1792*[1]

The Fascist and Nazi dictatorships were children of the age of mass
politics. They rested on mass mobilization and mass support. They
claimed legitimacy as revolutionary incarnations of genuine democracy against the purportedly inauthentic, plutocratic, and decadent parliamentary regimes of the Western powers. The two dictatorships and
the thirty years' war of 1914–45 that was their natural element illustrated the full extent to which the entry of the masses onto the stage
of world history had failed to produce the universal peace that philoso-
phers had foretold and optimists had celebrated.[2] That regrettable circumstance was no surprise to perceptive students of the dictatorship
and war without mercy that had attended the initial breakthrough of
mass politics in Europe, the revolution in France that had begun in
1789. For as the visionaries of the tumultuous *Assemblée Nationale* that
went to war against most of Europe in 1792–93 dimly perceived, mass
politics had changed statecraft forever. It had fused foreign policy and
domestic politics.

The Revolution overthrew both France's political order and its
external relations. In seeking to reconstitute them, the revolutionaries
concluded that they were "surrounded by snares and perfidy" and
threatened by a "volcano of conspiracies about to erupt." The coun-
terrevolutionary emigrés, the Austrian and Prussian monarchies and

---

1. "Une guerre est près de s'allumer, guerre indispensable pour consommer la révolu-
    tion"; similarly, Jacques-Pierre Brissot, 17 January 1792: *Archives Parlementaires de 1787
    à 1860*, première série, vol. 37 (Paris, 1891), pp. 85, 471.
2. And some political scientists: see among much other recent literature on democracy
    (and implicitly mass politics and modernity) as a remedy for war, Michael W. Doyle,
    "Kant, Liberal Legacies, and Foreign Affairs," *Philosophy and Public Affairs* 12 (1983),
    pp. 209–217, and "Liberalism and World Politics," *American Political Science Review*
    80:4 (1987); for the optimists, see Norman Angell, *The Great Illusion* (London, 1909),
    a work legendary for its poor timing.

1

armies, and the sinister inhabitants of the "catacombs" of conspiracy that metaphorically undermined "nearly all of France" were part of a single all-encompassing web uniting foreign and domestic enemies: ". . . all nobles, aristocrats, and those dissatisfied with the Revolution have united against equality; all the kings of the earth are leagued against us . . ."[3]

France's only apparent recourse was preemptive attack on this "party of despotism" both within and without. A holy war of "peoples against kings" would answer the impending war of "kings against peoples": "Free France [was] on the point of fighting against enslaved Europe." The revolutionaries' ultimate aim was nothing less than "universal liberty" and the salvation of "France and [of] the human race" through a "general rising of all the peoples." Secular apocalypse would answer the driving need – also deeply felt in later revolutions – for an end to the revolutionary process that would harmonize internal and external worlds: "We need a *dénouement* to the French Revolution."[4] Behind the rhetoric in which they fervently believed lay a structural impasse of which the revolutionaries were all too aware. They faced a royal and constitutional government that blocked their vocal demands for total power. The war of 1792 was their reply: a quest for popular mobilization and battlefield triumph that would "consummate" the revolutionary transformation of France and of all humanity.

The aspirations of the revolutionaries perished with them - at least provisionally – under the guillotine, "sword of equality." Their war became within a few years a prosaic national enterprise of conquest and plunder, and ended twenty-three years after it began with France's exhaustion and the restoration of the monarchy. The example of the great upheaval of 1792–1815 deterred great-power war for two generations, for the cautious statesmen who patched Europe together once more believed fervently that foreign and domestic disorder, war and revolution, were inextricably intertwined. Thereafter French weakness

---

3. Isnard, *Archives Parlementaires*, 34:541 (31 October 1791), 39:416 (6 March 1792)("presque toute la France est minée par des souterrains . . ."); similarly, 37:85. A lecture by Timothy Blanning at Princeton University in April 1989 on "Nationalism and the French Revolution" introduced me to the astonishing sources quoted here; see also his *The Origin of the French Revolutionary Wars* (London, 1986); for some of the background, see Carol Blum, *Rousseau and the Republic of Virtue* (Ithaca, NY, 1986); François Furet, *Interpreting the French Revolution* (Cambridge, 1981); and Jacob L. Talmon's indispensable *The Origins of Totalitarian Democracy* (London, 1952).
4. Isnard, *Archives Parlementaires*, 39:416 (6 March 1792), 35:442 (29 November 1791), 37:88 (5 January 1792); Guadet, 36:382 (25 December 1791); Brissot, 36:600 (29 December 1791); Cloots, 36:79 (13 December 1791); Isnard, 37:547 (20 January 1792), 35:67 (14 November 1791).

and the harsh limits that Bismarck set upon the German national movement prevented general European war, while in western Europe telegraphy, railways, repeating rifles, quick-firing artillery, and mass education made 1789-style urban insurrection obsolete.

Only the emergence of Prussia-Germany as a challenger to European and world order after 1890 made revolution practical politics once more. Japan, the most self-consciously Prussian of non-European states, helped. Its defeat of Russia in 1904–05 offered Russia's revolutionaries – among them adherents of a refined and pseudoscientific variant of the revolutionary faith of 1789–94 – the prospect of overthrowing a non-European autocracy ruling a backward peasant society. The revolution of 1905 collapsed, but Germany's bid for world power in 1914–18 opened boundless opportunities.

And not merely for Russian Marxists, although their most ruthless faction seized power by coup d'état in Petrograd and conquered all Russia in the revolutionary civil war of 1918–20. War, Bolshevik terror, and famine thereafter obliterated the shallow-rooted civil society imposed in the previous century on peasant Russia. Soviet dictatorship enserfed the peasantry anew, foreclosed any chance of recreating civil society, and set the mold for revolution and autocracy – in and after the second round of the thirty years' war – in conquered eastern Europe and in the peasant societies of sinified East Asia. The "party of a new type," the disciplined, centralized, militant sect of professional revolutionaries, stabilized the revolution for decades in ways the Girondins and their Jacobin rivals and executioners had – to their own doom – failed to imagine.[5]

The Great War likewise shook the political and social foundations of central and western Europe. Austria-Hungary fragmented into its component nationalities; civil society persisted, although often mutilated through the violent removal of groups suddenly declared alien in lands they had inhabited or ruled for centuries. At the other end of the spectrum of outcomes, the United States, Britain, and even France – which suffered the greatest losses in relation to population of any state in western Europe – emerged in 1918–19 with their social and political systems largely intact.

Italy and Germany, the powers in the middle, were less fortunate. Their civil societies, unlike Russia's, survived war and its aftermath.

---

5. V. I. Lenin, *What Is to Be Done?* (1902); efforts in recent decades by Western social historians of Russia to claim the Bolsheviks of 1917 for democracy while ignoring the determining role of Lenin's party concept are singularly unpersuasive.

But their political systems suffered dislocation or decapitation, and succumbed either soon or late to nationalist rather than Marxist dictatorship. In both cases, enough of the state remained intact that a coup d'état followed by the conquest or erasure of civil society was impractical. Fascist and Nazi dictatorships thus emerged from compromises with older political and social structures. The results were both peculiar and terrifying. Temporary containment of the revolutionary impulse led to an unconscious rediscovery of the mechanism of 1791–92, of the indispensable function of great wars in "consummating the revolution."[6] Why and how that happened, within what limits and with what consequences, is the subject of this book.

6. Readers may find the comparisons drawn here between Girondins, Bolsheviks, Fascists, and Nazis a breach of taste. Yet even before the putrescence of Communism exposed the vanity of its inherently ahistorical claim to be "progressive," it was clear that the widespread assumption that only the Left could make revolutions contained a hidden but indefensible teleology, a claim to know where history was going. When applied to twentieth-century events, that assumption also fell afoul of the obvious confusion between political extremes: were Stalin and Hitler "Left" or "Right"? The term *revolution* is historically meaningful only as a neutral analytical concept applied without fear or favor to any event that fits a clearly articulated definition: (for instance) a violent attempt to achieve rapid, fundamental changes in dominant values and myths, political institutions, social structures, leadership, and government policies (see, in general, Eugen Weber, "Revolution? Counterrevolution? What Revolution?," *Journal of Contemporary History* 9 [1974]: 3–47; Perez Zagorin, "Theories of Revolution in Contemporary Historiography," *Political Science Quarterly* 88 [1973]: 23–52, and "Prolegomena to the Comparative History of Revolution in Early Modern Europe," *Comparative Studies in Society and History* 18 [1976]: 151–74).

Part I

ORIGINS AND DYNAMICS

"Where do we come from, what are we, where are we going?": Paul Gauguin's despairing – or flippant – painting title of 1897 asks historical questions. The first chapter offers one set of answers, with regard to the Italian and German dictatorships, to Gauguin's first question. The second seeks to explore his second and third: the nature, structures, and dynamics of the dictatorships themselves. The first concentrates above all on broader historical forces; the second emphasizes the roles of the dictators and of their ideologies. If read sequentially, the two chapters offer a comparative overview that ranges from innocent beginnings in the 1860s to bloody end in 1945.

1

ITALY AND GERMANY FROM UNIFICATION TO MILITANT DICTATORSHIP, 1860–1933

Fascism and Nazism twisted, or ended, the lives of hundreds of millions of people. Interest in their origins has prospered even in the present era of historical *pointillisme*. The most disdainful adherents of poststructuralist theory or of the social microhistory of everyday life find it difficult to deny that dictatorship, global war, and genocide can ruin your whole day.

The overall structures of the national histories of Italy and Germany from territorial unification in 1860/71 to dictatorship in 1922/33 and defeat in 1943/45 consequently remain subjects of passionate debate. Yet analysts of the origins of the Western interwar "Great Dictatorships" have for the most part avoided systematic comparison as a tool for understanding each country's trajectory. A few scholars have explored resemblances between the processes and consequences of territorial unification in the two cases, or have studied the regimes' structures or particular sectors within them in a comparative way.[1] A vast body of writing linked to the concept of "fascism" (lowercase) has usually assumed a common parentage, sometimes due to shared features of the unification process and aftermath, although

---

1. See in particular Howard McGaw Smyth, "Piedmont and Prussia: The Influence of the Campaigns of 1848–49 on the Constitutional Development of Italy," AHR 55:3 (1950), pp. 479–502; for the movements and regimes, see the fine overviews of Wolfgang Schieder, "Das Deutschland Hitlers und das Italien Mussolinis: Zum Problem faschistischer Regimebildung," in Gerhard Schulz, ed., *Die Grosse Krise der dreissiger Jahre* (Göttingen, 1985)(Italian: *Passato e Presente* 9 [1985], pp. 39–65); "Die NSDAP vor 1933: Profil einer faschistischen Partei," *Geschichte und Gesellschaft* 19:2 (1993), pp. 141–154; "Fascismo e nazionalsozialismo nei primi anni trenta," pp. 45–56 in Angelo Del Boca et al., eds., *Il regime fascista: Storia e storiografia* (Bari, 1995); see also Gustavo Corni, "La politica agraria del fascismo: un confronto fra Italia e Germania," *Studi Storici* 28 (1987), pp. 385–421, and Charles S. Maier, "The Economics of Fascism and Nazism," in his *In Search of Stability: Explorations in Historical Political Economy* (Cambridge, 1987), pp. 70–120.

always within the framework of a generic concept that embraces other cases with entirely different origins and is itself prior to and independent of the evidence.[2]

But most interpretations have followed the well-trodden and exclusive paths of the national historiographical *Sonderwege*. Heinrich von Treitschke and his successors sanctified Germany's supposed distinctness from the West. Hans-Ulrich Wehler denounced it. Savoyard-patriotic orthodoxy proclaimed the uniquely Italian – and triumphant – character of Italy's *Risorgimento* and of the resulting national state. Antonio Gramsci, Communist founder and anti-Fascist martyr, damned that same *Risorgimento* as a betrayal, and Italy's subsequent history as a history of bondage and of permanent, structural estrangement of the Italian people from a state liberal in name only.

When reference to a broad European framework has seemed necessary, authors have usually looked westward rather than across the Alps for yardsticks. German scholars have preferred to compare Germany, whether favorably or unfavorably, to the British "nation of shopkeepers" or to the France that Germany invaded three times and conquered twice in seventy-five years. After 1945 they sometimes rejected comparison altogether, as inappropriate to a national history made forever unique by Auschwitz. Italian historians have sometimes looked wistfully to Westminster, but more often, whether in rejection or emulation, to revolutionary and republican France.

Yet for all the reluctance of the two parties to look southward or northward across the Alps, and for all the discontinuities, incongruities, and gaps between the two national histories and historiographies, common themes and kindred interpretive models have emerged. In Italy, Gramsci offered the most influential sketch of the links between the process of territorial unification, the nature of the unified state, and its dictatorial destiny. He embraced above all the fierce critique of military-monarchical unification under Piedmont enunciated by Giuseppe Mazzini and taken up by the bloodthirsty nationalist prophets of following generations, from the eccentric fin-de-siècle amateur historian-philosopher Alfredo Oriani, to Enrico Corradini of the Italian Nationalist Association, to Benito Mussolini of the *Partito Socialista Italiano*, who privately confessed an admiration for Oriani. Gramsci, Mussolini, and the Nationalists all agreed: the people had "been absent" from unification.

---

2.   Tim Mason, "Whatever Happened to Fascism," pp. 323–31 in his *Nazism, Fascism, and the Working Class* (Cambridge, 1995) offers the concept a decent burial. See also pp. 53-56.

Gramsci annexed that basic insight to Marxism by defining unification as a failed "bourgeois revolution," a *rivoluzione passiva* from above without mass participation. The democrats of the *Risorgimento* had failed to model themselves on the Jacobins, who had carried through France's allegedly exemplary bourgeois revolution by harnessing the peasantry with the all-powerful promise of land to the tillers.[3] The result in Italy, in Gramsci's savage and despairing indictment, was a miscarriage of the historical process. The monarchical "moderates" of the 1860s

> claimed that they sought to create a modern state in Italy, and instead produced a bastard. They sought to constitute a broad and energetic governing class, and they failed. [They sought] to situate the masses within the structure of the state, and they failed. The paltry political life from 1870 to the twentieth century, the elemental and endemic rebelliousness of the popular classes, the niggardly and stunted existence of a skeptical and cowardly governing elite are the consequence of that failure.[4]

Gramsci's overall interpretation of modern Italian history remained confusing and incomplete: his eccentric mixture of Marx and Benedetto Croce, his frequent rethinkings, and the fragmentation imposed by his imprisonment under the Fascist regime made it so.[5] His exegetes nevertheless imposed on his writings a coherent line that runs roughly as follows: the "moderates" and their successors cemented their domination by co-opting, through the infamous process of *trasformismo*, revolutionary democrats such as Francesco Crispi. They sometimes employed foreign expansion to fortify conservatism at home, as in Crispi's Ethiopian adventure of the 1890s, which while it worked "diverted into the boundless distance [*all'infinito*]" the land hunger of the southern peasantry. Above all, they brokered a permanent if informal sociopolitical bargain between northern industry and southern landowners. That *blocco storico* of structure and superstructure, re-cemented under Crispi through protective tariffs, was ostensibly the central political fact of united Italy and the paramount source of the alleged iron continuity between Liberalism and Fascism. For

3. As Luciano Cafagna and others have pointed out, this interpretation of Jacobin agrarian policy is untenable even in the light of work by Marxist scholars such as Georges Lefebvre (Cafagna, "Se il Risorgimento italiano sia stato una 'rivoluzione borghese,'" in his *Dualismo e sviluppo nella storia d'Italia* [Padua, 1989], p. 177).

4. Gramsci, *Il Risorgimento* (*Quaderni del carcere*, vol. 3) (Turin, 1974), pp. 94–95 (my translation).

5. See Luisa Mangoni, "Il problema del fascismo nei 'Quaderni del Carcere,'" in Franco Ferri, ed., *Politica e storia in Gramsci* (Rome, 1977), vol. 1, especially pp. 436–37.

two generations, Italian Marxist historians followed in lockstep the Gramscian vision of Mussolini's regime as a direct and logical continuation, in the new climate of mass mobilization after 1915–18, of Liberal Italy's "dictatorship without hegemony" over the Italian people. A "Prussian-style power bloc" had presided over Italy's road to the modern world.[6]

In Germany, the edifice that Hans-Ulrich Wehler erected on foundations laid by Eckart Kehr in the 1920s and by Hans Rosenberg, Fritz Fischer, and Helmut Böhme in the 1950s and 1960s likewise posited a national history radically distinct from the revolutionary-democratic "model" of England and France: "*Im Anfang steht keine Revolution.*"[7] Thereafter, Bismarck's revolution from above stabilized the domination of the *Junkers* over Prussia and Germany for a further half-century. His post-1871 regime was a "bonapartistic dictatorship" employing the black arts of "negative integration" – the conscious political exploitation of internal and external "enemies of the Reich" – within, and of social imperialism or the calculated export of the social question without. And after Bismarck's turn to protective tariffs in 1878–79, Prussia-Germany too rested upon a *blocco storico*, the infamous "marriage of iron and rye" of East Elbian Junkerdom and Ruhr industry. The resulting continuity, under the sign of the "primacy of internal politics," of "social-imperialist resistance against the emancipatory process of industrial society in Germany," and of the agrarian-industrial "power cartel" led in the end to Adolf Hitler. Nazism was nothing more than an "extreme social imperialism" that "sought by its breakthrough to the 'East' to hold off once again emancipatory progress within and divert [the masses] from their domestic unfreedom." The *Junkers'* manipulative resistance to the modern world was the fundamental source of German exceptionalism in the twentieth century.[8]

But it was the Harvard of the 1960s, in the person of Barrington

6. Gramsci, *Il Risorgimento*, pp. 77, 107; Mangoni, "Il problema del fascismo," p. 393; for "blocco di potere di tipo prussiano," see the very influential Giuliano Procacci, "Appunti in tema di crisi dello Stato liberale e di origini del fascismo," *Studi Storici* 6 (1965), p. 225.

7. Wehler, *Deutsche Gesellschaftsgeschichte* (Munich, 1989–), vol. 1, p. 35; for key elements of this interpretation, see Fischer, *Germany's Aims in the First World War* (New York, 1967); Hans Rosenberg, "Political and Social Consequences of the Great Depression of 1873–1896 in Central Europe," pp. 39–60 in James J. Sheehan, ed., *Imperial Germany* (New York, 1976); Böhme, *Deutschlands Weg zur Grossmacht* (Cologne, 1966).

8. Wehler, *Bismarck und der Imperialismus* (Cologne, 1969), p. 501; *The German Empire 1871–1918* (Leamington Spa, 1985); Fischer, *From Kaiserreich to Third Reich* (London, 1986).

Moore, Jr., that offered a grand comparative synthesis embracing both countries among several others, and combining Kehr's view of Germany with elements found in Gramsci. Moore's *Social Origins of Dictatorship and Democracy: Lord and Peasant in the Making of the Modern World* – which Wehler characterized as "brilliant" – put forward the essentially monocausal theory that the presence or absence of peasant revolution decided whether societies followed the democratic or the conservative-dictatorial road to modernity.[9] In Moore's scheme the revolutions from above of Cavour, of Bismarck, and of the samurai who hurled down the Tokugawa Shogunate in 1868 led with apparent inevitability through "conservative modernization" to "fascism and its wars of aggression, the consequence of modernization without a real revolution."[10]

These ambitious and elegant models now appear quaint. Neither Gramsci's innocent idealization of the bloodthirsty fanaticism of Jacobin France nor Wehler's Whig-theory-of-history model of Britain has aged well.[11] Nor have the authors' specific analyses of the Italian and German cases prospered. Gramsci's assumption that a revolution from below could have made a very different and truly united Italy, and his apparent assertion of the existence of a semipermanent *blocco storico*, as opposed to fleeting parliamentary alignments, rested on flat denial of Italy's immense regional diversity and especially of the pre-unification chasm of several centuries between North and South.[12] Exploration of the manifold divisions between, and the internal fractures of, German agriculture and industry has cast doubt upon the existence or importance of the "alliance of iron and rye" described by Wehler and others.[13] His central thesis, that the German dictatorship

---

9. Boston, 1966; see especially pp. 439–42 (including Moore's acknowledgement of Kehr's "brilliant analysis", p. 441 note 6); Wehler, *Bismarck*, p. 26 note 14. Moore does not refer to Gramsci, who had not yet been widely translated, but some of the latter's theses fit almost seamlessly into Moore's grand theory.
10. Moore, *Social Origins*, pp. 447–52, 506.
11. François Furet and Mona Ozouf, eds., *A Critical Dictionary of the French Revolution* (Cambridge, MA, 1989) offer a useful summary of the post-Marxist view of the French Revolution (see especially the entry for "Terror"); on Britain, see Geoff Eley and David Blackbourn, *The Peculiarities of German History* (Oxford, 1984), pp. 62–74, 98–117.
12. For the odd assertion that the peninsula enjoyed "a relatively homogeneous economic-political structure" after 1815, see Gramsci, *Il Risorgimento*, pp. 96–97; Lucy Riall, *The Italian Risorgimento* (London, 1994), especially pp. 48–49, offers an acute summary of the weaknesses of Gramsci's overall position.
13. See for instance Otto Pflanze, "'Sammlungspolitik' 1875–1886; Kritische Bemerkungen zu einem Modell," in his *Innenpolitische Probleme des Bismarck-Reiches* (Munich, 1983), pp. 153–93, and Henry Ashby Turner, Jr., "Alliance of Elites as a Cause of Weimar's Collapse and Hitler's Triumph?," pp. 205–214 in Heinrich August Winkler

ultimately derived from "social-imperialist" political and ideological manipulation by aristocratic elites, is likewise tenable only with difficulty, as Geoff Eley has suggested, in the light of the grass-roots origins of at least part of the pre-1914 "national opposition," and of that opposition's noisy nationalist hostility to the government of those same elites.[14] And in his latest work, Wehler has appeared to retract his assertion of the primacy of internal politics and has qualified his claims of aristocratic dominance through manipulation, while retaining Bismarck's "charismatic" rule as the deus ex machina that established the noble-industrial "power cartel" that ostensibly set Germany on the path to Hitler.[15]

Moore's cheerful if oblique endorsement of revolutionary bloodshed as the inescapable prerequisite for democracy has also not aged well. His grandiose interpretive scheme itself suffered from its monocausal core, from its erasing of necessary distinctions between his cases, and from its stunning lack of circumstantial detail. If the *Junkers* and their state were the backbone of Germany's conservative modernization, what and where were their Italian agrarian counterparts? Even in Italy's "east Elbia" south of Rome and in the islands, a politically and socially coherent landed interest, much less one whose existence was bound up with state and army, was exceedingly hard to find.[16]

If the prime culprit is not the aristocracy, the obvious remaining class villain, the allegedly unitary "bourgeoisie," seems even more miscast as the protagonist of Italian and German exceptionalism. All Western industrial societies are in some sense "bourgeois," but not all have developed dictatorships.[17] If Germany was just another bourgeois state, if the German bourgeoisie was as strong and well-adjusted as some of Wehler's critics have implied, then how did it give birth to or succumb to a movement and regime with counterparts only in Italy and Soviet Russia, and aiming at racist world revolution? If *fascismo* was simply a new version of "Liberalism" (the quotation marks are Gramsci's) adapted to the post-1914/18 age of mass mobilization, why

and Elizabeth Müller-Luckner, eds., *Die deutsche Staatskrise 1930–1933: Handlungsspielräume und Alternativen* (Munich, 1992).

14. See especially Eley, *Reshaping the German Right: Radical Nationalism and Political Change after Bismarck* (New Haven, 1980).

15. *Gesellschaftsgeschichte*, especially vol. 3, pp. 965–66, 985–89, 990–93, 1276–79, 1284–86; despite nuances, Wehler has saved the basic structure of his earlier interpretation.

16. Gregory Hanlon, *The Twilight of a Military Tradition: Italian Aristocrats and European Conflicts, 1560–1800* (London, 1998) is illuminating on Italy's lack of Junkers.

17. A point Geoff Eley has sought to answer by invoking selectively elements of his opponents' views: "What Produces Fascism?," pp. 254–82 in his *From Unification to Nazism* (Boston, 1986).

did it act in the European arena in such conspicuous defiance of anything recognizable as bourgeois virtues – one of which is elementary prudence?

The embarrassment both of the aristocratic "Prussian road" model of Italian and German aristocratic-conservative modernization leading to fascism, and of its antagonist, the "bourgeois-capitalist road" to fascism, has left a vacuum both at the level of the national histories and at that of comparative explanation. For Germany, Detlev Peukert's imaginative variant – by way of postmodernism and modernization theory – posited that Germany's uniqueness and the source of Weimar's collapse lay in the peculiarly "brutal and uncompromising form" that modernization took in Germany, and the "sudden and simultaneous presence of several different elements of crisis." Stripped of the exotic terminology, this "crisis of classical modernism" appears to revive the familiar social science schema of the superposition – in Germany, and sometimes in the Italy of 1915–22 – of several stages or crises of modernization that in more fortunate societies occurred separately – a view also advanced by Wehler as a corollary to his continuing insistence on the salience of the villainy of Germany's "premodern elites."[18] Peukert's emphasis on the potentially destructive nature of "modernity" is welcome although not new. The National Socialists' fanaticism based on mass literacy and their ballistic missiles built by slaves exemplified it.[19] But Peukert's apparent reduction of Germany's career of conquest and genocide to one extreme "development-possibility" of the modernization process that owed little or nothing to long-standing German peculiarities is neither intrinsically plausible, nor helpful in explaining the particular shape that the Nazi experiment took.[20]

The very real disparities between Italy and Germany and between the literatures about them, the ever-increasing and often lovingly cultivated fragmentation of historical knowledge, and the concentration in recent decades on issues remote from high politics and even from their social and intellectual underpinnings make the persistent explanatory vacuum increasingly difficult to fill. But perhaps the effort is not entirely hopeless.

---

18. Detlev J. K. Peukert, *The Weimar Republic: The Crisis of Classical Modernity* (New York, 1992), pp. 188, 280–81; see also Wehler, *Gesellschaftsgeschichte*, vol. 3, pp. 1292–95, which apparently prefigures that author's approach to Weimar.
19. See also (despite its fundamentally optimistic message) David Landes, *The Unbound Prometheus* (Cambridge, 1969), p. 7: "Change is demonic."
20. Peukert, *The Weimar Republic*, pp. 188, 281; *Max Webers Diagnose der Moderne* (Göttingen, 1989), especially pp. 81–82; see also the remarks of Peter Fritzsche, "Did Weimar Fail?," *Journal of Modern History* 68 (1996), pp. 648–49.

STATES, SOCIETIES, MYTHS

Any attempt at comparative history must start by justifying its choice of cases, which is never self-evident. Italy and Germany nevertheless seem fitted and fated for comparison by their nineteenth-century starting points as "geographic expressions" or stateless cultural nations, by their development of dictatorships in the wake of the war of 1914–18, and by their common ruin in 1943/45. They shared none of these three salient features with other major European societies. In addition, the key areas in the post-1918 gestation of the two dictatorial movements – Bavaria and northern Italy – were far more comparable in their respective levels of economic development than Germany's 5:3 aggregate superiority over Italy in per capita gross national product in 1913 suggests.[21]

The trajectories of the two states and societies divide almost inevitably into three distinct periods: from the era of territorial unification to war in 1914/15; the cataclysm of the Great War; and the aftermath that ended in dictatorship – four short years for Italy, fourteen for Germany. Analysis of the first period will also serve to lay down an overall comparative framework embracing state structures, societies and economies, and national movements and mythologies.

The state must come first, for in both cases it antedated and created the "nation" by acts of will very unlike the slow accretion practiced by the English and French medieval monarchies. The ambitions, diplomacy, and military force of the Piedmontese and Prussian states – in unequal and abortive alliance in 1866 – established the territorial framework within which national societies embodying the preexisting Italian and German high cultures could ultimately emerge from regional, linguistic, and (in Germany) religious fragmentation.[22]

Paradoxically, given their historic roles, both states were absolutist-military border principalities that were or had been eccentric, territorially and intellectually, with respect to their cultures. But there correspondences largely end. The effectiveness of Piedmont's army and state machine made it unique in an Italy that since 1494 had been a land of weak states dominated by foreign great powers, undermined by the Roman theocracy, and almost equally incapable of aggression or

21. For the 5:3 ratio, see Paul Bairoch, "Europe's Gross National Product, 1800–1975," *Journal of European Economic History* 5:2 (1976), p. 286.
22. The role of the two states does not, however, validate the claim of John Breuilly (*Nationalism and the State* [London, 1993], p. 96) that in Italy and Germany "nationalism was more important as a product than as a cause of national unification."

self-defense. Yet Piedmont's effectiveness was merely relative. As late as 1778 its proud aristocratic officer corps – a social formation unique in civic-mercantile Italy – quashed proposals for teaching its members subjects as bookish as mathematics, map making, and the art of fortification.[23] After 1815, repeated political purges, relentless surveillance, and a cult of blind obedience and barrack-square routine under stern clerical supervision stunted its already weak impulses toward learning from the Napoleonic experience. The wars of the *Risorgimento* revealed a stolid old-regime force, often stalwart in defense and capable of winning isolated engagements, but without a high command able to plan and execute a campaign or commanders with a grasp of operational art.[24] Of Italy's first three "wars of independence" – 1848–49, 1859–60, 1866 – the only one that did not end in military disaster and humiliation was the second, in which the French army provided campaign planning and over two-thirds of both troops and casualties. The Italian navy's contribution was the disaster at Lissa in 1866, in which an outnumbered and outgunned Austrian squadron defeated the Italian battle fleet. And despite attempts to "Prussianize" the army in following decades, disaster at Adua against the Ethiopians in 1896 and embarrassment in Libya in 1911 and after appeared to confirm the harsh verdict of 1866.[25]

The political consequences of military malpractice were deep and striking. The notable similarities between the Piedmontese and Prussian constitutions of 1848–49 remained inoperative in essential ways. Italian political culture had since the eighteenth century and especially since 1796 leaned more toward French and British models than had its German counterpart, but it was the military defeat of absolutism that counted most. Charles Albert and Victor Emmanuel II had personally squandered on the battlefields of 1848–49 and 1866 the prestige they needed to control the Liberals whose nationalism they had sought to exploit. Victor Emmanuel's irresponsible and inept handling of Garibaldi's two attempts on Rome in the 1860s and the monarch's hare-brained secret diplomacy, which almost took Italy to

23. Lucio Ceva, "Il problema dell'alto comando in Piemonte durante la prima guerra d'indipendenza," *Il Risorgimento* 37:2/3 (1985), p. 147; also Walter Barberis, *Le armi del principe: La tradizione militare sabauda* (Turin, 1988), Chapter 3.
24. On the Piedmontese army of the Napoleonic era and its lack of resemblance to that of Prussia, see especially Barberis, *Le armi del principe*, Chapter 4; for its performance in 1848, see Ceva, "Il problema dell'alto comando."
25. Nicola Labanca, *In marcia verso Adua* (Turin, 1993) offers acute analysis and much new evidence; for Italy's second major colonial war, see Francesco Malgeri, *La guerra libica* (Rome, 1970).

war against Prussia in 1870, did the rest. The monarchy retained vital residual prerogatives in foreign and military affairs, but its ministers, acting in and through parliament, thereafter had the upper hand.

Prussia took a different path. It had been a European great power since 1740, and utterly outclassed Piedmont in size, force, and efficiency even before the post-Napoleonic settlement gave it much of western Germany, including the as-yet undiscovered coal and iron of the Ruhr. Far more than in the case of Piedmont, the core and reason for being of the Prussian state was its army. Prussia was not merely an army with a state, as eighteenth-century wits had it. It reversed the usual "Western" relationship between military power and society: its army created and formed a society in its own image, first in Prussia's historic lands, then in its eighteenth-century conquests and annexations, then in its 1814/15 acquisitions, and finally in the new Prusso-German Reich after 1866/71.[26]

Contrary to its reputation for blind "corpse-obedience" acquired under Frederick the Great, that army was soon unequaled in its precocious professionalism and readiness to innovate. Shattering defeat at Napoleon's hands in 1806 had opened the road to military reforms in which the army revealed a rare aptitude for learning from experience and for corporate self-criticism, and a unique ruthlessness in purging incompetents.[27] The soldier-king William I took revenge for the demoralizing interlude of 1848–49, when his elder brother, Frederick William IV, had failed to follow expeditiously his generals' prompting to crush "the mob." In 1860 William reasserted through a military reform almost as dramatic as that of 1807–14 the primacy of war as the army's task and the supremacy of the army over society. This "Prussian revolution" brought closer to reality the theoretically universal service established in 1814.[28] The new force structure reduced to insignificance the corps of citizen-officers of the militia created in 1813–14, which had until then represented a significant encroachment upon the regular officer corps' monopoly of force. It also summoned up the decisive constitutional conflict with Prussia's Liberals, patriots all, yet intent on reasserting the primacy of society over the army. The army in retaliation brought in Otto von Bismarck and cowed or crushed its enemies both domestic and foreign in three swift wars. Bismarck and

---

26. Otto Büsch, *Militärsystem und Sozialleben in alten Preussen* (Berlin, 1962), remains the best analysis of the origins and character of the relationship between Prussian army and Prussian society.
27. See Chapter 5 of this volume.
28. For the "Prussian revolution" of 1860–67 and its significance, see especially Michael Geyer, *Deutsche Rüstungspolitik 1860–1980* (Frankfurt a. M., 1984), pp. 25–45.

Moltke the elder thereby rescued not aristocracy – despite their membership in it – but something far rarer historically, and far more dangerous: the supremacy of army over society.[29] But that supremacy, like the new Germany's own "semi-hegemonic" position in Europe, remained precarious.

Diplomacy and war could establish the territorial framework for national societies. But the limited Italian and Prussian wars "from above" of 1859–66, and even the German-national crusade against France in 1870–71, could not and did not create *nations* from populations divided by numerous inherited and deeply etched regional, social, and religious cleavages. The predominant divisions were different and of unequal depth in the two cases, but their net effect was and remained similar, marking these societies off from their far better integrated western neighbors.[30]

In Italy, vertical regional divisions cut deepest. Piedmont grudgingly acquired the South and South-Center in 1860 through what many northerners considered (and still consider) a historical accident or misfortune, the "Garibaldi effect." North and South, despite the misleading congruence of some of their economic statistics at unification, were and remained civilizations apart. By 1900 the North, which had for centuries been richer in agriculture, in banking and commerce, and in the civic culture of its city-states, had acquired mass literacy and a notable industrial core. The South, despite the enclaves specializing in agricultural exports emphasized in recent revisionist historiography, remained a land of destitute peasants, rapacious owners of *latifundia*, and parasitic preindustrial cities.[31]

Germany's regional divides were less deep, and ultimately less crippling to the long-term enterprise of "nationalizing the masses." Occupational distribution and per capita production differences between the industrial West and agrarian East were almost as great by the 1920s as those between the Italian North and South. Yet the developed and rapidly developing regions of Germany contained three-fourths of its population by 1910 – a structure that offered a sort of

---

29. For a similar suggestion, using different terminology and with emphasis on the role of industrialization, see ibid., p. 37.

30, Eugene Weber, *Peasants into Frenchmen: The Modernization of Rural France* (Stanford, 1976) emphasizes France's North-South division, but concedes that even in the most backward recesses of Languedoc, peasants had largely given way to "Frenchmen" by 1914.

31. For the underlying trends, see especially Cafagna, *Dualismo e sviluppo nella storia d'Italia*, pp. 187–220, and Vera Zamagni, *Dalla periferia al centro: la seconda rinascita economica dell'Italia 1861–1990* (Bologna, 1993), Chapters 1–2.

inverted mirror image of Italy, where in 1911 slightly over half the population lived in the Center, South, and islands.[32] And Prussia-Germany's schoolmasters and drill sergeants had imposed 99 percent literacy in German by 1900, a literacy that carried with it loyalties that transcended regional divisions.

The two societies' horizontal social cleavages reversed the relationship that existed between their regional divides. Lines of class and status etched north and north-central Italy, the area roughly comparable socially to Germany, far less deeply and lastingly than they did the German-speaking lands. A perceptive Habsburg functionary, seeking to explain Lombardy to his aristocratic superiors in Vienna in the early 1830s, had put it aptly if with inappropriate scorn: north Italy's nobility was an "artificial and fluctuating aristocracy of money."[33] Italy had a multiplicity of subtle social distinctions, but little – even in the South – resembled the face-to-face *Herrschaft* over "their" peasantry exercised by the East Elbian nobility even after emancipation of the serfs. Above all, nothing in Italy resembled the iron rigidity of German social gradations. The medieval terminology of "estates" or *Stände* showed enormous persistence; the absolutist state had created new functional estates such as officer corps and bureaucracy; and the new classes arising as industrialization advanced after 1840 took on much of the rigidity of the *Stände*.[34] The absence of revolution thus weighed unequally on the two societies. In Germany, as the nineteenth century wore on, mass education encouraged the spread of aspirations that were by definition at least partly blocked – for the German educational system paradoxically acted *both* as a path for social mobility between *Stände* and as a filter that narrowed admission to prized elites such as the officer corps.

Finally, religion divided both societies far more deeply than was the case with their neighbors, reinforcing regional divides and creating political ones. The Italian state's destruction of the Church's temporal power and "unjust, violent, null and void" annexation of Rome had set against the new national state the supreme head of the religion to which over 99 percent of Italy's population nominally belonged. The Church's initial refusal to allow the faithful to participate in national

---

32. See Richard Bessel, "Eastern Germany as a Structural Problem in the Weimar Republic," *Social History* 3 (1978), p. 207; Zamagni, *Industrializzazione e squilibri regionali in Italia* (Bologna, 1978), p. 206; SVIMEZ, *Un secolo di statistiche italiane: Nord e Sud 1861–1961* (Rome, 1961), p. 13.
33. Carl Czoernig, "Über die Ursachen der Revolution in Italien" (1833), quoted in Mario Meriggi, *Il Regno Lombardo-Veneto* (Turin, 1987), p. 110.
34. Wehler, *Deutsche Gesellschaftsgeschichte*, vol. 3, pp. 189, 843–4, is discerning on this.

politics undermined Italy's fitful attempts to expand its restricted electorate from the 1880s onward, and helped poison further the already tense relationship between state and peasantry.

In Germany, the religious division was different in character, but even more durably damaging to national integration in the eyes of many Germans. Catholicism was the religion of 36 percent of the population of the Reich at its founding, and increased slightly thereafter. Against the Roman Catholic Church, as in Italy, stood the state – an intermittent antagonist since jurisdictional clashes between the Rhineland clergy and the Prussian bureaucracy in the 1830s. But unlike the case of Italy or France, the renewed *Kulturkampf* against the Church that followed 1871 was not simply a conflict between the irreconcilable claims of Caesar and those of God. The Prussian Liberals who made their peace with Bismarck after 1866 indeed fought it as a struggle between modernity and the Middle Ages, rationality and obscurantism. But the core of the conflict, and the ultimate source of its intractability, lay in the clash between *two* theocracies, the Roman and the Hohenzollern. Gradual movement toward compromise in the 1880s and the emergence of the Catholic Center Party as a "state-supporting" force by the 1890s in no way diminished the Protestant character of the Prussian state and its role as defender of the faith of Prussia-Germany's Protestant majority. The state's claim to the mantle of Luther and Calvin, when added to the regional division between the almost exclusively Protestant North and East and the partially or predominantly Catholic West and South, gave German religious disunity a peculiarly bitter and lasting edge.

Cleavages in society do not inevitably become political fractures; the relative autonomy of politics is the first precondition for effective government.[35] Italian Liberalism survived after 1860 by incorporating southern local interests into its parliamentary majorities, and by tolerating the takeover of the state machine by the South's immense surplus of unemployed lawyers and *dottori*.[36] Yet in both Italy and Germany, the process of territorial unification and the advance of capitalist techniques, when superimposed on preexisting regional, social, and reli-

---

35. For this thesis, see Paolo Farneti's classic, *Sistema politico e società civile* (Turin, 1971), especially pp. 60–114, and his "Social Conflict, Parliamentary Fragmentation, Institutional Shift, and the Rise of Fascism: Italy," in Juan J. Linz and Alfred Stepan, eds., *The Breakdown of Democratic Regimes* (Baltimore, 1978), pp. 3–4.

36. On this *meridionalizzazione* of the state, see especially Sabino Cassese, *L'amministrazione centrale* (Turin, 1984); for the post-1860 South's overproduction of learned unemployed, see Massimo Barbagli, *Disoccupazione intellettuale e sistema scolastico in Italia (1859–1973)* (Bologna, 1974), pp. 62–63, 139–52.

gious divisions, produced a remarkably similar pattern of political fractures.

In both cases, a nationalist "majority subculture" – lay and liberal in
Italy, Prussian-monarchical and staunchly Protestant in Germany –
centered upon the unitary state. In both cases this subculture, in part
because it controlled the state, failed to develop a unitary mass party.
In Liberal Italy, the *"grande partito liberale"* hailed by luminaries such
as Antonio Salandra was no party at all, but an amorphous majority
formed with lip service to liberal values and imperfectly glued together by "favours received or indiscretions detected and overlooked."[37] In
Germany, National Liberals, Left-Liberals, and Conservatives split
the voters of the Prusso-German camp among them, and only the
Conservatives developed the beginnings of a mass-party base by orga-
nizing the peasantry after 1890 against foreign agricultural competition, cities, and Jews.

In both cases the national *"Lager"* – the German word for armed
camp seems peculiarly apt – faced two mighty and seemingly irreconcilable adversaries. First was organized Catholicism, with its organizational bases in the Church, the Catholic lay organizations and, in
Germany from the 1870s and Italy after 1919, in cohesive national
mass parties, the Center and the *Partito Popolare Italiano*. Second came
the socialists, who in Germany had divided from their would-be liberal patrons in the 1860s, and in Italy had emerged by the 1890s from
the seething radical republicanism and anarchism of areas such as
Emilia-Romagna. All four subcultures suffered early from persecution,
exclusion, or self-exclusion: the *Kulturkampf*, the enduring Roman
cold war between Liberal state and Vatican theocracy, Bismarck's anti-
socialist laws, and Liberal Italy's frequent use of administrative exile as
a political argument and of army firepower as a collective bargaining
tool. Each subculture emerged with its character set in fierce opposition to the existing order. And each began its political career in a system of stunted parliamentarism, in which the narrow electoral law
(Italy) or the federal structure, absence of electoral reapportionment,
and absolutist executive (Germany) deflected the full force of mass
politics, and secured the effortless domination of the national camp.

The third bundle of decisive forces acting on the trajectories of Italy
and Germany from the unification era to the Great War and after
derived from the national movements and mythologies. These had
originated and grown outside and in part in opposition to the states

37. As the British ambassador put it in early 1914 (quoted in Simon M. Jones, *Domestic
   Factors in Italian Intervention in the First World War* [New York, 1986], p. 36).

that ultimately presided over territorial unification. That was a condition virtually unique among great power or would-be great power nationalisms; it meant that neither of the two nationalist movements, in their crucial formative years, needed to accept or even acknowledge the constraints of domestic or international reality.

That freedom had perilous consequences. Mazzini, who virtually invented and formed (or deformed) Italian nationalism in his own image, proclaimed that politics was and must be a *fede*, a militant total faith to which all other aspects of life were and must be duly subordinate. He also claimed without apology a world mission for Italy. After the Rome of the Caesars and that of the Church, the "third Rome" of the Italian people was coming, and with it an age in which Italy would give "a new and more powerful Unity to all the nations of Europe." That "third and still vaster Unity" would not erase national distinctions within the harmonious "Europe of the peoples" of Mazzini's imagination, yet Rome would nevertheless be its center and its borders would unquestionably encompass all Italian-speakers as yet unredeemed. Mazzini was seemingly unable to imagine that nationalisms might conflict, that neighboring Germans and Slavs might resist, and that the naked ferocity of the "first Rome's" legions might be the only means of inducing Europe to accept Italian primacy. Yet his successors, from Oriani to the Nationalists to Mussolini, came soon enough to revel in the immense bloodshed demanded by the national mission and by its minimum requirement, that Italy become the true great power it still so clearly was not.

German nationalism was even more explosive. Its origins in the revolt of Germany's intellectuals – against French culture before 1789 and French domination after 1800 – gave it a bitterness not found in Italy, where the literate classes had tended to perceive French conquest after 1796, for all its bloodshed and exactions, as welcome release from inept or corrupt governments and from the crushing weight of the Church.[38] German nationalism possessed, thanks to its origins at the intersection of philology, post-Kantian philosophy, and the Protestant apocalypse, a certainty in its claims to world primacy that eluded rivals both in Italy and elsewhere. It had begun to develop, long before the arrival of Darwin in Germany, an exclusiveness based on blood and a definition of the nation that was inextricably intertwined with hatred of Europe's oldest minority: that which was German was that which

---

38. On the role of *ressentiment* as a core element of "late-comer" nationalisms, see Liah Greenfeld, *Nationalism: Five Roads to Modernity* (Cambridge, MA, 1992), pp. 15–17, 222–74 (Russia), 371–95 (Germany).

was not Jewish.[39] And it subsumed within the national cult the worship
of great men representative of the essence of the *Volk*, from Arminius
through Frederick Barbarossa-sleeping-under-the-Kyffhäuser to
Martin Luther. Its growing European territorial and world-power
aspirations, ably summed up at Frankfurt in 1848, were to erect "a
giant Reich of 70 millions, and if possible of 80 or 100 millions, and
plant the standard of Arminius in that Reich, to stand there armed
against east and west, against the Slavic and Latin peoples, to wrest
mastery of the seas from the English, and to become the most powerful *Volk* on this earth."[40]

The victories of Bismarck and Moltke did not found this tradition;
attempts to depict German nationalism as a comparatively harmless
and liberal phenomenon until diverted from its natural road to the
modern world by the intervention of *Junker* blood and iron are profoundly implausible in the light of the megalomania that the
Bildungsbürgertum, the German learned upper middle classes, so amply
displayed in 1848.[41] Prussia's triumphs were politically indispensable
to the eventual outcome: they created a militant military-minded
German Reich. But ideologically they merely confirmed and strengthened preexisting tendencies. World history, as the Protestant apocalyptic tradition had suggested, now indeed became the Last Judgment
("*Die Weltgeschichte ist das Weltgericht*"). The Germans were the most
"favored race in the struggle for life." Great men still walked abroad,
booted and spurred, doing God's work through German might. The
further expectations thus aroused made Mazzini's lunacy seem modest
and benign.

The nation-states that actually emerged could not have failed to disappoint movements such as these. Italian *literati* from Mazzini himself

39. Klaus Vondung, *Die Apokalypse in Deutschland* (Munich, 1988); Paul L. Rose, *German
     Question / Jewish Question: Revolutionary Antisemitism in Germany from Kant to Wagner*
     (Princeton, 1990), especially p. 41.
40. Count Friedrich Deym, in *Stenographischer Bericht über die Verhandlungen der deutschen
     constituirenden Nationalversammlung zu Frankfurt am Main* (Leipzig, 1848–49), vol. 4, p.
     2882. For the context, see Lewis Namier, *1848: The Revolution of the Intellectuals*
     (Garden City, NY, 1964), and the courageous work of Günter Wollstein, *Das
     "Grossdeutschland" der Paulskirche: Nationale Ziele in der bürgerlichen Revolution 1848–49*
     (Düsseldorf, 1977).
41. For Wehler's comforting identification of 1866–71 as the point at which German his-
     tory left the rails, *Gesellschaftsgeschichte*, especially vol. 3, pp. 1284–87; for some of the
     mass of contrary evidence, see, among much other work, Leonard Krieger, *The German
     Idea of Freedom* (Chicago, 1972), and Wollstein, *"Grossdeutschland" der Paulskirche*.
     Wehler's own occasional references to the undeniable peculiarity of the *Bild-
     ungsbürgertum* and the explosive character of German nationalism – both nonaristo-
     cratic features of the German *Sonderweg* with pre-Bismarckian origins – betray a cer-
     tain unease.

to the poet Giovanni Pascoli to Mussolini railed at the inadequacies of post-*Risorgimento* Italy: its alien Savoyard dynastic core, the drabness and corruption of its politics, its seemingly congenital inability to achieve genuine national integration, and its repeated battlefield failures. But those same *literati* had a sovereign remedy, widely held but best summed up by Oriani in 1889:

> War is an inevitable form of the struggle for existence, and blood will always be the best warm rain for great ideas. . . . The future of Italy lies entirely in a war which, while giving it its natural boundaries, will cement internally, through the anguish of mortal perils, the unity of the national spirit.[42]

Italy's conquest of Libya in 1911–12 perhaps served as "make-up exam," in the words of the young liberal-nationalist historian Gioacchino Volpe.[43] But it signally failed to bring unity, unleashing rather the revolutionary antinationalism of the Socialist *massimalisti* under Mussolini's fervent leadership. Nor could a passing colonial victory amid renewed evidence of military bungling erase the enduring shame of Custoza, Lissa, and Adua. Only a truly great war could satisfy the thwarted internal and external aspirations of the Italian national cult.

A similar quest for natural boundaries and beyond, and for the unity of the national spirit on a far greater scale and with far wider and deeper impact, was the essence of post-1871 German nationalism. Bismarck, like Cavour, had created a state that on sober reflection seemed almost the negation of the aspirations of a nationalist movement for which Germany's natural frontiers, at least since the Napoleonic era, ran "as far as the German tongue resounds."[44] In 1866 Bismarck had expelled the Germans of Austria from *his* Germany by force for good Protestant, Prussian, and *Junker* reasons. The Dual Alliance of 1879, celebrated by nationalists on both sides of the Austro-German border as a quasi-federal *Nibelung*-bond, was no substitute for the yearned-for Reich of 70 millions, nor could it protect the Germans of Austria-Hungary from ever-deepening submersion in a sea of lesser breeds.

Prussia's now-accomplished mission in Germany also clearly mandated, in good Hegelian fashion, a German mission in the world.

---

42. Oriani, *Fino a Dogali* (Bari, 1918 [1st ed. 1889]), p. 126; for this remedy's wide appeal, John A. Thayer, *Italy and the Great War* (Madison, 1964), especially Chapters 8–9; Mario Isnenghi, *Il mito della grande guerra da Marinetti a Malaparte* (Bari, 1970), Chapters 1–5; and Federico Chabod, *Storia della politica estera italiana dal 1870 al 1896*, vol. 1, *Le premesse* (Bari, paperback ed., 1971), pp. 31–33.
43. "Esame di riparazione": *Giovanni Belardelli, Il mito della "nuova Italia": Gioacchino Volpe tra guerra e fascismo* (Rome, 1988), p. 19.
44. Ernst Moritz Arndt, "Vaterlandslied" (1812), in his *Gedichte* (Halle, n.d.), pp. 86–87.

Treitschke proclaimed it in words that – doubtless consciously – echoed the navalist enthusiasms of the Frankfurt Parliament: a "final settling of accounts with England." Max Weber noted more guardedly in his famous 1895 inaugural that "the unification of the Reich was a youthful frolic that the nation . . . should have avoided, if it should merely prove to be the conclusion rather than the starting-point of a German world power policy." The era of the independent intellectual was now waning; mass agitation suited to the new age was becoming the order of the day. And the organization that best embodied the increasingly extreme world view of the German nationalist movement was the Pan-German League, founded in 1891 and steadily more influential in German politics to 1914 and beyond. Its foremost leader, Heinrich Class, was a sometime pupil of Treitschke who had imbibed some of his national spirit from a family friend, an old revolutionary of 1848 and "south German democrat of the first water." In his most famous work, a best-seller of 1912–14 hopefully entitled *If I Were the Kaiser*, Class insisted openly that Germany's external mission and internal salvation alike demanded blood: "Whoever loves his nation and seeks to hasten our present illness to its crisis, will yearn for war, the awakener of all the good, healthy, robust forces in the *Volk*."[45] Even a less bellicose figure than Class – the would-be political theorist Kurt Riezler, who as confidant and counselor to Chancellor Theobald von Bethmann Hollweg after 1909 complained guardedly of the naive "faith in violence" by-then universal among German nationalists – was moved as early as 1911 to note in his diary the widespread "authentically German idealistic (and correct) conviction that the *Volk* needs a war." "This conviction," Riezler significantly added, "Bethmann likewise shares."[46]

German convictions also included the expectation of mythic leadership. The foremost historian of his generation, Friedrich Meinecke,

45. Wolfgang J. Mommsen, *Max Weber und die deutsche Politik 1890–1920* (Tübingen, 2nd rev. ed., 1974), p. 74. On "borussianisches Geschichtsdenken" from Droysen to Treitschke and Lenz, see especially Wolfgang Hardtwig, "Von Preussens Aufgabe in Deutschland zu Deutschlands Aufgabe in der Welt," *Historische Zeitschrift* 231:2 (1980); for Class, see his *Wider den Strom*, pp. 19–20 and 14–16 ("Mir war Treitschke der Meister, der mein Leben bestimmte"), and (pseud. Daniel Frymann) *Wenn ich der Kaiser wär'* (Leipzig, 5th exp. ed., 1914), pp. 53–54, 182–83; also Peter Winzen, "Treitschke's Influence on the Rise of Anti-British Nationalism in Germany," pp. 155–56, 161–63 in Paul Kennedy and Anthony Nicholls, eds., *Nationalist and Racist Movements in Britain and Germany before 1914* (London, 1981).
46. Kurt Riezler: *Tagebücher, Aufsätze, Dokumente*, ed. Karl Dietrich Erdmann (Göttingen, 1972), p. 180; for Riezler on German nationalism, see his *Grundzüge der Weltpolitik in der Gegenwart* (pseud. J. J. Ruedorffer) (Stuttgart, Berlin, 1914), pp. 111–12.

was like Riezler a relatively moderate member of the *Bildungs-bürgertum*, yet he expressed the widespread discontent "with the notion of our nation as a great spiritual corporate body [*geistige Gesamtpersönlichkeit*]; for we long for a Führer for the nation, a Führer for whom we can march through fire."[47] And Heinrich Class, while calling for war, for depriving the German Jews of citizenship, and for a new Bismarck to replace the current "weakling [*unbrauchbares*] sovereign" (the Emperor William II), also ventured the chilling prediction that should the coming inevitable and yearned-for war bring defeat, "the present internal fragmentation [*innere Zerrissenheit*] will lead to such chaos that only the mighty will of a dictator will be able to bring order once more."[48]

The impact of nationalist doctrines in the two countries inevitably varied with the nature of those doctrines and of the surrounding culture, the strength of countervailing forces, and the extent of literacy – for reception of all such notions presupposed command of the written word. In Italy, the intelligentsia's lust for foreign conquest and integrative violence was weaker in its impact than in Germany for at least four reasons. First, the cultural building blocks available to Italian ideologues did not include *either* the Hegelian-Protestant philosophies of history *or* the pseudoscientific notions of race common in Germany. A deficit in fanaticism was the result. Second, Italian nationalism failed to develop an equivalent to the German cult of the national Führer. Rome and its emperors were impossibly remote. Garibaldi for all his military prowess was wise enough to recognize his own limitations as a political leader. Third, the Church provided both intellectual and structural barriers to the "nationalization of the masses" in Italy. It viewed religion rather than blood as the overriding division within the human species, and preached, without always practicing, the doctrine that "we are all brothers." Its supreme chief held a virtual monopoly of charismatic leadership on the peninsula. Except in the North, the secularization process that increasingly sapped the position of German Protestantism – leaving a vacuum that only nationalist belief could fill – had not appreciably weakened Italian Catholicism's millennial position as the focus of peasant loyalties. The absence of religious competition also made Italian Catholicism's position vis-à-vis the state immeasurably stronger than that of its German counterpart. Fourth and finally, Italy's relatively low levels of literacy proved an enduring

47. Quoted in Elizabeth Fehrenbach, *Wandlungen des deutschen Kaisergedankens* (Munich, 1969), p. 91.
48. Class, *Wenn ich der Kaiser wär'*, pp. 53–54, 182–83, 74–78, 222.

barrier to the popularization of the national cult, whereas mass education and secularization – the very foundations of modernity – were also the foundations of German nationalism's claim to total power.

THE HAMMER OF WAR, 1914–18

Historical development is in principal open-ended: much in politics, on the battlefield, and in everyday life turns on chance and individual peculiarities. But we also make our history not as we please but "under circumstances directly found, given, and transmitted from the past." And neither in Italy nor in Germany was participation in the Great War that made dictatorship possible entirely accidental.

The elites of both countries willed war in ways not found elsewhere. Germany willed it first, and thus made a great war possible for Italy and for all of Europe. And in Germany, two forces – the *Bildungs-bürgertum* and the army – willed it. The intelligentsia's contribution was indirect, in proclaiming over decades the sanctity of German violence and in fostering after 1900 an atmosphere in which, as Moltke the younger suggested hopefully in 1912, a suitable casus belli might move the nation to "unanimously and fervently [take] up arms."[49] The army's role was direct and decisive. Its leaders demanded war repeatedly after December 1912 – war to rescue the Reich from its worsening strategic position, but also to rescue the position of the officer corps at the apex of the German social pyramid. For once the armaments and strategic railways of the Russians and the French were ready in 1916–17, Germany had no hope of offensive victory, and the "first *Stand*" would no longer be able to claim that it alone held the key to national salvation. That unthinkable humiliation could only be prelude to demotion to the status of a mere functional elite, like the military establishments of other powers. Those who must have a German domestic social cause for the catastrophe of 1914–18 need look no further.

In Italy, "we two alone" – as Salandra smugly put it – Salandra and his foreign minister, the high conservative Sidney Sonnino, willed war with the approval of King Victor Emmanuel III. Their inspiration was the external and internal ambitions shared throughout the Italian educated classes, fear of the wrath of those same classes, and in Salandra's

---

49. Moltke memorandum, 16 December 1912, in John C. G. Röhl, "An der Schwelle zum Weltkrieg: eine Dokumentation über den 'Kriegsrat' vom 8. Dezember 1912," MGM 1/1977, p. 118.

case the aspiration – which one might at a pinch call "social-imperialist" – to give the Liberal regime through victory new foundations resistant to the advance of the Socialist and Catholic mass organizations.

But fear was the most powerful goad: fear that no regime could survive that spurned the chance to complete the *Risorgimento* through the conquest of Trento and Trieste, and to seize Adriatic supremacy and Ottoman and colonial booty. Italy's choices, as a member of the inner circle, Ferdinando Martini, put it, were ". . . to be a Great Power or not to be one; to remain monarchical or – with the fall of the monarchy – to place in danger even its [territorial] unity; to be masters in our own house, in *mare nostrum*, or condemned to centuries of servitude."[50] These perilous notions were a sort of unconscious echo, in a minor key, of German fears and ambitions: "world power or downfall," Italian style.

War when it came did not at first disappoint the nationalist prophets in either land. The mobilization of the German masses for bogus self-defense in the "August Days" of 1914 was the last great hour of the *Bildungsbürgertum*. For a brief instant it led an outpouring of national enthusiasm that seemed, both to its members and to outside observers, to have obliterated all regional, *Stand*, class, and religious cleavages. Four years and 2.5 million dead cooled German enthusiasm, but in a crucial respect the intoxication was lasting. The August Days seemed to show that national integration in Germany was *possible*. They offered a standard against which to judge and find wanting the Imperial regime and its eventual parliamentary successor.[51]

In Italy, the intelligentsia played a direct role in precipitating war that had been denied it in Germany. "We two alone," Salandra and Sonnino, were not enough – without unsolicited help from the piazza – to overcome the hostile majority in parliament left them by their great predecessor, Giovanni Giolitti, who had led Italy almost uninterruptedly from the turn of the century to 1914. In the "radiant May"

---

50. Sidney Sonnino, *Diario 1914–1916* (Bari, 1972), p. 18; Olindo Malagodi, *Conversazioni della guerra (1914–1919)* (Milan, 1960), vol. 1, pp. 31–32, 46; Ferdinando Martini, *Diario 1914–1918* (Milan, 1966), p. 407 (7 May 1915).
51. Recent attempts to debunk the "myth" of the August Days betray a degree of naiveté. That German war-enthusiasm was less than total – although demonstrably more intense than in France – is no great surprise. What is significant is that so many of those who passed through the August Days believed that national integration, however briefly, had in fact been achieved – and could be achieved again. See the useful analysis of Peter Fritzsche, *Germans into Nazis* (Cambridge, MA, 1998), pp. 17–30; Jean-Jacques Becker, *1914: Comment les français sont entrés dans la guerre* (Paris, 1977), offers a standard of comparison.

of 1915, the poet-aesthete Gabriele D'Annunzio, the Mazzinian-republican and syndicalist agitators, the fiery defectors from Socialism led by Mussolini, and the Nationalists all combined to conquer the squares of Italy's cities for the cause of war. Their enthusiastic violence coerced Giolitti, parliament, and ministers and king alike. D'Annunzio, who virtually invented the hitherto nonexistent role of Italian nationalist Führer, put the issue then and later in terms borrowed directly from Oriani: war was "a baptismal font to purify [Italy] of the filth, pusillanimity, and cowardice of centuries"; only "an immense slaughter" could bring the necessary "steel-like unity."[52]

That unity was even more partial and short-lived than its German counterpart. Both countries, for reasons deriving from their geostrategic situations and foreign policies as well as from their internal politics, fought the war up to, and in Germany's case beyond, the edge of political disintegration. Their civil societies survived, but war deepened old cleavages and opened new ones, exacerbating in both cases beyond all previous experience the *innere Zerrissenheit* that war was to have healed. And in the end, war made both countries ungovernable.

The simple bipartite clash between Prusso-German elite and German masses, between Hindenburg-Ludendorff high command and Independent Socialists, between "victory-peace" and "peace of reconciliation" proposed by historians from Arthur Rosenberg to Jürgen Kocka, is wholly inadequate to describe 1914–18 reality in Germany, much less to explain the revolution without revolutionaries of 1918.[53] By 1917 the Reich had fractured *politically* – within rather than between its parties, and into small irreconcilable groups or tendencies – under the crosscutting of multiple and distinct conflicts over war aims, conduct of the war, reform of the franchise and executive, and the gospel emanating from revolutionary Petrograd. Germany likewise fractured *socially* under the hammer of war: fear, death, semistarvation, separation, and the claustrophobia of a continent-wide siege. The estrangement between elites and urban masses was only one of many deep gulfs that opened: between Catholics and Protestants, Jews and Gentiles, Prussians and Bavarians, gaunt city dwellers and sleek peasants, *Frontkämpfer* and "rear-echelon swine" – a much-hated category that included Germany's entire male industrial workforce. Above all,

52. Quoted from Tommaso Gallarati Scotti, "Idee e orientamenti politici e religiosi al Comando Supremo: appunti e ricordi," in Giuseppe Rossini, ed., *Benedetto XV, i cattolici e la prima guerra mondiale* (Rome, 1963), p. 513.
53. Arthur Rosenberg, *Imperial Germany: The Birth of the German Republic 1871–1918* (Boston, 1964 [1928]); Jürgen Kocka, *Klassengesellschaft im Krieg: Deutsche Sozialgeschichte 1914–1918* (Göttingen, 1973).

the war was the hour of Germany's anti-Semites, who had no Italian counterparts. In a society besieged by what it perceived as a ring of demonic enemies, the agitation of Class and his associates swiftly gained ever-wider acceptance.[54]

In Italy, "radiant May" had been a phenomenon of the northern cities and the Roman mob, of the *literati* and students and agitators who imposed and fought Italy's war as a civil war. The *interventisti* had cowed but not destroyed the Socialist party, which with its slogan of "neither support nor sabotage" took a position from the beginning far distant from the measured faithfulness to the national cause of the Social Democratic Party of Germany (SPD). Italy's warrior-agitators had ridiculed and defied the Vatican and had browbeaten organized Catholicism. And through the state they had helped plunge into war, they had coerced the peasants who ultimately suffered three-fifths of Italy's casualties.[55]

But those who had launched Italy's war by intimidation in pursuit of an idea failed to dominate either parliament or the masses with that idea. Italy's intervention and disputes over the conduct of war irretrievably clove the Liberal ruling class. Parliament's only potential governing majority deferred to Giolitti and his "friends" in parliament, who with an ambiguity that drove the *interventisti* to frantic charges of treason, resolutely evaded sharing responsibility for the war. The *interventisti* themselves fractured into a multiplicity of groups over war aims and methods in the Adriatic and beyond.[56] And the government allowed Italy's Erich Ludendorff, General Luigi Cadorna, to bully it mercilessly until his removal by defeat in November 1917.

In society at large, the strains of war further estranged Catholics from *interventisti*; the Pope's August 1917 description of the war as a "useless massacre" tarred the Catholic subculture in both Italy and Germany with the brush of treason. Above all, the war cracked open the city-country and North-South cleavages. Peasant infantrymen,

---

54. See in general Werner Jochmann, "Die Ausbreitung des Antisemitismus," in Werner E. Mosse, ed., *Deutsches Judentum in Krieg und Revolution 1916–1923* (Tübingen, 1971), and Uwe Lohalm, *Die Geschichte des Deutschvölkischen Schutz- und Trutz-Bundes 1919–1923* (Hamburg, 1970), pp. 46–76.

55. On peasant casualties, see Virgilio Ilari, *Storia del servizio militare in Italia* (Rome, 1989–), vol. 2, p. 437, and Arrigo Serpieri, *La guerra e le classi rurali italiane* (Bari, 1930), p. 42.

56. Vittorio De Caprariis, "Partiti politici e opinione pubblica durante la Grande Guerra," *Atti del XLI congresso di storia del Risorgimento italiano* (Rome, 1965), pp. 73–149, offers by far the most acute analysis of Italian politics in 1915–18; see also Piero Melograni, *Storia politica della grande guerra 1915/1918* (Bari, 1969), and Roberto Vivarelli, *Storia delle origini del fascismo* (Bologna, 1991), vol. 1, especially the discussion of war aims, Chapter 2, sections 1–2, and Chapter 3, section 1.

many of them from the South, faced with perplexity and distrust an officer corps drawn from the landowning classes who governed Italy, and greeted with outright hatred the *interventista* volunteers in their own ranks. But above all, and in flagrant defiance of Leninist orthodoxy, the peasant infantry hated the urban workers – whose bewildered Turin insurrection of August 1917 they unquestioningly drowned in blood.[57]

In both Italy and Germany, armies and societies nevertheless proved capable of final supreme efforts. Italy's Bainsizza plateau offensive of August 1917 almost broke the Austro-Hungarian army. When the Germans, aided by the inadequacies of the Italian army's higher leadership, cracked the front at Caporetto in October 1917, 294,000 of Italy's peasant soldiers surrendered with little apparent shame. But other Italian units – cut off for once by swift movement and communications failure from the influence of the high command – slowed and then stopped the Germans short of Venice and Verona with a flexible and tenacious defense. At home, defeat galvanized the *interventisti* to organize Italian nationalism, for the first time in its history, into a genuine if amorphous mass movement. A "*fascio* of national defense" in parliament linked to "committees of internal resistance" at the periphery stood firm with Jacobin zeal against "enemies without and saboteurs within" in the expectation of final victory.[58] And victory was not denied. For in the Battle of Vittorio Veneto of October 1918 that crowned Italy's war, the army high command, after much prodding from the politicians, for once laid down a sound operational concept and executed it with skill and drive.

In Germany, the national camp likewise mobilized in 1917–18 against Catholic and Socialist threats, and gave birth to a far mightier organization than the "*fascio* of national defense." The "German Fatherland Party" proclaimed by Admiral Alfred von Tirpitz, father of the German battle fleet, on Sedan Day, 2 September 1917, was with-

---

57. Labanca, *Caporetto* (Florence, 1997), and Labanca, Giovanna Procacci, and Luigi Tomassini, *Caporetto: Esercito, Stato e Società* (Florence, 1997) provide useful introductions to the immense literature; on the Turin events, see especially Alberto Monticone, *Gli italiani in uniforme* (1915–1918) (Bari, 1972), pp. 89–144; Paolo Spriano, *Torino operaia nella Grande Guerra* (Turin, 1960), Chapter 10; Luigi Ambrosoli, *Né aderire né sabotare 1915–1918* (Milan, 1961), pp. 229–37; on the infantry's pervasive contempt for the workers, see the testimony of Leonida Bissolati, in Malagodi, *Conversazioni*, vol. 1, pp. 165–66.

58. See especially Giovanna Procacci, "Aspetti della mentalità collettiva durante la guerra: L'Italia dopo Caporetto," pp. 261–89 in Diego Leoni and Camillo Zadra, eds., *La Grande Guerra: Esperienza, memoria, immagini* (Bologna, 1986), and Franck Demers, "Caporetto e il sorgere del fascismo a Cremona," *Storia Contemporanea* 8:3 (1977), pp. 533–48.

in a year the largest mass organization in Germany, with up to 800,000 followers to the SPD's war-shrunken 243,000. The *Vaterlandspartei* in both ideology and membership was the concentrated essence of the Protestant-north German national *Lager*. It sought to "rekindle the burning enthusiasm of August 1914," and in countless leaflets and speeches it hammered home the message that at this culminating moment of the war the sole hope of Germany's enemies was Germany's internal disunity: "Germany Awake! Thine hour of destiny has arrived."[59]

Indeed it had. Defeat in the West despite the supreme last effort of Ludendorff's spring 1918 offensives destroyed utterly a national morale that had held up in the expectation of victory, despite all Germany's fragmentation. With the realization that sacrifice no longer had a purpose, the German army melted away through desertion. The remaining bonds holding Germany's social groups together and to the national cause broke. Navy mutinied and army crumbled in a vast military strike, and Woodrow Wilson's apparent insistence on withholding peace from Germany's "military masters and monarchical autocrats" forced the Kaiser's abdication and flight. Not social and political polarization – for where was the storming of the Tuileries or even of the Winter Palace? – but a sort of despairing negative unanimity was the source of the monarchy's almost bloodless collapse.

Despite the apparent differences between Italian victory and German defeat, both political systems and societies emerged from 1914–18 with unhealing wounds. In each case, society remained fragmented and politics shattered, although the survival of the Italian monarchy helped the Italian establishment preserve more cohesion than its German counterpart. In each case, the national movements remained radically and bitterly unsatiated. Italy's ungrateful allies mutilated – in D'Annunzio's famous phrase – its far-reaching war aims, and those same allies mutilated Germany territorially while temporarily demoting it from great power status. In both cases, although with far greater force and a radical anti-Semitic coloration in Germany, the myth of the *Frontkämpfer* as a new and pure elite stabbed in the back by the Left and the home front arose and flourished. In both cases, the

---

59. Tirpitz speech at Königsberg, 2 September 1917, in Fischer, *Germany's Aims in the First World War*, p. 432 (an eerie sound recording also exists); *Vaterlandspartei* founding proclamation in Heinz Hagenlücke, *Deutsche Vaterlandspartei: Die nationale Rechte am Ende des Kaiserreichs* (Düsseldorf, 1997), endpaper (pp. 180–87 for membership figures and composition); manifesto of the Brandenburg branch, 3 November 1917, in Ralph H. Lutz, ed., *Documents of the German Revolution: Fall of the German Empire, 1914–1918* (Stanford, 1932), vol. 1, p. 371.

peace of 1918 was merely the perpetuation of nationalist wars both foreign and domestic.[60]

In Germany two further conditions added to the explosiveness of the postwar situation. The decapitation of the state and the army's treaty limitation to 100,000 officers and men destroyed the strategic, political, and social preeminence the army had established over the previous two and a half centuries. Defeat, as an assistant of Luden-dorff's put it in October 1918, meant a world in which German offi-cers would "eke out their existence impoverished and but little regard-ed."[61] That was a world for the overthrow of which the officer corps, re-tempered in defeat as in 1807, would spare no effort and shrink from no sacrifice whether or blood or of principles. And German defeat also intensified beyond previous measure the culturally and politically overdetermined yearning for a Führer. On 11 November 1918, Germany's blackest day, a prominent Prussian pastor expressed in a letter to his son a widely felt sentiment: ". . . we were without lead-ership, that was our cruel fate and in vain we stand here: God give us a man!"[62] That was a prayer too soon answered.

THE "COLLAPSE OF LIBERAL REGIMES"?

The immediate causes of the advent of dictatorship in both societies in 1919–33 have occasioned much spilled ink over the allegedly inherent terminal iniquities and dysfunctions of capitalism, the mechanisms of the "collapse of liberal regimes," and Germany's alleged "crisis of clas-sical modernity." The first line of interpretation is too indiscriminate to explain why Germany and the United States, the advanced capital-ist societies hardest hit by the Great Depression, received Adolf Hitler and Franklin Delano Roosevelt respectively as their rulers in 1932–33. The third – at least as advanced by Peukert – likewise fails to register certain obvious distinctions between Germany and other societies that also exemplify the nebulous concept of "modernity." And the second line of investigation too often rests on the Whiggish assumptions that

---

60.   Bernd Ulrich and Benjamin Ziemann, eds., *Krieg im Frieden: Die umkämpfte Erinnerung an den Ersten Weltkrieg* (Frankfurt am Main, 1967) offers a useful sampler of the war's persistence in Germany.
61.   Albrecht von Thaer, *Generalstabsdienst an der Front und in der OHL* (Göttingen, 1958), p. 240 (9 October 1918).
62.   Friedrich Lahusen (Berlin) to his son, 11 November 1918, quoted in Arlie J. Hoover, *God, Germany, and Britain in the Great War* (Westport, CT, 1989), pp. 120–21.

liberal parliamentarism is the norm, and that functioning parliamentary regimes existed in post-1918 Italy and Germany.

In reality, neither country had enjoyed parliamentary government based on mass politics before 1914/15. The war, by arousing or inflaming appetites and spreading myths that no liberal regime could satisfy or fulfill, made the early creation of such governments improbable. The central historical issues are less why dictatorship came than why it was so long delayed in Germany, and why in each case it took the form it did.[63]

The Italian and German paths from parliamentary government to a cabinet formed around the leader of a paramilitary nationalist party were remarkably similar, once allowances are made for key differences between the two societies and their politics. In each case, three broad phases are discernible: a period of parliamentary instability and increasing fragmentation and paralysis (summer 1919–summer 1921 in Italy; the far longer 1919–1930 interlude in Germany). There followed a period of swift deterioration driven by the Fascist military conquest of north and central Italy on the one hand and by Nazi electoral triumphs *and* street violence on the other (summer 1921–summer 1922 in Italy, March 1930–May 1932 in Germany). Then the final crises (July–October 1922, June–January 1932–33) consumed the last of the ever-fewer alternatives to Mussolini and Hitler.

The first phase emerged with seeming inevitability from the war, which had deepened each country's preexisting cleavages, created new ones, and helped to make fiercely political those cleavages that were not already so. Italy's postwar elections, held in November 1919, were the country's first under unrestricted universal male suffrage and proportional representation, which the Socialists and Catholics had demanded and which the Liberals had grudgingly conceded in the hope of rescuing some shred of their former predominance in the Socialist and Catholic strongholds of north Italy.[64] The masses, maddened by years of privation and sacrifice and by the prospect of

---

63. Pessimism about Weimar's long-term prospects has at last belatedly ousted the bizarre recriminations of the 1960s and 1970s about the Republic's alleged betrayal by the SPD; see especially the judgment of Gerald D. Feldman that Weimar was a "gamble which stood virtually no chance of success" ("Weimar from Inflation to Depression: Experiment or Gamble?," in Feldman, ed., *Die Nachwirkungen der Inflation in der deutschen Geschichte* [Munich, 1985], p. 385).

64. See Serge Noiret, *La nascita del sistema dei partiti nell'Italia contemporanea: La proporzionale del 1919* (Bari, 1994) and "Riforme elettorali e crisi dello Stato liberale. La 'proporzionale' 1918–1919," *Italia Contemporanea*, March 1989, pp. 29–51.

revenge, saw the election as a referendum for or against the "war of the *signori*." The result was cataclysmic.

In place of the still-comfortable 1913 liberal majority of three-fifths of the Chamber of Deputies, three great camps emerged almost equal in strength (170-odd Liberals, 100 Catholics, and 159 Socialists out of 508 seats) and utterly irreconcilable in their beliefs and leading personalities. The Liberals had long divided ideologically along the Left-Right spectrum. Bitter personal rivalries estranged Giolitti, Salandra, Vittorio Emanuele Orlando, Francesco Saverio Nitti, and their followers. And war had cloven the Liberals into *interventisti* and neutralists, each bent on vindication and revenge. Not even the Socialist threat or shared hostility to the Catholics could overcome these divisions. The new *Partito Popolare*, for its part, announced its intention of wresting the state from the Liberals and reconquering Italian society for Catholicism – an objective both Liberals and Socialists were bound to contest bitterly. And the Socialists emerged from the war dazzled by the light from the East, by the prospect of "doing like Russia." With parliament thus savagely divided, no stable governing majority was possible.[65]

But from the beginning parliament took second place to the streets and the countryside. The downtrodden peasantry took literally the government's wartime promise of land to its peasant infantrymen, and sought in 1919–20 to seize and divide the great estates of the South and center, and to revolutionize land rights and ownership in the North. Socialist agricultural and industrial unions in the Po Valley imposed, with the frequent use of force, increasingly draconian terms on landlords, tenant farmers, and shopkeepers, while laying siege to the remaining liberal positions in local politics. On the Right, mutinous army units and young officers occupied the Adriatic city of Fiume – perched uneasily between Italy and Yugoslavia in the absence of an agreed border – in September 1919 under the histrionic leadership of D'Annunzio. The Socialists' verbal revolutionism in the national arena and vengefulness and spite at the local level made them political pariahs. The failure of their unplanned quasi-insurrectionary seizure of industrial plants across north Italy in September 1920, and their local election defeats in most important northern cities that autumn marked the culmination of their inept assault on the social and political order.

65. On the autism of the Socialists and the ambitions of the *Popolari*, see especially Vivarelli, *Origini del fascismo*, Chapter 2; Farneti, "Rise of Fascism," pp. 8–12 (1919–20), 23–26 (1921–22), provides an acute summary of the mutual hostilities of and internal divisions within all three blocs.

Giolitti, who had returned to power for the last time in June 1920, waited confidently for the Socialists to subside, and crushed D'Annunzio's mutiny with naval gunfire during the "Christmas of Blood" that December.

Stabilization in the course of 1921 should have ensued. But it did not. The Socialists had failed to seize power in the streets. Socialists and Catholics, divided by bitter ideological conflict, by local rivalries in the northern countryside, and by Socialist violence, were incapable of combining in parliament to take power jointly. And even the formidable Giolitti proved unable to rule in 1920–21 without a majority that he could only have secured at a price unacceptable to an old anticlerical accustomed to effortless domination over all non-Liberal forces. Yet Italy's problems could not wait: state, economy, and industry had emerged from the war in need of comprehensive and painful structural reforms, a requirement made more acute by severe recession in 1920–21. The need to balance the budget, shore up the balance of payments, stabilize the lira, postpone or pay war debts, rehabilitate a tottering banking system, and salvage or downsize in an orderly way the overextended heavy industrial complexes that had grown chaotically during the war would have taxed any statesman or governing coalition.[66]

In postwar Germany, by contrast, leftist and rightist insurrection, political assassination, French invasion, and hyperinflation failed to make orderly government impossible. The eclipse of the monarchy had so shattered the north-German Protestant nationalist *Lager* that it lost control of the executive, if not of army and bureaucracy. The Catholics and majority Socialists, through their stalwart if not universally appreciated participation in the 1914–18 war effort, could lay effective claim to the succession. With the SPD leading, they hesitantly stepped in to rule. Friedrich Ebert, SPD union leader and former saddler (as his enemies never tired of repeating), became the first president of the German Republic. SPD and Catholic willingness to collaborate with one another both in the Reich and in Prussia – where they governed jointly until 1932 – neutralized both Left and Right extremists, and saved parliamentary government for a decade.

Yet the Republic's seeming stability was deceptive. The third pillar of the "Weimar coalition" of 1919, the left-Liberals of the German Democratic Party, swiftly collapsed in the catastrophic election of June 1920, and fragmented thereafter under the influence of the ultra-pro-

66. See especially Douglas J. Forsyth, *The Crisis of Liberal Italy: Monetary and Financial Policy, 1914–1922* (Cambridge, 1993), Chapters 6–7.

portional Reichstag electoral law of 1920, which permitted – or
encouraged – the rise of the numerous splinter parties that diverted
votes from the parties of government.[67] The electoral disaster of 1920
had effects less severe than Italy's 1919 election, but the Republic
lacked coherent majorities for the rest of its fitful existence: during the
celebrated golden age between consolidation in 1924 and the fall of
the Müller government in 1930 no fewer than seven cabinets came and
went. All rested only on ad hoc majorities formed around individual
issues. And the electoral outcome also showed conclusively how few
non-Socialist and non-Catholic democrats Germany possessed; the
national *Lager*'s voters and the majority of its leaders overtly or covert-
ly rejected the Republic. Field Marshal Paul von Hindenburg's triumphant campaign for the Reich presidency in 1925, a sort of electoral reunion, brokered by Tirpitz in person, of the constituency of the
Vaterlandspartei, drove that message home.[68]

This precariousness could not lead to disaster – yet – largely because of the Versailles Treaty so often damned as the root cause of
Weimar's destruction. Versailles left the German elites, despite their
lamentations over its allegedly boundless iniquities, with something
vital still to lose: the territorial unity of Bismarck's Reich. The foremost threat to that unity was the French army standing guard in the
Rhineland; while it remained, the national *Lager* could not coalesce
around a militant alternative to the German Republic without risking
preventive war and partition.

It was during this preliminary phase that challengers inevitably
arose in both countries to claim the vacant leadership of the nationalist camp. The preexisting national myths and the impact of the war
determined their character. The Italian and German nationalist "parties of a new type" of 1919 and after bore a relationship to their precursors analogous to that between the Bolsheviks and the parties of the
Second International. But unlike the Soviet case, war was all-important to their genesis and nature, not merely to their triumph. In Italy

---

67. See especially the contrafactual simulations of Jürgen W. Falter, *Hitlers Wähler*
    (Munich, 1991), pp. 126–35, which graphically illustrate the electoral system's contri-
    bution to the Republic's instability: in a first-past-the-post system, the Weimar coali-
    tion would probably have preserved absolute majorities until 1932. Giovanni Sartori,
    "The Influence of Electoral Systems: Faulty Laws or Faulty Method?," pp. 43–68 in
    Bernard Grofman and Arend Lijphard, eds., *Electoral Laws and Their Political
    Consequences* (New York, 1986), offers satisfying analysis of the underlying theoretical
    issues.
68. On the politics of the 1924–28 period, Michael Stürmer, *Coalition und Opposition in der
    Weimarer Republik 1924–1928* (Düsseldorf, 1967) remains useful; for the 1925
    Hindenburg majority and its close correspondence to the 1930 and 1932 Hitler votes,
    see Falter, *Hitlers Wähler*, pp. 123–25, 359–63.

and Germany the war not only persisted into "peacetime," but also offered a new politics, a new individual and organizational model: the "political soldier." That term, wielded by figures as superficially unlike as Giuseppe Bottai – assault troop commander and literary Fascist – and Heinrich Himmler, defined the essence of the new nationalist politics and the new nationalist warfare that was its core. That warfare was by definition total, annihilational, and omnidirectional, at once against the "internal enemy" and the external world. It aimed simultaneously at that true national integration missed or only momentarily grasped in the Great War and at the now twice-frustrated external goals of the two national cults.

The war also offered, even in Italy where the role was not overdetermined by history, models of charismatic leadership. The youthful leaders – of infantry platoons, companies, and battalions – who survived the great slaughter had learned somehow to inspire their men. The *Arditi*, Italy's picked assault troops and prototypical political soldiers, developed a style of military leadership based on professional skill, dash, personal magnetism, and ideological commitment that was entirely foreign to the passive obedience unto death that the Piedmontese-Italian *Regio Esercito* prized. That new style had its postwar political uses. And at least one individual seized upon the war he had helped to launch in order to create a personal cult. D'Annunzio had spent 1915–18 happily drunk on words and blood – "The Italians must be driven by fury to seek nourishment from the brains of their enemies." He had greeted wrathfully "the ghastly stench of peace."[69] The role he had created for himself as poet-warrior and national prophet outlived both peace and ultimate fiasco at Fiume. His example and his liturgy lacked the broad resonance guaranteed by Germany's "expectation of a Führer," but D'Annunzio nevertheless offered a model that a more politically astute leader could exploit. Without "the Poet's" example Mussolini might have remained what he initially was to the turbulent Po Valley chieftains, "the guy with the newspaper."[70]

War and aftermath opened the road to the two movements by creating new constituencies and reshuffling old ones. Demobilization flooded both countries with "military desperadoes" – whose neglect, in

---

69. Quotations: Tommaso Gallarati Scotti, "Idee e orientamenti . . . al Comando Supremo," p. 513; Mario Silvestri, *Isonzo 1917* (Milan, 2nd ed., 1971), p. 51.
70. "Quello del *Popolo d'Italia*": Emilio Gentile, *Storia del partito fascista 1919–1922: Movimento e Milizia* (Bari, 1989), p. 295; Richard A. Webster, "La vocazione messianica di Gabriele D'Annunzio," *Nuova Antologia* 2194 (April–June 1995), pp. 88–101, is instructive on the origins of D'Annunzio's role as national *vate*.

most interpretations of the demise of Liberal Italy or of Weimar, Wolfgang Sauer once noted with the jibe that "the military is apparently still not a category for social analysts."[71] Both countries also produced a student generation, avid for violence, that had just missed the war. Students and veterans of the *Arditi* were the most prized of Mussolini's recruits to his new movement in winter–spring 1919, and former junior officers and students provided the backbone of the Fascist gangs of 1920–21. In Germany, the returning warriors and disappointed youth made the open and then covert civil war of 1919–23. The reduction of the army to 100,000 by the Versailles Treaty, the inherited confusion between social and military rank, the much-heightened postwar barriers to entry into the *Offizierstand*, and the enduring military-mindedness of the German young built in a structural pressure for nationalist violence that persisted until the Republic's successor sated those appetites to the very fullest.

In both countries the old enemies of the national camp were likewise the enemies of the new dictatorial-revolutionary movements. The *Fasci di Combattimento* met with toleration or support from prefects, police officials, officer corps, and Liberals of all stripes, but also appealed to a far wider constituency. The Socialist rural offensive of 1919–20 rested above all on the landless laborers, and threatened not only the landowning *signori* of the urban middle classes but also the numerous landed peasants who had done well in the war. That strategic error sealed the Socialists' fate. The Fascist movement, infinitely more expert in violence than the Socialists who had so long ranted about revolution, found a rural mass base in 1920–21 through its attack on the Slovenes and Germans of the newly conquered borderlands and on the Socialist and Catholic peasant unions and local administrations of the Po valley. Its structure was above all paramilitary, even after its transformation into a political party, the *Partito Nazionale Fascista* (PNF), in November 1921. Its aims were a seamless mixture of nationalist revenge on the alleged saboteurs of the war effort and mutilators of victory, and class war against the Socialist agrarian unions and local leaders. Social and ethnic geography confined it, as a native growth, to north Italy and the few regions in the South that the Socialists had penetrated. By mid-1921 it was nevertheless over 200,000 strong, and confident and well-armed enough to claim to lead the nation, and to create its internal unity and external glory through violence.[72]

71. Sauer, "National Socialism: Totalitarianism or Fascism?", AHR 73:2 (1967), p. 411.
72. See in general Adrian Lyttelton, *The Seizure of Power: Fascism in Italy, 1919–1929* (Boston, 1972), pp. 54–71; Gentile, *Movimento e milizia*, Chapters 1–3; Renzo De

In Germany, the "Marxists" and "political clerics" were likewise the new movement's targets, while Wilhelmine judges blinked at nationalist murders and generals eager for rearmament beamed upon the "splendid youths" of the nationalist militias. Yet the German state and army held firm against nationalist temptation. The Right rose twice, in the essentially traditionalist Berlin Putsch of March 1920 of Wolfgang Kapp, founder of the *Vaterlandspartei* alongside Tirpitz, and in the Munich "Beer Hall Putsch" of the new right-radicalism, led by Adolf Hitler and inspired by the Italian example of nationalist revolution, in November 1923. Both broke on the rock of the Reich presidency and the abstention or counteraction of the army, which remained grudgingly neutral in 1920 and enforced Ebert's authority and the constitution through a long period of martial law in winter 1923–24. Failure and temporary imprisonment after its Putsch forced the Nazi leadership, much against its inclinations, to abandon thoughts of an insurrectionary "march on Berlin," to confine its paramilitary violence to targets on the far Left, and to seek local and national power primarily through the creation of a mass party that would conquer the electorate for the "National Socialist Idea."[73]

The National Socialist German Workers' Party (NSDAP) refounded after 1925 fiercely repudiated and denounced all sectarian appeals, whether to religion or to class. Even as it broke out northward from its south German birthplace, it far transcended the Protestant-national subculture that nevertheless voted for it disproportionately from 1930 onward. It proclaimed itself the militant mass party of German nationalism, of revolt against the verdict of 1918 and against the innere Zerrissenheit of Empire and Republic that had allegedly led to and perpetuated defeat. It promised the restoration of national unity and power, and to its followers it offered above all the career open to talent – or criminality – that its Führer himself symbolized.[74] It was Germany's first genuinely modern political party, in its unsurpassed agitational techniques, its appeal to the future rather than the past and

Felice, *Mussolini il fascista* (Turin, 1966–68), vol. 1, pp. 8–9 (table) and Chapter 1; for the extremist foreign policy aspirations of the early movement, Giorgio Rumi, *Alle origini della politica estera fascista (1918–1923)* (Bari, 1968).

73. Schieder, "Fascismo e nazionalsozialismo nei primi anni trenta," pp. 46–51, documents the extent to which Hitler and his associates saw, and sometimes publicly invoked, the Italian dictatorship as a model before 1933.

74. Much recent sociological work on the pre-1933 NSDAP and electorate, for all its sophistication in handling data, rests on primitive and ahistorical assumptions about the determination of voting behavior by material interests: see especially William Brustein, *The Logic of Evil: Social Origins of the Nazi Party, 1925–1933* (New Haven, CT, 1996) and Thomas Childers, *The Nazi Voter: The Social Foundations of Fascism in Germany, 1919–1933* (Chapel Hill, NC, 1983). Richard F. Hamilton, *Who Voted for Hitler?* (Princeton, 1982) and Falter, *Hitlers Wähler*, offer more sophisticated views.

to mobility rather than Stand, and in its recruitment across class and confessional lines. By 1929 it was ready to bid for supremacy within the national camp.

Attempts by leaders in that camp to redraw a political map they had come to view as intolerable opened the second phase of the process that led to dictatorship in both countries. By spring 1921, Giolitti found his footing in the 1919 parliament too narrow to support the drastic economic reforms that Italy's postwar situation demanded. He therefore called early elections for May 1921 in the hope that Fascist violence had cut the Socialists and *Popolari* down to size and would force them to accept his leadership on his terms. He also courted the Fascists themselves with marked benevolence, and legitimized their violence by including them in the government-sponsored "national bloc" election lists. Mussolini's movement, which had failed to gain entrance to parliament in 1919, thereby conquered 35 seats: Mussolini himself demonstrated his mastery of the Liberals' middle-class constituency by accumulating 370,000 votes and finishing first in both the Milan and Bologna areas. And contrary to Giolitti's expectations, the new parliament proved even more fragmented and less capable of supporting stable Liberal government than its predecessor.

That outcome and Giolitti's consequent swift resignation in June 1921 effectively ended parliamentary rule in Italy. Giolitti's puny successors, Ivanoe Bonomi and Giolitti's chief lieutenant, Luigi Facta, failed either to secure reliable majorities or to govern. A banking crisis and sharp recession further sapped the government's position in winter 1921–22. The *Popolari* flatly vetoed Giolitti's return until too late, while the PNF seized and held the political initiative, manipulating the ambitions of conservative Liberals and Catholics and the infantilism of the Socialists to block the formation of a hostile parliamentary coalition. At the periphery, the Fascist *squadre* destroyed what little remained of the government's power and prestige; in summer 1922 large-scale motorized raids, their passage "marked by lofty columns of fire and smoke," smashed the few remaining Socialist strongholds in the Po Valley and north-central Italy, and unhinged Facta's cabinet in Rome.[75]

In Germany, the second phase opened with more deliberation and less publicity than in Italy – and before the full impact of the Depression that is too often invoked as the decisive cause of dictatorship.

---

75. For the phrase, and vivid description of the reality, see Italo Balbo, *Diario 1922* (Milan, 1932), especially pp. 95–110.

Unlike the situation in Italy, but with much significance for the future shape of Europe, it was the army that forced the issue. The *Reichswehr* had since the mid-1920s evolved a phased rearmament plan designed – with the utmost professionalism of which that supremely professional organization was capable – to reestablish German hegemony in Europe. The first phase, from 1928 to 1932, was still – although barely – compatible with Weimar's budgetary and political framework. But the "second rearmament plan," designed to run from 1933 to 1938 and drafted from 1927–28 onward in increasingly detailed form, was something else again. It aimed at a "minimum objective" – on the road to far greater things – of an army and air force "of assured fighting power and operational capabilities with modern equipment and adequate logistical support."[76]

The road to that goal led through a mobile twenty-one-division army – roughly three times the permitted Versailles Treaty strength – as a first "provisional" milestone. Yet even that lesser objective required the total subordination of Weimar's foreign and budgetary policy to *Reichswehr* requirements, and the removal of Versailles Treaty restrictions on military training for Germany's youth. Progress beyond twenty-one divisions – a force equal to Poland's army alone – would in the planners' view require the complete reconstruction of German society and politics, in accordance with the notions of the total war of the future developed by army theorists since 1919.[77]

The foremost barrier to the realization of this grandiose vision was not the Western powers, whose feeble objections to German rearmament the army easily swept aside in 1932–33. It was internal: as recently as 1926 a key SPD figure had denounced to the Reichstag the army's violations of the Versailles Treaty and its clandestine ties to the Red Army, and the SPD had fought the 1928 election successfully with the slogan "meals for kids, not pocket battleships." Then the party had resumed its decisive governmental role at the Reich level by providing the chancellor, Hermann Müller, for the Grand Coalition of 1928–1930.

---

76. For all this, see Geyer, "Das Zweite Rüstungsprogramm (1930–1934)," MGM 17 (1975), p. 135 and (for the quotations, from the record of an internal ministry conference of December 1931) p. 149.
77. See Wilhelm Deist, "The Road to Ideological War: Germany, 1918–1945," in Williamson Murray, MacGregor Knox, and Alvin Bernstein, eds., *The Making of Strategy: Rulers, States, and War* (Cambridge, 1994), pp. 358–65; Geyer, *Aufrüstung oder Sicherheit: Die Reichswehr in der Krise der Machtpolitik 1924–1936* (Wiesbaden, 1980), pp. 76–97, 211–12; and the useful summary of *Reichswehr* aims in Jürgen Förster, "Das Verhältnis von Wehrmacht und Nationalsozialismus im Entscheidungsjahr 1933," *German Studies Review* 18:3 (1995), pp. 471–80.

By the end of 1929, the army's political leaders, under pressure from the planners' deadlines, began to press a receptive Reich president to eject the SPD from government. A Reich government that met the army's requirements would have to rule against the parties, or at the very least against the Left. Then the Grand Coalition not unexpectedly collapsed in March 1930, after a difficult winter and rising tension between the doctrinaire left wing of the SPD and Germany's increasingly militant business interests; the occasion was a seemingly trivial squabble over funding for the unemployed. The army and a variety of agrarian and antirepublican interests and groups arrayed behind Hindenburg now had their chance, as the SPD voluntarily relinquished power at the national level. The new cabinet, swiftly assembled under a conservative Catholic politician, Heinrich Brüning, received from the ancient field marshal (at that point eighty-two) the mission of leading a nonparty cabinet equipped to defy the Reichstag and rule through presidential emergency decrees.

Brüning nevertheless preferred a degree of parliamentary support. But the SPD refused to accept his Depression-inspired austerity budget, and a Reichstag majority rescinded the Article 48 decrees with which he sought to force it through. In summer 1930, like Giolitti in 1921, he therefore sought to recast the legislature to create a durable center-right majority that would exclude the Left from power. Also like Giolitti, Brüning acted while a nationalist mass movement was swiftly gaining strength: winter 1929–30 was the NSDAP's point of electoral breakthrough in a series of crucial contests in the lesser German federal states.[78] And Brüning neglected a further critical fact: the last French troops left the Rhineland in June 1930, depriving Versailles of its powerful restraining effect on German domestic politics. The voters of the nationalist *Lager* could now safely choose genuinely radical solutions.

That September, after a Reichstag election campaign that in the words of the British ambassador "brought into the open, through one party or another, all that Germany hopes for and intends to strive for in the field of external affairs," they did just that. The NSDAP succeeded to Hindenburg's 1925 electorate, and became the second largest party in Germany.[79] The NSDAP's appeal, thanks to preexist-

78. See the analysis in Jung, "Plebiszitärer Durchbruch 1929? Zur Bedeutung von Volksbegehren und Volksentscheid gegen den Young Plan für die NSDAP," *Geschichte und Gesellschaft* 15 (1989), pp. 502–05.
79. Argument, and quotation, from Sally Marks, *The Illusion of Peace: International Relations in Europe 1918–1933* (New York, 1976), pp. 112–14; likewise Erich Eyck, *A History of*

ing traditions and universal literacy, was far more powerful and total than that of its Italian counterpart. The party, after its reemergence from political obscurity in 1929–30, offered nothing less than a systematic attempt to recreate the national euphoria of August 1914 in everyday life. It exploited and believed in the German national cult's mythology of social unity. It mercilessly derided the Weimar "Jew-Republic" as symbol, cause, and perpetuator of Germany's fragmentation and defeat. The Führer and his cult gained through the deepening Great Depression an apocalyptic edge; Nazism's triumphant claim to be "the opposite of everything that now exists" was a compelling appeal against which Brüning had no defense.[80] And in the presidential election of March–April 1932 Hitler captured from the venerable field marshal – despite his electoral Pyrrhic victory – the uncontested leadership of the national *Lager*.

In the third and final phase, from July to October 1922 and from June 1932 to January 1933, the two movements came to power as the mass parties of the national camp in similarly structured compromises with establishments incapable of ruling further without mass backing – and thus committed, implicitly or explicitly, to ending parliamentary government. In this final phase, contingency and the idiosyncrasies of individuals played a heightened role, alongside inherited determinants that included the violence of the national myths, the tripartite division between national, Catholic, and Socialist blocs, and the more immediate political and social fractures imposed by war and aftermath.

The key factors in the final phase of the path to dictatorship common to the Italian and German cases were four: crises that further accentuated the political paralysis inherent in the tripartite division of politics, while progressively sapping what little public support the Liberal state and the Weimar Republic still retained; elites whose mentalities largely precluded the understanding that *fascisti* and National Socialists claimed and were capable of exercising total power; armies whose institutional and professional interests, political calculations, and ideological affinities moved them to bargain with rather than suppress nationalist insurgents; and the interaction of the opportunism, illusions, and fears of the heads of state and their advisers with the tactical skill of the PNF and NSDAP leaderships.

In Italy the final crisis opened with the collapse of the first Facta

the Weimar Republic (Cambridge, MA, 1967), vol. 2, pp. 275–77. For the electoral details, Falter, *Hitlers Wähler*, pp. 30–34.

80. Gregor Strasser (speech of 20 October 1932), quoted in Karl Dietrich Bracher's still unsurpassed *Die Auflösung der Weimarer Republik* (Düsseldorf, 5th ed., 1984), p. 98.

government in mid-July 1922. Massive Fascist "punitive expeditions" at the periphery and Facta's inability and unwillingness to crush them provoked the *Popolari* to pull the cabinet down.[81] Yet they did so without any prospect of creating a *Popolare*-Socialist coalition to block Fascism at the center. Orlando and Ivanoe Bonomi predictably failed to form cabinets commanding a parliamentary majority – in part because Giolitti and others sought spitefully to punish the *Popolari* by reimposing Facta once more, in part because many Liberals still saw Fascist violence as a legitimate answer to Socialist and Catholic encroachment, and feared that the "return to legality" that they claimed to seek would leave them defenseless against the two mass parties.[82]

Facta's hastily patched together second cabinet was scarcely in place before Socialists offered up their own contribution to the final dissolution of the parliamentary order: a general strike intended as a protest against Fascist violence and the state's complicity. The strike (1–3 August 1922) sought to paralyze transport in much of urban Italy. It gave the Fascists the initiative, which they did not subsequently relinquish, and a further pretext for reprisals carried out in place of a state that had "once more demonstrated its impotence."[83]

Facta sought only to hang on until his patron Giolitti could be lured back from an extended sulk in France, Switzerland, and the Italian Alps.[84] D'Annunzio, whose ascendancy in the nationalist camp might have allowed him to contest Mussolini's increasingly insistent claims to rule, temporarily removed himself from play by fracturing his skull during a romp about his villa in mid-August. Political humiliation and internal strife crippled *Popolari* and Socialists; Giolitti greeted the belated lifting of the Catholic veto upon him with silent contempt. Above all, no Liberal leader now dared – and almost none desired – to rule against the Fascist movement. Giolitti put it bluntly in a famous open letter published on 26 July: a "genuine civil war" would be the

81. On the much-debated question of the authorities' complicity with Fascist violence, an issue complicated by the deliberate ambiguity of much of the documentation, see Danilo Veneruso, *La vigilia del fascismo: Il primo ministero Facta nella crisi dello stato liberale in Italia* (Bologna, 1968), pp. 319–73; De Felice, *Mussolini il rivoluzionario* (Turin, 1965), pp. 602–06; *Mussolini il fascista*, vol. 1, pp. 27–42; and Vivarelli, "Bonomi e il fascismo in alcuni documenti inediti," *Rivista Storica Italiana* (March 1960), pp. 147–57.

82. See especially the merciless analysis of Veneruso, *Vigilia del fascismo*, Chapter 6 and conclusion.

83. Proclamation by the leadership of the PNF, 31 July 1922, in Antonino Répaci, *La marcia su Roma* (Milan, rev. ed., 1972), pp. 629–30.

84. See the Giolitti and Facta correspondence in Répaci, *Marcia su Roma*, pp. 618–622, 625, 672–73.

inevitable result of any attempt to suppress Fascism. By September 1922 all that remained to decide was whether the Fascists would enter the cabinet under Giolitti, Salandra – or Mussolini.

In Germany, the army took the lead in provoking the final crisis, as it had in urging an end to parliamentary government. Until spring 1932, a wide variety of outcomes were possible: Brüning's power rested on parliamentary toleration by the SPD as well as on Hindenburg's favor. A return to parliamentary government was theoretically possible, Hindenburg permitting, once the economic emergency passed. But Hindenburg had committed himself to ruling against the Reichstag in 1930, and now took furious umbrage at being involuntarily cast by his advisers as the Left's candidate against Hitler in the spring 1932 presidential election. Simultaneously, Brüning's *Reichswehr* minister and minister of the interior, General Wilhelm Groener, belatedly concluded that Nazi paramilitary violence was an intolerable threat to the state's monopoly of force, and must be suppressed. Groener's short-lived ban of the SA and SS in April 1932 led to his downfall at the instigation of his devious protegé and chief political operator, General Kurt von Schleicher, who had sought persistently – and long with Groener's support – to "tame" the Nazi movement politically and to annex its paramilitary formations in support of the *Reichswehr*'s overriding priority, the coming rearmament plan.

Brüning's fall soon followed Groener's. Hindenburg withdrew his confidence from a government tolerated by the SPD and invidious to his fellow East Elbian landowners.[85] *His* governments must stand irreproachably on the Right. The two minority cabinets that followed, those of a Hindenburg favorite, the renegade Catholic and extreme authoritarian Franz von Papen (June–November 1932), and of Schleicher himself (December 1932–January 1933), had – unlike Brüning – no appreciable Reichstag backing.

They came by this condition honestly. The NSDAP had secured powerful pluralities in the elections of March–April 1932, including a Nazi-Communist negative majority in the Prussian legislature. Yet

---

85. The putative behind-the-scenes role of the East Elbian landed class in removing Brüning in 1932 and in bringing Hitler to power in January 1933, like the allegedly parallel role of industrial malefactors of great wealth, has occasioned much historiographical speculation over many decades about the supposed contribution of "premodern elites" to Germany's ostensibly straight path from Bismarck to Hitler. For more dispassionate and empirically grounded views, see Wolfgang Zollitsch, "Adel und adlige Machteliten in der Endphase der Weimarer Republik. Standespolitik und agrarische Interessen," and Turner, "Alliance of Elites," pp. 205–214 and 239–256 respectively in Winkler and Müller-Luckner, eds., *Die deutsche Staatskrise.*

Papen, deluded by Nazi assurances of support in return for the rein-statement of the SA and new national elections, and intent for his own part on destroying all basis for party government, nevertheless dissolved the Reichstag. As the election approached, Papen made his own claim to leadership of the national *Lager* by destroying with presidential decrees backed by *Reichswehr* troops the one remaining institutional support for parliamentary government in Germany, the SPD-led minority coalition in Prussia.

Hitler and the NSDAP campaigning machine put on their supreme performance for the 31 July election. National unity as the prerequisite for economic recovery and future greatness was the party's central theme, and Hitler relentlessly damned Nazism's adversaries, Left and Right, for seeing it as "typically German to have thirty parties." He by contrast proclaimed that his "life's goal [was] to annihilate and exterminate [*zu vernichten und auszurotten*] these thirty parties" and to make the nation whole.[86] The NSDAP emerged as the strongest party in the Reichstag, with 230 seats and a negative majority against the Republic in combination with the 89 Communists. The only majority coalition now conceivable required the unlikely coupling of the NSDAP and Center parties.[87] Attempts in mid-August by a shaken Reich president and by Schleicher to induce Hitler to lend his constituency to Papen failed utterly. Only the chancellorship – and Hindenburg's undertaking to support the new cabinet, as he had Brüning and Papen, with his decree powers – offered in Hitler's view a station appropriate to his unique personal qualities and historically unprecedented mass support.

Hindenburg's indignant refusal and deep mistrust enraged Hitler, who scornfully announced that he would outwait Papen and Hindenburg: "I know they are convinced that they are all far cleverer than we are . . . Let them be clever. *We* are the more determined. [And] I am the most unrelenting of all."[88] Papen's attempt, after all else had failed, to exhaust the NSDAP with a new national election in November reduced the NSDAP plurality. But the Nazi-Communist negative majority remained in place, and now not even an NSDAP-

---

86. Hitler, 27 and 21 July 1932, HRSA 5/1:275–76, 249; for the thirty (or "forty or fifty parties, associations, and petty groups") and the Party's longstanding mission to restore national unity as a central Hitler theme throughout spring–summer 1932, ibid., 5/1:3, 17, 22, 45, 89, 96, 180, 207, 218, 261, 278, 280, 285–6, 289, 293.

87. For the electoral arithmetic (and much else), Bracher, *Auflösung*, Chapter 10 (table, p. 565).

88. HRSA, 5/1:349 (7 September 1932); for the Hitler-Hindenburg talks, Thilo Vogelsang, *Reichswehr, Staat und NSDAP: Beiträge zur deutschen Geschichte 1930–1932* (Stuttgart, 1962), pp. 497–80.

Center coalition promised a governing majority. Papen's cabinet recoiled in horror at the most promising remaining alternative, that of suspending the Reichstag and much of the constitution, declaring a state of emergency, and ruling by presidential decree until economic recovery had made Germany more governable. The *Reichswehr* helpfully announced that it could not master a simultaneous confrontation with Communists, Nazis, and Poles. It was thus that Schleicher, with the grudging support of a Reich president mortally irritated by the loss of his "comrade" Papen, found himself chancellor with no more parliamentary support than his predecessor, and less of Hindenburg's confidence.

The "old gentleman" had so far vetoed a Hitler chancellorship as sternly as he had insisted that the Left be excluded from government. But if Schleicher failed to secure appreciable Reichstag support by January 1933 and Hitler maintained his refusal to back the government except as its leader, no constitutionally legitimate and politically feasible alternative except new elections would remain.[89]

In Italy, the post of prime minister was by September 1922 Mussolini's to lose. He skillfully kept in play all those who might cross him, courting D'Annunzio, Nitti, Salandra, Giolitti, Facta, and the king with a view to assuming a share of power by invitation and consolidating it through new elections. But he did not neglect the violence that had brought his movement this far: by mid-October feverish preparations were under way for the greatest punitive expedition of all, a march on Rome by the united Fascist *squadre* of north and north-central Italy. This twin-track approach required all of Mussolini's tactical skill, and depended for its success above all upon speed. The Fascist movement could not sustain its control of north Italy or maintain its own cohesion without conquering power nationally, and the lies and mutually contradictory blandishments with which Mussolini had plied his would-be allies would eventually be found out. Fascism must act before Facta's cabinet collapsed spontaneously, or Giolitti stepped in – Mussolini's greatest fear, for in his view only Giolitti had the political courage to turn the army's machine guns on Fascism.

In the final week of October, after a triumphant party rally at Naples, Mussolini's associates mobilized the *squadre*, seized the cities of the North, and launched their improvised and disorderly expeditionary forces southward, while Mussolini himself held the political

<hr>

89. See Bracher, *Auflösung*, p. 565 (table); AdR, Schleicher, pp. 235 (Schleicher: a majority cabinet requires Hitler's support), 241–42 (*Reichswehr* ministry summary of options other than new elections: all are breaches of the constitution).

threads in Milan. Facta, faced with the civil war he had so long sought
to avoid, belatedly sought to fight; the Rome army command was confident of blocking and dispersing the Fascists far from the city. The
king at first appeared to stand firm behind the government's proclamation of a state of siege. Then Victor Emmanuel III buckled, for reasons that remain unclear, but among which the view of General
Armando Diaz, victor of Vittorio Veneto, and of other senior military
figures that the "army will do its duty, but it would be best not to put
it to the test" was apparently decisive.[90] Violence *within* the national
camp was in the end not an option.

Mussolini himself, stiffened by the timely obduracy of his secretary
of the party, Michele Bianchi, repudiated all his earlier assurances that
he would enter a government under Giolitti or Saladra – the king's
first choice – and demanded and obtained the prime ministership. His
coalition cabinet included Diaz as minister of war, hostages from a
chastened *Partito Popolare*, and sheepish Liberals. It was as yet far from
the *Regime Fascista* of the future. But it was the decisive step.

The final agony of the German Republic evidenced the same narrowing of options as in Italy. By December 1932 those around
Hindenburg feared yet another election because of the apparent danger that the Nazi bubble might suddenly burst and many of Hitler's
supporters defect to the Communists – whose inexorable advance
since spring appeared to them a far greater threat to the social order
than the NSDAP. The *Reichswehr*'s leaders resented their newfound
political exposure under Schleicher. They were willing to impose martial law and to enforce it if Hindenburg so ordered. But such an outcome was diametrically opposed to their professional imperative of
"remilitarizing" the nation in pursuit of rearmament, and the erection
of a military dictatorship would pit them against their natural constituency. Schleicher himself was distinctly queasy at the prospect –
which he claimed Papen would have realized had he remained in office
– of thrusting the *Reichswehr* "into the streets with machine guns
against nine-tenths of the *Volk*."[91]

---

90.   See above all Répaci, *Marcia su Roma*, pp. 504–08, 580–86, 922; Brian R. Sullivan, "A
      Thirst for Glory: Mussolini, the Italian Military, and the Fascist Regime, 1922–1936"
      (Ph.D. dissertation, Columbia University, 1984), Chapter 1, section 6, and Chapter 2,
      section 1; Giorgio Rochat, *L'esercito italiano da Vittorio Veneto a Mussolini (1919–1925)*
      (Bari, 1967), pp. 403–07.
91.   Quotation: Schleicher briefing (corps and division commanders), 13–15 December
      1932, in Vogelsang, "Neue Dokumente zur Geschichte der Reichswehr 1930–1933,"
      VfZG 2:4 (1954), p. 427. Wolfram Pyta, "Vorbereitungen für den militärischen
      Ausnahmezustand unter Papen/Schleicher," MGM 51 (1992), pp. 385–428, and
      Eberhard Kolb and Pyta, "Die Staatsnotstandsplanung unter den Regierungen Papen

As Schleicher frittered away the initiative, Papen reemerged in January 1933 to sabotage his successor by secretly assembling a cabinet that would include himself, Hitler, and the German Nationalist Party leader Alfred Hugenberg. Schleicher himself still harbored the delusion that Hitler – whatever he might say in public – would accept a lesser post than the chancellorship, and also failed to perceive that Papen had thoroughly undermined what little remained of his own standing with Hindenburg. On 23 January, as Papen's clandestine negotiations were close to success, Schleicher sought and was refused the power to set aside the constitution and postpone the Reichstag's meeting by presidential decree – the same course which Papen had sought to pursue and which Schleicher had warned would lead to the very civil war for which Hindenburg explicitly refused to take responsibility.[92]

The Reich president would not tolerate a government resting on the Left – which had ruled out Schleicher's acceptance of an almost-despairing alliance offer from the leader of the deposed SPD government of Prussia in early January. Hindenburg was also unwilling to formally breach the constitution – especially to preserve that constitution's democratic essence, in which he, as a Prussian field marshal born in 1847, decidedly did not believe. He was evidently weary of his responsibilities; a cabinet resting on a majority, even one made up largely of National Socialists, seemed in the end preferable to provoking further the Prussian-Protestant *Lager* from which he had come, and which was now baying for Hitler. Even Schleicher and the far from pro-Nazi army commander-in-chief, Eduard von Hammerstein, came in the end to view a Hitler chancellorship as preferable – naturally with Schleicher staying on as *Reichswehr* minister – to Papen's return. And Hindenburg had a further safeguard alongside Papen's profuse assurances that Hitler had been "hemmed in" with conservatives in the new cabinet: a general of his own choice to replace the now-despised Schleicher as *Reichswehr* minister. That the general, Werner von Blomberg, former army chief of staff (1927–29) and a member of the "total war" faction in the army leadership, was also – not entirely coincidentally – an admirer of Hitler was either unknown

---

und Schleicher," pp. 155–182 in Winkler and Müller-Luckner, eds., *Die deutsche Staatskrise*, are excellent on *Reichswehr* planning for martial law, but fail to place it within the context of the *Reichswehr*'s institutional objectives.

92. See AdR, Schleicher, p. 232 (16 January 1933), for Schleicher's fatuous underestimation of Hitler; for Papen's negotiations, see Turner, *Hitler's Thirty Days to Power: January 1933* (London, 1996), Chapters 5–6; Bracher, *Auflösung*, Chapter 11.

to Hindenburg or did not trouble him. Hindenburg administered the oath of office to Blomberg behind Schleicher's back just after 9:00 A.M. on 30 January 1933. The rest of the Hitler cabinet, its internal frictions lubricated and conservative doubts assuaged or silenced by the smooth patter of the new vice-chancellor, Papen, followed around 11:30. The new Reich chancellor was in private gloatingly confident that he could outwit his coalition partners and erect the same dictatorship over Germany that had long existed within the NSDAP. Mussolini had shown the way.

CONCLUSION

If explanations that emphasize the role of groups are absolutely imperative, it might be useful to set aristocracy and bourgeoisie aside, and examine closely the nature and role in both Italy and Germany of the intelligentsia and the officer corps. The *literati*, as authors and guardians of the national myths, gave form before 1914/15 to the aspirations that ultimately shaped the PNF and NSDAP and smoothed their roads to power. And the ambitions and skills of the officer corps contributed mightily to the shape and scope of those aspirations and determined above all the extent to which they could be carried out.

The outcomes of 1922 and 1933 were made possible – if not necessary – by features inherited from the period of territorial unification and its aftermath. Both countries' national movements arose outside and in part against existing states, without suffering the slightest restraining experience of political responsibility. The two countries' "latecomer" status accentuated the inevitable disjunction between aspirations and realities, between the incompleteness of the existing national states on the one hand, and European cultural hegemony and true great power status (Italy) or world power status and world domination (Germany) on the other. Internally, both were torn regionally and socially, and among their deepest cleavages were those that divided each into three great blocs: a beleaguered national camp facing Catholic and Socialist adversaries. Nationalist demands for transcendent social unity made more intense than elsewhere by belated and incomplete territorial unification faced a degree of *innere Zerrissenheit* that only blood sacrifice could seemingly cure.

In the German national cult, Protestant, Hegelian, and pseudo-Darwinian philosophies of history, Bismarck's victories, and continental economic supremacy added a hard edge of certainty to the national sense of mission, while ancestor worship and the yearning for unity were embodied in a thirst for mythic leadership – with the whole nurtured and spread by generations of *literati* and schoolmasters. In Italy, by contrast, a *Risorgimento* made above all – as the intellectuals never ceased to lament – by diplomatic deception and foreign arms inspired caution along with burning resentment. The expectation of a Führer was far weaker, the literacy needed to brand such notions upon the popular consciousness far less pervasive. The Church monopolized the loyalties and values of at least half the nation. And military-economic weakness likewise had a restraining – although not sufficiently restraining – effect.

The Great War, by splitting both societies and political formations into incoherent fragments, rendered them ungovernable irrespective of victory or defeat. War decapitated the state in Germany. In both countries war, and ensuing elections that at last accurately reproduced and gave full political weight to the many fractures within the two societies, led to paralysis either open or latent. War decapitated or shook to its foundations a national camp that had never before needed, and had failed to develop, a mass party. War had created the mold for militant "parties of a new type" that claimed to incarnate and lead that camp. And in the end, those parties achieved a virtual monopoly of the national mythology and domination of the nationalist activists and electorate.

Yet these movements would neither have found the political space needed to grow and prosper, nor have succeeded in erecting dictatorships without the confluence of many structural factors, and the assistance or acquiescence of many individuals. In the first phase, from mid-1919 to spring 1921 in Italy and from 1919 to spring 1930 in Germany, stable parliamentary government might eventually have emerged, had the political landscape been less fractured and the major parties more capable of compromise, and had key decision makers such as Giolitti and Hindenburg been determined to rule with rather than against the parties. In the second phase, from summer 1921 to summer 1922 and from spring 1930 to summer 1932, parliamentary government might still have been restored, given the will to defend it by force. But that will was almost entirely absent, for the chief threat came in each case from within the national camp. In the third phase, those with the power to bar the future dictators' roads to Rome and Berlin succeeded, through a series of staggering but unsurprising misjudgments, in so narrowing their options that they faced in the end only the apparent choice of accepting their adversaries as heads of gov-

ernment, or of fighting them in the streets. Everyone in authority –
Victor Emmanuel III, Hindenburg, Giolitti, Papen, Schleicher, the
Italian generals – in the end came to view the new governments of
"national concentration" as the path of least resistance. Teleology, in
this final phase, was inherent in events, not a retrospective construct.[93]

Even after Fascists and Nazis had devoured their coalition partners
in 1922–25 and 1933–34, the compromise settlements between conservatives and revolutionaries reached in October 1922 and January
1933 exerted a structural pressure for external violence not found any-
where else. Hitler by 1934 was more powerful than Mussolini ever
became, but even he could not simply abolish the Wilhelmine allies
and the civil society that he had inherited. That galling situation
proved an unfailing goad to ever-greater risk. The national myths that
had acclaimed bloodshed as the source of true national integration
thus took on a new form that in Germany – in the absence of cultural
or political restraints, in the presence of a social structure with an
enduring rigidity that invited revolt, and with the army's enthusiastic
and expert help – promised almost limitless destruction. Both movements' drives for mastery abroad and for total power at home, for the
destruction of inherited and hated political and social orders and the
ascent of their followers, demanded war. And only a truly large war
would serve.

93. Turner, *Hitler's Thirty Days*, Chapter 7, emphasizes the "strong elements of contingency in the events that brought Hitler to power" (p. 166). But after all due regard is paid
to the importance of Papen's role in inducing Hindenburg to accept Hitler as chancellor and in securing Hugenberg's grudging participation in the new cabinet, the situation after Brüning's dismissal, and especially after the July 1932 election, was anything
but open. Given (1) a Reichstag incapable of furnishing a governing majority without
the NSDAP; (2) Hindenburg's refusal to govern on the Left, which ruled out a
Schleicher bargain with the SPD; (3) Hindenburg's weariness at his own political exposure, reluctance to sanction formal breaches of the constitution, and rejection of "civil
war" against the NSDAP; (4) Hitler's refusal to accept anything less than the chancellorship; and (5) the *Reichswehr's* rearmament priorities, lack of vocation for military dictatorship, and (after November 1932) distrust of Papen, a Hitler chancellorship, while
not foreordained, was the most probable outcome.

2

CONQUEST, FOREIGN AND DOMESTIC, IN FASCIST ITALY AND NAZI GERMANY

> . . . between Germany and Italy there exists a community of destiny. . . . [Germany and Italy] are congruent cases.
>
> — *Benito Mussolini, 1936*

> The brown shirt might perhaps not have arisen without the black shirt.
>
> - *Adolf Hitler, 1942*[1]

FASCISM, GENERIC AND HISTORIC

Mussolini and Hitler were not alone in emphasizing the common origins, features, and destinies of Fascism and National Socialism. Theories of "fascism" – that elusive generic phenomenon with a small "f" – have proliferated with abandon ever since the 1920s. Definitions have ranged from the Third International's "open terroristic dictatorship of the most reactionary, chauvinistic, and imperialistic elements of finance capital" through Ernst Nolte's militant anti-Marxism, to the modernization theorists' "mass-mobilizing developmental dictatorships under single-party auspices." And a historian of ideas has recently described fascism as a "genus of political ideology whose mythic core . . . is a palingenetic form of populist ultranationalism."[2]

Voices of caution have occasionally sounded, urging the "deflation" of a concept that "exists in faith and is pursued by reason," or suggesting that fascism fails to encompass adequately the ultimate evil of National Socialist Germany.[3] Yet the notion is still with us, even if no two theories of fascism coincide. Marxists have normally equated fascism and capitalism "in the final analysis," but have divided over fascism's precise degree of subservience to capital. In cases such as Ger-

---

1. Quotations: Strunk minute, 31 January 1936, NARA T-454/56/000226; Hitler, *Monologe im Führerhauptquartier 1941–1944* (Hamburg, 1980), p. 43.
2. Nolte, *Three Faces of Fascism* (New York, 1966), pp. 20–21; Roger Griffin, *The Nature of Fascism* (London, 1991), p. 26.
3. Gilbert Allardyce, "What Fascism is Not: Notes on the Deflation of a Concept," *American Historical Review* 84 (1979), pp. 367–88; Berndt Martin, "Zur Tauglichkeit eines übergreifenden Faschismus-Begriffs," VfZG 29 (1981), pp. 48–73.

many's, where the evidence is overwhelming that the "fascists" actually ran the country, flexible Marxists have had recourse to "Bonapartism," that independent dictatorial executive over rather than of the bourgeoisie.[4] But the Bonapartism Marx described in his *Eighteenth Brumaire* was not a mass movement like Fascism or National Socialism, and although Marx apparently did not realize it, once he conceded even temporary autonomy to politics, his essentially monocausal philosophy of history would cease to illuminate events.

Tim Mason attempted to resolve that dilemma with a Marxist version of Hermann Rauschning's *Revolution of Nihilism*.[5] The primacy of politics over economics in Nazi Germany, Mason argued, meant that the Nazi state was by nature outside history, incapable of "social reproduction," and thus doomed to self-destruction for violating the historical "law of motion" Engels claimed Marx had discovered. Sadly, the real Nazi Germany was so unself-destructive that it nearly achieved total victory in 1940–41, and defied a world of enemies that included the three remaining world powers for three years thereafter. Its enemies literally had to blast it flat; destruction was its most striking characteristic, but it was the destruction of others.

Ernst Nolte's *Three Faces of Fascism* opened the post-1945 theoretical debate by attempting to define fascism as the "epochal phenomenon" of interwar Europe, a violent, militarily organized anti-Marxism that Great War and Bolshevik Revolution had conjured up. Nolte's definition had the advantage of eliminating from consideration figures such as Khaddafi, Castro, and Perón. But the societies in which the remaining fascisms arose were embarrassingly diverse, and the movements themselves even more so. A concept that united Nazis, Action Française, the Romanian Iron Guard, and the Estonian Association of Freedom Fighters stretched belief. Nor was the lowest common denominator or "fascist minimum" that Nolte chose, that of militant anti-Marxism, peculiar to the interwar movements or to regimes generally called fascist, and it implicitly contradicted Nolte's chronological boundaries. Nolte's expansion in the 1980s of his original notion that Nazism was a reaction to Bolshevism into the claim that Auschwitz "was above all a reaction, born of fear, to the genocidal pro-

4. Particularly August Thalheimer, "Über den Faschismus" (1930), in Wolfgang Abendroth, ed., *Faschismus und Kapitalismus* (Frankfurt, 1967); see also Jost Dülffer, "Bonapartism, Fascism, and National Socialism," *Journal of Contemporary History* 11 (1976), pp. 109–28.
5. Mason, "The Primacy of Politics: Politics and Economics in National Socialist Germany," pp. 53–76 in his *Nazism, Fascism and the Working Class* (Cambridge, 1995); Rauschning, *The Revolution of Nihilism* (New York, 1939).

cesses of the Russian Revolution" aroused widespread revulsion and ridicule.[6]

Anti-Marxism may help explain the origins of many of the movements, but it was clearly not as central to their ideologies or policies as Nolte's definition requires. Hitler, the prophet of race, did not so much object to Marxism as to its purported Jewish essence. The anti-Marxism of his post-1919 world view was actually a compound of racialist anti-Semitism and geopolitics, and he rejoiced in 1941 at the "good turn" the Soviet regime had done him by enslaving Russia's peasants even before the coming of the *Herrenvolk*. Nor was the anti-Marxism of the ex-Socialist Benito Mussolini central to his world view; it fluctuated in intensity depending on its momentary usefulness.[7]

The third major approach has been that of the social scientists, who have attempted to relate fascism to the process of modernization. But that term has acquired almost as many definitions as fascism and is equally vague. It tends either to include everything that has happened in the West since the Renaissance – and is thus analytically useless – or it rests on essentially arbitrary choices of indicators whose relationship to one another is unclear and whose measurement is problematic. At worst, the concept confuses chronology with morality, and becomes a normative, teleological Whig theory of history, unreflectively derived from the West, and imposed on the rest.[8]

Modernization theory has nevertheless given rise to four principal fascisms. Barrington Moore, Jr., as suggested in the previous chapter, described it – implausibly especially for Italy – as the outcome of conservative-aristocratic modernization. Others have argued that fascism is a political alternative characteristic of the stage of economic growth at which industry begins to outweigh agriculture, a theory that at best

---

6. Nolte, "Zwischen Geschichtslegende und Revisionismus? Das Dritte Reich im Blickwinkel des Jahres 1980," in *"Historikerstreit"* (Munich, 1987), pp. 32–33; Nolte continued: ". . . the so-called annihilation of the Jews was a reaction or a distorted copy, and not the first act or the original."

7. Hitler: *Monologe*, p. 62 (17–18 September 1941); Mussolini (at the founding meeting of the *fasci*): Bolshevism "would not scare us if it demonstrated to us that it could guarantee a nation's greatness" (OO 12:325, 23 March 1919); his fall 1939 remark that Stalin's regime was "a kind of Slavic Fascism" (Ciano, 16 October 1939); and Philip V. Cannistraro and Edward D. Wynot, Jr., "On the Dynamics of Anti-Communism as a Function of Fascist Foreign Policy, 1933–1945," *Il Politico* 38 (1973).

8. For a noteworthy example of all these defects, see Horst Matzerath and Heinrich Volkmann, "Modernisierungstheorie und Nationalsozialismus," pp. 86–102 in Jürgen Kocka, ed., *Theorien in der Praxis des Historikers* (Göttingen, 1977). In the ensuing discussion (pp. 102–16), Kocka suggests that the only alternative to constructs such as modernization theory is "myths and ideologies" – a remark establishing both a false dichotomy and a distinction without a difference.

fits only Italy and Argentina.[9] A third possibility is that fascisms are "modernizing dictatorships." That category also rules out Hitler, since Germany was highly industrialized by 1933, and includes everyone from Nkrumah to Mao, giving the concept all the rigor of india rubber while eliminating the single most powerful and dangerous regime commonly considered fascist.[10] Finally, modernization theory provides a possible negative definition of fascism as a revolt against the modern world, a utopian antimodernism. But regrettably for its opponents, the chief example of that sort of fascism was Nazi Germany, a regime infatuated with high technology and social engineering. That recognition has prompted one commentator to describe the Nazis as "reactionary modernists," a paradoxical category that suggests that analyzing fascisms in terms of modernization is unrewarding.[11]

Nor can reducing generic fascism to a "genus of political ideology," as Roger Griffin has suggested, necessarily save a failed concept. Generic fascism's "mythic core" might serve as part of a historically useful definition, and Griffin's selection of the rebirth – palingenesis – of the nation as the essential feature of that myth is ingenious.[12] But it is far from clear why that particular lowest common denominator is the essential one, and in any case a persuasive definition of generic fascism cannot ignore political structures and deeds.

After seventy-five years of debate, the scene resembles a desert battlefield littered with the burnt-out, rusting hulks of failed theories. Yet comparative history, despite a complexity in execution that mirrors the reality it seeks to describe, offers a way around the conceptual difficulties just outlined. And inevitably the obvious candidates for comparative treatment, among the phenomena usually understood as generically fascist, are the two principal "historic fascist" regimes in Italy and Germany. Both arose in relatively advanced societies – northern Italy was different from Bavaria, but only marginally more backward economically. Both were in part responses to affronts to the self-esteem of nations that were relative latecomers to unification and

---

9. See A. F. K. Organski, "Fascism and Modernization," pp. 19–41 in Woolf, ed., *The Nature of Fascism*.
10. See particularly A. James Gregor, *Italian Fascism and Developmental Dictatorship* (Princeton, 1979), and Gregor's other works mentioned therein.
11. See Henry Ashby Turner, Jr., "Fascism and Modernization," pp. 117–39 in Turner, ed., *Reappraisals of Fascism* (New York, 1975); Jeffrey Herf, "Reactionary Modernism. Some Ideological Origins of the Primacy of Politics in the Third Reich," *Theory and Society* 10 (1981), pp. 805–32.
12. See Griffin, *The Nature of Fascism*, especially p. 26.

industrialization, and that suffered from deep social, regional, and, in Germany, religious cleavages. Finally, both were the creation of leaders who combined conspicuous talents as agitators, political tacticians, and ideological visionaries.

That last quality implies a collision between vision and reality. Comparison of those visions and of their respective collisions with reality offers insight into the nature of both movements and regimes, and into possible distinctions between them and other varieties of political evil. But any attempt to analyze Fascist and National Socialist ideologies, final goals, and political actions raises a variety of issues. Did the movements have ideologies worthy of the name? If they did, whose pronouncements are authoritative sources, and which of those pronouncements are irrelevant, which are tactical, and which are fundamental? Attempts to answer the first question have frequently encountered two pitfalls: "mirror-imaging" and radical skepticism. Victims of the first pitfall have unreflectively applied conventional categories of liberal and Marxist social thought to phenomena that liberalism and Marxism are ill-equipped to explain. They have attempted to understand Fascist and National Socialist ideologies as social ideologies expressing the attitudes of particular classes and addressing the problems those classes faced in adapting to modern industrial society.

Unfortunately for that approach, Fascist and National Socialist ideologies were not expressions of particular classes and groups, but – like Marxism – above all the creation of individuals: Mussolini and Hitler. Despite Rosenbergs and Gentiles, Feders and Himmlers and Bottais, the two dictators were the sole unimpeachable creators and interpreters of the doctrines of their movements. The dictators were the doctrine, the word made flesh, and understanding the success of their ideologies requires both appreciation of the role of charismatic leadership in hammering doctrine home, and analysis of the context in which they flourished. No pat social interpretation ("the revolt of the petite bourgeoisie") can help explain extreme nationalist political religions the first principle of which was the denial of class, and which appealed to all classes, although to varying degrees.

Nor has the widespread assumption that an ideology must be social encouraged fruitful inquiry. Commentators have seized on whatever scraps of doctrine fit their assumptions about what an ideology must contain, especially Mussolini's "Doctrine of Fascism" essay, written in collaboration with Giovanni Gentile. But that pompous exercise had less to do with Fascist ideology than with Mussolini's intermittent tactical attempts to achieve intellectual respectability. And even the Mussolini-Gentile essay proclaimed that the true test of manhood and nationhood was war – a curiously antisocial social ideology.[13] Fascist corporativism, which the regime itself touted as the answer to the social needs of the age, remained a sickly plant in which Mussolini himself took little interest. And in the German case, nothing even resembling a conventional answer to the social problems of an industrial society ever emerged.

Discarding the assumption that an ideology must be a variety of conventional social thought allows the examination of Fascist and Nazi ideologies and goals on their own terms. But any such attempt inevitably comes up against the second pitfall: the temptation to dismiss everything as propaganda. In the Italian case, radical skepticism has been especially fashionable. Roberto Vivarelli claimed in a witty essay on Mussolini's transition from Socialism to Fascism that no logical connection existed between the man's words and deeds, "which does not mean that 'words' counted for little in Mussolini's life."[14] Renzo De Felice, whom Vivarelli was attacking, also concluded in the early volumes of his monumental Mussolini biography that the Duce was always the man of day-to-day improvisation, of "absolute relativism," of power for power's sake.[15] At least one prominent Italian Communist historian concurred, and another described Mussolini as a mere "gang leader preoccupied with holding onto power."[16] In the German case, scholars have tended to take Hitler's ideological efforts more seriously; he did after all write a book. But some historians have gamely denied that Hitler had ideas, or argued that whatever ideas he had were irrelevant to his political course.[17]

---

13. "The Doctrine of Fascism," in Adrian Lyttelton, ed., *Italian Fascisms from Pareto to Gentile* (New York, 1973), p. 47.
14. Roberto Vivarelli, "Benito Mussolini dal socialismo al fascismo," *Rivista storica italiana* 79 (1967), p. 448; also his *Origini del fascismo*, vol. 1, pp. 260, 263–64, 299–300; on p. 333 Vivarelli hints at the "social thought" argument.
15. De Felice, *Mussolini il rivoluzionario*, p. xxvi; *Mussolini il fascista*, vol. 1, pp. 168, 464–65, 537.
16. Paolo Spriano, *Sulla rivoluzione italiana* (Milan, 1978), p. 56; Ernesto Ragionieri, *Storia d'Italia*, vol. 4 (Turin, 1976), p. 2215.
17. See particularly A. J. P. Taylor, *The Origins of the Second World War* (New York, rev. paperback ed., 1966), pp. 70–72, and Norman Stone, *Hitler* (Boston, 1980), pp. 16, 67. Hans Mommsen, "National Socialism," in *Marxism, Communism, and Western Society* (New York, 1973), vol. 6, p. 67, finds Schumpeter's "aimless expansion" the best description of National Socialist policy. Gerhard Schulz, *Aufstieg des Nationalsozialismus* (Frankfurt, 1975), p. 218, argues on the basis of a *Mein Kampf* passage (p. 170) that Hitler was a mere "*Machiavellist*" who did not care whether his ideology was "true or false" (see also pp. 212–13). But the *Mein Kampf* passage actually establishes only that

The case of the radical skeptics would be stronger if Hitler and Mussolini had displayed the sort of erratic opportunism consonant with the absence of ideology and the nihilistic pursuit of power. But in both cases the dictators expressed at the beginnings of their careers coherent ideologies that were not necessarily entirely popular or plausible, and continued to profess those ideas both publicly and privately throughout. The steady radicalization of their policies suggests an attempt to bring practice into line with theory, and implies that their increasingly rare moderation was tactical and their extremism genuine. In the end, both leaders provoked catastrophe by persisting, despite steadily increasing risks, in their attempts to bend the world to fit the idea. If that was opportunism and nihilism, it was clearly a strangely elaborate and consistent variety.

From Mission to Program

The Italian case is the more ambiguous of the two. Mussolini's pilgrimage from Socialism to Fascism, and his apparently sincere although private criticisms of Hitler as a doctrinaire, imply an unwillingness to take principles seriously.[18] The well-attested influence of Nietzsche, Sorel, and of the prophet of the "rape of the crowd by political propaganda," Gustave Le Bon, might suggest that for Mussolini, any myth would do. In a December 1914 attack on critics of his conversion from Socialist pacifism to rabble-rousing *interventismo*, he proclaimed that "the absolute d[id] not exist except in cold and unfruitful abstraction." And in the summer of 1920 he insisted that "nothing is eternal," neither political regimes nor modes of production nor systems of ideas; time and chance happened to them all. But both these apparent confessions of relativism were no more than Mussolini's habitual way of attacking the millenarian delusions of the Socialists.[19] Mussolini himself, both as Socialist and Fascist, had a world view that rested on one underlying assumption, and two political myths. The fixity of these ideas suggests that they were not simply Nietzschean conceits or expressions of a nihilist will to power, but ideas in which he

---

Hitler thought Marxism "false"; he viewed his own theoretical task as the establishment of "absolute truth" (MK, p. 210).

18. See De Felice, *Mussolini il duce* (Turin, 1974–78), vol. 1, p. 496.
19. OO 7:81 (13 December 1914); 15:86–87 (11 July 1920). For more on Mussolini's supposed relativism, see Emilio Gentile, *Le origini dell'ideologia fascista (1918–1925)* (Bari, 1975), pp. 143–44, 147, 425.

actually believed. What Mussolini failed to do was to assemble his ideas into an all-embracing intellectual system or into a monocausal, teleological philosophy of history.

The later Duce's underlying assumption, derived from sources as varied, if mutually reinforcing, as Heraclitus, Nietzsche, Darwin, Marx, Pareto, and Alfredo Oriani, was that life was struggle. History was an endless succession of conflicts between elites, states, or tribes. In each epoch a particular elite or state set the tone. By definition, dominant elites or states were the fittest, a conception Mussolini took not as a rationalization for resignation, but as a call to battle.[20]

Mussolini's myths of revolution and the nation determined the nature of that battle. The first was inevitably that of revolution, the myth of Mussolini's childhood and youth in the red Romagna, reinforced by Marx, Sorel, and a career as Socialist journalist-agitator. The Marx that Mussolini preferred was inevitably Marx the revolutionary; for Marx the philosopher of history, the economic theorist, the historian, the German patriot, or the heir of the Enlightenment Mussolini had little use. These latter Marxes he identified with the pedestrian beliefs of the reformist Socialists. What Mussolini instead proclaimed was Sorel's "barbarous notion of socialism," a revolution by an elite of primitives who would inaugurate a "new civilization" of joyous paganism.[21] That was precisely what Mussolini later attempted as a Fascist. Even the terminology remained the same, as did most of Mussolini's enemies: the reformist Socialists, the bourgeois establishment, the monarchy, the military hierarchy, and the Church.

Mussolini's second fixed idea was that of the nation and its mission, an idea also acquired as a Socialist. Revolutionary expectations and adaptation to prevailing Socialist dogma prompted occasional antinational outbursts, such as his famous 1910 declaration that the national flag was "a rag that should be planted on a dung-hill," or his neutralist September 1914 party manifesto. But behind protestations that the proletariat had no fatherland lurked the convictions of a radical nationalist. The Socialist Mussolini displayed an unsocialist appreciation of Mazzini, and of Giuseppe Prezzolini and his circle of quasi-

---

20. Pareto, elites: OO 1:6–7, 73–75, 128 (1904–08); 3:26 (1910); Marx and Darwin: 2:9–10 (1909); Oriani: note 23 following. For Pareto and Marx, see especially Gregor, *The Young Mussolini and the Intellectual Origins of Fascism* (Berkeley, 1979).
21. Barbarous socialism: OO 3:66 (1910); "I am a primitive," 4:183 (1912); paganism (Nietzsche): 1:174–84; new civilization: 3:87 (1910); revolutionary elite: 1:128 (1908), 3:26 (1910).

nationalist litterateurs grouped around *La voce*. That journal's attempt
to further "the spiritual unity of [all] Italians" met with Mussolini's
apparently unfeigned approval.[22] He occasionally let fly an anti-Aus-
trian barb sharpened by his experience as an agitator in the Trentino
and his association with the irredentist Socialist, Cesare Battisti. Finally, from 1909 if not earlier Mussolini was an "assiduous and devoted reader" of the works of Oriani, the bloodthirsty recluse who not
only insisted that only war could make post-*Risorgimento* Italy whole
but also demanded that the nation take up Rome's historic mission in
Africa and the Mediterranean. That last enthusiasm did not possess
Mussolini until the war years, but he could scarcely have proclaimed
himself "*un orianista*," as he did in 1909, without sharing many of
Oriani's ideas.[23]

It was the shock of European war in 1914 that removed the theoretical opposition between the revolutionary and national myths. Mussolini greeted the collapse of the Socialist International with something approaching glee. When his attempt to lead the Socialists into
support of a "revolutionary war" failed, his last speech to his comrades
before they expelled him from the party in November 1914 was purest
Oriani:

> If Italy remains absent, it will be once more the land of the dead, the land
> of cowards. I tell you that the duty of Socialism is to shake this Italy of
> priests, pro-Austrians, and monarchists. . . . Despite all your howls of
> protest, the war will flatten the lot of you [*vi travolgerà tutti*].

In the following months, Mussolini fused the myths of revolution
and of the nation. War, and war alone could assuage the national inferiority complex and make the nation whole. "A nation old with fifty
centuries of history and young with fifty years of national life" could
not behave like "a nation of rabbits." War must destroy "the ignoble
legend that Italians do not fight, it must wipe out the shame of Lissa
and Custoza, it must show the world that Italy can fight a war, a great
war; I say again: *a great war*." No longer would foreigners see Italy as
a land "of travelling storytellers, of peddlers of statuettes, of Calabrian

---

22. Antimilitarism and internationalism: OO 2:7, 2:169–70 (1909), 3:137 (1910); 4:53
    (1911); Mazzini: 3:68 (1910); national unity: 2:55 (1909); 38:11–12 (1909).
23. Nationalism: OO 2:75 (1909), 3:266–67 (1910), 6:58–60 (20 January 1920); Oriani:
    38:45–46; 2:128 (1909). Gentile, *Ideologia*, p. 37, assumes that Oriani's nationalism, and
    hence Mussolini's, was cultural – a charitable interpretation that ignores both ideo-
    logues' thirst for blood.

banditi." And war could also be a kind of revolution. The day Italian bayonets crossed the Ringstrasse in Vienna, "the Vatican's death knell [would] sound."[24]

Under the sign of perpetual struggle, internal and foreign policy, revolution and war merged. The barbaric new man of Mussolini the Socialist became the "impatient and generous youth," the "young rebels" of *interventismo*.[25] And despite stalemate and catastrophe at Caporetto, the war, as Mussolini put it in early 1918, had proved that this "small, despised people," this "army of mandolin players," could fight. Combat and the fact that Italy had willed it by deliberately entering the war confirmed in turn the nation's historic mission and claim to "higher destinies." Those destinies Mussolini identified with the Roman past and the "myth of empire" that derived from it.[26] The imperial heritage that Liberals such as Orlando also invoked, Italy's newfound confidence through victory over Austria-Hungary, Italy's teeming millions (favorite theme of "precursors" and Nationalists) all demonstrated that Italy was bound for Mediterranean domination, and would become "once again . . . the beacon of civilization for the world."[27] The nation might of course choose to become an "archaeo-logical bordello or an Anglo-Saxon colony." But the example of Rome, which had "laid out roads and drawn boundaries and given the world the eternal laws of its legal codes" placed modern Italians under "another universal duty."[28] For no one, in Theodor Mommsen's words, could "remain at Rome without a universal idea." Rome must again become "the leading city of the civilization of all of western Europe" and Italy "the leading nation of world history."[29]

The political content of that "new civilization" was clear from very early in Mussolini's career as a Fascist. The world, Mussolini announced in 1921 and 1922, was moving rightward, and Fascism itself was "scarcely at the beginnings of its mission."[30] By mid-1925, Mussolini had taken to characterizing Fascism as "one of the few cre-ative ideas of this tormented historical period." Italy, the last of the

---

24. OO 6:429 (10 November 1914); 7:70 (11 December 1914); 7:197 (14 February 1915); 7:418 (24 May 1915); 7:394 (16 May 1915).
25. OO 7:57 (29 November 1914).
26. OO 18:331; 10:434–35, 11:91–92, 12:77.
27. The war and Italy's mission: OO 11:86 (19 May 1918); 13:147 (24 May 1919); 18:200 (5 May 1922); 21:443 (4 November 1925); 23:248 (4 November 1928); beacon of civi-lization: 12:77 (20 December 1918); 16:128 (25 January 1921).
28. OO 14:22 (24 September 1919); also 15:70, 16:106, 17:148; Rome: 15:217–18 (24 September 1920).
29. OO 15:70 (1 July 1920), 16:159 (6 February 1921); 18:144 (6 April 1922).
30. OO 17:18 (30 June 1921); see also 18:69, 71; 16:142 (2 February 1921).

great powers to achieve maturity, was the first to construct a truly modern state. Like the French Revolution, the Fascist revolution would have worldwide influence and epochal significance. By late 1926, the Duce had become self-assured enough to claim grandiloquently that his movement was the bearer of a "new type of civilization." The twentieth century would not merely be the "century of Italian power," it would also be the century of universal Fascism.[31]

Mussolini's fundamental ideas were not entirely unsystematic. But Hitler's "rock-hard convictions" amounted to a philosophy of history, an all-embracing, all-explanatory system of belief. Its first principle, from which Hitler never wavered after his first recorded enunciation of it in 1919, was pseudobiological racism, the "anti-Semitism of reason."[32] Race, he claimed in January 1921, was "the driving force of world history"; later, in *Mein Kampf*, he described it as "the key not only to world history, but to all human culture." History was the history of race struggle. National Socialism was ultimately a science.[33]

Some historians have argued that attempts to interpret Hitler's ideology "as if it were systematic" are futile; others have suggested that in the end the ideology's function as a tool of totalitarian manipulation was essential and its "intellectual substance" unimportant.[34] But Hitler was neither a trendy relativist, nor a man who lacked respect for convictions. In his way – and to the dismay of more up-to-date NSDAP ideologues such as Alfred Rosenberg – Hitler was a nineteenth-century positivist with ideas at least as systematic as those of the Marx who asserted that history was the history of class struggle. Both Marxism and Hitler's world view were millenarian religions of world salvation: salvation for man as a species reborn from the proletariat in one case, salvation for the reborn Aryan species of man in the other.[35] Both required the pitiless elimination of groups: the class enemy for Marxism, the racial enemy for Nazism. Nor did Nazism's

31. OO 21:389 (24 September 1925); 22:109 (7 April 1926); 22:187 (early August 1926); 22:12 (18 November 1925), 22:135 (23 May 1926); and in general Michael Ledeen, *Universal Fascism* (New York, 1972).
32. HSA, p. 89 (16 September 1919); a dearth of sources has so far prevented detailed reconstruction of Hitler's views before 1919.
33. HSA, p. 301 (27 January 1921); MK, p. 339.
34. Mason, "The Primacy of Politics," p. 193; Karl Dietrich Bracher, in Bracher, Wolfgang Sauer, and Gerhard Schulz, *Die nationalsozialistische Machtergreifung* (Cologne, 2nd rev. ed., 1962), pp. 262, 271, 286; Schulz, *Aufstieg des Nationalsozialismus*, pp. 218, 421; Martin Broszat, *The Hitler State* (London, 1981), p. 218; Mommsen, "National Socialism," p. 68.
35. On the eschatological core of Marxism, see Robert C. Tucker, *Philosophy and Myth in Karl Marx* (London, 1961), and Leszek Kolakowski, *Main Currents of Marxism*, vol. 1 (Oxford, 1978).

alleged "lack of intellectual substance" prevent German intellectuals from embracing it with an enthusiasm that could not have been wholly feigned.

Hitler's system naturally did not spring suddenly from the aspirant Führer's brow, although scholars have sometimes overestimated the length of time Hitler took to weld his ideas together.[36] Much later, Hitler conceded to his entourage that "in the early days of the movement I found myself compelled to act from intuition." Only during his post-Putsch imprisonment in 1924, he maintained, did he have the time to "confirm his ideas by the study of natural history [*den Gedanken naturgeschichtlich zu begründen*]."[37] But Hitler's early speeches suggest that it required roughly three years, from the fall of 1919 to the winter of 1922, for the "anti-Semitism of reason" to harden into a genuine world system, complete with a visionary program for action, of which more later.

Hitler's starting point was the "recognition" (the English is pale and inadequate beside the German *Erkenntnis*) that the "race-tuberculosis of nations," the Jews, were responsible for the 1918 revolution and thus for Germany's defeat in the Great War. By the late spring of 1920 Hitler had taken a further, decisive step. Perhaps under the influence of his revered friend, the drunkard poet Dietrich Eckhart, and of the *Protocols of the Elders of Zion*, which appeared in German in January 1920, Hitler began to enunciate an all-embracing interpretation of world history.[38] He now recognized the Jews from Moses to Lenin, or "from Joseph to Rathenau," as the essence of triumphant evil from the Bronze Age to the Weimar Republic. Jewish "robber nomads," the "most national race of all the ages," lived by parasitically corrupting other peoples while seeking world mastery for themselves. Only Germany stood in the way: "Jewry . . . knew well that its domination could only be broken by a national force as strong as itself, and that would be the German *Volk*." Hitler's solution, as early as April 1920, was simple and drastic: he proclaimed "the inexorable resolve to strike

---

36. Common practice is to ascribe canonical status to *Mein Kampf* (1924–26). The early sources in HSA show that all decisive elements in *Mein Kampf* had emerged by the end of 1922.
37. *Monologe*, p. 49 (July 1941); see also p. 262.
38. HSA, pp. 88–90, pp. 156, 176. Hitler freely and gratefully admitted Eckhart's early influence (MK, p. 687, and *Monologe*, p. 208 [1942]). For Hitler as a "pupil" of the *Protocols*, see Walter Laqueur, *Russia and Germany* (Boston, 1965), pp. 103–04, 340 note 54; Norman Cohn, *Warrant for Genocide* (New York, 1966), p. 193. Hitler's first recorded mention of the *Protocols* dates from August 1921 (HSA, p. 452); his speeches suggest earlier acquaintance with their contents.

the evil at its root and exterminate it root and branch."[39] That this was at least potentially a project on a world scale was clear from the insistence with which Hitler spoke of the Jews' own "world power plans" and "eternal Jewish goal – world domination." His remarks about German aims widened correspondingly, from the conventional nationalist (and NSDAP program) demand for the unification of all Germans in one state "from Memel to Pressburg, from Königsberg to Strassburg," to the more grandiose if vaguer project of creating a "Germanic empire of the German nation."[40]

By March 1921 his aim was no longer defense, but offense: it was Germany's mission to "heal" a sick world.[41] In the spring of 1922, Hitler began to make that claim a major element in his speeches. Only two alternatives existed for Germany: "either victory of the Aryan side or its annihilation and victory of the Jews." Germanic blood was gradually becoming exhausted, and the future of the world was grim unless Germany "liberated" itself. The nation's "greatest deed" lay ahead of it: "to be leader [*Führer*] in the coming battle of the Aryans against the Jewish world peril." Germany, he insisted in the next months, must be "the foundation of an Aryan world order." That was Germany's "historic mission."[42] Such an order would mean an end to history in the conventional sense. In *Mein Kampf* Hitler made the point explicitly:

> And so the folkish philosophy of life corresponds to the innermost will of Nature, since it restores that free play of forces which must lead to a continuous mutual higher breeding, until at last the best of humanity, having achieved possession of this earth, will have a free path for activity in domains which will lie partly above it and partly outside it.

Even the iron law of struggle might fall into abeyance: ". . . the pacifistic-humane idea is perfectly all right perhaps when the highest type of man has previously conquered and subjected the world."[43] Mankind would achieve biological apotheosis. Hitler had fused pseudo-Dar-

---

39. HSA, pp. 137–38, 145–46, 184–204 (31 May, 11 June, 13 August 1920); HSA, pp. 119–20 (6 April 1920): ". . . es beseelt uns die unerbittliche Entschlossenheit, das Übel an die Wurzel zu packen und mit Stumpf und Stiel auszurotten (lebhafter Beifall)."
40. Jewish world domination: HSA pp. 195, 220, 254, 273, 464 (among others); uniting all Germans: pp. 106, 126, 128, 180, 242.
41. HSA, p. 354 (19 March 1921); Hitler borrowed from a nineteenth-century tag: "und es mag am deutschen Wesen / einmal noch die Welt genesen."
42. HSA, pp. 620, 623, 631, 698, 779 (12 April 1921; 28 September 1922; 3 January 1923); see also p. 694.
43. MK, pp. 383–84, 288.

winist anti-Semitism and German nationalism into a religion of world redemption.

On a fundamental level, the beliefs of Hitler and Mussolini were thus different in kind. Mussolini's assumption that struggle was the father of all things and his revolutionary and national myths were not cut from the same cloth as Hitler's political religion. Mussolini did not propose to rescue the world for good but merely to establish the new Rome's dominant place in it. Nevertheless, the internal and geopolitical programs the two leaders drew from their ideologies were rather more similar than the beliefs themselves.

By 1926–27, Mussolini's program was fixed in all essential details. Internally, he proposed to create a fanatical following for the national myth – a new sort of Italian – while consolidating his own unchallenged power as dictator. The war had undoubtedly accelerated the "process of consolidation of the national consciousness." But given Italy's fragile traditions and short existence, *italianità* remained a "privilege limited to a relatively small minority."[44] And only a new elite could enforce the unity and discipline necessary for external self-assertion.

Here the war itself had helped. It had divided the fittest nations, including Italy, from the unfit, and had divided the Italians themselves into those who "had been there," and those who had not. The former, the "lords of the trenches [*trincerocrazia*]," would rule. But that vision soon proved a disappointment; the mass of returning veterans did not rally to the *Fasci di Combattimento* that Mussolini founded in March 1919.[45] The early Fascists, Mussolini ruefully concluded in 1919, were also far from a unified force: "their utter lack of respect for authority [*strafottanza*] and dynamism make it hard for them to form a block even with themselves." Mussolini therefore made tactical concessions to the spirit of the hour by describing his new movement as "ultra-libertarian," and denounced all dictatorships except that of "will and intelligence."[46]

But once "the hour of Fascism" came in the summer of 1920 with the Trieste *Fascio*'s ruthless assault on the Slovenes of the newly annexed areas, Mussolini felt safe to celebrate hierarchy and discipline. The turbulent chieftains of provincial Fascism must submit to him, "if

44.   See particularly OO 13:147–48 (24 May 1919); 16:20 (20 November 1920).
45.   OO 8:272, 10:140 (22 December 1916; 15 December 1917); on the veterans' movement, see Giovanni Sabbatucci, *I combattenti nel primo dopoguerra* (Bari, 1974).
46.   OO 14:71, 133 (18 October, 15 November 1919); also 14:151; 12:326–27 (23 March 1919).

[Fascism] wants, tomorrow, to impose discipline on the entire nation."[47] He made no secret of his conviction that parliamentary democracy was a miserable nineteenth-century relic; that was yet another link between Mussolini the Socialist and Mussolini the Fascist.[48] In March 1923, after becoming prime minister, he openly proclaimed that the PNF would entrench itself "and defend itself against all comers." And in the spring of 1924 he described the newly elected Chamber of Deputies, despite its Fascist majority assured by an electoral law devised for that very purpose, as "the last parliamentary experiment Italy [would] make."[49]

He was not afraid to pronounce the word *dictatorship* without qualification – and with approval – as early as November 1921. At a November 1923 press conference, he remarked that "every century [had] its history, its institutions; an intelligent dictatorship could last a long time." The "essential thing . . . [was] to set up the machinery; once it was set up, an operator could always be found." The new regime would be no mere personal dictatorship; it would inaugurate a new age in government.[50]

The full urgency of his task came to Mussolini only in the summer 1924 crisis that followed the murder – at Mussolini's order – of the Socialist deputy Giacomo Matteotti.[51] The spontaneous revulsion of much of Italian opinion showed the superficiality of the conversion to Fascism that had so far taken place. After shutting down the opposition from 3 January 1925 onward, he laid claim to total power throughout Italian society with a new insistence and openness. To the PNF congress of June 1925, he trumpeted "our ferocious totalitarian will . . . to Fascistize the nation, so that tomorrow Italian and Fascist, more or less like Italian and Catholic, will be the same thing." The Duce proposed to spawn the new man "in the laboratory":

> to create . . . the class of the warriors, who are always ready to die; the class of the inventors, who pursue the secrets of the mysteries [of nature]; the class of judges; the class of the great captains of industry; of the great gov-

47. OO 18:391–92, 412–13 (7 and 20 September 1922); for the "hour of Fascism," 15:152 (21 August 1920).
48. OO 17:18, 268–69 (30 June, 22 November 1921); 18:66–72 (25 February 1922).
49. OO 19:196 (March 1923); 20:295 (27 May 1924).
50. OO 17:268 (22 November 1922); 20:80 (1 November 1923). De Felice's contention (*Mussolini il fascista*, vol. 1, pp. 537–38 ; see also pp. 465, 591, 594, 602, 618, and vol. 2, pp. 9–10, 34–35, 67, 128–29, 342) that Mussolini did not seek a one-party dictatorial regime before late 1925 does not fit the evidence.
51. See Mauro Canali, *Il delitto Matteotti: Affarismo e politica nel primo governo Mussolini* (Bologna, Il Mulino, 1997), pp. 429–38.

ernors. It is through this sort of methodical selection that one creates the
great elites that in turn establish empires.[52]

Dictatorship, Mussolini added in the autumn of 1925, might have
overcome the old "image of the Italian people, repeated abroad, . . . of
a small nation, disorderly, noisy, and fidgety." But what Mussolini
described as "the weaknesses of the Italian character: . . . shallowness,
fecklessness, the belief that everything will go well," still remained.
These "traditional defects" must give way to "tenacity, perseverance,
and methodical work."[53] The regime must sweep away "the sediments
deposited in those awful centuries of political, military, and moral
decadence that r[an] from 1600 to the rise of Napoleon." It must in
other words complete the *Risorgimento*, which – Mussolini reiterated –
was "only the beginning, the work of a tiny minority." The "new man"
who would ultimately emerge from the PNF youth organizations
would revel in a "virile warrior education," and display a "sense of
virility, of power, of conquest" – and a brutish xenophobia.[54] He would
know neither fear, nor guilt, nor pity, and would owe loyalty to the
Duce, not king or Pope.

The path Mussolini eventually laid down toward that goal was the
logical extension of the tradition of Oriani and of the other post-
Risorgimento yearners for a great war to make Italy whole. Mussolini
had already called in 1914–15 for war as a kind of revolution. All revolutions, he remarked in 1920 in commenting on events in Russia,
were "fated to be imperialist." And in the same 1925 speech in which
he insisted on the creation of new elites, he affirmed that revolution
and war, domestic and foreign policy, reciprocally interacted:

> War and revolution are two terms that are almost always linked. Either war
> produces revolution or it is revolution that leads to war. Even the strategy
> of the two movements is alike: as in war, in revolution you do not always
> attack. Sometimes you must make more or less strategic retreats.
> Sometimes you must rest for long periods on positions you have conquered.
> But the goal is there: empire.

His ensuing protestations that empire need not be "territorial," but

---

52. All from OO 21:362–63 (22 June 1925).
53. OO 22:23, 100, 117, 246 (5 December 1925; 28 March, 15 April, 28 October 1926);
    23:78–79 (17 December 1927).
54. OO 24:75–76, 101; for Mussolini on the imperative of hatred toward foreigners, see
    Grandi diary, 1929–32, entry for 15 February 1929 (microfilm, Georgetown University
    Library, Washington, D.C.).

could be "political, economic, spiritual" rang hollow after all the talk of war.[55]

Mussolini was fully aware that his movement's weakness had so far prevented the upheaval to which he aspired. In a frank moment in 1924, he admitted to his Party subordinates that the March on Rome had been "a revolutionary deed and a victorious insurrection, [but] not a revolution. The revolution comes later." According to reports from Mussolini's "closest confidants" that reached the German ambassador in late 1924, Mussolini had chosen "another, rather more protracted method" of seizing total power than the antimonarchical coup feared at the time of the March on Rome. The real Fascist revolution would come in and through a great victorious war that would free Mussolini "to have himself acclaimed emperor while easily pushing aside the unwarlike king."[56]

Mussolini's starting point in the quest for total power through external violence was inevitably the Great War, which even before its end had made Italy an "imperial" nation, fully entitled to the Adriatic victory Slavs and Allies sought to deny. Both history and the fact that the Italian people were "prolific and hard-working" gave the right to expansion in the Mediterranean, "the sea of Rome." Imperialism, Mussolini insisted unseasonably on the first day of January 1919, in the midst of his countrymen's brief enthusiasm for Woodrow Wilson, was "an eternal and immutable law of life."[57] At the inaugural meeting of the *Fasci di Combattimento* that March, Mussolini proclaimed with statistics in hand that Italy's narrow and mountainous land and rapidly multiplying forty millions entitled it to a greater share of the Earth. Should the Allies of 1915-18 cheat Italy at the peace table, Mussolini threatened in the following weeks, Italy should join Germany. From its position athwart Britain's Mediterranean lines of communication it should shatter the British Empire in Africa and Asia.[58]

Mussolini took up with a vengeance Enrico Corradini's myth of the international class war. Italy should challenge the "quintessentially plutocratic and bourgeois" alliance of French, British, and Americans.

55. OO 21:362–63.
56. OO 44:10; Neurath to Auswärtiges Amt, 2 December 1924, GFM 6059/E447588–94 (quotation: E447591); see also OO 21:362–63 (22 June 1925): only the total "Fascistization" of the nation would give Fascism the right to call itself a revolution.
57. OO 10:434–35 (7 April 1918); 11:91–92 (28 May 1918); 12:77, 101 (20 December 1918, 1 January 1919).
58. OO 12:323 (23 March 1919); 15:184–85 (5 September 1920); 13:71, 76 (20, 23 April 1919).

The French, at least, were demographically exhausted. Italy would follow the Spain of Charles V and the France of Louis XIV and Napoleon as the "dominant nation of the entire Latin world," thanks to its demographic dynamism and the "virtues of our race [*stirpe*]."[59] Versailles was transitory. Demographic equilibria were shifting. The "immense wave" of Slavdom would wipe away the small states of central Europe, while the 70 to 80 million Germans would move westward into France to rectify that decadent nation's regrettable "imbalance between territory and population." As for Italy, it was after Russia and Germany the "most compact and homogeneous national bloc" in Europe. By 1950 that bloc would number 60 million, including the Italian population of the Mediterranean-African colonies and the emigrants across the oceans. Italy, "to be free," must throw off its economic dependence on the Anglo-Saxons by achieving self-sufficiency in grain and energy. It could then "become the dominating nation of the Mediterranean basin and discharge on the African shores of that sea the majority of its population and energies." The areas Italy was destined to conquer were "extraordinarily thinly settled" – an insight that would have come as a surprise to their inhabitants. But some "human tidal waves [*straripamenti di masse umane*]" were "inevitable and necessary," the "fertilizing reversals of history."[60]

Demography continued to furnish a major argument for expansion. But by the mid-1920s Mussolini had turned the argument in a direction unthought-of by Corradini and other prophets of the imperialism of the prolific poor. Once in power, Mussolini discovered that pride in the "riotous development" of Italy's population was misplaced.[61] Some areas of Italy, he recognized as early as mid-1923, resembled the despised French in their "demographic decadence." By 1927, once precise statistics had become available, Mussolini had become alarmed. In his marathon Ascension Day speech of May 1927, he surveyed the demographic decline of France and Britain, and insisted that the same decline – in other words, the usual demographic pattern of industrial societies – was a threat to the future of Italy as well. "Demographic potency" was the fundamental ingredient of national power; 40 million Italians were too few compared to the 40 million French, the 46 million British, the 90 million Germans, the 200 million Slavs,

59. OO 13:109, 147–49 (9 and 24 May 1919).
60. All from OO 16:105–06 (8 January 1921): "Per essere liberi."
61. Demography (among others): OO 16:335, 18:180, 19:191, 20:74 (1921–23) and particularly 21:97 (4 October 1924); "decadence" in some areas of Italy: 19:285 (22 June 1923).

and the 540 million inhabitants of the British and French colonial empires. Italy, "if it [were] to count for something," would have to "approach the threshold of the second half of th[e] century with a population no smaller than 60 million inhabitants." The alternative was renunciation of Italy's mission: "If we diminish in numbers, gentlemen, we will not found an empire, we will [instead] become a colony." The tenacious resistance to "the pernicious currents of contemporary civilization" by Basilicata, one of Italy's most miserably poor and populous regions, was an act of foreign policy.[62]

Mussolini's ensuing campaign to "ruralize Italy, even if it takes billions and half a century," was thus no more than a small part of a grand design that stretched far beyond the confines of the Italian state of the 1920s. It was an attempt to create the demographic conditions for Mediterranean primacy. The "battle for grain" of 1925 and later years, which many historians have interpreted as a propaganda stunt or as largesse to landed interests, was a related and conscious attempt to provide the economic prerequisites for Italy's "freedom":

> In an Italy entirely reclaimed [*bonificata*], cultivated, irrigated, and disciplined, in other words a Fascist Italy, there is space and bread for another ten million men. Sixty million Italians will make the weight of their numbers and their power felt in the history of the world.[63]

The geographic and strategic requirements of Italian freedom, and of empire, were as much on Mussolini's mind as the economic and demographic ones. The Great War had resolved the problem of Italy's land frontiers; the future lay on the waters. Only Italy was a truly Mediterranean nation. The French and Spaniards had Atlantic ports. Mediterranean preponderance [*predominio*] was therefore Italy's "by right of its geographic configuration and the maritime traditions of its race [*stirpe*]." The inland sea must become an Italian lake, "expelling those who are . . . parasites." Asserting Italy's rights would require breaking "the chains of hostility that surround[ed] Italy in the Mediterranean," and might also require "the demolition of the British

---

62. French decadence: especially OO 38:396 (22 June 1923); the rest from 22:364–67 (26 May 1927) (the "discorso dell'Ascensione").
63. "Ruralize Italy": OO 40:298 (24 March 1927); the rest from 23:216 (September 1928). De Felice's assumption that Mussolini's foreign and domestic programs were mutually exclusive alternatives (*Mussolini il fascista* [Turin, 1968], vol. 2, pp. 359–60; *Mussolini il Duce*, vol. 1, p. 179; *Mussolini il Duce*, vol. 2, p. 155) fits neither Mussolini's words nor the regime's actions. Carl Ipsen, *Dictating Demography: The Problem of Population in Fascist Italy* (Cambridge, 1996), analyzes the implementation and totalitarian implications of Fascist demographic policy.

Empire." The British guarded the principal exits from the Mediterranean at Gibraltar and Suez, and thus had a stranglehold over
Italy's supplies of food and raw materials.[64] By 1926–27, as described
in the following chapter, Mussolini had elevated that insight into a
general law of geopolitics that mandated a "march to the ocean" across
African territory that the Western powers controlled, in fulfillment of
Italy's mission of becoming a genuine great power. The Germans were
the most likely ally in that quest: despite their defeat in 1918, "the axis
of European history passe[d] through Berlin."[65]

Hitler's vision had many similarities to Mussolini's, but was different in three fundamental ways. First, Hitler's unified, monocausal
world view allowed him to derive everything from the central dogma
of race. Second, that dogma's world wide implications inevitably
pushed any program drawn from it in the direction of world domination and biological utopia, while Prussia-Germany's tradition of blood
and iron and its barely thwarted "grasp at world power" in 1914–18
made such a program inherently plausible to some Germans.
Mussolini's nationalism, by contrast, aspired only to Mediterranean
mastery and a century or two of European cultural and political hegemony on the model of Rome, or of France from Louis XIV to
Napoleon III. And Italy's weakness made even that aim seem visionary.

From the beginning, Hitler showed greater theoretical rigor than
Mussolini. Even the beer-hall agitator of 1920–21 conceived his internal goals, the "nationalization of the masses," race purification, and
the creation of a pitiless nationalist dictatorship, as a unified whole.[66]
Germany's class, religious, and tribal cleavages must disappear, as they
had in the euphoria of August 1914 and in the trenches of the Great
War. *Klassen- und Standesdünkel*, religious mistrust, and Prussian-
Bavarian enmity all weakened the Germanic Aryan race's struggle
against the Jewish world conspiracy. Internal divisions were themselves the product of racial mixing and Jewish parasitism: class consciousness was a Jewish disease, a form of false consciousness that the
Jews, that "most national race of all the ages," deliberately and sys-
tematically spread, but did not share.[67]

---

64. In order: OO 13:143 (22 May 1919); 15:289–90 (20 August 1920); 16:300–01 (3 May
    1921); 18:439 (4 October 1923); 15:37 (15 June 1920)(see also 15:29, 18:459); 18:432
    (1 October 1922); 21:273 (2 April 1925).
65. Axis: OO 18:120; also 20:29; for detailed analysis of Mussolini's geopolitics and quest
    for the German alliance, see Chapter 3 of this volume.
66. For the phrase, MK, p. 336; for some of the background, George L. Mosse, *The
    Nationalization of the Masses* (New York, 1975).
67. HSA, pp. 136–38, 145–46, 151 (31 May, 11 and 24 June 1920).

The remedy was simple: a "revolution in convictions [*Revolution der Gesinnung*]" that would sweep away class distinctions and inculcate the "blind, rock-hard, unshakable *belief* in the irresistible power of the German *Volk*" and in a better future. "For this reason, the aim of the National Socialists from 1920 on was "*not to become a class organization, but rather a Volk movement.*"[68] And hence Hitler's "socialism": the term was more than mere demagogy, even if Hitler did at one point remark that the movement's title of "workers' party" was a consequence of the need to "have the workers behind us."[69] What Hitler meant by "socialism" was not a society based on a nineteenth-century theory of political economy, but a new egalitarian style and unprecedented social mobility. The National Socialist revolution would not merely transform consciousness. It would liberate those Germans who until then had had no chance to rise. Ossified distinctions of birth, education, and wealth, according to Hitler, profited only the Jewish parasites. "Make way for talent!" was a corollary of anti-Semitism, the chief social ingredient of National Socialism, and one of its most effective appeals. Hitler, the self-proclaimed and self-evident "most capable man" of the Party, was simultaneously the prophet of the career open to talent, and its prize exemplar. His demand that the world judge him "by performance alone" was as unanswerable while success lasted as his sincerity was undeniable when he insisted that every true German "carried his marshal's baton in his knapsack."[70]

The career open to talent had a negative side. By 1923 Hitler had come to the conclusion that those without talent – the requisite pedigree or physical attributes – must vanish. Germany would expel its Jews, if they were lucky, and take measures against the deformed, the mentally ill, syphilitics, and drunkards: "The preservation of a nation is more important than the preservation of its unfortunates." The *völkisch* state would see to it that "only the healthy beget children." By 1923–24, in connection with the evolution of his foreign policy ideas, Hitler had also come to the conclusion that the healthiest of the healthy were the peasantry: "The slums of the cities were responsible

68. HSA, pp. 239, 255, 156 (24 September, 26 October, 3 July 1920).
69. HSA, p. 105 (16 January 1920).
70. HSA, p. 296 (12 January 1921): "Freie Bahn dem Tüchtigen!"; p. 461 (26 August 1921); Hildegard von Kotze and Helmut Krausnick, eds., *"Es spricht der Führer"* (Gütersloh, 1966), pp. 215–16 (1937); HSA, p. 158 (6 July 1920) for Hitler's favorable early assessment of the French revolution ("national und aufbauend"). For Hitler on revolution and equality of opportunity, see Rainer Zitelmann, *Hitler: Selbstverständnis eines Revolutionärs* (Hamburg, 1987), Chapter 2 and Chapter 3, section 2, as well as pp. 208, 213-14 of this volume.

for nine-tenths, alcohol for one-tenth, of all human depravity." The countryside, not the cities, had provided the "healthier section of the *Volk*" that had crushed the 1919 red terror in Munich.[71] But he came to the mysticism of blood and soil relatively late, as a consequence rather than a cause of his vision of eastern conquest. He secretly mocked the full-blown agrarian sentimentalism of Himmler, Walther Darré, and Martin Bormann.[72]

The final ingredient in Hitler's internal vision was inevitably a political revolution to accompany the revolution of convictions, the career open to talent, and the repudiation of the last shreds of Judeo-Christian morality. Germany, Hitler proclaimed as early as April 1920, needed "neither monarchy nor republic, but the form of state that is the best for the [German] people. We need a dictator who is a genius." He demanded "a [man with an] iron skull, with muddy boots, perhaps, but with a clear conscience and a steel fist, who will end the blathering of these [Reichstag] drawing-room heroes, and give the nation a deed."[73] Once Hitler had received from his own party the "dictatorial powers" he demanded in the summer of 1921, his utterances on that score took on new authority. In a "Germanic democracy," the best brain decided, not the "sluggishness of the majority." Hitler had already cast himself in the part. He might describe himself as a mere "drummer" when flattering nationalist notables, but he also claimed for his movement the right to provide the "strong man" Germany needed. As early as February 1922 he insisted the NSDAP would lead Germany "when the rotten edifice [of the Republic] finally collapse[d]."[74]

Mussolini's example was a powerful help. Hitler apparently first took public note of the Duce in August 1922, and was soon proclaiming that Mussolini "had shown what a minority can do, if a holy national will inspires it": the Fascists had smashed "Jewish-Marxist terror" and dragged a lethargic majority with them. The National Socialists, he now repeatedly proclaimed, likewise aspired "to take the *Volk* in hand."[75] In the course of 1923 he sometimes veiled his claim to

---

71. HSA, pp. 646, 1023, 1026, 1116 (22 June 1922; before October 1923; 28 February 1924); MK, p. 403.
72. HSA, pp. 1023, 1116, are apparently the only pre-1925 Hitler references to the life-giving qualities of the peasantry.
73. HSA, pp. 126, 127 (27 April 1920); also p. 443; "iron skull": p. 333 (6 March 1921).
74. HSA, p. 438 (14 July 1921); p. 622 (12 April 1922); pp. 643 and note 6, 753–54 (29 May, 4 December 1922): "Wir brauchen einen starken Mann, und den werden die Nationalsozialisten bringen"; p. 565 (2 February 1922).
75. HSA, pp. 683, 726, 704, 711 (17 August, 9 November, 22 and 25 October 1922); see

supreme leadership. ("We must forge the sword; the Almighty will give us the man for this sword.") But in predicting to the *Daily Mail* in October 1923 that if a German Mussolini came, "people would fall down on their knees and worship him," Hitler could only have had himself in mind.[76] In his speeches at his trial after the November 1923 Putsch, he openly claimed political leadership of the *völkische* movement and of a nationalist revolution. His later outline in *Mein Kampf* of the constitutional implications of the Führer principle was no more than confirmation of views he had held at least since 1921–22.[77]

Hitler's early sense of his vocation as Führer was never more apparent than in the foreign policy that accompanied and complemented his internal revolutionary goals. From very early, as with Mussolini, unity and leadership at home were the indispensable prelude to expansion abroad in fulfillment of the nation's mission: "Nations are only capable of great advances when they have carried through the internal reforms that make it possible to project the entire race toward foreign policy goals."[78] But unlike the geography that made Italy "prisoner of the Mediterranean" and ultimately prescribed a war against the Western powers, Germany's position and traditions did not foreordain the direction of its expansion. Hitler was set on war from the beginning – the NSDAP's January 1920 program demanded "land and soil for the nation" – but it took until 1922 to work out whom to conquer.

Hitler began with the staid Wilhelmine program of naval and economic expansion he later denounced as naive and unworkable. Germany, a "thickly populated state with highly developed industry, [was] necessarily impelled toward the world economy and overseas self-assertion [*Weltgeltung*]."[79] He celebrated Germany's rise to industrial might in his early speeches, and his provisional conclusion of late 1920 was that a modern state could only exist through participation in the

---

also pp. 795 ("heads will roll"), 806, 950. As early as February 1921, Hitler had claimed that the movement's swastika flag was the only appropriate one for a future "Germanic state of the German nation" (p. 323).

76. HSA, pp. 966, 1027.
77. HSA, pp. 1007, 1128, 1188, 1210; MK, pp. 449–50. For a different view, see Albrecht Tyrell, *Vom "Trommler" zum "Führer"* (Munich, 1975); similarly, Ian Kershaw, *Hitler, 1889–1936: Hubris* (London, 1998), pp. 169–70. Tyrell's stress on the role of Hitler's surroundings and followers in creating the Führer role is well taken. But Tyrell also reads Hitler's comparative modesty between 1919 and 1921–22 as a self-doubt conspicuously absent from the man's speeches, and ignores the more plausible possibility of tactical reticence.
78. HSA, p. 269 (30 November 1920).
79. HSA, pp. 207–08, 218 (25 August 1920).

world market, which in turn required the reestablishment of Germany's power position.[80]

But Hitler was far from finished. It was a short step from the NSDAP program's demand for soil to the claim that the causes of Germany's present misery included population increase. An aspiring nation that scorned birth control (an expedient that allegedly reduced nations to the "plaything [*Fangball*] of others") faced three choices: colonies, but Germany was admittedly a latecomer; emigration, which led to the permanent loss of the best blood to others; and industrial export. Pre-war Germany had taken the third course, and had failed because of England's envy, "the innermost root cause of the outbreak of war." In 1921 Hitler offered no remedy other than resistance to Versailles.[81] But by the end of December 1922, he had developed a coherent vision that remained essentially unaltered thereafter. His increasingly full-throated espousal of a German mission as "Führer of the Aryans" had brought with it the need for a commensurate foreign policy.

Even before the French occupation of the Ruhr in January 1923, which usually passes as the catalyst that impelled him to define his foreign policy program, Hitler's ideas had set. In a remarkable December 1922 conversation with an emissary of the then-Reich Chancellor Wilhelm Cuno, Hitler outlined with only slight reticence his ideas on both internal and foreign policy.[82] Internally, he was tactically circumspect, in deference to his audience. The nationalist dictatorship required to smash the Left could eventually give way to a monarchy; the solution of the Jewish question need not involve violence. His other views were less restrained:

> In foreign policy Germany must adjust itself to a purely continental policy, while avoiding the harming of English interests. We should attempt the carving up of Russia with English help. Russia would provide soil enough for German settlers, and a broad field of action for German industry. Then, when [we] settle accounts with France, England would not get in the way.

Hitler also mentioned Italy as a possible ally; even before hearing of Mussolini's movement he had been alive to the chance for exploiting

80. HSA, p. 271 (8 December 1920).
81. HSA, pp. 384, 421–22, 426–27 (10 and 31 May 1921); for his increasingly radical critique of Wilhelmine policy, pp. 505, 511 (21 October 1921).
82. Conversation with Eduard Sharrer, HSA, pp. 770–75; for the importance of the document, see pp. 34–35 of Geoffrey Stoakes, "The Evolution of Hitler's Ideas on Foreign Policy, 1919–1925," in Peter D. Stachura, ed., *The Shaping of the Nazi State* (New York, 1978).

Italian aspirations to "predominance in the Mediterranean." After discovering the Fascists, he defied German nationalist orthodoxy by proclaiming in November 1922 and thereafter that the Italian alliance required an end to "empty protests" over South Tyrol, which Italy had annexed in 1918.[83]

Hitler's December 1922 remarks included all the essential elements of the program he later outlined in the second volume of *Mein Kampf*, written in 1925–26: the violent reestablishment of domestic unity; expansion at Russia's expense; a settling of accounts with France; England and Italy as allies; and the most un-Wilhelmine conception of isolating enemies and destroying them one step at a time. The order of the steps in this *Stufenplan* remained problematic, however.[84] What the Ruhr occupation apparently did for Hitler was to make the elimination of France his highest priority; eastern expansion could only come after that preliminary step. But that was a minor change. The foundations of Hitler's program were in place. His subsequent elaborations of his vision in an essay of April 1924, in *Mein Kampf*, in his unpublished "second book" of 1928, and in campaign speeches of 1928 and 1930 in which he unambiguously claimed world mastery for Germany, brought only two new elements. The first was Hitler's discovery of America – the recognition that the United States might prove his final adversary. In that contest, Hitler concluded, Germany's greater concentration of Aryan stock would carry it to victory.[85] The second novelty was the recognition, even more explicit than Mussolini's, that foreign and domestic policy were inextricably linked:

> Domestic policy must secure the inner strength of a people so that it can assert itself in the sphere of foreign policy. Foreign policy must secure the life of a people for its domestic political development. Hence domestic policy and foreign policy are not only most closely linked, but must also mutually complement one another.

Translated into cruder terms, revolution was a prerequisite for expan-

---

83. HSA, pp. 118, 122, 168, 728 (29 March, 17 April, 1 August 1920, 14 November 1922); Jens Petersen, *Hitler-Mussolini* (Tübingen, 1973), pp. 65–68.
84. For Hitler's insistence on the need to proceed by stages, see especially MK, 249–50, and von Kotze and Krausnick, eds., *"Es spricht der Führer"*, pp. 147–48 (April 1937); for the Stufenplan metaphor, see Andreas Hillgruber, *Hitlers Strategie* (Frankfurt, 1965); Klaus Hildebrand, *The Foreign Policy of the Third Reich* (Berkeley, 1973); and Jost Dülffer, *Weimar, Hitler und die Marine* (Düsseldorf, 1973).
85. For the chain of utterances that links the Hitler of 1924 with the Hitler of 1933, see Jochen Thies, *Architekt der Weltherrschaft* (Düsseldorf, 1976), pp. 41–61, and Dülffer, *Marine*, pp. 204–20.

sion, and expansion for revolution. That insight was as important to
Hitler's program as his external *Stufenplan*.[86]

The foundations of the world views of Hitler and Mussolini were
thus different, but the visionary programs they developed had much
in common. Internal domination and foreign expansion, demography
and geopolitics, were intertwined. Both leaders hoped to proceed by
stages: consolidation at home, then exploitation of the rivalries of
other powers to gain freedom for conquest. And both leaders,
although Hitler was more rigid – or open – in laying down the alliances and stages by which Germany would climb to world mastery,
envisaged Italy and Germany as partners in destroying world order.

EXPANSION AND REVOLUTION: COUNTERFEIT PEACE

Comparative analysis of the collision between these visions and the
external world, and of the interplay of domestic politics and foreign
policy in the two regimes, must begin with the contexts in which the
two leaders operated. Those contexts had both similarities and decisive differences. Mussolini could draw to some extent on ancestor worship, thanks to the megalomania of Gioberti, Mazzini, and post-
Risorgimento ideologues such as Oriani. If the Liberal establishment
could routinely invoke Rome, as did Orlando when he hailed the victory in 1918 as a *"vittoria romana,"* Mussolini could invoke it with
greater conviction and skill.[87] And Mussolini could exploit, in ways the
establishment could not, the gap between Roman example and Italian
achievement, between Rome's status as center of the world and Italy's
relative backwardness and weakness in the age of industry and true
world empires. For the consequence, at least in the eyes of many educated Italians, of the gulf between national claims and reality, between
Roman victories and Liberal defeats at Custoza, Adua, and Caporetto,
was a national inferiority complex that only imperial self-assertion
could soothe. And when "Roman victory" failed to move the Allies at
the Paris peace conference to concede the territories Italy demanded,
the myth of the "mutilated victory" further intensified the frustrations
that fed the success of the Fascist movement.

86. Adolf Hitler, *Hitler's Second Book* (New York, 1961), p. 34; similarly, pp. 24, 46–47, 79,
    210. See also Martin Broszat, "Betrachtungen zu 'Hitlers Zweitem Buch,'" VfZG 9
    (1961), p. 422; the only systematic attempt to interpret Hitler's later policies in these
    terms is Dietrich Orlow, *The History of the Nazi Party*, vol. 2 (Pittsburgh, 1973).
87. Quoted in Vivarelli, *Origini del fascismo*, vol. 1, p. 236 note 207.

Internally, the Roman myth had an undoubtedly useful side: Caesar and Augustus personified its potentially dictatorial uses (for the virtues of the Republic, other than discipline, Mussolini had little use). But the myth also had an unfortunate aspect, which Mussolini's piously authoritarian Nationalist allies exploited to the full. Rome had given the West a legal and bureaucratic tradition that contained inherent if not always operative restraints on arbitrary personal power.

The ideologies and traditions of the principal competitors of dictatorial nationalism – Socialism and the Church of Rome – also stood in the way of the "barbarous" revolutionary dictatorship Mussolini sought. If German Social Democracy, in the words of one of its founders, was a "preparatory school for militarism" that took its organizational cues from the Prussian army, Italian socialism was a preparatory school for anarchy.[88] The fissiparous tendencies of the Italian labor movement and the ineffectually intransigent *massimalismo* that Mussolini himself had helped create made the nationalization of the masses a herculean task. The Vatican's ideological grip was far stronger even than that of the Socialists. "Catholic totalitarianism," as Pius XI half-jokingly described it in a 1932 conversation with Mussolini, demanded its due.[89] Nor could the Church entirely abandon the main tenets of Judeo-Christian ethics or its own claims to educate the young. Those claims conflicted directly with the regime's project of forging a new man.

Institutional structures and the war's impact also conspired to limit Mussolini's scope. Liberal Italy, despite a casual brutality in its dealings with the *popolo*, had always respected the rights of its elites. Cavour had trampled on liberal principles in the heat of political struggle, but he was not an admirer of Mill and Bentham for nothing. Giolitti's regime had acquired a low moral reputation, and had failed to command the loyalty of the young, the Nationalists, and the avant-garde who proclaimed with increasing vehemence the necessity of an authoritarian "new state."[90] But the cataclysm of 1915–18 had neither destroyed the parliamentary system outright, nor – despite the opening that war gave to Mussolini – given much promise of the ecstasy of national integration that nationalist Germans had glimpsed in and after the August days of 1914.

The one bright spot for an aspirant to dictatorship was the

88. For the remark (by August Bebel), see A. J. P. Taylor, *The Struggle for Mastery in Europe, 1848–1918* (Oxford, 1954), pp. xxxiii–xxxiv.
89. OO 37:129.
90. See Gentile, *Il mito dello Stato nuovo dal antigiolittismo al fascismo* (Bari, 1982).

Piedmontese-Italian state's authoritarian tradition in foreign and military policy, those most closely held of the *arcana imperii*.[91] For both constitutional and practical purposes that area had remained out of bounds to parliament, as Salandra, Sonnino, and the king had demonstrated in May 1915. But unfortunately for Mussolini, these arbitrary powers were not ones he could easily appropriate; by definition they belonged ultimately to the monarchy. And the king and his generals and admirals remained jealous of the authority and autonomy that war and victory had reinforced. Even after 1925, the monarchy remained the state's center of legitimacy for Italians who considered the state legitimate at all. Above all, the monarchy remained the center of legitimacy for the army, the only institution in Italy that could throw Mussolini out.

Finally, the political circumstances in which Mussolini took power were in some ways far from promising. The Liberals, from Orlando to Nitti to Giolitti to Bonomi to Facta, had failed to govern, had connived at Fascist violence, and had ultimately capitulated to Mussolini. But the crisis of the Liberal state was in no sense as cataclysmic as the German crisis of 1930–33; the Italian Liberals remained in parliament as the far from discredited "flankers" of a PNF that until the rigged election of May 1924 had mustered only 35 seats of the 535 in the Chamber of Deputies. Even after the abolition of the remaining non-Fascist parties in November 1926, conservative ex-Liberals in black shirts, along with Mussolini's Nationalist allies, helped set the tone in the Chamber and above all in the Senate. That tone was anything but *totalitario*. Even that implicit prophet of authoritarianism Vilfredo Pareto left behind a political testament, published in 1923, that urged Mussolini not to abolish parliament.[92] Italy's establishment remained in its heart committed to liberal forms, if not to liberal principles. It embraced the "cult of the Duce" gingerly because the Duce left it no choice – in both 1922 and 1925 – between acquiescence and a civil war the Fascists might not win, but which might open the road for the vengeful revival of Socialist *massimalisti* and Communists.

The Fascist Party itself was also of little help. Despite its paramilitary origins, it was at first anything but a centralized *Führerpartei*, and until 1926 it preserved an internal apparatus of committees and elec-

---

91. See Brunello Vigezzi's illuminating "Politica estera e opinione pubblica in Italia dal 1870 al 1945," *Nuova rivista storica* 63:5/6 (1979), pp. 548–54.
92. "Pochi punti di un futuro Ordinamento Costituzionale," *La vita italiana*, September–October 1923, pp. 165–69.

tions that smacked suspiciously of liberalism.[93] The Grand Council of Fascism, despite the role Mussolini assigned it as spearhead in the "partification" of the state, was a collegial body and an implicit check on Mussolini's authority; in the end its vote against the Duce on 24–25 July 1943 gave king and generals their pretext to overthrow the regime. The PNF contained figures whose politics ranged from violent monarchism (De Vecchi di Val Cismon) to syndicalist corporativism (Massimo Rocca) via brutal *squadrismo* (Roberto Farinacci, Italo Balbo). PNF intellectuals such as Bottai openly aspired to a liberalization of Party and regime. Above all, the turbulent local chieftains defied Mussolini's authority again and again, until after 1925 he finally bent them to his service by calling it the service of the state.[94] Thereafter he expressed his distrust of his own party most strikingly in the succession of summary mass dismissals of ministers and PNF potentates known as "changes of the guard." That was a leadership style very different from Hitler's tenacious and reciprocated loyalty even to followers as supremely disreputable as the sometime *Gauleiter* of Nuremberg, Julius Streicher.

Germany was indeed far more promising territory. Ideologically, German myths placed far fewer restrictions on arbitrary power than did the myth of Rome. The German tribal myth allowed Hitler to clothe his power, which German constitutional theorists recognized as "omnicompetent and total," in a veil suitable to the age of mass politics: "Germanic democracy."[95] The myths of the medieval Reich and the Prussian tradition of historic great men inspired awe for leadership and exacerbated the perceived gap between gray Weimar reality and past glory.[96] Finally, the miserable failure of the Second Reich to live up to widespread expectations of mythic leadership left open the role that Hitler eventually filled.[97] And unlike Mussolini, Hitler found in *völkisch* racism a preexisting radical ideology with wide resonance. The

---

93. See the 1921 and 1926 Party statutes, in Alberto Aquarone, *L'organizzazione dello Stato totalitario* (Turin, 1965), pp. 315–29, 386–92.
94. See Lyttelton, *Seizure of Power*, Chapter 11.
95. Ernst Rudolf Huber, *Verfassungsrecht des Grossdeutschen Reiches* (Hamburg, 1939), p. 142; HSA, p. 622 (12 April 1922).
96. Schulz, *Aufstieg des Nationalsozialismus*, pp. 65–66.
97. See Wolfgang Horn, *Führerideologie und Parteiorganization in der NSDAP (1919–1933)* (Düsseldorf, 1972), pp. 25–98. For the antecedents, see Class, *Wenn ich der Kaiser wär'*, pp. 54 (prophesying dictatorship should Germany lose the coming war), 242, 263 ("In Erwartung des Führers"); Schulz, *Aufstieg des Nationalsozialismus*, pp. 19–21, 127–28, 133–34; and F. L. Carsten, "Die historischen Wurzeln des Nationalsozialismus," in E. J. Feuchtwanger, ed., *Deutschland, Wandel und Bestand* (Munich, 1973), pp. 156–58.

already organized nationalism of small-town Germany, land of *Stamm-tisch* and rifle club, of combat veterans' leagues and patriotic beer-hall singing groups, did the rest.[98] The ideological alternatives to extreme nationalism, the SPD and Catholic subcultures, were also far more integrated into the nation than their Italian counterparts. And although the wartime interparty truce had broken down in 1917–18, the SPD and much of the working class harbored a noteworthy dislike of "Bolshevism" and a latent susceptibility to nationalist appeals.[99]

Finally, the ideology of the Prussian Protestant subculture – which included the *Reichswehr* – proved particularly welcoming to Hitler's blandishments after 1929. As Hitler himself put it, Protestantism, thanks to its origins and traditions, was better suited than Catholicism to defending "the interests of Germandom."[100] The decapitation of the state in 1918 had left the Protestant churches, celebrants of the mystical union of Throne and Altar, of "Potsdam and Bethlehem combined," without a focus for earthly loyalties at a time when they already had difficulty holding onto their flocks in the face of urbanization and the unsettling effects of the war. The Nazi movement offered insecure Protestant clergy a chance to draw closer to the *Volk* by participation in a great popular movement.[101] Hitler's cult was a conscious creation, but it was rooted, far more than that of the Duce, in native soil.

Institutionally as well, Hitler faced a more promising situation than his Italian predecessor, thanks to the decapitation of the state, the fierce vengefulness against the Left that pervaded bureaucracy and army, and the relative lack of cohesion of the German establishment. And Germany faced after 1930 an economic cataclysm, not the relatively mild Italian recession of 1921.

All these differences affected the nature of the compromises the two movements struck in order to gain power, and the dictators' subsequent freedom of movement. Mussolini, despite the clubs, daggers, pistols, and hand grenades of the *squadre* behind him, faced as prime

98. See the description in William S. Allen, *The Nazi Seizure of Power* (New York, 2nd ed., 1973), Chapter 2, and, for Bavaria to 1924, Harold J. Gordon, Jr., *Hitler and the Beer Hall Putsch* (Princeton, 1972), pp. 3–119; on the rifle clubs, Mosse, *Nationalization of the Masses*, pp. 148–54.
99. On the KPD, the SPD, and Germany's "Tory workers," see Hamilton, *Who Voted for Hitler?*, pp. 287–308, 387–89.
100. MK, p. 112.
101. For the phrase (Friedrich Naumann's), see Bracher, Sauer, and Schulz, *Machtergreifung*, p. 329; on Protestant electoral behavior, see particularly Hamilton, *Who Voted for Hitler?*, and Falter, *Hitlers Wähler*.

minister an establishment shaken in its self-confidence and prerogatives but still deeply entrenched: the monarchy, the army, the Church,
and the conservative "flankers" of Fascism in the Chamber of Deputies. Even after the one-sided 1924 election, he was dependent on a
parliamentary majority to an extent that Hitler, even before the Enabling Act of March 1933, was not.

What Mussolini could and did do was to consolidate control over
the PNF, and attempt to insert it into the state to counterbalance his
conservative flankers.[102] The first step, taken in mid-December 1922,
was the establishment of a Fascist "parallel cabinet," the Grand Council of Fascism. That marked the beginning of his attempt to create a
PNF sector of the state under his own control. The Grand Council
proceeded to decree the establishment of the Fascist Militia (MVSN).
The MVSN was not merely a device to control the unruly *squadre* by
placing them under formal military discipline. It was indeed, as Mussolini later billed it, the first step toward the "*Stato totalitario*," the first
attempt to breach the old state's monopoly of organized force.
Mussolini also moved adroitly to coopt and dominate the "flankers"
closest to him, the Nationalists, by inviting them in late 1922 to fuse
with the Fascist Party. Fusion increased Mussolini's social respectability and newfound appearance of monarchical loyalism, helped him
take control in the South, where the Nationalists were strong, and
provided the legal and political experts that provincial Fascism had
failed to produce. The Duce also took immediate steps to conciliate
the great economic interests. He flattered the major military leaders of
the Great War and reassured them that the MVSN would serve primarily as a police force. The Vatican did not remain exempt from his
attentions: while the Po Valley *squadristi* attacked Catholic labor
unions, Mussolini made clear in Rome his readiness to strike an advan-
tageous compromise, and he supervised the government bailout of the
Church's ailing Banco di Roma. In return, Mussolini could dispense
with the Democratic and *Partito Popolare* ministers he had accepted
into his cabinet, split the Catholic conservatives from the *Popolari* with
tacit Vatican assistance, and push through the electoral law that assured the government list an ironclad majority.[103]

In practice Mussolini still depended on the Liberal and Catholic
deputies. And despite the MVSN, he remained a royal prime minister.

---

102. The best account of Mussolini's tactics and relationship with his flankers is Lyttelton,
Seizure of Power, Chapters 5, 10.
103. See particularly Sabbatucci, "Il 'suicidio' della classe dirigente liberale. La legge Acerbo
1923–1924," *Italia contemporanea* no. 174 (1989), pp. 57–80.

The PNF was too weak politically to inaugurate a reign of terror in the absence of establishment support – even if terror could have achieved the unity Mussolini desired. Middle-class opinion lost its enthusiasm for castor oil once the Socialist mass organizations were crushed. An open trial of strength with the monarchy would have ranged the army and the vast majority of the politically active population behind the king. The crisis after Mussolini's bodyguard of thugs murdered Matteotti in June 1924 made clear the relationship of forces. His ante-chamber, the Duce later complained, emptied magically overnight; parliament rang with the accusation that he was the murderers' accomplice. The Liberals who made up much of the government majority publicly demanded an end to violence and respect for the constitution. D'Annunzio, inventor of the balcony speech and Mus-solini's principal rival as national mythmaker, described the tottering regime as a "fetid ruin."[104] The army, which despite assurances had taken amiss the creation of a Fascist fourth service, repeatedly claimed dominance over the MVSN. Mussolini had to concede; the MVSN swore loyalty to the king, while the Duce appointed additional gener-als to its command positions.

Mussolini's threat, made in cabinet, to "oppose any successor with all his forces" in the piazza ultimately carried the day, and opened the road, along with an opportune revolt by extremist MVSN leaders, for the suppression of the opposition and its press. The monarchy, through its military ministers and its Nationalist representative in the cabinet, Luigi Federzoni, preferred to save Mussolini rather than risk the civil war averted in 1922. Consolidation of the dictatorship in 1925–26 came with the tolerance of the establishment, and the result-ing balance was one Mussolini could not easily shift. He attempted to tilt the system slowly in his favor: that was the significance of his much-quoted slogan of 1925: "*durare.*"[105] Fascism had endured, had outlasted its enemies; now it must outlast its allies.

The Liberals proved easiest to eliminate. Mussolini's powers to leg-islate by decree steadily increased, and by 1926 he had no need of Salandra or Giolitti or their friends. The monarchy and its Nationalist and military following was not so easy to shake: they survived to remove Mussolini in July 1943. The Duce was able to insert the Grand Council of Fascism, like the MVSN, into the structure of the state. The law of 1928 that sanctioned its new authority as organ of the

---

104. De Felice, *Mussolini il fascista*, vol. 1, pp. 681 note 3.
105. OO 21:388 (24 September 1925).

regime as well as of the PNF also arrogated to it the right to regulate the royal succession.[106] The king was furious, but his own version of the strategy of endurance ultimately dictated acquiescence. In his relations with the armed forces, Mussolini likewise combined circumspection with gradual encroachment. When his 1924 choice for the war ministry, General Antonino Di Giorgio, ruffled the army's corporate feathers with proposals for military reform, Mussolini abandoned him and fulsomely praised the army establishment. He also temporarily adopted the thesis of the senior generals that defense of the Alpine frontiers had highest priority – a conception that cut across both his own Mediterranean projects and the navy's corporate interests.[107] These concessions to the army, and the rivalry between his two chief military assistants, Marshal Pietro Badoglio and General Ugo Cavallero, permitted Mussolini, who assumed all three service ministries in 1925, to achieve an uneasy position as arbiter. But military dilettantism and a hidden timidity in the face of expert opinion prevented him from imposing his own Mediterranean vision and priorities on the immobile army bureaucracy, while Di Giorgio's defeat at the hands of the army's conservatives made further attempts at reform from within the army itself improbable.[108]

Mussolini fared somewhat better with the king's men in government, the Nationalist notables. Fusion with the Fascist Party eliminated them as an organized, autonomous group, an outcome upon which Mussolini had insisted.[109] He also put important Nationalists to use. Federzoni, although he had supported Salandra for prime minister in October 1922 and had momentarily wavered before the imposition of dictatorship, made a first-rate minister of the interior and guardian of the state against PNF extremism. Alfredo Rocco, the legal brain of the Nationalists, produced a juridical edifice crowned with the famous Unified Law on Public Security of November 1926, a law so convenient for the police that much of it survived Fascism. But the Nationalists were also a long-term liability. A revolution to make

---

106. See Lyttelton, *Seizure of Power*, p. 431, and De Felice, *Mussolini il fascista*, vol. 2, pp. 310–11.
107. OO 21:312–13 (18 May 1925), with vigorous interruptions by Grand Admiral Paolo Thaon di Revel.
108. On Mussolini's military dilettantism and the army's peculiarities, see Knox, *Mussolini*, pp. 7–8, 16, 25–30, and Chapter 4 of this volume; on Di Giorgio's failure and its implications, Rochat, *L'esercito italiano da Vittorio Veneto a Mussolini*, Chapter 9, and Sullivan, "A Thirst for Glory," Chapter 2, section 2.
109. See Mussolini's comments in Franco Gaeta, *Il nazionalismo italiano* (Bari, rev. ed., 1981), pp. 242–43.

Italians into joyous pagan barbarians was unlikely if some of the revolutionary elite believed – with the ex-Nationalist and sometime secretary of the PNF, Giovanni Giuriati – that a revolution was "a juridical
construction, in other words, a far-reaching reform of internal public
law."[110]

The Church was an even more formidable obstacle than the Nationalists to any such revolution. Pius XI drove a hard bargain in the
negotiations that led to the "conciliation" of Roman Church and
Italian state in the Lateran Pacts of 1929. The regime, to the dismay
even of the king, conceded far more than any Liberal government
could have. In return, Mussolini gained major advantages. The deal
with Pius XI harnessed the Church's prestige to Mussolini's cult of
personality. He was now "the man Providence ha[d] placed in Our
path." The Church had blessed the regime with all the weight of its
centuries of authority; Italy's overwhelmingly Catholic population was
now free to support Fascism without reservation. And the Vatican was
itself caught: once it had made its pact with Mussolini, it had an investment in the regime's continued existence. The Pope's blessing of Mussolini meant that later Vatican protests against the regime's 1931 attack
on Catholic Action youth groups and against the racial persecution
Mussolini ordered in 1938 did not carry conviction. But the Lateran
Pacts also entailed constant Church interference in the most varied
political and educational questions. The Vatican's legal rights under
the treaties in some ways made it a more dangerous competitor for the
loyalty of the population after 1929 than before.

Internationally, Mussolini faced a web of restraints at least as daunting as those at home. The Great War had indisputably improved
Italy's power position. Austria-Hungary had disintegrated, and the Yugoslav successor state could neither challenge Italy at sea nor threaten
it on land. That gave Italy both Balkan opportunities and freedom for
Mediterranean expansion without worry about its rear. In other
respects the position was less favorable. Germany's temporary eclipse
had removed the time-honored counterweight to French power.
England, Italy's "traditional friend," was no more likely than it had
been before 1914 to underwrite an Italian imperial expansion that
would ultimately conflict with its own interests. Italy's immense
wartime debt and endemic balance of payments deficit rendered Mussolini as financially dependent on London and Washington as Liberal

110. Giuriati to Mussolini, 17 July 1943, in Giovanni Giuriati, *La parabola di Mussolini nei
    ricordi di un gerarca* (Bari, 1981), p. 221.

Italy had been on Paris and Berlin. That weakness, the narrow and parochial character of Italy's industrial base, and the far-from-pleasant memory of the Great War made the armaments expenditure required for conquest unpalatable to his domestic allies. The regime barely succeeded in stabilizing the lira in 1926–27, and that hard-won stability, which depended in large part on the favor of the house of Morgan, counselled caution.[111] In the event, only the navy and the newly created air force put the 1920s to best use; the army largely stagnated.[112]

Finally, before Mussolini could strike out on his own, he had to clear up Liberal Italy's colonial legacy: Libya, whose Arab inhabitants had driven Italy's garrisons back to coastal enclaves in 1915–18. The last Liberal government had begun the reconquest. But not until 1931–32 could Mussolini and his associates announce that the "rebellion" was "definitively crushed." The regime, consolidated at home, and fresh from killing or starving perhaps a third of the population of Cyrenaica, was free to look for new conquests – just as the Great Depression ended American financial tutelage, enfeebled the British, and produced, through Hitler, the German revival that Mussolini had foreseen would give Italy freedom. The Duce had from the mid-1920s on tried the patience of his advisers with projects for attacks on Turkey and sweeps into Croatia or France.[113] Now, ten years after the March on Rome, the road to empire began to open.

Hitler faced some of the same restraints that ensnared Mussolini, but the restraints themselves were weaker and the power of the Nazi movement within Germany and of Germany in the world notably greater than in the Italian case. The overwhelming force of the economic crisis that had helped bring the Nazis to power eased the dictator's task. Radical solutions seemed more plausible than in the Italy of 1922–25. The size and unsatiated radicalism of SA, Party, and infant SS made a purge of enemies unavoidable, even had Hitler wished to avoid it. The Party and its organizations were also large enough, and had attracted enough middle-class support, to provide adequate if often crude cadres for many of the key positions in the regional governments, for new national organizations such as the propaganda ministry, and for the expansion of Party and SS into areas reserved for state and establishment. And that state and establishment were themselves

---

111. When Mussolini heard that his Ascension Day 1927 prophecy of European war between 1935 and 1940 (OO 22:386) had appalled his New York bankers, he back-pedaled vigorously (DDI 7/7/236; see also OO 23:177).
112. See Knox, *Mussolini*, Chapter 1, and Chapter 4 of this volume.
113. See Chapter 3 of this volume.

less unified, more in tune with the dictator's goals, and far more capable of realizing them than their Italian counterparts.

At the top, instead of Victor Emmanuel III, tenacious defender of the centuries-old prerogatives of his house, stood Hindenburg. The field marshal had in 1932 assured an acquaintance that he would not hand Germany over to Hitler "like a laboratory rabbit." But after 30 January 1933 he did just that, through miscalculation of Hitler's intentions, the weariness of age, and the effects of Hitler's deferential and persuasive handling.[114] Some in the army looked to Hindenburg for a lead, but received none. General von Blomberg, far from guaranteeing the *Reichswehr*'s independence, soon showed himself convinced of Hitler's historic mission. The army, in the words of Blomberg's more calculating assistant at the *Reichswehr* ministry, Walther von Reichenau, sought to "enter the new state" to reassert its own time-honored position.[115] The Nazis indeed solved the army's major political problem. They apparently offered the more traditional officers organized popular backing for military-mindedness and for the old values the army could no longer successfully propagate on its own. And for the military specialists, the apostles of "total war" who demanded the wholesale reconstruction of society for war-making, the Nazis offered a vehicle for mass mobilization.[116] The specialists could therefore devote themselves to the "second rearmament plan" and the vistas beyond without political distractions.

General Werner Baron von Fritsch, who became army commander-in-chief in early 1934, took the traditionalist view. Fritsch saw what he took to be Hitler's anti-Marxism and military-mindedness in a favorable light, and was implicitly willing to use the SS, police, and Party to curtail the subversive influences to which the restoration of conscription would expose the army.[117] But he conspicuously lacked Blomberg's enthusiasm. That divergence ultimately worked in Hitler's favor; had Fritsch and Blomberg stood together, the army's defense of its prerogatives might have been far more effective than it was. As for the navy, its "1918 complex" – the officer corps' rage and remorse over the fleet mutinies that had touched off the 1918 revolution – helped

---

114. See Hitler's retrospective account: *Monologe*, pp. 211–12 (1942).
115. Klaus-Jürgen Müller, *Das Heer und Hitler* (Stuttgart, 1969), p. 53.
116. Andreas Hillgruber, "Militarismus am Ende der Weimarer Republik und im Dritten Reich," p. 146, in his *Deutsche Grossmacht- und Weltpolitik im 19. und 20. Jahrhundert* (Düsseldorf, 1977).
117. Müller, *Heer*, pp. 43, 165–67.

produce thoroughgoing commitment to the regime.[118] The new air force, founded under the command of Hitler's ponderous associate, Hermann Göring, was of necessity National Socialist in ethos and in interservice politics. Finally, the state bureaucracy saw in the Nazis the new force needed to recreate the authoritarian state it aspired to serve and rule. But unlike the services it lacked an ostensibly apolitical territory, like rearmament, within which to maintain a measure of independence. The bureaucrats succeeded only in mounting a rearguard action in defense of legal niceties.

The absence of establishment cohesion was particularly noticeable in the implementation of Hitler's central early policy: rearmament. All flankers agreed in principle that Germany must again become the dominant European power; but there agreement ended. Blomberg failed to impose order on his own bureaucracy, much less on the services or industry. Until Hindenburg's death, Hitler himself probably did not have the authority to impose programs or allocate resources in unpopular ways. Thereafter he showed a singular lack of interest in rigid long-term planning. His leadership style – the encouragement of "political free enterprise" among his followers – derived both from Darwinist principle and from the German army's cult of individual initiative, which Hitler had absorbed during four happy years of war. His goals were in any case so far-reaching that he could not have enunciated a coherent program without appalling even the true believers among his subordinates. Instead, he preferred to encourage those below to "work toward the Führer" while himself raising targets and setting goals incrementally on an ad hoc basis.[119] Admiral Erich Raeder, the navy chief, initially proposed the modest goal of naval parity with France, and by 1938–39 found himself cast as a "reluctant Tirpitz," building a fleet ultimately aimed at world domination and based on a strategic concept the Führer had not yet deigned to reveal.[120] Instead of rationalized, centralized planning, rearmament

---

118. Walter Baum, "Marine, Nationalsozialismus, und Widerstand," VfZG 11:1 (1963), pp. 44–45.
119. Political free enterprise: see the fundamental article of Ronald Smelser, "Nazi Dynamics, German Foreign Policy, and Appeasement," in Wolfgang J. Mommsen and Lothar Kettenacker, eds., *The Fascist Challenge and the Policy of Appeasement* (London, 1983), pp. 31–47; the army and initiative: Chapter 5 of this volume; "working toward the Führer": Kershaw, *Hitler*, pp. 529–31.
120. See Dülffer, *Marine*, pp. 457–58; Wilhelm Deist, "Zum Problem der deutschen Aufrüstung 1933–1936," *Francia* 5 (1979), pp. 564–65; Deist, in Deist et al., *Germany and the Second World War*, vol. 1, *The Build-Up of German Aggression* (London, 1990), pp. 472–80.

went forward as a struggle between temporary alliances of the various potentates and powers – Blomberg, Fritsch and his chief of staff Ludwig Beck, Göring, Raeder, Hjalmar Schacht of the ministry of economics and Reichsbank, the sometimes reluctant barons of heavy industry, and the eager new machine, electrical, optical, light metal, and chemical industries. Hitler could graciously await the bids of the contenders for his favor. In the relatively few cases in which the targets the armed forces proposed were insufficiently megalomaniacal, or financial strain and raw material shortages produced stalemate, as in the summer of 1936 and in 1938, he intervened to demand more of everything.[121]

Even before rearmament got under way, Hitler had eliminated his flankers – Papen, Hugenberg, and associates – from politics. Their appalling ineptitude was a final, vital difference between the processes of consolidation in Germany and Italy. The political balance of forces was admittedly far less favorable to the flankers than in Italy. Hugenberg's Nationalists (DNVP), the Nazis' sole electoral allies, received only 8 percent of the vote in the March 1933 elections to 43.9 percent for the NSDAP. But the flankers failed above all within government, which they counted on dominating by right of expertise and birth. By mid-summer 1933, Hitler had removed them from effective power, and Hugenberg – with the blessings of Neurath and the foreign office – from the cabinet. He then outlawed all other parties, a step Mussolini had needed four years to accomplish.

The NSDAP was a help in consolidating power rather than the necessary inconvenience the PNF usually represented for Mussolini. Hitler himself had a far closer relationship with his *Gauleiter* than Mussolini with the provincial Fascist *ras*. In the lean years after the refounding of the NSDAP in 1925, Hitler had personally appointed his paladins on the basis of loyalty and proven effectiveness.[122] That relationship was not solely the result of Hitler's personal magnetism; German traditions of military obedience, the war experience, and the yearning for a Führer that Hitler had drawn on since the beginning helped. By 1933 the NSDAP also had a major advantage, other than numbers, that the PNF lacked. The Nazis came to power while establishment and middle classes still thought them necessary to smash the Left. The violence with which Hitler's proconsuls consolidated their

---

121. Deist et al., *German Aggression*, part 3; Michael Geyer, "Rüstungsbeschleunigung und Inflation," MGM 2/1981, pp. 121–47.
122. See Horn, *Führerideologie*, Chapter 4.

grip in the provinces appeared a salutary blow against "Bolshevism" rather than a brutal invasion. And the crushing of the left-wing parties left the Nazis in command of much of the government machine. But Hitler was careful not to overreach. The revolution, he announced to the *Gauleiter* in late June 1933, was over; the NSDAP's primary duty was not to fight, but to educate.[123]

When Ernst Röhm, the supreme SA leader, instead challenged the officer corps for control of the coming mass army, Hitler struck. In June 1934 he had Himmler's SS troops shoot Röhm, his associates, and an assortment of former or potential opponents that included the retired General von Schleicher and his former assistant. The army, in its glee at the SA's demise, overlooked the death of two of its own and the future SS threat to its monopoly of force; Blomberg could cite the massacre to Prussian traditionalists as evidence of Hitler's loyalty to the army. Upon the long-expected death of Hindenburg in August 1934 Hitler received his reward. Blomberg, apparently on his own initiative, had the armed forces swear unconditional personal loyalty to Hitler in person. Given the officer corps' passion for technique, narrow horizons, stern conception of duty, and aspirations to European hegemony, that step was decisive. In the eyes of most officers it deprived resistance to the regime of moral validity.

By the summer of 1934, with the military oath and the constitutional change that fused the offices of chancellor and Reich president, Hitler had achieved a position far stronger than Mussolini ever enjoyed. That power position was nevertheless utterly inadequate to the tasks Hitler had set himself; it was as yet no "foundation that [could] guarantee the life of the *Volk* for many centuries."[124] The bureaucracy remained capable of passive resistance, and after Hindenburg's death Hitler again gave the *Gauleiter* license to attack it. Given the difficulty of finding enough qualified National Socialist recruits, he foresaw that it would require ten years to produce the responsive instrument he sought.[125] The army and the economic magnates remained at least partially beyond his grasp. He needed their expertise, and as in Italy, the army remained the only institution with the power to destroy the regime.

Worst of all, Hitler faced the ideological resistance of Germany's

123. See Broszat, *The Hitler State*, pp. 111–12; Orlow, *Nazi Party*, vol. 2, pp. 79–80.
124. Speech at the Berlin Sportspalast, 22 January 1933, in Max Domarus, ed., *Hitler: Reden und Proklamationen* (Munich, 1965), p. 182.
125. Conference minute, 1 November 1934, in Hans Mommsen, *Beamtentum im Dritten Reich* (Stuttgart, 1966), pp. 145–46.

subcultures. The effectiveness of that resistance and the extent of Nazi penetration of German society remains imperfectly understood. Clearly, not everyone embraced the new gospel; the population of the large industrial centers remained particularly unreliable. The "yes" votes from Hamburg and "red Berlin" in the August 1934 plebiscite that sanctioned Hitler's replacement of Hindenburg were well below the 75 percent mark, and nothing suggests that the attitudes and convictions that produced those figures altered with any rapidity in the ensuing years.[126]

The churches and their flocks were an even more serious obstacle to ideological control than the industrial workers. As late as 1939, about 94 percent of Germany's inhabitants were members of a Christian church – a proportion that rose slightly when the regime deported Germany's remaining Jews to their deaths in 1941–42. By his own later account, Hitler's initial hope was to fuse Catholics and Protestants into a German national church in the regime's service.[127] The first step in that project was the attempt to annex the Protestants through the creation of a semiofficial "German Christian" movement. But the German Christians' clumsy attempts to "de-Judaize" Christianity and to take over Lutheran Church organizations produced an inevitable backlash. The Protestant pastors, unlike their coreligionists in the officer corps, refused en masse to take an oath to the Führer.[128] The fanatical nationalism of most Protestants prevented an open political breach with the regime, but by mid-1934 Hitler had clearly lost the ideological battle on that front.

He fared even worse with the Catholics. Politically, he outmaneuvered the Center Party, securing its support for the March 1933 Enabling Act with promises of a concordat, then dissolving the party with Vatican approval in return for concluding that same concordat. But ideologically, especially in the deeply Catholic areas of south Germany and the Rhineland, the Church remained an almost insuperable obstacle. Its unfriendly reception of the regime's July 1933 law on sterilization of the insane and congenitally ill, which Hitler pushed through

126. Figures: Bracher, Sauer, and Schulz, *Machtergreifung*, pp. 358–59. For more on National Socialist penetration of society, see (among others) Martin Broszat et al., eds., *Bayern in der NS-Zeit*, 4 vols. (Munich, 1977–81); Detlev Peukert and Jürgen Reulicke, eds., *Die Reihen fast geschlossen* (Wuppertal, 1981); Kershaw, *Popular Opinion and Political Dissent in the Third Reich: Bavaria 1933–1945* (Oxford, 1983); and David F. Crew, ed., *Nazism and German Society, 1933–1945* (London, 1994).
127. Figures: Bracher, Sauer, and Schulz, *Machtergreifung*, p. 347; national church: Gerhard Engel, *Heeresadjutant bei Hitler* (Stuttgart, 1974), p. 49 (18? June 1939).
128. Bracher, Sauer, and Schulz, *Machtergreifung*, p. 338.

the same cabinet meeting that ratified the concordat, was symptomatic of the limits of Catholic support. As a connoisseur of mass psychology, Hitler "did not underestimate the suggestive power of the churches."[129] He was also aware that success in the 1935 Saar plebiscite depended on the Catholic vote. Consequently he urged tactical restraint on the Party, while demanding of the churches, at a minimum, that they leave politics – a field he defined in the broadest possible terms – to Party and state. The NSDAP must secretly prepare for final confrontation; the Party's ultimate loyalty must be to him, not to the churches.[130]

The internal obstacles to the full realization of Hitler's program were thus substantial, even if less weighty than those that oppressed Mussolini. Internationally, the position was less daunting. Germany was inherently far stronger than Italy. And although defeated in 1918, it had like Italy improved its long-term strategic position in the war. Versailles had left the core of Bismarck's Germany's untouched, and the collapse of the two eastern empires left the Reich facing a motley collection of *Saisonstaaten* incapable of either individual or collective self-defense.[131] The withdrawal from Europe of the United States, the power that had robbed Germany of final victory in 1917–18, rounded out this favorable picture. Hitler, despite his railing at Versailles, was well aware of the true correlation of forces. Germany had a second chance at world mastery if it acted swiftly.

To exploit that chance, Germany must mobilize its potential, and thus perhaps rouse France, its most dangerous immediate adversary. They would soon see "if France has statesmen," Hitler told the military leaders four days after his appointment as chancellor: "if it does, it will not allow us time [to rearm] but will attack us . . ."[132] The French had no statesmen. Western feebleness helped foster the close congruence that persisted until 1936 between the conservative-nationalist instincts of generals, diplomats, and economic magnates, and the preliminary stages of Hitler's vision of racist world revolution. With each success – Germany's departure from the Disarmament Conference and the League of Nations, the February 1934 nonaggression

---

129. Engel, *Heeresadjutant*, p. 30 (6 August 1938).
130. Alfred Rosenberg, *Das politische Tagebuch Alfred Rosenbergs aus den Jahren 1934/35 und 1939/40*, ed. H.-G. Seraphim (Göttingen, 1956), pp. 32, 56.
131. See Gerhard L. Weinberg, "The Defeat of Germany in 1918 and the European Balance of Power," *Central European History* 2:3 (1969), pp. 248–60 – an article fundamental to understanding interwar Europe.
132. Liebmann minute, 3 February 1933, in Vogelsang, "Neue Dokumente," p. 435.

pact with Poland that unhinged France's alliance system, the Saar plebiscite, the announcement of universal military service and of the Luftwaffe, the Anglo-German naval treaty – Hitler's ascendancy over the establishment grew.

The remilitarization of the Rhineland in March 1936 produced the first open divergence over tactics between Hitler and his military and foreign office flankers. It was also the latest in a series of foreign policy triumphs intended to galvanize public opinion. The recipe had worked in the fall of 1933 when Germany left the League, but since then the regime had lost popularity. Rearmament brought full employment but also increasing strains and shortages. The reintroduction of conscription in 1935 was not universally popular – that year the regime mounted no general elections or plebiscites. The NSDAP, although increasingly successful at preventing the bureaucracy from administering, proved relatively inept at remolding the public into good National Socialists; enforced enthusiasm was not contagious.[133] Hitler conceded openly to his foreign policy advisers that his decision to act resulted in part from a need to distract the public from domestic difficulties.[134]

The flankers, although still in agreement with Hitler's immediate revisionist goals, began to find his methods excessively risky. Blomberg, in particular, warned of dire consequences from the Rhineland coup. When news of French and British unhappiness began to filter back, he beseeched Hitler to withdraw the troops. Hitler himself suffered an attack of nerves, but held to his course.[135] When the French predictably caved in, Hitler could preen himself on his superior judgment; perhaps his too-cautious military advisers were outliving their usefulness. Active expansion would clearly call for men of sterner stuff.

Similarly, the struggle throughout the spring and summer of 1936 over economic priorities – essentially a contest in which Hitler, Göring, and the army defeated Schacht and those economic magnates who deplored the increasing strain of rearmament – marked the parting of the ways between Hitler and another important group of flankers. Fortunately for Hitler, the two main sources of opposition were themselves at odds both internally and with one another. The generals split into traditionalists and total war theorists, overt pro-Nazis and self-

---

133. See for instance the description in Allen, *The Nazi Seizure of Power*, Chapter 17.
134. Hassell notes, in Esmonde Robertson, "Zur Wiederbesetzung des Rheinlandes 1936," VfZG 10:2 (1962), pp. 202–05.
135. Friedrich Hossbach, *Zwischen Wehrmacht und Hitler* (Göttingen, 2nd ed., 1965), pp. 84–85.

proclaimed unpolitical soldiers of the old school. In industry, firms such as I. G. Farben that benefited from autarchy and accelerated rearmament divided from much of the rest of heavy industry, which was increasingly reluctant to build new plants when reason dictated that Germany would eventually run out of currency and raw materials. Hitler demonstratively slapped down industrial and financial foot-dragging by placing Göring in charge of much of the economy in September 1936. But the military and foreign policy establishment was less accommodating. By late 1937 Hitler had discovered that foreign adventure was impossible without a further measure of revolution at home.

EXPANSION AND REVOLUTION: UNHOLY WAR

Mussolini's transition to active expansion aroused less resistance than Hitler's; the Duce's chosen victims seemed less capable of defending themselves. Nevertheless, the decision to attack Ethiopia in 1935 has found a variety of interpretations. Determinists have argued that the Depression and consequent need to reflate the economy prompted expansion. Another popular claim is that Mussolini sought to "relaunch" a flagging regime and cement the loyalty of the younger generation by foreign adventure.[136] Renzo De Felice, while rejecting the economic argument and demonstrating persuasively that the regime was at the height of its popularity, has suggested that failure to transform society at home impelled Mussolini into previously unsought imperial adventure. The decision for war, in all these views, was a choice for second best, and Ethiopia no more than a target of opportunity that German revival impelled the frightened French to offer Mussolini. Finally, Jens Petersen has argued that what happened between 1932 and 1935 was that international alignments at last permitted Mussolini to implement a long-held expansionist program. German rearmament and French fear, along with the Depression's severing of financial dependence on Washington at last gave Mussolini his chance.[137]

Mussolini's repeated, almost monotonous references to the goal of

---

136. Franco Catalano, *L'economia italiana di guerra* (Milan, 1969), p. 7; Giorgio Rochat, *Militari e politici nella preparazione della campagna d'Etiopia* (Milan, 1971), pp. 105–07.
137. *Mussolini il fascista*, p. 359; *Mussolini il duce*, vol. 1, pp. 179, 466–67; Petersen, "Die Aussenpolitik des faschistischen Italien als historiographisches Problem," VfZG 22:4 (1974), pp. 417–57.

empire from 1918 on support the last interpretation. But it was more than a foreign policy program that moved him to action. Only war, whose uncivilizing effects he well remembered, could help break the old society's resistance to the new paganism, make Italy the "militarist" nation he demanded, and further undermine monarchy and Church.[138]

Ethiopia was not Mussolini's initial choice of target, although he had expressed interest in acquisitions there as early as 1925. Only after it became clear in winter 1932–1933 that France was unwilling to tolerate Fascist conquests in the Balkans did Mussolini begin planning to avenge Adua, the humiliating defeat of Fascism's alleged precursor Crispi. In the end, Ethiopia was the one enemy Mussolini's flankers and the other European powers would reluctantly permit him to conquer.[139] The flankers too felt the shame of Adua, and assumed that the Italy that had in the end broken Austria-Hungary could defeat a landlocked, half-tribal, half-feudal kingdom with perhaps a quarter of Italy's population. The other powers seemed likely to tolerate an Italian aggression outside Europe that did not directly touch their own possessions.

Mussolini nevertheless faced and overcame major obstacles in launching his Fascist imperial war. Internally, he had to sap the tenacious resistance of the army, the king, and of a conservative establishment that abhorred risk. The Duce complained in 1936 that the monarch bore no responsibility for victory: "*He* didn't want to go – I had to force him." Mussolini complained later that many, many important people came to him and said, "You have already done great things. Now [you should] pull in your oars."

Mussolini's knowledge of British fleet unpreparedness – on which he bet too heavily – and Whitehall's craven reluctance to force the issue allowed him to hold his course. But the attack on Ethiopia remained, in the words of overcautious advisors Mussolini later quoted, "a gamble [*un'avventura*], a great gamble."[140] The establishment's reluctance may not have been entirely a consequence of Mussolini's external risk taking. Defeat at the hands of British, or stalemate in Ethiopia, would risk far more than Italy's reputation and international position. It would risk the regime, and with it, the advantages the establishment had secured through its forced compromise with Mus-

---

138. OO 26:308 (24 August 1934) (the "discorso del carro armato").
139. For full analysis of the turn toward Ethiopia, see pp. 132-40 of this volume.
140. All from OO 44:325 (17 April 1943).

solini. Conversely, victory would excessively reinforce the regime and increase Mussolini's chances of receiving the blind obedience to which he aspired. Nor did Mussolini miss opportunities to make victory popular and Fascist rather than military and dynastic. General Emilio De Bono, his original choice as commander in East Africa, was despite loyalty to king and army a man who owed his position to "Fascist merits."[141] The MVSN mobilized, with army help, to provide specifically Fascist units whose combat performance the propaganda apparatus could then inflate. The new empire, Mussolini proclaimed to frenetic applause on 9 May 1936, was a Fascist empire that "bore the indestructible marks of the will and power of the Roman *fasci.*" By implication Italy's new imperial status owed little or nothing to the old order.[142]

Victory indeed had consequences both domestic and foreign. Mussolini, as "founder of the empire," could now impose on his subordinates, without being laughed at, the reverence he aspired to. His subsequent policy – open hostility to the Western powers in the Mediterranean, the intervention in Spain, the racial laws, a fierce if involuntarily comic PNF campaign against upper-middle-class mores, the annexation of Albania, and the plunge into war in 1940 – was only possible thanks to domestic reinforcement through African victory and to the license for aggression which increasing German preponderance brought. Far from representing a falling off from the famous "realism" that his propagandists ascribed to him, Mussolini's later policies were simply ever more risky attempts to implement his program within his own lifetime. It was his mission to remake "the character of the Italians through combat." Revelation of a long-held vision, not the "involution" of personality and will that some scholars have discerned, presided over Italy's road to the Second World War.[143]

African victory naturally did not remove all obstacles. Mussolini was able to put the League of Nations' sanctions to good use in convincing the great economic interests that autarchy – the breaking of Italy's remaining ties to the world market – was the only feasible course. And although autarchy proved "too tight a shirt" for the export industries, the increasing stream of armaments contracts helped ease their pain.

141. His replacement in November 1935 by Badoglio was consequently an internal setback for Mussolini – but winning on the battlefield took immediate priority.
142. OO 27:268–69 (9 May 1936).
143. Mussolini's words: Ciano, 13 November 1937. For the involution thesis, which resembles the folk wisdom of the day (". . . se dopo l'Etiopia, si fosse fermato . . ."), see De Felice, *Mussolini il duce*, vol. 2, Chapter 3.

Italy's massive dependence on imported energy and strategic raw materials made genuine autarchy impractical, but furnished yet another argument for expansion. In both domestic and foreign policy, Mussolini moved with increasing self-confidence. He plunged into Spain apparently without consulting the king; when the army chief, General Federico Baistrocchi, objected and Badoglio grumbled, he sacked one and demanded that the other show approval publicly. Spain, however, provided anything but the expected easy victories, and the disaster at Guadalajara in March 1937 allowed the king to level veiled reproaches at Mussolini.[144] But humiliation passed with the summer 1937 victories in the Basque country. By early 1938, the German example – Hitler made himself commander-in-chief of the armed forces on 4 February – prompted emulation. The PNF, presumably on Mussolini's secret instructions, pushed through Chamber and Senate a bill making both Duce and king "First Marshals of the Empire." Demotion of the monarch to Mussolini's level produced wrath at the Quirinal.[145] Mussolini also promulgated in 1937–38 laws that formally wrote the PNF into the constitution, and in January 1939 the Chamber of Deputies became the Chamber of *Fasci* and Corporations. Only the Senate remained as a relic of the liberal-monarchical past, and it owed its considerable staying power to its life tenure and royal appointment.

Mussolini and his entourage began looking forward with increasing anticipation to the removal of the king, perhaps even as early as the end of the Spanish war. It was only right, the Duce commented cynically in 1936 when exempting the king's foreign assets from the nationalization that League sanctions made necessary, to leave him "a well-protected nest-egg"; the fate of monarchies was frequently uncertain.[146] The Duce's private remarks suggest an ever-growing resolve to smash the internal and foreign policy restraints the monarchy still imposed.[147]

The military establishment, like the monarchy, failed to show the necessary enthusiasm for Mussolini's increasing taste for risk. Although he had achieved de facto direction of the armed forces during the Ethiopian war, Mussolini remained a prisoner of their institu-

144. Knox, *Mussolini*, p. 30.
145. De Felice, "Mussolini e Vittorio Emanuele III Primi Marescialli dell'Impero," in Università degli Studi di Messina, *Scritti in onore di Vittorio De Caprariis* (Rome, n.d.), pp. 347–68.
146. De Felice, *Mussolini il duce*, vol. 2, p. 16 (in general, pp. 14–21).
147. See particularly ibid., p. 40, and Bottai, 23 June, 12 July, 13 June 1938.

tional structures. Major surgery, such as the 1933 and 1936–37 plans for a tri-service defense ministry that would restrict the services' autonomy, was impossible without diminishing both the traditional primacy of the army and the monarchy's prerogatives.[148] Both the rigidity of service promotion procedures and the caste resistance of the senior generals inhibited the injection of fresh and necessarily Fascist blood into the higher reaches of the armed forces. In strategic planning, Mussolini had his way for a while. In 1936–38 the army, under Baistrocchi's successor, General Alberto Pariani, harbored grandiose visions of an assault on Egypt from Cyrenaica. But after the shock of the Munich crisis, Badoglio reasserted his prerogatives as Mussolini's chief military adviser and killed the plan. If France were also hostile, Italy was too weak to seize Suez. Badoglio's refusal to permit planning "that d[id] not correspond to the situation" meant that when the situation changed, Italy had no plans. In the event, Mussolini had to trick his generals and admirals into war in 1940 with the assurance that they need not fight.[149]

Less dangerous for Mussolini than the recalcitrance of monarchy and armed forces, but still inconvenient, was the Church. The Vatican, despite its compromise with Mussolini, made difficulties about what Pius XI denounced as "pagan state idolatry." The Church overwhelmingly supported the Ethiopian campaign and Mussolini's ostensibly anti-Bolshevist intervention in Spain. It evinced qualified approval even of the annexation of Albania.[150] But when Mussolini's concern with the "purity of the race" came home from the colonies, and in deference to the Germans attacked Jews as well as blacks, the Vatican became uneasy. The Church was not averse to religious discrimination, and avant-garde Jesuits urged segregation of the Jews. But the 1938 racial laws promulgated in emulation of Hitler's Nuremberg Laws of 1935 included Catholic converts, and exceeded their German model in pseudobiological rigor.[151] At the same time, the German alliance and the increasing risk of general war added to the Church's reservations about the regime. War – apart from death and destruction – would lead either to an Axis defeat that would endanger the Lateran

148. Knox, *Mussolini*, pp. 17–18.
149. Ibid., pp. 18–19, 58, 119–23, and Knox, "L'ultima guerra dell'Italia fascista," in Bruna Micheletti and Pier Paolo Poggio, eds., *L'Italia in guerra 1940–43* (Brescia, 1991), pp. 24–27.
150. Knox, "L'ultima guerra dell'Italia fascista," p. 11.
151. See De Felice, *Storia degli ebrei italiani sotto il fascismo* (Turin, rev. ed., 1972), pp. 204–05, 286–87; Michele Sarfatti, *Mussolini contro gli ebrei* (Turin, 1994), pp. 125–26.

Pacts, or to a victory that would bring pagan racist revolution in earnest. Hence the papal protests and peace messages against which Mussolini increasingly railed between 1938 and 1940.

The upper middle classes, too, began to distance themselves subtly from Mussolini as he moved to implement his vision. It required the shock of defeat to consummate the divorce Italian style between the regime and what Mussolini described as a bourgeoisie riddled with "cowardice, laziness, [and] love of the quiet life." But the origins of that divorce lay in Mussolini's post-Ethiopian activism both at home and abroad. Italy's forced "nonbelligerence" in September 1939 was thus not an example of Mussolini's purported realism, but rather the establishment's last victory over the regime's revolutionary expansionism. The Pope and Badoglio, diplomats, industrialists, and king, all coalesced behind Mussolini's son-in-law and foreign minister, Galeazzo Ciano, to hold back Mussolini and the Party enthusiasts. But the victory was a Pyrrhic one. Mussolini remained in control of the machinery of government. Only a coup, which the king briefly contemplated in March 1940, could remove him. When the king failed to move, the members of the quasi-coalition of "moderates" remained prisoners of their separate bargains with the Duce and of their own cautiously expansionist appetites.

The great German victories in the West in May 1940 enabled Mussolini to activate that expansionism with the promise that Italy need not fight. He himself sought instead a swift but decisive conflict that would free Italy from its Mediterranean imprisonment and give him the prestige to crush his flankers. That was why the regime insisted – contrary to common sense, which dictated the mobilization of all strands of Italian nationalism – that this war was "*la guerra fascista*." It was to be a war of internal as well as foreign conquest. And when Italy's independent war ended in the winter of 1940–41 in disaster at Taranto, in the Albanian mountains, and in the sands of Beda Fomm, Mussolini's revolutionary project died with it.[152] The regime survived until the "moderate" Fascists revolted against Mussolini and the king and generals overthrew him in July 1943. But the crushing defeats of 1940 and Italy's humiliating new status as first satellite of the Reich had broken the prestige Mussolini needed for internal transformation. In the end, the flankers, emboldened in defeat, repudiated the regime in the name of the same Italian nationalism, and the same interests, that had once led them to support it.

---

152. Knox, *Mussolini*, Chapters 3, 6, and Conclusion.

Hitler fortunately also failed, but his failure was infinitely bloodier than Mussolini's. Hitler had written in *Mein Kampf* that Germany would "either be a world power, or cease to be." He almost achieved the first, and barely failed at the second. His starting point in blending revolution and territorial expansion was his discovery in November 1937 that Germany's growing if foreseeably temporary preponderance in armaments had not convinced Blomberg, Fritsch, and Neurath that Germany could, should, and must strike soon. A lamentable lack of faith emerged from their alarmed protestations at the 5 November 1937 Reich Chancellery conference at which Hitler revealed for the first time that he intended to seize Austria and smash Czechoslovakia, situation permitting, as early as 1938. Fritsch and his subordinate Beck objected not only to the risks involved, but above all to Hitler's implicit claim to be Germany's sole font of strategic leadership.

Hitler confirmed his 5 November prediction of war two weeks later in a speech to NSDAP officials. New tasks awaited Germany, "for the living space of our *Volk* is too narrow." And he again stressed the identity of foreign and domestic policy: just as the National Socialists had "led the nation upwards" internally, so they would achieve for Germany abroad "the same rights to existence as other nations."[153] Two months later, he dismissed both Blomberg and Fritsch, and for good measure Neurath and the ambassador to Italy, Ulrich von Hassell. Blomberg's mésalliance with an ex-prostitute and damaging though bogus SS charges of homosexuality against Fritsch allowed Hitler to dispense with both, and take over Blomberg's position in person. Civilian control of the armed forces and Clausewitz's heretical notion that war was a tool of politics thus came at last to Prussia-Germany, through the dictator whom Heinrich Class had once prophesied should the monarchy fail in the coming great war.[154]

In the aftermath of the 4 February coup, many high officers seethed with indignation at the preposterous accusations against Fritsch, but foreign policy came to Hitler's aid. Developments in Austria allowed him to distract the army with a military task: the Anschluss. The resulting personal triumph allowed him to brush off army pressure for Fritsch's reinstatement, while the public, consulted in the first plebiscite since the Rhineland coup, returned an overwhelming vote of

---

153. Domarus, *Hitler*, p. 760 (21 November 1937).
154. See especially Müller, *Armee und Drittes Reich 1933–1939* (Paderborn, 1987), pp. 40–41; for Class, see note 48 to Chapter 1.

confidence. Foreign policy had first demanded domestic upheaval, then blessed it with success.

But obstacles remained. The credulous acceptance of the Führer's mission and quasi-supernatural gifts by his new military assistants, Wilhelm Keitel and Alfred Jodl, was far from general in the upper reaches of the officer corps. Throughout the summer, as preparations to attack Germany's next victim, Czechoslovakia, went forward, Hitler gave vent to a stream of complaints against the generals. Most of them "had rejected [his leadership], and continued to reject it." They "as yet did not understand the meaning of the new age," and were far inferior in élan to his trusty *Gauleiter*. Delays in the army-supervised construction of the *Westwall* fortifications led him to threaten to turn that enterprise over to Martin Bormann, "whom he could at least rely on."[155] Fritz Todt, another NSDAP luminary, actually got the job. And several months later, Hitler apparently intimidated a reluctant Admiral Raeder with the not entirely incredible threat that if further delays slowed the gargantuan naval program, he would turn procurement over to Todt.[156]

The real issue of the summer, however, was what Hitler characterized as "*Angst* and cowardice in the army": the refusal of Beck and the hesitation of other senior officers to accept the dictator's strategic leadership and the risks the Czech enterprise would involve. Fortunately for Hitler, Beck was isolated both in his high assessment of the risk of general war and his dogged insistence on the co-responsibility of the army chief of staff for Germany's strategic decisions. Nevertheless, Hitler felt obliged to harangue his top commanders twice in mid-August to counteract Beck's influence and steel their nerves for the struggle. Conveniently for Hitler, Beck cracked under the strain and resigned. His successor, Halder, toyed briefly with conspiracy, but did not dare open contradiction. Even more fortunately for Hitler, the West surrendered Czechoslovakia without fighting. Bloodless triumph cut the ground from under doubters and plotters. Munich also raised Hitler higher in public esteem than ever before – the German people had nationalist triumph without war.[157]

The crisis had other effects besides strengthening Hitler internally.

155. Engel, *Heeresadjutant*, pp. 20, 26, 32 (20 April, 25 June, 18 April 1938).
156. Dülffer, *Marine*, pp. 500–01, 512, 541.
157. Müller, *Heer*, Chapters. 7–8; Christian Hartmann, *Halder, Generalstabschef Hitlers 1938–1942* (Paderborn, 1991), Chapter 5, section 1; Williamson Murray, *The Change in the European Balance of Power, 1938–39* (Princeton, 1984), Chapters. 5–7; Kershaw, *The 'Hitler Myth': Image and Reality in the Third Reich* (Oxford, 1987), pp. 138–39.

He had passionately sought war against the Czechs both to steel the young and to test the newly minted *Wehrmacht*. Only at the last moment did he accept the negotiated surrender of the Sudetenland. On the evening of 27 September, Hitler watched motorized units on their way to the border roll through central Berlin, as he had ordered. The public stood, silent and sullen; no cheers or "German greetings" honored the Führer's appearance at the Reich Chancellery balcony.[158] The delirium of August 1914 did not repeat itself. After the public euphoria attending the Anschluss, this may have come as a shock. The unfeigned enthusiasm of German crowds for Chamberlain added insult to injury.[159] Hence Hitler's post-Munich rage at the British ("we will no longer tolerate the supervision of governesses") and his diatribe to German press representatives on 10 November, demanding indoctrination that would "free the *Volk* of doubts that make it unhappy" and inculcate "*fanatical* belief" in final victory. The nation must stand like "formed-up troops" behind his decisions. The "intellectual strata" – by which he meant those educated Germans, including officers, who still refused to accept him on faith – were unfortunately still necessary: "otherwise one could exterminate them, or whatever."[160]

Hitler could have been under no illusion that propaganda alone would consolidate internal unity behind him. As he harangued the press, the SS and police were supervising the cleanup of the debris from synagogues and Jewish shops burned out in the *Kristallnacht* pogrom. Hitler had inspired that action as a hint of things to come and a salutary release for NSDAP radicalism, but he was too shrewd a judge of public and elite opinion to associate with it openly. Generals were still heard to mutter about hanging "this swine, Goebbels," who was ostensibly responsible.[161] The time of the Jews was nevertheless coming, Hitler hinted in his 30 January 1939 Reichstag speech. That of the churches, he had said privately the previous August, had not yet come; he still had "too many other problems."[162]

Yet as his insistence on his cyclopean building program and his acceleration of the already breakneck pace of naval construction suggest, Hitler had already left the confines of the interwar German state far behind (symptomatically, Germany proper now became the

158. Telford Taylor, *Munich* (New York, 1979), p. 877.
159. See the editors' remarks in *"Es spricht der Führer"*, pp. 230–31.
160. "Governesses": speech at Saarbrücken, 9 October 1938, in Domarus, *Hitler*, p. 956; the rest from von Kotze and Krausnick, eds., *"Es spricht der Führer"*, pp. 283, 281–82.
161. Fedor von Bock, quoted in Müller, *Heer*, p. 385.
162. Domarus, *Hitler*, p. 1058; Engel, *Heeresadjutant*, p. 30 (6 August 1938).

"*Altreich*"). The immense Nazi eagle with a globe in its claws that Hitler ordered to crown his gigantic Berlin great hall was no mere ideological metaphor. Germany, he told a group of senior officers in early February 1939, was bound for world mastery; the triumphs of 1938 were not the end of the road but the beginning. Germany could best preserve the reputation and prestige acquired since 1933 by "without letup exploiting every opportunity, however small, to move immediately toward a new success."[163] He would tolerate no more "warning memoranda" – an apparent reference to Beck's attempts to thwart him the previous summer. The "hot-house intellectualism" of the general staff since Schlieffen's day was outdated; he demanded "believing officers" with "trust and blind confidence."[164]

The next major success, Hitler decided shortly after his bloodless absorption of rump Czechoslovakia in mid-March 1939, must come in war against Poland. The origins of that war, which contrary to Hitler's intentions eventually became a world war, have inevitably provoked vast controversy. But until Tim Mason's work on the regime's relationship with the industrial workers, few scholars have had much to say about the internal ramifications of Hitler's decision. Mason opened the question up by suggesting that Hitler took the plunge largely to escape the economic and political crisis that rearmament had created. Conquest was "an end in itself," an improvised defensive "flight forward" to escape intolerable domestic problems. The argument is not persuasive.[165] Hitler had passionately wanted to fight in 1938, before the crisis reached full intensity. Politically, the regime was hardly on its last legs, either in the public or in the official mind. The Ruhr miners, on whose efforts all of German industry relied, had a lower absentee

163. Speech of 10 February 1939, printed in Jost Dülffer et al., *Hitlers Städte: Baupolitik im Dritten Reich* (Cologne, 1978), p. 313.
164. Quoted in Müller, *Heer*, p. 383.
165. See Mason, "Innere Krise und Angriffskrieg 1938/1939," pp. 158–88 in F. Forstmaier and H. E. Volkmann, eds., *Wirtschaft und Rüstung am Vorabend des Zweiten Weltkrieges* (Düsseldorf, 1975); also his *Arbeiterklasse und Volksgemeinschaft* (Opladen, 1975), pp. 119–166. For the criticisms, see Jost Dülffer, "Der Beginn des Krieges 1939: Hitler, die innere Krise, und das Mächtesystem," *Geschichte und Gesellschaft* 2 (1976), pp. 443–70, and Ludolf Herbst, "Die Krise des nationalsozialistischen Regimes am Vorabend des Zweiten Weltkrieges und die forcierte Aufrüstung," VfZG 26:3 (1978), pp. 347–92 (particularly pp. 376–82), as well as Mason, "The Domestic Dynamics of Nazi Conquests: A Response to Critics," pp. 295–322 in his *Nazism, Fascism and the Working Class*. For public opinion, see Kershaw, *Hitler Myth*, pp. 139–47, which suggests that only fear of war marred the popularity Hitler had achieved through foreign success in 1938–39.

rate in 1938 than in 1929, and later showed remarkable aptitude for supervising slave labor.[166]

As for the economic crisis, the evidence does not suggest that anyone except a narrow circle recognized it as such. Hitler merely argued, in prodding his generals toward war, that Germany could hold out only "for a few more years."[167] That was less a prediction of imminent catastrophe than a ploy to egg the reluctant onward by reminding them of difficulties that they had helped him create. Mason also claimed in support of his thesis Hitler remarks in both 1937 and 1939 that Germany faced a choice between expansion and degeneration. But those remarks were merely Hitler's standard justification, fixed since 1921–22, of the need for *Lebensraum*.[168] The economic strains of 1938–39 were for him no more than further confirmation of that insight.

But the foremost difficulty with Mason's theory was that it isolated the events of 1938–39 from those preceding, and thus interpreted as cause a phenomenon that was first of all effect. As Jost Dülffer pointed out, internal strain derived from Hitler's ever-increasing demands on the economy for armaments and for his immense building program.[169] Those demands led directly to war, with no need for an intervening *deus ex machina* in the form of internal crisis. Only war could transmute armaments into Lebensraum and world mastery. Only war, along with the new Reich's cyclopean monuments and incessant propaganda, could fully nationalize the masses. The 1938–39 crisis was above all a symptom of Hitler's offensive forward thrust toward war and revolution rather than a driving force behind it.

Three considerations were decisive for the timing of the attack on

---

166. John Gillingham, "Ruhr Coal Miners and Hitler's War," *Journal of Social History*, summer 1982, pp. 637–53; Alf Lüdke, "The Appeal of Exterminating 'Others': German Workers and the Limits of Resistance," *Journal of Modern History* 64 (supplement)(1992).

167. Hitler speech summary, 22 August 1939 (probably from stenographic notes by Canaris), ADAP D/7/168. A second version, written that evening by Admiral Boehm, suggests even less urgency: "perhaps 10–15 years." Mason preferred the Lochner document (ADAP D/7, pp. 171–72 note), which ascribes to Hitler a lament that "the Four Year Plan has failed and we are finished, without victory in the coming war." But the Lochner version will not bear too much weight. Its provenance, its divergences from all other accounts, and its piquant fabricated details (a Goring war dance on the conference table) mark it as an Abwehr/resistance concoction for Western consumption. (On the sources, see Winfried Baumgart, "Zur Ansprache Hitlers vor den Führern der Wehrmacht am 22. August 1939," *VfZG* 16:2 [1968], pp. 120–49).

168. Mason, "Innere Krise," pp. 182–84.

169. Dülffer, "Beginn des Krieges," p. 464.

Poland. First and least important was the pact with Stalin, which secured Germany's rear and checkmated the remaining doubters among the generals. Second came a broader consideration, which Hitler repeatedly emphasized in his 1939 harangues to his military leaders. Rearmament had created a brief window of opportunity for Germany; after 1941–42 that window would close as the other powers caught up. Finally, of course, came Hitler's ever-growing obsession with the short time left to him personally; as he told his generals "in all modesty" in November 1939, he alone possessed the nerve [*Entschlusskraft*] to fulfil Germany's mission.[170]

He lost no time in putting war to use. Within the Reich, he secretly ordered the killing of the congenitally ill and insane in state institutions. Poland offered an even greater opportunity to implement his internal programs for Germany – using Poles as "laboratory rabbits." As Heydrich crudely explained it to the army, "we want to spare the little people, but nobility, clergy, and Jews must be killed."[171] The generals recoiled in pious horror, then sheepishly yielded responsibility for the occupied territories.

The generals did make a brief stand on the sole issue they could not evade: Hitler's demand, made immediately after Poland's collapse, for an immediate offensive to smash the French and British. The army's resistance, which included yet another hesitant Putsch conspiracy in which Halder again took fleeting interest, was the last twitch of the organized German establishment. It was short-lived. This time, no one dared openly question Hitler's strategic judgment as Beck had done; instead, the generals took refuge in technical arguments that inevitably lost force as army readiness improved and French ineptitude and demoralization became apparent. Hitler's tirades terrorized Brauchitsch and Halder, and the repeated postponements of the attack due to weather allowed the generals to prepare it with the thoroughness that was their trademark.[172] The pathetic April 1940 showing of British and French in Norway did the rest. When army and Luftwaffe crossed the western borders on 10 May, the doubters had long fallen silent or joined the ranks of the converted.

In mid-January, even before the *Wehrmacht* rolled, Hitler had made clear to some of his associates the internal consequences of victory: "The war is in this respect, as in many other matters, a favorable

170. ADAP D/7/168 (22 August 1939) and D/8/348 (23 November 1939).
171. Müller, *Heer*, p. 427.
172. See especially Hartmann, *Halder*, Chapter 6, sections 2, 3.

opportunity to dispose of it (the church question) root and branch." In the ancient world entire peoples had been liquidated, and the Soviet Union was setting the example in the present. But the old German "proclivity for mysticism" still thwarted him:

> If he did nothing now against the rebellious parsons, then it was not least out of concern for the *Wehrmacht*. There they ran to the field chaplains, and a trooper who was brave with the good Lord was always more useful to him than one who was cowardly without Him. But here the indoctrination of the SS, which was now proving in war that ideologically schooled troops could be brave even without the Lord, would outline the necessary development.[173]

In conversation with Rosenberg, his expert on religion, Hitler foresaw the possibility of smashing the churches by force (*"ein harter machtpolitischer Eingriff"*) – but that would be feasible only when Germany was "fully independent internationally"; "otherwise the resulting blaze of internal political controversy could cost us our existence."[174]

The *Wehrmacht*'s crushing victory over France in May–June 1940 did not secure the full measure of freedom Hitler sought. But he now commanded the confidence of the military elite as never before or after. Symptomatic of that confidence was the pleasurable anticipation with which many senior generals prepared to tackle the next intriguing military problem Hitler set them, operation *Barbarossa*: the destruction of the Soviet Union and the physical elimination of its "Jewish-Bolshevik intelligentsia." A few had doubts, but now took refuge not in plotting but in irony; Field Marshal Gerd von Rundstedt saw off a fellow army group commander with a cryptic "Well, see you in Siberia."[175] The public, sullen during the phony war, went "berserk with success" after French collapse; in the words of one jaundiced eyewitness, Germany's cafes were full of "beer-soaked old pinochle players dividing up continents over their steins."[176]

Yet Hitler still lacked the prestige to impose his vision in its entirety inside Germany. The attack on the Soviet Union was thus more

---

173. All from Engel, *Heeresadjutant*, pp. 71–72 (20 January 1940); see also p. 52 (8 July 1939).
174. Rosenberg, *Tagebuch*, p. 98 (19 January 1940).
175. See Helmut Krausnick, "Kommissarbefehl und 'Gerichtsbarkeitserlass Barbarossa' in neuer Sicht," VfZG 25 (1977), pp. 685, 718–20, 757, and Andreas Hillgruber, "The German Military Leaders' View of Russia Prior to the Attack on the Soviet Union," pp. 169–85 in Bernd Wegner, ed., *From Peace to War: Germany, Soviet Russia and the World, 1939–1941* (Providence, 1997).
176. Friedrich Percyval Reck-Malleczewen, *Diary of a Man in Despair* (New York, 1970), pp. 109, 103.

than merely a response to Churchill's incomprehensible obduracy and to United States support for Britain, or another momentous step in Hitler's foreign policy *Stufenplan*. It was also a further mighty thrust toward the internal barbarization of Germany itself. *Lebensraum* and foreign policy "freedom" would at last enable him to crush that "reptile," the churches.[177] The war of racial annihilation in the East would harden German youth to destroy the old society at home, while the lavish rewards of victory would still whatever unquiet consciences remained.

Yet even as the *Wehrmacht* struck deep into Russia, the bishop of Münster, Count Galen, raised his voice publicly against the euthanasia program. The regime had already identified and killed over 70,000 inmates of hospitals and institutions, and Galen's words did not prevent the program from going forward thenceforth in a lower key and under camouflage. Hitler nevertheless raged in private: this affront would appear in the churches' final bill. As he remarked in October 1941, he had also had to tolerate the Jews for a long time; now, though he left it unsaid, their extermination had begun.[178]

That last foundation of his program was indeed all that remained once the *Wehrmacht* failed to take Moscow in November–December 1941. In Jodl's words, "long before anyone else in the world, Hitler suspected or knew that the war was lost," and that suspicion drove him to give the Final Solution an ever-higher priority, a priority that soon eclipsed the fighting of the war itself.[179] Internally, SS and Party vied in radicalism, while the furtive half-knowledge of Germany's eastern crimes and of coming retribution bound the public to the regime to the end. What remained of the establishment had lost in 1938–40 all capacity to put the brakes on Hitler. The final despairing gesture of some of its members, the botched bomb plot of 20 July 1944, if anything strengthened the regime. Barbarous revenge ended the history of Prussia, while miraculous survival fleetingly refurbished Hitler's defeat-tarnished charisma.[180] Hitler's revolution, unlike that of

---

177. "Reptile": *Monologe*, p. 337 (11 August 1942).
178. Ibid., p. 108 (25 October 1941). Hitler frequently remarked that the ideal solution would be to let the churches die out naturally (ibid., pp. 40–41, 67, 82–85), but he clearly intended to help them along (see especially ibid., p. 272).
179. Jodl memorandum, October 1946, in Percy Ernst Schramm, *Hitler: The Man and Military Leader* (Chicago, 1971), p. 204; Hillgruber, *Hitlers Strategie*, pp. 551–54 and note 84; Hildebrand, "Weltmacht oder Niedergang: Hitlers Deutschland 1941–1945," in Oswald Hauser, ed., *Weltpolitik II 1939–1945* (Göttingen, 1975), pp. 308–13.
180. See Kershaw, *Hitler Myth*, pp. 215–19.

Mussolini, had made itself irreversible from within. And the temporary allies who met across the rubble of Greater Germany could not restore Bismarck's Reich, even had they wished it.

CONCLUSION

From the perspective of results, Mussolini's claim that Italy and Germany were "congruent cases" was an exaggeration. It also cannot erase the many differences between the societies over which the two regimes arose, and between their myths, traditions, and institutions. The degree of freedom of action achieved differed markedly between the two regimes because of these underlying conditions, and not merely because of the frequently invoked but partly illusory gap in ruthlessness and dynamism between the dictators. The two leaders' visions, despite the differences between their underlying ideologies, were indeed congruent in their mixture of demography and geopolitics, if not in Hitler's racialist philosophy of history. Above all, the relationship between foreign and domestic policy in the two regimes was similar. Foreign policy was internal policy and vice versa; internal consolidation was a precondition for foreign conquest, and foreign conquest was the decisive prerequisite for revolution at home that would sweep away inherited institutions and values, Piedmontese-Italian and Prusso-German military castes, the churches with their claim to deep popular loyalties and their inconvenient if not always operative Christian values, and, last but not least, the putatively decadent and cowardly upper middle classes.

In the end it is this identity of foreign and domestic policy that distinguished these two regimes from the other despotisms of the century of war and mass murder. Revolutionaries who seized power through civil war in predominantly peasant societies – from Lenin and Stalin to Mao and Pol Pot – could have "revolution in one country": millions shot or starved at will without the need for territorial aggrandizement. Millenarian ideologies and the need to harmonize the internal and external worlds might dictate eventual expansion, but in practice foreign conquest was a bonus, not an indispensable prerequisite for internal transformation. And as those regimes aged, expansion often became a conservative, even "social-imperialist" exercise aimed at demonstrating their continuing vitality and at depriving their wretched subjects of hope of deliverance. Only Mussolini and Hitler, like the men of 1792 before them, faced societies that required a great war to "consummate the revolution." That path helped ensure that their regimes, unlike those of their Marxist-Leninist rivals, did not live to grow old.

Part II

Foreign Policies and Military Instruments

Implementing the dictators' visions required foreign policies designed to camouflage aggressive intent while wooing similarly ambitious allies, and armed forces capable of the wide-ranging offensive warfare needed to destroy the international order. Scholars have studied numerous aspects of Italian foreign policy in the Fascist period. But unlike the German case, coherent overviews are rare.[1] Chapter 3 attempts to provide one, organized around an issue that since the 1960s has been thoroughly explored north of the Alps, the nature and extent of the continuities linking the foreign policy of the regime with that of its predecessors.[2] The essay focuses on the restraints under which Mussolini labored, the difficulties encountered in choosing Fascist Italy's first victim, and the search for allies – especially for the

---

1. Nothing remotely resembling either Gerhard L. Weinberg, *The Foreign Policy of Hitler's Germany*, 2 vols. (Chicago, 1970–1980), or Hans-Adolf Jacobsen, *Die Nationalsozialistische Aussenpolitik 1933–1938* (Frankfurt a. M., 1968), exists for Fascist Italy. C. J. Lowe and Frank Marzari, *Italian Foreign Policy, 1870–1940* (London, 1975) nevertheless remains useful. Arianna Arisi Rota, *La diplomazia del Ventennio: storia di una politica estera* (Milan, 1990), and H. James Burgwyn, *Italian Foreign Policy in the Interwar Period, 1918–1940* (Westport, CT, 1997) are insufficiently analytical and fail to set Italian policy persuasively in its domestic, ideological, and strategic contexts. Among the studies of particular periods, Ennio Di Nolfo, *Mussolini e la politica estera italiana 1922–1933* (Padua, 1960); Fulvio D'Amoja, *Declino e prima crisi dell'Europa di Versailles: Studio sulla diplomazia italiana ed europea 1931–1933* (Milan, 1967) and *La politica estera dell'Impero* (Milan, 1967); and Giampiero Carocci, *La politica estera dell'Italia fascista 1925–1928* (Bari 1969), stand out. For the early debates, Jens Petersen, "La politica estera del fascismo come problema storiografico," in Renzo de Felice, ed., *L'Italia fra tedeschi e alleati* (Bologna, 1973), is vital.
2. See Andreas Hillgruber, *Germany and the Two World Wars* (Cambridge, MA, 1981); Hildebrand, *Foreign Policy of the Third Reich*; and Wolfgang Michalka, "Der 30. Januar 1933. Kontinuität oder Bruch in der Deutschen Aussenpolitik," pp. 183–205 in Christoph Gradmann and Oliver von Mengersen, eds., *Das Ende der Weimarer Republik und die Nationalsozialistische Machtergreifung* (Heidelberg, 1994).

vengeful German nationalist ally required to free Italy for Mediterranean domination.

The armed forces and industrial establishment that Mussolini inherited received short shrift in the great war that he found at last in 1940. Chapter 4 charts the nature, extent, and impact of their inadequacies through analysis of the wartime career of the largest and most influential service, the Italian army. Chapter 5, although very different in structure and chronological range, seeks to explain why the outcome in the German case was infinitely more bloody. Nazi Germany's unique "fighting power" derived on the one hand from the peculiar leadership tradition that the Prussian and Prusso-German army acquired after its traumatic encounter with Napoleon in 1806–07, and on the other from Nazi revolutionary egalitarianism. A unique blend of military professionalism, racist fanaticism, and the military-ideological "career open to talent" – in conscious imitation of 1793 – condemned the Europe of 1942–45 to the deadliest three years of war in history.

3

FASCISM AND ITALIAN FOREIGN POLICY: CONTINUITY AND BREAK

> Whatever diplomacy and maps may say, we do not intend to remain eternally as prisoners in the Mediterranean.
>
> – *Mussolini, 30 March 1939*[1]

Senatore Salvatore Contarini, secretary-general of the Ministry of Foreign Affairs until 1926 and Mussolini's first and only diplomatic mentor, thought he knew the place of Fascism in Italian foreign policy: "We must use Mussolini like the blood of San Gennaro: exhibit him once a year, and then only from afar."[2] Contarini's formula, and still more his dismal failure to hold his master to the assigned role, suggests that the advent of Fascism in 1922 marked some sort of break in Italian foreign policy. As in Germany, where the nature and extent of the analogous break in foreign policy in 1933 has exercised immense attraction for historians as part of a wider debate about the shape of modern German history, understanding the balance between tradition and novelty in Italian foreign policy after 1922 is vital to situating the Fascist experiment historically. Yet Mussolini's foreign policy is poorly understood, and much vital evidence has remained unexplored or insufficiently exploited.[3] The literature and sources that have so far emerged nevertheless suggest three fundamental questions: What, if any, were the distinctive characteristics of Fascist foreign policy? What were the constraints upon its implementation? What led to war and ruin after 1936?

1. OO 44:229.
2. Mario Luciolli, *Palazzo Chigi: anni roventi* (Milan, 1976), p. 53.
3. Hildebrand, *Foreign Policy of the Third Reich*, and Günter Wollstein, *Vom Weimarer Revisionismus zu Hitler* (Bonn, 1972), are helpful introductions; for Italy, see especially the remarks of Richard A. Webster, "Autarky, Expansion, and the Underlying Continuity of the Italian State," *Italian Quarterly*, Winter 1964; Rumi, *Alle origini della politica estera fascista*; De Felice, *Mussolini il duce*, vol. 1, pp. 323, 340, 439–40; R. J. B. Bosworth, *Italy, the Least of the Great Powers* (Cambridge, 1979), pp. 418–20; Knox, *Mussolini*, pp. 110–11, 363–64 note 10; Alan Cassels, "Was There a Fascist Foreign Policy?," *International History Review* 5:2 (1983); Sergio Romano, "Diplomazia nazionale e diplomazia fascista: continuità e rottura," *Affari Esteri* 16 (1984), pp. 440–54.

Any attempt to deal with the first question, the singularity of Fascist foreign policy, requires analysis of Italy's pre-1922 traditions. Scholars otherwise widely differing in premises and interpretations have concurred that Fascism for the most part recapitulated, in blackshirt, the wilder aspirations of Liberal Italy. Testing that proposition requires some description of those aspirations, which were indeed not small. Liberal Italy's foreign policy elite sought to make Italy a true great power, consolidated in its real or supposed national territory, dominant in the Mediterranean, equipped with vast colonial perquisites, universally respected, and – most important – feared.[4]

Since the 1870s intemperate spirits had invoked war, a great war, as the necessary means to achieve great power status and to "make Italians" at home. Colonial enthusiasts had proposed that "race must be substituted for race" in East Africa to accommodate Italy's overflowing population; performance fortunately lagged behind aspiration.[5] After the turn of the century, the Italian Nationalist Association, literary antisocialists turned international social Darwinists, urged that "proletarian" Italy take up the external class struggle, and proclaimed the absolute primacy of foreign over domestic policy while paradoxically demanding a great war to consolidate domestic authority.[6]

The half-yearned-for coming of the Great War expanded official Italy's horizons. Colonial ministry bureaucrats projected Italian domination of Ethiopia and a *Mittelafrika italiana* from Libya to Lake Chad – and perhaps to the Gulf of Guinea. From the foreign ministry, Sidney Sonnino sought annexations in Dalmatia and Turkey that would make Italy master of the Balkans and eastern Mediterranean.[7] Nationalists preached both sets of aims with a vehemence that has led one commentator to suggest that "even Mussolini, in the most 'dynamic' period of Fascist foreign policy, never achieved either the mindless thirst for empire of the Nationalists, or their irresponsibility."[8]

---

4.   Chabod, *Storia della politica estera italiana dal 1870 al 1896*; Bosworth, *Least of the Great Powers*; and the trenchant summary of Federico Curato, "Aspetti nazionalistici della politica estera italiana dal 1870 al 1914," *Il Politico* 47:2 (1982).
5.   Ferdinando Martini, in Bosworth, *Least of the Great Powers*, p. 82.
6.   Nationalists on war and authority: Brunello Vigezzi, *L'Italia neutrale* (Milan, 1966), pp. 440–41, 963; primacy of foreign policy: 1918 nationalist manifesto, *Politica* 1:1 (December 1918), pp. 16–17.
7.   Italy still awaits its Fritz Fischer, but see especially Robert L. Hess, "Italy and Africa: Colonial Ambitions in the First World War," *Journal of African History* 4:1 (1963) and Sidney Sonnino, *Diario* (Bari, 1972).
8.   Franco Gaeta, *Il nazionalismo italiano* (Bari, 2nd rev. ed., 1981), p. 189.

But if Nationalist territorial ambitions embraced both the Crispi-colonial ministry line of African-Mediterranean expansion *and* the Sonnino concept of Adriatic, Balkan, and Near Eastern annexations and hegemony, the Nationalists nevertheless remained children of Liberal Italy.[9] Enrico Corradini might rail at the bourgeoisie ("like a garbage scow it makes the rounds of the sewer outlets disgorging malevolent filth, and takes everything on board, until it sinks"), imply that his own monarchism was conditional on the king's fulfilling the imperial mission, and claim with unconscious paradox that nationalism was "an instrument of internal revolutionary reform." The Nationalists' descent to the piazza in spring 1915 to call for war and their plotting with D'Annunzio and dissident generals after 1918 scarcely stood as models of order and legality. Nevertheless, the Nationalists remained true believers in state and monarchy, army and navy. Even after fusion with Fascism in 1923, most remained wedded to the idea of a "new state" founded on constitutional though undemo-cratic government.[10]

If the Nationalists were thus something less than totalitarian, the Liberal governments of the Great War's aftermath proved less than Nationalist in their breadth of ambition. The mirages of an Adriatic that was Italian on both shores, of a lodgment in Turkey, of vast African gains, of Italian suzerainty over the Caucasus, and of indepen-dent access to oil, coal, and grain soon dissolved. Reality – internal tur-moil, external isolation, and economic weakness – prevailed.[11] Sober heads such as Giolitti ultimately cooled the belligerence of D'An-nunzio and of the Nationalists' military friends. Moderation would serve best in expanding Italian influence in southeastern Europe and the Mediterranean, in rivalry with the one remaining great power on Italy's borders: France. Italy cut its losses in Albania and sought to patch up relations with its new eastern neighbor, Yugoslavia. It was

9.   See Vigezzi, *L'Italia neutrale*, especially pp. 557, 561–63; Bosworth, *Least of the Great Powers*, p. 46.
10. Corradini, *Discorsi politici* (Florence, 1923), pp. 10, 131; John A. Thayer, *Italy and the Great War* (Madison, 1964), p. 200; Vigezzi, *L'Italia neutrale*, pp. 564, 663–64; Corradini's political testament, in Luigi Federzoni, *L'Italia di ieri per la storia di domani* (Milan, 1967), p. 17; Alfredo Rocco, *La trasformazione dello Stato* (Rome, 1927), pp. 5–6; Gentile, *Mito dello stato nuovo*.
11. DDI 6/1/393; Francesco Coppola, "La pace italiana," *Politica* 1:1 (December 1918); C. A. Roselli, "Il necessario impero d'oltremare," *Politica* 1:2 (January 1919); Marta Petricioli, "L'occupazione italiana del Caucaso," *Il Politico* 1971:4, 1972:1; Webster, "Una speranza rinviata: L'espansione industriale italiana e il problema del petrolio dopo la prima guerra mondiale," *Storia Contemporanea* 11:2 (1980).

this line of Liberal foreign policy, with a touch of colonial ambition, to which Contarini was heir, and to which he attempted to hold Mussolini.

Mussolini's ultimate refusal to be held implies that his foreign policy differed from that of his predecessors. Many scholars have nevertheless resolutely denied that Mussolini had a *foreign* policy at all. Even Marxists have succumbed to Gaetano Salvemini's seductive notion, born in the heat of political combat, that Mussolini's diplomacy was no more than a series of improvisations that served internal propaganda purposes.[12] That *Primat der Innenpolitik* reductionism has not survived unscathed the slow opening of the archives. Its Leninist rival, the theory of Fascist "imperialism" as agent of Italian capitalism, also fell on hard times even before the collapse of the Soviet empire.[13] The dominant "anti-anti-Fascist" orthodoxy has emerged from a convergence between the Mario Toscano school of technical diplomatic history and the massive Mussolini biography of Renzo De Felice. That orthodoxy rests on De Felice's claim that Mussolini's underlying concept was the traditional aspiration of the House of Savoy and Liberal "*Italietta*": the role of arbiter of the balance of power, the "decisive weight" that could, in the elegant 1930 formula of Dino Grandi, Mussolini's foreign minister, "sell [itself] dearly in the hours of the great future crisis." Mussolini purportedly hoped to use this central position to give Italy its long-overdue empire in Africa while keeping the peace in Europe.[14]

Such a program may indeed place Mussolini firmly in the seamless continuity of Italian foreign policy. But the difficulty with the "*peso determinante*" and peace in Europe thesis, as with its domestic counterpart, De Felice's early interpretation of Mussolini's domestic policy as mere *trasformismo* in blackshirt, is that it explains little of the evidence.[15] It fails to account for Grandi's sometime insistence, of which

12. Salvemini, *Mussolini diplomatico* (Bari, 1952), especially Chapter 28; Giorgio Rochat, "Dal nazionalismo all'imperialismo: la politica estera italiana da Corfù alla guerra d'Abissinia e di Spagna (1923–38)," in Aldo Alessandro Mola, ed., *Dall'Italia giolittiana all'Italia repubblicana* (Turin, 1976), pp. 199–202.

13. As Giampiero Carocci put it, in Italy "the only great force whole-heartedly interested in imperialism was the State" (*Politica estera*, p. 13); see also his "Contributo alla discussione sull'imperialismo," *Il movimento di liberazione in Italia* 23 (1971), p. 12.

14. DDI 7/9/234 (Grandi); De Felice, "Alcune osservazioni sulla politica estera mussoliniana," in De Felice, ed., *L'Italia fra tedeschi e alleati*; also *Mussolini il duce*, vol. 1 (Turin, 1974), and, more cautiously, vol. 2 (Turin, 1981); on both historiographical and factual issues, see Knox, "The Fascist Regime, Its Foreign Policy and Its Wars: An 'Anti-Anti-Fascist' Orthodoxy?," *Contemporary European History*, 4:3 (1995).

15. *Trasformismo*: De Felice, *Mussolini il fascista* (Turin, 1966–68), especially vol. 1, pp. 537–38, 588, 591, 594, 618; vol. 2, pp. 8–10, 67.

more later, that Italy's role as "arbiter" involved European war, perhaps against France. And it offers no plausible answer to the decisive question: why did Fascist Italy progress from small wars, to bigger ones, to ruin at the side of Hitler's Germany?

The search for concepts underlying Mussolini's foreign policy can benefit from taking at least a few of Mussolini's utterances at face value, and making some effort to distinguish the Duce's aims from his diplomatic and propaganda tactics and from the frequent attempts at conciliation and negotiation of his increasingly terrified subordinates. For although Mussolini had neither occasion nor inclination to write a *Mein Kampf* before coming to power in 1922, visionary goals and a program consistent with his later actions, as suggested in the preceding chapter, emerge from his remarks both public and private between 1919 and 1927.

In the course of his pre-1914 career as Socialist agitator, Mussolini had affirmed Sorel's "barbarous notion" of socialism, accepted Mazzini's dangerous theory that politics should be a kind of religion, and secretly harbored the conviction that "we must create the spiritual unity of all Italians." The Great War resolved Mussolini's ambiguities, and much else. Mussolini publicly and enthusiastically embraced Oriani's conception of the nation's creation through bloodshed, and added to it in the course of the war the aspirations to Adriatic and Mediterranean empire of Italy's policy elite, both Liberal and Nationalist. After coming to power, and even before he openly assumed dictatorial prerogatives in January 1925, Mussolini concluded that those aspirations, if realized, might also allow him to grasp the total power at home that the monarchy, the Church, and civil society seemed stubbornly intent on denying him. The warrior indoctrination of Italy's youth, artificially stimulated demographic growth, and the beginnings of autarchy were likewise intended to fit Italy for empire.

From the beginning, the creation of that empire meant making Italy "the predominant nation of the Mediterranean basin."[16] And as early as April 1919 Mussolini discerned Italy's ultimate adversary: the "plutocratic and bourgeois" West; Corradini's myth of the international class struggle between poor, populous Italy and bloated, declining France had taken on new and broader meaning. War had made clear Italy's vulnerability to "the blackmail of grain and coal." War's aftermath revealed to the full what Mussolini and much of the Italian elite took to be the selfish obstinacy of Italy's ex-allies. And Mussolini,

16.   OO 16:106; also 12/77, 15:185, 16:128, 159, 301, 335, 18:439, 459.

unlike vacillating Nationalists such as Francesco Coppola, repeatedly sounded a note of fierce hostility to "those who are parasites living off the Mediterranean." It was in Italy's interest "to help demolish" the British Empire, Mussolini proclaimed publicly; privately, soon after achieving power, he offered support to Indian revolutionaries while professing unshakable resolve to "drive the English out of the Mediterranean."[17]

Mussolini apparently derived from the Nationalists and the navy one further essential element of his program: geopolitics. Postwar Adriatic friction with Yugoslavia and France increasingly led the Nationalists to frame their description of Italy's plight in geopolitical terms. By the end of 1919 Attilio Tamaro was denouncing Malta, Biserte, and Toulon as "a chain of formidable strongholds that surround and can blockade Italy."[18] By autumn 1921, as the Italian navy prepared for the Washington Naval Conference, its staff planners concluded that the real geopolitical threat derived from the choke points at Gibraltar and Suez rather than from hostile bases closer in. The combination of resource dependence and "geographic position in an enclosed sea" rendered Italy extremely vulnerable. The navy thus found a convenient rationale for its Washington demand for parity with France and for its claims on the armaments budget. Coppola likewise lamented British domination of the "gates of the Mediterranean" in the Nationalist journal *Politica*. And in August 1922 the navy's former war leader, Grand Admiral Paolo Thaon di Revel, forcefully summarized the position to the Senate. Four-fifths of Italy's imports came by sea from outside the Mediterranean: "with Suez and Gibraltar barred, Italy will soon be at the mercy of its adversary."[19]

Mussolini adopted these themes, which complemented his notions of Italy's Mediterranean mission, as early as June 1920. Giolitti's evac-

---

17. OO 18:439, 432; also 13:71, 75–76, 109, 142–46 (which did not appear in print until 1937, and may have suffered emendation), 14:220, 471, 16:104–06, 300–01, 18:180; PRO FO 371/8889, C9802 (a detailed and convincing SIS "Report on relations between the Italian Government and Indian revolutionaries . . .," 31 May 1923)(warm thanks to Brian R. Sullivan for a copy of this document).

18. Tamaro, "L'Italia tradita nell'Adriatico," *Politica* 3:3 (January? 1920), p. 339; Francesco Coppola, "L'intesa è finita," *Politica* 4:11–12 (April 1920), p. 163. The notion of geopolitical encirclement by France had pre-war precedents: see Corradini, "Dall'italianismo al latinismo," *Il regno*, 1 May 1904, p. 2, and Giovanni Pascoli, "La grande proletaria si è mossa," November 1911, in Rochat, ed., *Il colonialismo italiano* (Turin, 1974), p. 88.

19. Chief of naval staff memorandum, 23 October 1921, in Giovanni Bernardi, *Il disarmo navale fra le due guerre mondiali* (1919–1939) (Rome, 1975), p. 46; Coppola, "La paralisi della storia" (21 November 1921), *Politica* 3:29 (1921), p. 187; AP, Senato, 1921–22, 3:3834 (14 August 1922).

uation of Valona led Mussolini to declaim against the "chain of hostility that surround[ed] Italy in the Mediterranean." The outcome of his first genuinely Fascist foreign policy act, the August–September 1923 attempt to annex Corfù, presumably confirmed that insight. Britain objected, and Mussolini grudgingly permitted Contarini and his ambassadors to extricate him from a potential confrontation with the crushingly superior Royal Navy. Publicly, Corfù was a Fascist triumph, but the Italian navy's private confession that shipping and coastal cities were largely defenseless may have come as a shock.[20] Thaon di Revel, by then navy minister, reiterated in December 1924 and March 1925 his earlier claims to the Senate. The postwar situation required priority in armaments for navy rather than army; otherwise Italy "would remain a prisoner in the Mediterranean."[21]

It was at that point, in March 1925, that Mussolini's 1920 notions about an Italy encircled "in its own sea" apparently began to harden into dogma. With a "fixed stare" resembling "that of a fanatic," Mussolini informed an appalled Contarini on 6 March that

> Gibraltar, Malta, Suez, Cyprus represent a chain that permits England to encircle, to imprison Italy in the Mediterranean. If another link, Albania, were welded to [that chain], we would have had to break it with a war. A short war; it would not have lasted more than a few weeks, for Italy today is no longer the Italy of the days of Giolitti . . .

On 2 April, in the Senate, Mussolini echoed Thaon di Revel: "the Mediterranean has only three approaches, and these three approaches are well guarded." Blockade would render Italy's food situation "extremely difficult."[22]

By autumn 1926 Mussolini had transmuted these merely practical insights into a monocausal theory of international politics, a geopolitical dogma. In a leap that carried him far beyond the parochial concerns of the naval staff or Nationalist complaints of "encirclement," he derived from that dogma an uncompromising program, announced to an assemblage of senior officers in late 1926 or early 1927:

20. "Catena": OO 15:37; also 15:29. Corfù: see especially Di Nolfo, *Mussolini e la politica estera italiana*, pp. 85–98; Cassels, *Mussolini's Early Diplomacy* (Princeton, 1970), Chapter 4; Matteo Pizzigallo, *Mediterraneo e Russia nella politica italiana* (Milan, 1983), Chapter 1; and DDI 7/2/347, 348.
21. AP, Senato, 1924, 1:915–16 (20 December 1924); AP, Camera, 1925, 3:3151, 3171 (30 March 1925); Thaon di Revel to Mussolini, 28 March 1925, in Bernardi, *Il disarmo navale*, pp. 215–217.
22. Mussolini, 6 March 1925, in the memoirs of an eyewitness, Ugo Sola (Sola typescript ms., pp. 184, 188–89)(see also Carocci, *Politica estera*, p. 265 note 3); OO 21:273.

A nation that has no free access to the sea cannot be considered a free nation; a nation that has no free access to the oceans cannot be considered a great power. Italy must become a great power.[23]

Mussolini held to that visionary goal. He told his ministers in late 1929 that Italy "could not remain voluntarily imprisoned" in the Mediterranean. It must choose: "to founder, or to achieve mastery." The goal reappeared in confidential remarks to naval officers on the eve of the Ethiopian war, in his secret speech of 4 February 1939 to the Grand Council of Fascism, in his 31 March 1940 war directive to the armed forces, in further secret remarks in April 1940, and in his 10 June 1940 balcony performance announcing Italy's plunge into the Second World War. Italy must become a true great power by breaking the bars of its prison: Corsica, Tunis, Malta, Cyprus. It must overawe or crush the smaller states in its way. It must "march to the ocean" across British or French colonial territories.[24] Given the anti-Western nature of his ultimate objective, Mussolini was understandably guarded in public, but his dogged insistence that Italy was a prisoner in the Mediterranean repeatedly betrayed his underlying aim.[25]

Escape from Italy's prison required rearmament, the selection of intermediate objectives in Europe and Africa, the securing of allies, and the camouflage of the dictator's long-term goals until both he and Fascist Italy were strong enough to avow them openly. Rearmament, which scholarly opinion has in general discerned only after 1935, began fitfully in the 1920s.[26] Total military expenditure as a proportion of national income rose from a modest 2.6 percent in 1923–25 to 3.4 percent in 1927 and 5.4 percent in 1931. Thereafter it rose sharply to 18.4 percent in 1936, and declined only slightly in 1937–38 before rising again with the Second World War. Until 1931 Italy's expenditure in relation to national income ran only slightly below that of France, western Europe's most heavily armed state. Then Italy surpassed the French. Between 1926 and 1940 Italy also spent proportionately more than Britain, despite the latter's worldwide commitments. Actual

---

23. Mussolini speech to military leaders, autumn 1926–early 1927 (source: General Arturo Vacca-Maggiolini, quoted in Emilio Canevari, *La guerra italiana* [Rome, 1948–49], vol. 2, p. 211). Rochat, *Badoglio* (Turin, 1974), pp. 557–58, places the speech in autumn 1926; see also OO 40:51–52.
24. Minutes, 8 November 1929, ACS, Verbali del Consiglio dei Ministri, vol. 18: "L'Italia o sfonda o resta padrona"; Romeo Bernotti, *Cinquant'anni nella Marina militare* (Milan, 1971), p. 232; OO 37:151–57, 29:403–05; Knox, *Mussolini*, pp. 40, 96; DDI 9/3/669.
25. See especially DDI 7/8/323; OO 24:235, 26:323.
26. On military policy, see Sullivan, "A Thirst for Glory," and Lucio Ceva, *Le forze armate* (Turin, 1981).

expenditure, as opposed to expenditure as a percentage of national income, rose from a third of France's in 1923 to roughly three-fifths in 1933–34. Then Ethiopian and Spanish wars carried Italian expenditure past that of France even in absolute terms.[27]

The gradual increase in the military budget after 1925 bought an air force which until the mid-1930s was one of the world's largest. The navy increased from 403,000 tons of mostly pre-war and wartime vessels in 1926 to 600,000 tons of predominantly new or modernized ships by 1934. The fleet might not equal that of France, Mussolini told his Navy undersecretary in 1927, but it should at least represent "for France what the German navy represented – and shall represent again, in good time – for Britain: a nightmare and a menace." French internal disintegration and the "aggressive and tenacious Fascist spirit" would do the rest. The army, despite the continuing weaknesses to be explored in the following chapter, overcame the organizational crisis into which demobilization, budgetary stringency, and innate conservatism had plunged it. It passed from a mobilizable force of perhaps nine to ten divisions in 1923 to an ostensible figure of forty divisions by summer 1933.[28] Mussolini aspired to use them.

The choice of intermediate objectives was not without difficulty. The lands bordering the Mediterranean and its exits were already spoken for. One potential victim was Ethiopia, the key to a consolidated Italian empire in East Africa that would command the Red Sea and threaten Britain at Suez. As early as July 1925 Mussolini foresaw the need "to prepare ourselves militarily and diplomatically in order to profit from a future [*eventuale*] disintegration of the Ethiopian empire." But in Africa Mussolini was willing to wait: "we cannot achieve

27. 1923–30 averages: Italy 3.15 percent, France 3.65 percent (but Italy surpassed France in 1926 and 1929); 1931–38 averages: Italy 10.16 percent, France 5.93 percent. Figures based on the sources cited in Knox, *Mussolini*, p. 296, and Robert Frankenstein, *Le prix du réarmement français* (Paris, 1982) p. 35; F. A. Répaci, *La finanza italiana nel ventennio 1913–1932* (Turin, 1934), pp. 109–110, 129 (*Carabinieri* and MVSN counted as military; Italian fiscal years averaged to calendar years).

28. OO 40:436; nine to ten divisions: Mussolini, in notes by General Pietro Gàzzera (undersecretary, then minister of war, 1928–33), 22 July 1932, Gàzzera papers microfilm; I am deeply indebted to Brian R. Sullivan for a copy of this indispensable source, and for other documents vital to this chapter. For a description of the material, including some items not found on the microfilm, see "Le guerre segrete di Mussolini," *La Stampa*, 9 January 1982, and Sergio Pelagalli, "Il generale Pietro Gàzzera al ministero della guerra (1928–1933)," *Storia Contemporanea* 20:6 (1989). Forty divisions: Gàzzera, "Efficienza dell'esercito al 22 luglio 1933 A. XI," Gàzzera papers microfilm. For the army's organizational travail and gradual growth, see Badoglio, "Memoria sull'organizzazione dell'esercito italiano...," October 1925, ACS, Carte Badoglio, box 2, and Gàzzera's exhaustive annual reports to Mussolini and the king for 1929 through 1933, Gàzzera papers microfilm.

a total violent solution [*soluzione integrale violenta*] unless there is chaos in Europe."[29]

Albania instead became Mussolini's first "Fascist trophy."[30] The Yugoslavs had responded to their 1923 loss of Fiume to Mussolini by sponsoring Ahmed Zogu's December 1924 Albanian revolt; Mussolini could counterattack with Contarini's acquiescence. The result was a semicolonial economic agreement that fastened on Albania in March 1925 what Mussolini described as an Italian "*main-mise,*" and treaties in 1926–28 that he boasted to D'Annunzio gave Italy "the gate of the bitterest sea."[31] But even as Italy sought to consolidate its hold on Albania, Mussolini in winter 1925–26 apparently also contemplated a Corfù-style descent on Turkey. The coming to power of a military dictator, Theodoros Pangalos, transformed Greece from victim into potential junior partner, and the Anglo-Turkish dispute over the oil of Mosul similarly metamorphosed Britain from an adversary into an apparent ally. But Italian preparations to ship an expeditionary force from Naples, and Mussolini's inflammatory speeches during his Tripolitanian tour in mid-April 1926, alerted the intended victims. Atatürk ordered a partial mobilization that apparently compelled Mussolini to shelve the project.[32]

That left Yugoslavia. Mussolini had accepted on sufferance Contarini's 1924 Italo-Yugoslav friendship treaty; it ratified Italy's annexation of Fiume.[33] But in the long run he was only willing to tolerate Yugoslavia as an Italian satellite. Contarini, who thought differently, departed in early 1926; Mussolini had by then consolidated his dictatorship and felt strong enough to let him go. And when the Yugoslavs reacted to Italian encroachments in Albania by reluctantly seeking a security treaty with France, Mussolini began to contemplate dealing them "one of those lessons that suffice to correct the mental and polit-

---

29. OO 39:465; Giuliano Cora, "Un diplomatico durante l'era fascista," *Storia e Politica* 5:1 (1966), p. 92.
30. For the phrase, see H. James Burgwyn, *Il revisionismo fascista* (Milan, 1979).
31. Alberto Pirelli, *Taccuini 1922/1943* (Bologna, 1984), p. 66; DDI 7/4/60; OO 40:535. Pietro Pastorelli, *Italia e Albania, 1924–1927* (Florence, 1967) argues that Mussolini sought Albanian independence (indeed he did – from Yugoslavia, not Italy); Giovanni Zamboni, *Mussolinis Expansionspolitik auf dem Balkan* (Hamburg, 1970) is more penetrating.
32. Detailed evidence on spring 1926 plans against Turkey has not yet surfaced, but see the retrospective remark in Grandi diary, 15 October 1929. In addition, OO 22:112–18; DDI 7/4/298, 377, 475; ADAP B/3/99; GFM 2784H/D538343, D538357; DBFP 1a/2/207, 248; army staff, "Principali questioni trattate dall'Ufficio Operazioni durante la permanenza di S.E. il Maresciallo Badoglio allo S.M. dell'Esercito," 15 February 1927, ACS, Carte Badoglio, box 2, and Sullivan, "A Thirst for Glory," pp. 197–99. For earlier Mussolini ambitions in Anatolia, DDI 7/3/604.
33. Mussolini, in Carlo Umiltà, *Jugoslavia e Albania* (Milan, 1947), pp. 27–28, 48.

ical deformities of any people." In early 1927 he apparently intensified support for Macedonian terrorists operating against southern Yugoslavia. In April of the same year he contracted with revisionist Hungary secret understandings directed at least in part against Belgrade, and promised the Hungarians arms.[34]

Then, in July 1927, he called together his chiefs of staff and their aides for what he described as "the first meeting for the systematic preparation for war." War, he insisted, would come "soon or perhaps less soon, but it will certainly come." And Fascist Italy's first war plan would be an "*offensive* war plan" against Yugoslavia: "the attack must be aggressive, unexpected." France and the Little Entente, he anticipated, would accept a fait accompli if Italian action were swift and ruthless. He and Marshal Badoglio set 1932 as the target date for readiness. Mussolini's relish for destroying Yugoslavia inevitably suggests ambitions beyond Italy's eastern border far more extensive than the modest defensive aims frequently invoked in the literature.[35]

War in Europe required allies. Albania assured Italy's grip on the mouth of the Adriatic and potentially threatened Yugoslavia from the south. The quasi-alliance with Hungary in 1927 and joint Italo-Hungarian support for Croat terrorism against Belgrad from 1929 on served the same purpose. The 1928 attempt to construct a triple alliance between Italy, Greece, and Turkey that netted a pair of unwelcomely bland friendship treaties was a further failed step in the same direction. Support of a "March on Vienna" by the Austrian Right in 1928–29 and later had a similar aim. In a December 1930 conversation with his minister of war, General Pietro Gàzzera, Mussolini was explicit about his purposes, although for Gàzzera's benefit the Duce attempted to make Italy appear the injured party: "When in [19]33–34 the encirclement of Yugoslavia will be complete (with Austria, Hungary, Bulgaria, Greece a benevolent neutral, Albania), and we are sure of Turkey, which will let us pass the Straits, it will be time to finish off Yugoslavia, a power that threatens us."[36]

Alliances with small powers were nevertheless of limited use.

---

34. GFM K449/K130369–71; DDI 7/4/446, 7/5/78, 123, 157, 333.
35. Minutes of meeting, and Badoglio letter, 18 July 1927, in Antonello Biagini and Alessandro Gionfrida, eds., *Lo Stato Maggiore Generale tra le due guerre (Verbali delle riunioni presiedute da Badoglio dal 1925 al 1937)* (Rome, 1997), pp. 104–05, 108 (emphasis in original). For the relentlessly provocative character of Mussolini's Yugoslav policy, the judgment of Grandi, who helped implement it, is conclusive: Grandi diary, especially 2 December 1930, 3 April 1931 and final entry (a long retrospective discussion, dated 8 August 1932, of events between April and July 1932; the first page or pages are apparently missing).
36. Mussolini, in Gàzzera notes, 23 December 1930.

Liberal Italy had needed great-power allies to secure even the relatively modest acquisitions of 1918. Fascist Italy aspired to turn the Mediterranean basin upside down, and required alliance with a great power of equally revolutionary ambitions. That power, Mussolini apparently saw from the beginning, could only be Germany, chief threat to the postwar settlement. With an openness and vehemence that few in Italy's political elite matched, Mussolini repeatedly announced in April–May 1919 that the West's avarice at the Paris peace conference would drive Italy to join the Germans in order to achieve the Mediterranean domination that was Italy's due. His interest in the Reich persisted. It was to Berlin, not Paris, that he traveled in early March 1922 in his first unofficial foreign policy venture.[37]

Once in power, he soon moved to increase and exploit the German threat to the international status quo. In September 1923, after vague feelers from Stresemann about a "common policy," he sought German military backing against France should the seizure of Fiume lead to war with Yugoslavia. The German chancellor politely evaded. That and later rebuffs led Mussolini to doubt that Stresemann, that "putrid freemason and . . . parliamentarized political dilettante," was a fit ally for Fascist Italy, although the Duce never entirely gave up hope.[38] But Mussolini had also already inaugurated a practice more and more familiar in later years: pursuit, through parallel diplomacy outside foreign ministry control, of ideologically based alliances with forces that appeared to share his revolutionary goals. Beginning in early 1923 he apparently delivered weapons to the German army. In February 1924 he sent General Luigi Capello to Berlin to explore the vehemently expressed desire of the German army and Right for a war of revenge against France.[39] Military weakness and the Right's temporary incoherence brought that hope to naught, but at the height of the Matteotti crisis Mussolini, according to the German ambassador to Rome, still considered a nationalist Germany his ally of choice. Sooner

37.   OO 13:71, 109, 14:470–71, 16:106; see also 18:120, 20:29. For another 1919 call for a
      German alliance – and war for Tunis – see Orazio Pedrazzi (later Fascist consul in
      Jerusalem), "Le iniquità coloniali della conferenza di Parigi," *Politica* 2:2 (May 1919),
      p. 319. Coppola, whose credentials as Nationalist extremist are not in doubt, merely
      thought a strong Germany necessary for Italy's freedom of movement. ("Accademia
      sinistra," *Politica* 2:2 [May 1919], pp. 229, 254.)
38.   DDI 7/2/360 and note 3; 7/2/373; 7/5/228; Vera Torunsky, *Entente der Revisionisten?*
      (Cologne, 1986), pp. 48–52.
39.   Torunsky, *Entente*, pp. 52–54; Jens Petersen, *Hitler-Mussolini* (Tübingen, 1973), pp.
      11–13.; DDI 7/2/489 and note 2; 7/3/39, 3/43 and note 1; Capello report, March 1924,
      in De Felice, ed., *Mussolini e Hitler* (Florence, 1983), pp. 70–115.

or later Versailles would collapse, and "in the . . . new war between France and Germany, the Italy led by Mussolini would place itself at Germany's side, in order to crush France jointly."[40]

The expiration in 1935 of the decisive provisions of Versailles, French occupation of Rhineland and Saar, even allowed Mussolini to prophesy the date. In his long-remembered Ascension Day speech of May 1927 he affirmed that "a crucial point in European history" would arrive between 1935 and 1940. Italy would then "make [its] voice heard and see [its] rights recognized." That prophecy, and Mussolini's accompanying fulminations about five million men under arms and an air force powerful enough to "blot out the sun," aroused considerable alarm abroad. He was careful not to repeat his prophecy publicly in the same bellicose terms.[41] And waiting for Germany was tedious, despite the promising relationship that Mussolini and his air chief, the ex-leader of *squadristi* Italo Balbo, developed behind Grandi's back after 1927–28 between the Italian air force and its clandestine German counterpart. From the vantage point of June 1929, Mussolini confided to Gàzzera that the Germans had so far disappointed him: "Germany is disarmed – we cannot negotiate for possible cooperation against France (Capello in 1924)."[42]

Mussolini's estimate that war would "perhaps become . . . necessary or inevitable" by the mid-1930s remained in force until 1931–32, and he continued to expect German help. His remarks to Gàzzera in 1929 and 1930 were unequivocal:

> We must look forward within a period of four to six years to the wars with France and Yugoslavia. . . . We have already completed two steps, Budapest and Vienna, toward Berlin. We shall complete the last. But we must *give* to the Germans, not *receive*. We must . . . tow them, not be towed by them.

The Germany that Fascist Italy proposed to tow also had a particular ideological coloration. Five months after Hitler's September 1930 election triumph, Mussolini predicted to Gàzzera that the "accession to power of the German Right" would come in 1934–36. And as early as 1927 he had dared name the price that Italy would pay for German backing against the West: Anschluss. A Germany stretching from the

---

40. Neurath to Auswärtiges Amt, 2 December 1924, GFM 6059/E447588–94 (quotation: E447591); Neurath ascribed his information at least in part to Mussolini himself.
41. OO 22:386; see also DDI 7/5/236 and OO 23:177.
42. ADAP B/7/232 note 3; Petersen, *Hitler-Mussolini*, pp. 21–24; Grandi diary, 10 January 1931; Mussolini, in Gàzzera notes, 11 June 1929.

Spree to the Danube, Mussolini told his Hungarian allies, would threaten only France.[43]

While waiting to take that last step toward Berlin, Fascist Italy nevertheless had to live in the despised world of Western bourgeois respectability. Domestically, Mussolini's ambiguous status as royal prime minister hobbled him, although PNF attempts to sap the power of the establishment made gradual progress. In the realm of economics, the regime required the cooperation of the industrial and financial magnates of Milan and Turin, who on the whole sought peace, a docile labor force, and protection from the rigors of the market. The public, despite occasional boasts by Mussolini that it would gleefully welcome war, was profoundly weary after the immense outpouring of blood and treasure in 1915-18.

Externally, Mussolini inherited from his predecessors both an unenviable degree of economic dependence and a shortage of political freedom for maneuver. The "battle for grain" could not free Italy of reliance on foreign and mostly seaborne supplies of coal and oil. Resource dependence, apart from its danger in war, brought in peacetime a constant drain on the balance of payments that helped weaken the lira drastically after December 1924, a difficulty ultimately removed by loans from the Morgan Bank. The financial tutelage of New York and Washington was preferable to that of London or Paris, but it nevertheless bound Mussolini to the status quo.[44]

Strategic and political weakness paralleled economic inadequacy. British sea power, linked with that of France, indeed dominated the Mediterranean and its exits. London's toleration of Mussolini, although conspicuous under Austen Chamberlain until 1929 and under his Labour successors thereafter, was conditional on the Duce's pretending to love peace. On land, the Franco-Yugoslav agreement of November 1927 placed Italy in a strategic vise. Before that pact, the army staff had estimated that Italy could mobilize more troops at a faster rate than Yugoslavia. But French advisers and materiel in the east and the French threat to Italy from the west totally transformed the situation. The aims of Mussolini's military buildup seemed to

---

43. "Necessary or inevitable": Mussolini to *federali*, 25 October 1928, in Attilio Tamaro, *Venti anni di storia* (Rome, n.d.), vol. 2, p. 308; block quotation: Mussolini, in Gàzzera notes, 30 June 1930 (emphasis in original); see also 7 August 1929; German Right: Mussolini, in Gàzzera notes, 27 January 1931; Anschluss: DDI 7/5/123 and Maria Ormos, "L'opinione del conte Stefano Bethlen sui rapporti italo-ungheresi (1927–31)," *Storia Contemporanea* 2:2 (1971), p. 300.

44. On the United States connection, see especially Claudia Damiani, *Mussolini e gli Stati Uniti 1922–1935* (Bologna, 1980).

recede ever further the more Italy armed. After 1929 the combined forces of France and Yugoslavia, as seen from Rome, outnumbered Italy's by ratios of 2:1 or better, even after deducting French and Yugoslav units needed to secure other borders.[45]

Mussolini nevertheless strove mightily to maintain the planning assumption that France would not intervene in an Italian war of aggression against Yugoslavia. But in winter 1928–29 his undersecretary of war and his army chief of staff, Generals Gàzzera and Alberto Bonzani, compelled him to accept their view that for the moment a single-handed war in the east was unrealistic. Mussolini, with apparent encouragement from Badoglio, continued to toy with the notion that "if we were to act very swiftly, perhaps France would not intervene," and with projects for an offensive through Austria to outflank Yugoslav border defenses. In mid-1930 he even contemplated a surprise descent on southern France.[46] Clandestine Italian support for the Croat terrorist movement of Ante Pavelic and Gustav Kosutic, including weapons and explosives after early 1929, also appeared to offer hope. Mussolini himself met Kosutic in mid-October 1929 and committed himself to what Grandi, with overstatement calculated to appeal to his master, described to the Italian council of ministers as "making Croatia." Pavelic and Kosutic in turn promised vassalage to Italy.[47] But the Croat project offered little hope of short-term success; in practice Mussolini had to accept strategic paralysis.

In this unpromising situation Mussolini inevitably followed a foreign policy version of the two-track tactic that had served so well domestically between 1921 and 1925.[48] As he remarked to Gàzzera in 1929, "verbal pacifism" was merely verbal: "We shall bleat with the

45. Army staff memorandum, 13 April 1927, ACS, Carte Badoglio, box 2; Ferrari to Mussolini, 31 January 1928, in Canevari, *Italia 1861–1943* (Rome, 1965), vol. 1, p. 420; 1929–33 ratios: Gàzzera to Mussolini, 11 June 1929; Gàzzera annual reports for 1929–33, Gàzzera papers microfilm: 1929 = 2.5:1, 1930 = 2.25:1, 1931 = 2.4:1, 1932 = 2.8:1, 1933 = 2:1.
46. Bonzani to Gàzzera, 2 RP, 11 March 1929; Bonzani to Mussolini, 3 RRPP, 14 March 1929; Mussolini, in Gàzzera notes, 16 March 1929; Mussolini to Bonzani, 3 RRPP, 17 March 1929 (drafted by Gàzzera); Mussolini to Badoglio, 11 RRPP, 20 March 1929, all in Gàzzera papers microfilm. Mussolini quotation (and continued Badoglio planning for single-handed war): Gàzzera notes, 18 November 1929. For surprise attack on France, see Gàzzera notes, 14 July 1930, and Emilio Faldella, *L'Italia e la seconda guerra mondiale* (Bologna, 1960), p. 16 (1931).
47. Grandi diary, 27, 29 January; 7, 12 February; 16, 18 October 1929; Grandi to Gàzzera, 12 November 1929, with Forges Davanzati minute of 13–14 October 1929 talks with Pavelic and Kosutic; Gàzzera to Grandi, 6937/73, 27 November 1929, all in Grandi papers, roll 10; Grandi speech to Council of Ministers, 5 November 1929, NARA T-586/1295/112735: "Abbiamo fatto l'Albania, dobbiamo fare la Croazia."
48. "We must anesthetize . . . the opposition and also the Italian people" (OO 44:10).

sheep, and howl with the wolves." In that spirit he had signed the 1924 friendship treaty with Yugoslavia. In 1925 he had laid down that Italy must "narcotize [*cloroformizzare*] the world of Ethiopian officialdom" while waiting for Ethiopia to collapse, and had consequently concluded a meaningless Italo-Ethiopian friendship treaty in 1928.[49] Occasional soothing words and interminable negotiations with France in 1928–29 and Yugoslavia in 1930–32 likewise served to anesthetize until Germany revived and Fascist Italy could howl.

Multilateral security agreements such as Locarno or the 1928 Kellogg-Briand Pact Mussolini resisted, for they threatened to bind Italy to the status quo. He signed grudgingly rather than suffer isolation, then happily scoffed at the rapid deterioration of the "spirit of Locarno" and at the spectacle of the "diplomacy of the *arrivés* questing after the phantoms of perpetual peace."[50] His proposal to disarm – or arm – to the level of the most armed continental state, unveiled in June 1928, was in Grandi's words a mere "straw man." Mussolini's purpose was to delude the naive Anglo-Saxons and pillory the French, who sensibly declined to disarm in the face of German and Italian hostility.[51]

Verbal pacifism had major domestic disadvantages. It conflicted with the aim of Mussolini and the Fascist Party of molding the young into a warrior race thirsting for conquest. It also threatened loss of faith in the ranks of the PNF itself. Mussolini therefore attempted to reconcile the contradictory imperatives of international respectability and domestic barbarization by speaking in code: "revision" of the supposedly iniquitous peace treaties was a recurring theme from 1919 on. That sham goal was more acceptable to Mussolini's diplomatic advisors than the open espousal of aggression would have been; it was the foreign policy counterpart to the myth of the state with which Mussolini camouflaged from his conservative flankers his drive toward total power. His diplomats might carp at the threat to Italy from *German* revisionism, but that was the very revisionism that Mussolini himself hoped would help him destroy – not revise – both peace and settlement.[52]

---

49. Mussolini, in Gàzzera notes, 11 June 1929; OO 39:465; DDI 7/10/38 and note 1 suggests that Mussolini's 1925 directive remained the core of Italian policy in East Africa.
50. OO 22:385–86, 23:271, 40:543, 41:138–39.
51. DDI 7/9/234; also 7/8/315 and 7/11/37, p. 68; OO 23:184.
52. OO 14:31, 214 (1919); for the puzzlement Mussolini's revisionism caused even the most intelligent of his diplomats, see Vitetti memorandum, July 1932, in De Felice, *Mussolini il duce*, vol. 1, pp. 848–49, and Raffaele Guariglia, *Ricordi* (Naples, 1949), pp. 79, 82.

By 1929, however, Mussolini had grown weary of the frustrations of the day-to-day conduct of foreign affairs, and of the need to profess peaceful intentions personally. He handed the foreign ministry over to his undersecretary, Dino Grandi, that most plausible of Fascist chieftains. Judging from his diary, Grandi had been full of Fascist fervor as undersecretary. But as foreign minister he reversed himself abruptly: Mussolini's aggressive Balkan policy and implacable hostility to France had driven Italy into a perilous dead end. Grandi and his army colleague Gàzzera agreed that Italy might soon face a two-front preventive war. Yugoslav action against Albania would trigger an Italian landing to uphold Italy's protectorate; then France would intervene in the resulting Italo-Yugoslav war in order to crush Fascist Italy before it rearmed, and before a resurgent Germany recalled French power to the Rhine.[53]

Grandi, worried sick, requested permission in December 1929 to make over Italy's image. Mussolini was presumably not entirely unaware of the panic among his subordinates, and had his own trepidations about the lira. He readily authorized Grandi to mouth pacifist platitudes as impudently as necessary. He himself would continue to speak as he chose, and the substance of Italian policy would change little. Mussolini ordered irredentist agitation for Dalmatia quieted, but continued clandestine support for Croat terrorism and resisted efforts by Grandi to negotiate détente with Yugoslavia.[54]

Then Mussolini, as pedagogue of the Revolution, made his inflammatory May 1930 speeches in Tuscany: "words are beautiful things, but rifles, machine guns, ships, aircraft, and cannon are still more beautiful." The pacifist façade Grandi was laboring to construct crumbled.[55] A further Mussolini speech in the month following Hitler's September 1930 election victory made explicit earlier hints that Fascism was indeed "for export." Grandi noted in his diary that he might as well close up shop at Palazzo Chigi. Who needed a foreign ministry, with ideology in command and Cavour relegated to the attic?[56] Mussolini might proclaim his realism – a claim some post-1945

53. Pride in policy since 1926: Grandi diary, 27 January, 6 February 1929; fear of French preventive war: 22 October, 1, 6, 28 November 1929 (talk with Gàzzera); errors of policy since 1926: 24, 25 December 1929; for the Albania-Yugoslavia-France worst-case scenario, see also Gàzzera notes, 6 November 1930.
54. Grandi diary, 2, 25 December 1929; minute of Mussolini-Grandi talk, 27 December 1929 (Grandi papers, roll 10); lira: Grandi diary, 20 October 1929.
55. OO 24:235; also 24:227–28, 243–44, 278–85; Grandi diary, 18, 20 May 1930; also Grandi in DBFP 2/1/210.
56. OO 24:283; Grandi diary, 28 October 1930.

Italian scholarship has imprudently echoed.[57] But the dictator, Grandi morosely recognized, was in truth a revolutionary fanatic who saw both international relations and domestic politics through the same ideological lenses. His master, as Grandi put it in 1933, "consider[ed] himself not only the chief of the Italian government but [also] the Pope of Fascism."[58]

Mussolini nevertheless eventually recognized that pseudo-pacifism only worked if he appeared to back it personally. Italy's increasingly difficult economic situation required that he so appear: the Great Depression hit hard in early 1930. Foreign credit tapered off after 1928; foreign trade declined by about a third between 1929 and 1934. The Depression ultimately imposed a degree of autarchy and state economic control that Mussolini could never have achieved on his own. But in the short term it also cut the funds available for rearmament and made investors nervous. The 1930 machine-gun speech panicked the middle classes into dumping government bonds; the regime spent 50 million lire on price support. The former Fascist Party boss of Milan gloomily reported that the masses were anything but "prepared in spirit" for war.[59] By autumn 1930 Mussolini had also apparently decided that Gàzzera's doomladen predictions of a two-front war arising from conflict in Albania were plausible. Finally, he faced renewed attack on the lira and the need to refund a major portion of the national debt in May 1931. The regime could scarcely avoid economic disaster if Italy's small investors withheld their savings.[60]

Mussolini therefore grudgingly took up pseudo-pacifism personally in a new year 1931 radio address in English, while Grandi carried the same line, with an anti-French twist, to the League of Nations. Throughout 1931 Mussolini generally gave Grandi his head, and even allowed him some control over the Italian press. With his master's

57. See Knox, "An Anti-Anti-Fascist' Orthodoxy?".
58. Grandi diary, summer–autumn 1930, but especially 24 August and 12 September 1930; for Mussolini's unrealism, see also 6 January 1931; quotation: Skirmunt (London) to Beck, 9 March 1933, in Jósef Lipski, *Diplomat in Berlin* (New York, 1968), p. 61.
59. For attempts by Mussolini and Gàzzera to increase the army budget despite conditions of extreme stringency, see especially Gàzzera notes, 7 August, 11 October, 27 December 1929; 30 May, 30 June, 2 July 1930; 29 January 1931; Gàzzera annual reports for 1929–1932; and Gàzzera correspondence on the issue, all in Gàzzera papers microfilm. For Mussolini and the Depression: Grandi diary, 1 January, 24, 31 May 1930; Florence speech reaction: Grandi diary, 26 May 1930; public opinion: Giampaoli, in De Felice, *Mussolini il fascista*, vol. 2, pp. 443–44.
60. Gàzzera notes, 11 October 1929, 6 November 1930, 27 December 1930, 5 May 1931 (Mussolini and the worst case), 29 January 1931 (pseudo-pacifism); Mussolini on the lira and the debt: Grandi diary, 16 December 1930, 21, 23, 28 March, 3 June 1931.

sometimes reluctant backing Grandi played off the unsophisticated Anglo-Saxons against the French, and convinced worthies such as Arthur Henderson and Henry L. Stimson of Mussolini's love of peace.

Grandi nevertheless remained uneasy. Mussolini never confided to him the general objectives of Italian policy.[61] The dictator was realist enough not to reveal his megalomania fully even to close subordinates. Left to his own devices, Grandi therefore apparently fell back on the advice of his staff, and perhaps on the perusal of back numbers of the Nationalist house organ *Politica*. The result was the now-famous *politica del peso determinante*, the "policy of the decisive weight." Italy's weakness, Grandi concluded by mid-1930, left no alternative but to avoid definite commitment while awaiting the inevitable Franco-German war hinted at in Mussolini's 1927 Ascension Day speech. Then the Italians could be "the arbiters of the war on the Rhine."[62]

The basis of Grandi's conception was an un-Fascist admiration for the Liberal tradition of Triple Alliance and intervention against Austria-Hungary, and a most un-Mussolinian reverence for Locarno, which Grandi considered the foundation of Italy's postwar great-power position.[63] Grandi's strategy was not incompatible, he thought, with tactical agreements with France or Germany and with a final option for either one. France was sometimes his chosen – but before mid-1931 apparently unattainable – partner. But up to that point Grandi generally preferred the thought of a German-Italian war against France after a ten-year détente that would allow the Fascist revolution, "an idea that has not yet found bayonets," to acquire some. Only the *German* alliance could bring Italy Corsica and Tunis.[64]

---

61. See Grandi's complaints, Grandi diary, especially 12 September, 28 October 1930, and final entry.
62. Compare Coppola, "La Francia e noi," "Equilibrio europeo," *Politica* 5:40–41, 42 (1923), pp. 50–51, 220, and "Ginevra e Locarno," *Politica* 18 (1925), p. 30, with Grandi, DDI 7/9/234.
63. From Locarno to the *peso determinante* theory: Grandi diary, 5, 6 February, 8 October 1929 (1914 example); 25, 26 August, 25 December 1930; 1 January, 5 March 1931; DDI 7/9/234, 7/10/272. Grandi found his master's contempt for Locarno incomprehensible: Grandi diary, 5 March, 2 April 1931.
64. For Grandi's hope for a future German alliance, see especially Grandi diary, 24 December 1929; 18, 25, 26 August 1930 (Corsica and Tunis); 28 March 1931; "bayonets": DDI 7/11/37, p. 68. The diary and its accompanying papers cast doubt on the authenticity of two purported Grand Council speech texts (2 October 1930, 5 March 1931) by Grandi on which De Felice and others have built their view of moderate Italian goals in Europe coupled with expansion in Africa (compare *Mussolini il duce*, vol. 1, pp. 370–74, 377–80, 382 note, and Dino Grandi, *La politica estera dell'Italia dal 1929 al 1932* (Rome, 1985), pp. 277–327, 340–64, with Knox, "I testi 'aggiustati' dei discorsi segreti di Grandi," *Passato e Presente* 13/1987, pp. 97–117, and 16/1988, pp. 190–92.

In the spring of 1931, however, Grandi belatedly began to recognize how dangerous to Italy his prospective ally might soon become. He began to urge on Mussolini "equilibrium" and "equidistance" for their own sake, rather than as a means to drive up the price the Germans would have to pay for Italy's support in war.[65] The massive vote for Hitler of September 1930 and the spring 1931 Austro-German customs union project also concentrated the minds of the French, who were now terrified enough to pay for Italian friendship. Pierre Laval, who lacked the inhibitions of his predecessors as French prime minister, suggested *"l'Etiopie par exemple"* when in July 1931 Grandi mentioned Italy's unappeased colonial appetites. Grandi and his advisers thereupon began pressing hard, with the help of General Emilio De Bono at the colonial ministry, for agreement with France in Europe, and for war in Africa.[66]

But unlike Grandi, Mussolini was not resigned to impotence in Europe. As late as January 1931 he was still telling Gàzzera that "we will have to see if at a certain point it would not be useful to attack ourselves."[67] Mussolini discouraged Laval's summer–autumn 1931 advances, and when Grandi urged him in February–March 1932 to seek agreement with France, he flatly refused. To Grandi he insisted that French offers of Ethiopia were a trap designed to immobilize Italy in Europe just as German revival opened new prospects.[68] In mid-March 1932, to Grandi's chagrin, Mussolini torpedoed any hope of negotiations with Paris through his noisy press support for Hitler against Hindenburg in the first round of the German presidential election. In early April, Mussolini informed the Grand Council of Fascism of the French "serenades," but made clear his lack of enthusiasm: "When the right time comes we shall have to stop and think about them." He suggested that the outcome of the second round of the German election might give Italy its cue. His own choice was obvious; to the Grand Council he disparaged "Fascists who do not approve of Hitler" and listed the Führer's accomplishments at length. Then the Duce unceremoniously dismissed Grandi in late July 1932. Grandi had no doubt, as he departed for gilded exile as ambassador in London, that Hitler's advent was the reason for his going.[69]

---

65.   Grandi diary, 25 March, 26 April 1931; 22 February 1932; DDI 7/10/397.
66.   DDI 7/10/413; also 385, 423, and, in general, Giovanni Buccianti, *Verso gli accordi Mussolini-Laval* (Milan, 1984).
67.   Gàzzera notes, 29 January 1931.
68.   Grandi diary, 20 February, 4 March 1932.
69.   Grandi diary, 13, 20 March 1932, and final entry; DDI 7/11/315; "Address by Mussolini to the Fascist Grand Council, 7/8 April 1932," Allied Forces Headquarters,

Mussolini felt briefly free to be himself. The Depression made a degree of autarchy both necessary and politically possible; trade and finance would no longer tie his hands. The Japanese, to his delight, had run amok in Manchuria. Two days after firing Grandi, Mussolini ordered Gàzzera to "study" the conquest of Corsica. When informed that the army had reached its target figure of forty mobilizable divisions, he complained that "when we had nothing we did Fiume and Corfù; now that we are stronger we are more prudent." "Better that way," Gàzzera claimed to have replied.[70]

Prudence still demanded a respectable front. To replace Grandi Mussolini brought in as undersecretary Fulvio Suvich, who unlike most Nationalists was more bureaucrat than ideologue. While dismissing five ambassadors, he grudgingly consented to give the career diplomats one last chance.[71] And he retained a pseudo-pacifist fallback position: the project for a consultative pact of the four European great powers to oversee both peace and treaty revision. Mussolini and the Germans had first toyed with the notion in 1931 as a tactical counter to the hated *Paneuropa* of Briand, and Mussolini relaunched it as a trial balloon in an October 1932 speech. One purpose of the pact was to authorize a German rearmament that would "keep France respectful," while slowing that rearmament to a pace that Italy could match.[72] Mussolini now judged that the years lost during the Depression would delay the inevitable German war of revenge until 1938, when he hoped to be ready.[73] In the intervening period, the pact would above all provide insurance against the French preventive war that German rearmament and the coming Italo-German ideological alliance might otherwise summon up. "Reciprocal consultation

G-2, 16–18 July 1945 (NARA, Record Group 331, reel 476A) (thirty pages of translated excerpts from Italian minutes of the 7 and 8 April 1932 meetings [see also OO 25:92–94 and NARA T-586/1122/074698–702]. The Italian originals, which were evidently among Mussolini's papers on capture, have not surfaced.) The dictator's anti-Yugoslav and anti-French bellicosity, his ideological predilection for Hitler (documented exhaustively in Grandi's diary), his rejection of France's initial advances over Ethiopia, and his apparent willingness to concede Austria to Hitler in 1933 contradict the suggestion of Burgwyn ("Grandi e il mondo teutonico: 1929–1932," *Storia Contemporanea* 19:2 [1988], pp. 220–22) that Mussolini sought to use Hitler only to blackmail France into agreement.

70. Gàzzera notes, 22 July 1932; Mussolini on the Japanese: Aloisi, 13 September 1932.
71. Last chance: Aloisi, 26 July 1932.
72. Mussolini, in Gàzzera notes, 3 September 1932, 4 January 1933, and Aloisi, 4 October 1932.
73. Inevitable war in 1938: Mussolini talk with Gömbös, 10 November 1932, in Lajos Kerekes, *Abendämmerung einer Demokratie* (Vienna, 1966), p. 119; Mussolini held to the date: see Ludwig Jedlicka, "Mussolini und Österreich 1936," *Österreich in Geschichte und Literatur* 6 (1962), p. 416.

. . . between great powers," Mussolini remarked to his diplomats, was a "formula" to put the democracies to sleep.[74]

Pseudo-pacifism did not extend to Yugoslavia. King Alexander, who had vainly sought détente with Italy since 1930 through a variety of channels, had in February 1932 offered Mussolini the only terms the Duce was willing to accept: an alliance with Italy and an end to Yugoslavia's French ties. Negotiations behind Grandi's back in the spring of 1932 led to an incognito visit to Italy by Alexander, apparently in late July or early August. No alliance resulted. Instead, Mussolini concluded that Yugoslavia was "on the eve of disintegration" and that the French commitment was weakening.[75] In September, the terrorists of Pavelic and Kosutic raided Yugoslavia from the Italian Dalmatian enclave of Zara, hoping to set off a Croat revolt. The raid failed dismally, but Mussolini continued to expect "revolution in Croatia."[76] He also responded at last, personally, to French offers to Grandi. In November 1932 he told an emissary from Paris that he would abandon to France the Italian settlers in Tunisia if France "would leave Italy free in southeastern Europe."[77] That was Mussolini's personal prototype for the Franco-Italian bargain of January 1935 that sealed the fate of Ethiopia. He initially sought a free hand for war in Europe, not Africa, and understandably gave no assurances that Italy would back France against Germany.

French willingness to listen to such demands, and a Hungarian report that the French had told the Little Entente "that in case of war between Italy and Yugoslavia, France would not be able to aid Yugo[slavia]," apparently convinced Mussolini at the beginning of 1933 that the hour of Croatia had come. "If there is war between us and Yugoslavia, France *will not move*," he triumphantly informed Gàz-

---

74. Mussolini, in Aloisi, 3 January 1933.
75. Mussolini, in Gàzzera notes, 11 August 1932: "Re Aless[andro] è incerto. E' venuto in questi giorni in Italia col nome di Conte Availa – S.E. [Mussolini] è convinto che si è alla vigilia dello sgretolamento." For the Italo-Yugoslav negotiations, see especially Gàzzera notes, 23 September 1930, 8 August 1931, 30 January 1932; Grandi diary, 21 March, 12 July 1931; 4, 20 March 1932; DDI 7/8/302, 370, 7/9/148, 234, 7/10, p. 46 note 1; 7/10/30, 52, 276, 309, 386, 416, 420, 446, 7/11/66, 105, 122, 213 (alliance offer), 234, 256, 281, 7/12/15, 34, 189, 357; for the Yugoslav side, Jacob Hoptner, *Yugoslavia in Crisis* (New York, 1962), pp. 19–20.
76. Mussolini, in Aloisi, 28 November 1932; see also DDI 7/12/414. For the *Ustascha* and their place in Mussolini's policy, see Teodoro Sala, "Le basi italiane del separatismo croato (1929–1941)," in *L'imperialismo italiano e la Jugoslavia* (Urbino, 1981).
77. Mussolini, in Gàzzera notes, 4 January 1933; also Aloisi, 12 November 1932, and DDF 1/2/182, p. 390; Mussolini later gave Aloisi (14 January 1933) a misleadingly bland version of the conversation; see also DDI 7/12/343, 374, 400, 432, 453.

zera.[78] Mussolini ordered the foreign ministry to prepare to implement the "Croat plan" for an uprising followed by Italian intervention
as – in Mussolini's phase – the "paladins of law, of the oppressed."[79]
Then, on 8 January 1933, the Duce announced to Gàzzera that
Yugoslavia was preparing to attack Italy. Gàzzera dismissed that absurd
claim out of hand; Mussolini replied "What then are we waiting for?"
Gàzzera was firm. French intervention was likely, and would "give us
a lesson that would last us for a century." But Gàzzera evidently did
not think that he had carried his point, for the next day he called upon
the king, whom he predictably found "opposed to a war by us against
Yugo[slavia]: France awaits just such an opportunity to jump on us."[80]

Royal authority, the recalcitrance of Gàzzera, and perhaps also tim-
orous disapproval from his immediate foreign ministry subordinates,
Suvich and Baron Pompeo Aloisi, apparently induced Mussolini to
shelve the Croat adventure.[81] He nevertheless told Gàzzera that
Pavelic's men were the only ones in his stable of terrorist groups "that
had up to now produced anything"; he was raising their monthly
stipend.[82] Yet barring a genuine internal collapse in Yugoslavia – for
which Mussolini continued to hope until the murder of King Alexander in October 1934 failed to produce one – Mussolini after January
1933 could only fight in Africa.[83]

Reinforcing Gàzzera's warnings and the king's apparent veto came
an increasing measure of apparent external threat. Croat agitation, the
coincidental discovery of clandestine Italian arms shipments to Hungary, and Hitler's accession to power on 30 January 1933 amid unre-
strained jubilation in the Italian press triggered a "violent Italophobe
campaign" in Paris and a troop call-up in Yugoslavia. By early March
Rome seethed with rumors that General Maxime Weygand, whom
Grandi had once described as the Conrad von Hötzendorff of the

---

78. Mussolini, in Gàzzera notes, 4 January 1933.
79. Aloisi, 30 December 1932; see also 29 December; "paladins": Gàzzera notes, 13
    January 1933.
80. Gàzzera notes, 8 January 1933 (Mussolini-Gàzzera); 9 January 1933 (Gàzzera–Victor
    Emmanuel III).
81. Gàzzera notes, 13 January 1933: "Piano croato – lo trovo sacrosantamente vivo –
    [Mussolini] [l]o illustra confermandolo. Mi dice di darlo agli Esteri ché lo diano ai
    croati – Dico che non conviene e *che ormai la decisione è in quel senso.* [Mussolini]
    [a]pprova le mie proposte circa l'utilizzazione dei croati." (my emphasis; the "decision"
    was presumably the king's).
82. Mussolini, in Gàzzera notes, 14 February 1933.
83. Repeated Yugoslav bids for a rapprochement in 1933–34 led only to a crude Mussolini
    demand for Yugoslav territory, as part of a treaty that would have reduced Yugoslavia
    to a vassal state (DDI 7/14/217, 218, 224, 228, 236, 452, 465).

French army, was urging preventive war against Italy or Germany or both. The French, Mussolini conceded, were "nervous, hysterical."[84]

To soothe them, he retreated to his Berchtesgaden in the hills above Forlì, hastily drafted his Four Power Pact, and released it to a grateful world on 8 March. As ostensible proof of Mussolini's pacifism it was an immediate success. Niggling over its details occupied all four great powers throughout spring and summer 1933, and saved Mussolini both from his Yugoslav policy and from his deliberate identification with Hitler.

Mussolini's relationship with Berlin, in the event, proved a bitter disappointment. In the autumn of 1932 he had sought to beguile his new subordinates at Palazzo Chigi with protestations of "equidistance": "On the Rhine we are against France, on the Danube with France."[85] But privately he had looked forward to the end of Weimar as a step toward Italy's freedom. He had encouraged Hitler's rise by propaganda support and political advice. He had publicly prophesied in late October 1932 that "in a decade, Europe will be Fascist or *fascistizzata!*" He had allowed Balbo to visit Berlin in December 1932 and to meet semipublicly with Hermann Göring, soon to be Balbo's German counterpart as air force chief. He had ordered his press to celebrate Hitler's coming as Fascist Italy's own triumph.[86] He had prepared an agenda for face-to-face talks with Hitler in which revision of Germany's eastern borders and Anschluss figured prominently. And on 3 March 1933 he reportedly told Grandi that he was "prepared not only to agree to Anschluss but to place this problem before the international forum on Italy's initiative"; his aim was "the closest contact between the Fascist and Nazi regimes." Grandi claimed to friends to have dissuaded Mussolini from such a drastic step, but expressed deep foreboding about the future to the British foreign secretary.[87] Once Hitler was in power Mussolini took up clandestine air cooperation with Germany with renewed alacrity. On 11 April 1933 Hermann Göring and his principal air subordinate, Erhard Milch, met in Rome with their Italian counterparts. On Mussolini's behalf Balbo agreed to

---

84. Grandi diary, 9 December 1930; Aloisi, 13, 16, 17 February, 5 March 1933; Gàzzera notes, 17–18 February, 4, 14 March 1933; on the Weygand rumors and Yugoslav military preparations, see also Aloisi, 25 December 1932; OO 25:197–98; DDI 7/13/28, 95, 114, 148; De Bono diary, 31 March 1933, ACS.

85. Aloisi, 4 October 1932; also 14 January 1933.

86. DDI 7/11/79, 99, 7/12/532; De Felice, ed., *Mussolini e Hitler*, pp. 241, 248–50; OO 25:148, 199–200, 37:364; Petersen, *Hitler-Mussolini*, pp. 114–16.

87. DDI 7/13/153 for Mussolini's agenda; Skirmunt to Beck, 9 March 1936, in Lipski, *Diplomat in Berlin*, pp. 60–61, and DBFP 2/5/38 for Grandi's alarm; also DDF 1/2/421, and, for the date, DDI 7/13/205.

a German proposal for a new and massive covert program of pilot training in Italy. He also stressed Italy's "identity of views" with Göring over the need, imposed by demography, for eastward expansion by Germany and colonial expansion by Italy.[88]

Fascist Italy's pursuit of the German alliance broke down through no fault of Mussolini's. Hitler signally failed to take the Duce's pressing advice to soft-peddle the "Jewish question."[89] Far worse, Göring disclosed abruptly during his April visit that the new Germany had no intention of postponing the Anschluss for a decorous interval. Under the scrutiny of Suvich, who was as fiercely anti-German as any former subject of Austria-Hungary, Mussolini reacted to this frontal challenge. The Duce's hold on his subordinates and ultimately on establishment opinion was at stake. He provisionally concluded that Italy would have to resist, and that he might even have to woo the despised Yugoslavs for a Rome-Belgrade-Budapest combination to bar Germany's way on the Danube. But Mussolini's conversion was half-hearted; to Gàzzera he confided on 1 May that "We have these cards in hand: Italy-Austria-Hungary-Germany; or if not, to restrain Germany, Italy-Yugoslavia-Hungary, Italy-Greece-Bulgaria-Turkey."[90]

Despite repeated pleas and warnings from Rome, Hitler failed to hold back the Austrian National Socialists and their friends in the Reich, even while expressing awe of Mussolini's historic stature and protesting a newfound willingness to delay Anschluss for ten to thirty years.[91] In October 1933, without consultation with Mussolini, Hitler left both Disarmament Conference and League, destroying the last shreds of the Four Power Pact. Mussolini, for his part, moved in the course of summer 1933 to take charge of Austria; the price he exacted for his protection of the regime of Chancellor Engelbert Dollfuss was the destruction of the Vienna Social Democrats in February 1934 and the erection of pseudo-Fascist institutions.[92]

Conflict with Hitler did not inhibit Mussolini's search for a war of conquest, although after the experience of January–March 1933 he was careful to fall back on a target that flankers and monarchy would

88. DDI 7/13/406; see also 195.
89. See especially DDI 7/13/327, 339, 343, 427.
90. Aloisi, 12, 13, 17 April 1933; Rudolf Nadolny, *Mein Beitrag* (Wiesbaden, 1955), pp. 134–35 (source: Soragna); DDI 7/13/327, 339, 343, 442, 479; Mussolini, in Gàzzera notes, 21 April 1933, 1 May 1933; Suvich and Göring: DDI 7/13/515; also DBFP 2/5/144.
91. DDI 7/13/605, 921, 942.
92. See Petersen, *Hitler-Mussolini*, Chapters 5, 8; Kerekes, *Abendämmerung*; DDI 7/13/923, 7/14/21, 111, 585, 589, 683.

let him attack. That could only be Ethiopia, which some of his subordinates were all too willing to press upon him as a sort of prize for good behavior in Europe. Grandi, in the months before his sudden departure from the foreign ministry in July 1932, unofficially urged Gàzzera to look into the requirements for the war of aggression in East Africa that a French alliance would make possible. Gàzzera found Mussolini's movement toward Germany as alarming as did Grandi, and complied.[93] De Bono and his subordinates at the colonial ministry had been actively exploring the lineaments of an East African war since early 1932, while colonial enthusiasts in the foreign ministry such as Aloisi and Raffaele Guariglia likewise pressed for action. After initiating army and air force staffs in November, De Bono presented Mussolini with a joint-service plan in mid-December 1932. Mussolini approved it, and set a tentative date of 1935, but on the precondition – highly doubtful at that point in view of the Croat plan – that Italy be "completely free in Europe."[94]

The Ethiopian project apparently remained in that limbo through most of 1933. Only Mussolini's dismissal of all three service ministers and his assumption of their posts himself in summer and autumn presaged some sort of action; Gàzzera would not thwart him again. In January–February 1934, as his Austrian client Dollfuss moved to crush the Social Democrats in Vienna, Mussolini ordered the beginning of concrete preparations to smash Ethiopia in 1935; a December 1933 Croat assassination plot launched from Italy against King Alexander had failed.[95] In Africa, Mussolini could overcome the military and monarchical caution that had checked him in Europe. He had the backing of the colonial ministry and of influential foreign ministry figures from the start, and acquired that of navy, air force, a reluctant army staff, Badoglio, and the Nationalists. The dying Nationalist architect of the Fascist police state, Alfredo Rocco, touchingly thanked Mussolini for letting him see Adua avenged.[96] By July–August 1934 the French appeared ready for a summit at Rome in the autumn, thus

93. Grandi diary, 22 February 1932; this is perhaps the origin of the mysterious army staff "Progetto O.M.E." of 1932; see also Gàzzera notes, 11 June 1932.
94. Rochat, *Militari e politici*, pp. 26–31 and 276–93; DDI 7/12/38, 138, 222, 223, 248, 393, 449; De Bono diary, 15 December 1932, ACS; Aloisi, 3 January 1933.
95. De Bono diary, 8 February 1935, ACS, and Rochat, *Militari e politici*, pp. 39–40 and Chapter 2; DDF 1/5/161 and Vladeta Milicevic, *Der Königsmord von Marseille* (Bad Godesberg, 1959), pp. 47–51; DDI 7/14/514, 518, 536, 551, 602, 608, 696, 739.
96. De Felice, *Mussolini il duce*, vol. 1, pp. 632–41; Rochat, *Militari e politici*, Chapters 2–4; Bottai, 5 December 1935.

encouraging establishment hopes that Mussolini's war might take place with international approval.

The only apparent obstacle to action, paradoxically, was Germany, whose rise was the fundamental precondition for an Italian war. Hitler's Austrian subordinates murdered Dollfuss on 25 July 1934, little more than a month after Duce and Führer had met for the first time at Venice. The ensuing Italo-German crisis emboldened Badoglio to tell a service chiefs' meeting that "the game [was] not worth the candle" in Africa.[97] The shadow of the reluctant monarch behind him was perceptible.

Yet the Austrian confrontation also hastened Italy's war in Africa: it helped convince Paris that Italy was so committed against Germany that Franco-Italian agreement was possible. Then, on 9 October, the Croats at last succeeded in assassinating King Alexander of Yugoslavia – and France's foreign minister, Barthou – immediately before the latter's planned visit to Rome. Mussolini confided to the Hungarians his hope that Yugoslavia would collapse, or otherwise provoke Italian intervention. War in Europe would put off readiness for Ethiopia by a year.[98] No war came. But as Mussolini had also anticipated, Barthou's replacement, Laval, was the very man to step nimbly across the corpse of his predecessor. The January 1935 Rome agreements with France

97. Minutes of 27 July 1934, in Biagini and Gionfrida, eds., *Verbali delle riunioni presiedute da Badoglio*, p. 301 (see also DDI 7/15, pp. 733–34 note); similar, more tentative Badoglio remarks to Mussolini (12 May 1934) in Rochat, *Militari e politici*, p. 325.

98. The published version of Aloisi's diary (27 April; 1, 29 August; 1 September; 1 October [postponement of Ethiopia]; 3, 6, 9, 10 October 1934) gives the impression that Mussolini fobbed off Palazzo Chigi with claims that he planned to drop the Croats, and covered himself publicly with a conciliatory remark about Yugoslavia in a speech three days before the murders. For his regret that war did not come, see Ormos, "Sur les causes de l'échec du pacte danubien," *Acta Historica* 14:1–2 (1968), pp. 31–32 and note 12; see also Mussolini's remarks to Gömbös in DDI 7/16/112. In 1944 Aloisi testified – before partially retracting, perhaps under pressure from military intelligence – that "[w]hile undersecretary Suvich attempted a rapprochement with Yugoslavia . . . Mussolini in secret ordered the assassination of King Alexander." (Clara Conti, *Servizio segreto* [Rome, 1946], pp. 20–21, 165; *Il processo Roatta* [Rome, 1946], pp. 41–42, 45–46, 55; also Sullivan, "A Thirst for Glory," Appendix 2). Italian support of Pavelic and plans to attack Yugoslavia, now as a response to any tightening of economic sanctions, continued throughout 1936: Aloisi, 7 January 1936; Pirelli, *Taccuini*, p. 190; minute of talk with Mussolini, 6 December 1936, and Szabó notes ("Summary of Events") on repeated meetings with Mussolini and Pariani about a possible attack on Yugoslavia, May 1936–January 1937, both in papers of László Szabó, 1936, K100, Foreign Ministry Archive, Hungarian National Archives, Budapest (my warmest thanks to Brian R. Sullivan for copies and translations). For a different – but unsupported – view of Mussolini's intentions toward Yugoslavia in this period, see De Felice, *Mussolini il duce*, vol. 1, pp. 514–16.

gave Mussolini the famous free hand in Ethiopia, while pledging him to cooperate with France in defending Austria.[99] He did not consider himself bound forever. Before signing with Laval he had apparently confided to the Hungarian prime minister an interest in reestablishing the "old relationship" with Berlin, and had reportedly insisted that "the Italo-French conflict could never be entirely patched over; he would exploit the French, if they offered him anything, without becoming dependent upon them."[100]

Apparently certain of closing the deal even before Laval's arrival for the final talks, Mussolini had drafted for his subordinates a directive dated 30 December 1934 that established Fascist Italy's immediate objective: *"the destruction of the Ethiopian armed forces and the total conquest of Ethiopia."*[101] Within weeks of the French agreements, Mussolini sent De Bono to East Africa, and followed him with an ever-increasing stream of Italian units and materiel. Ethiopia was simply the first step, he confided in March 1935 to one of his diplomats and to the industrial magnate Alberto Pirelli: "And afterwards we shall conquer Egypt and the Sudan!" Italy, he insisted, sought "an empire that stretched from the Mediterranean to the Indian Ocean."[102]

Yet the British, whom Grandi had suggested were decadent, proved unexpectedly stubborn. London's opposition was confused and strangely diffident at first, apparently in order not to startle Mussolini out of the transitory anti-German front of the Western powers that had convened at Stresa in April. But London became more decisive as spring 1935 drew on into summer. The king, Badoglio, and the chiefs of staff also raised their voices in August–September; the seemingly inevitable clash with Britain, Badoglio warned, would "reduce us to a Balkan level."[103] Mussolini held to his course. His answer, to the British and presumably to the crown as well, was an ostentatious fatalism. The massive buildup in Eritrea and Somalia had committed Italy and the regime. Those who opposed him should choose: either sub-

---

99. For Mussolini's expectation that Laval would give him a better deal than Barthou: De Bono diary, 13 October 1934, ACS; for negotiations and agreement: Buccianti, *Verso gli accordi Mussolini-Laval*; Enrico Serra, "Dalle trattative sul confine meridionale della Libia al baratto sull'Etiopia," *Nuova Antologia*, July–September 1980; De Felice, *Mussolini il duce*, vol. 1, pp. 506–33; DDI 7/16.
100. ADAP C/3/310, C/4/311 (Gömbös retrospective remarks); also Ormos, "Pacte danubien," pp. 37, 44–45.
101. Printed in Rochat, *Militari e politici*, pp. 376–79 (emphasis in original).
102. Mussolini, in Cora, "Un diplomatico," p. 94, and Pirelli, *Taccuini*, pp. 123–24; likewise Ugo Ojetti, *I taccuini* (Florence, 1954), p. 484.
103. Badoglio to Mussolini, September 1935, in Rochat, *Militari e politici*, p. 229.

mission to his will, or the collapse of the regime and chaos both at home and abroad.[104]

The king apparently yielded grudgingly at the last moment, perhaps comforted by London's perverse assurances to Mussolini that it would not use force to stop him in Africa. Britain failed either to dissuade Mussolini through its display of naval might, or to propitiate him with a pseudo-compromise that delivered Ethiopia by slices. To ward off oil sanctions and to hold wavering subordinates and flankers in line, Mussolini kept open the possibility of negotiation throughout autumn–winter 1935–36.[105] But his first aim was the long-foreseen *"soluzione integrale violenta."* Despite slow military progress in the first months and gradually tightening League sanctions, his hostility to the Hoare-Laval compromise plan and his relief at its shipwreck were obvious.[106] Expansion overseas, revolution at home, and the war of national effort that he had consequently imposed on his armed forces demanded nothing less than total victory.

Nor did the consequences of that victory for Italy's relations with France and Britain cause him anguish. He continued long into 1936 to dupe the French with protestations of yearning for a return to Stresa, but actions spoke louder than words.[107] By autumn–winter 1935, Mussolini was weary of his links to the status quo powers, to those "age-weakened" forces that sought to drag down the young upward-striving nations.[108] Sanctions actually helped him; they justified severing many of Italy's remaining ties to the world market and embittered even non-Fascists against the West. Germany now became, and remained until the end, chief supplier of the all-important coal that powered Italian industry.[109] Highly secret contacts with Hitler through an

104. See especially Rochat, *Militari e politici*, pp. 225–29; DBFP 2/14/284, 297, 320, 463; Aloisi, 28 May, 5 August 1935.
105. See DDI 8/1/289 for Mussolini's minimum terms, enunciated in May 1935 (direct rule of the Ethiopian periphery, protectorate over the Amhara core); thereafter 431 (war will mean "wiping Ethiopia from the map"), 433, 8/2/124, 331, 357, 366, 770, 788, 795.
106. Renato Mori, *Mussolini e la conquista dell'Etiopia* (Florence, 1978), politely demolishes the central claim of De Felice (*Mussolini il duce*, vol. 1, Chapter 6, especially pp. 609–10, 635, 642, 686–92, 706–10, 719, 738, 743) that Mussolini sought above all a diplomatic compromise; see also DDI 8/2/842, 854–56, 863.
107. DDF 2/1/239, 518; 2/2/17, pp. 33–34, 2/2/90, 173, 234, 275 (which slyly compares Mussolini's language to Hitler's peace speeches).
108. Mussolini, in ADAP C/4/322; for the role of demography in Mussolini's calculations in 1935 and after, Bottai, 1 September 1936; Ciano, 3 September 1937, 29–30 September 1938; ADAP D/1/2.
109. German coal as a percentage of Italian coal imports: 1933, 23.0; 1935, 51.8; 1936, 63.9;

Italian acquaintance of Hans Frank in summer and autumn 1935 paved the way for the decisive step toward an Italo-German alliance that Mussolini took on 6 January 1936. In conversation with the German minister in Rome, he invited Hitler to make Austria "in practical terms a satellite of Germany" while saving face for Italy by conceding sham independence. That policy led to Austria's alignment by treaty with Germany in July 1936, and ultimately to Anschluss in 1938.[110]

Mussolini held to his January 1936 suggestion to the Germans despite increasingly desperate pleas from Suvich, who clearly did not share French delusions that Mussolini sought a return to Stresa.[111] At the end of January, behind the back of Palazzo Chigi, Mussolini told a Hitler emissary that

> Italy cannot at this point lay its cards on the table. We cannot openly show France and England our attitude toward Germany. Not yet! It must happen slowly and cautiously. Nevertheless between Germany and Italy there exists a community of destiny. It will become ever stronger. It cannot be denied. They are congruent cases. One day we shall meet, whether we want to or not! But we want it! Because we must! (Mussolini strikes the table with his fist).[112]

And when Hitler approached him in late February 1936 with the news that Berlin contemplated tearing up Locarno and destroying the European strategic balance by remilitarizing the Rhineland, the Duce encouraged the Germans to move.[113]

The Rome-Berlin Axis that took shape between spring and autumn 1936 was thus a goal for which Mussolini actively strove, rather than the consequence of some arcane and impersonal "force of circumstances" after the 7 March Rhineland coup, as Mario Toscano and others have argued.[114] Mussolini deliberately encouraged Hitler to replace him as Austria's protector and to smash the European balance,

---

1937, 59.0; 1938, 58.2 (Elizabeth Wiskemann, *The Rome-Berlin Axis* [London, 1966], p. 76).

110. DDI 8/1/505, 720, 854, 8/2/48, 204, 232, 608, 656, 718; ADAP C/4/485; see also 486; on Mussolini's subsequent attitude toward the Austro-German agreement of July 1936, DDI 8/4/208, 503, 514.

111. ADAP C/5/90; Suvich in DDI 8/3/131, 194; Petersen, *Hitler-Mussolini*, pp. 470–71, 482–83.

112. Robert H. Whealey, "Mussolini's Ideological Diplomacy," *Journal of Modern History* 39 (1967), p. 435 (document: Strunk minute, 5 February 1936, NARA T-454/56/000225–33; my translation).

113. Mussolini, in ADAP C/4/579 (see also pp. 1146–47 note), and DDI 8/3/275.

114. Toscano, *The Origins of the Pact of Steel* (Baltimore, 1967), pp. 188–89; see also the apparent insistence of De Felice (*Mussolini il duce*, vol. 2, p. 338) that Mussolini dur-

as steps toward an Italo-German revolutionary alliance against the West.

He had long looked forward to that alliance. But it was only the April–May 1936 victory in Ethiopia, along with establishment rancor over sanctions and fear of British revenge, that gave him the authority to push it through. Suvich found himself isolated, humiliated, and bypassed. The first of the many contretemps that punctuated Mussolini's movement toward Hitler and world war – Berlin's purely tactical post-Rhineland offer to reenter the League just as Mussolini was threatening to leave it – did not deter the Duce for long. Rome disavowed Grandi for too-close cooperation with the Locarno powers in London, and on 1 April signed a secret pact with Heinrich Himmler covering police cooperation against "Bolshevism." Three days later Mussolini greeted Hans Frank, in Rome as Hitler's personal envoy, with outspoken contempt for French decadence and the now-habitual geopolitical grievance against Britain: "England is our jailer: it wants to hold us shackled in the Mediterranean."[115]

The new crown prince of the regime, Galeazzo Ciano, returned from bombing Ethiopian villages to claim the foreign ministry in June 1936 and officially inaugurate the policy of close alignment with Germany that he, his deputy Dino Alfieri, and the Italian ambassador in Berlin, Bernardo Attolico, had upheld in the Duce's service through the winter.[116] Ciano was destined to pass through the same cycle as his predecessor and rival Grandi: from euphoria at the drive toward empire, through doubts over Mussolini's contempt for diplomatic finesse, to impotent dismay at the consequences of his master's dogmatic radicalism.

As he moved toward Berlin, Mussolini reiterated to Aloisi his long-held aim of linking Libya to East Africa and freeing Italy from "the slavery of the Suez canal."[117] His "totalitarian solution" in Ethiopia and the coming march to the ocean demanded German backing; had

ing this period shared the "clearly hostile" attitude of Suvich toward rapprochement with Germany.

115. Mussolini's fury at Hitler: ADAP C/5/18, 41, 45, 75, 161; DDI 8/3/421, 440; and Renato Mori, "Verso il riavvicinamento fra Hitler e Mussolini," *Storia e Politica* 15:1 (1976), pp. 109–11. Grandi: Aloisi 20, 21 March 1936, ADAP C/5/185, DDI 8/3/500, 509, 514. Himmler-Bocchini pact, Frank: Petersen, *Hitler-Mussolini*, pp. 438–42, 479–80; Hans Frank, *Im Angesicht des Galgens* (Munich, 1953), pp. 228–29; DDI 8/3/589.

116. See Mori, "Verso il riavvicinamento"; Petersen, *Hitler-Mussolini*, pp. 461–66; ADAP C/4/486; for Attolico's advocacy, see DDI 8/2/187, 620, 8/3/202, 253, 407.

117. Mussolini, in Aloisi, 8 May 1936.

Mussolini sought mere security, London and Paris would even at this late date have been delighted to receive him.[118] But the "pendulum" of Italian policy – to use a Grandi and De Felice metaphor – failed to swing westward.

Within three months of the annexation of Ethiopia, Italy was again at war in Spain, in secret and ultimately unfruitful pursuit of the keys to the western Mediterranean, the Baleares and Ceuta.[119] Bleating with the sheep was now too implausible to ward off Western counter-action. Mussolini, Ciano, and Hitler therefore raised instead the banner of anti-Bolshevism as a tactical cloak for Axis expansion.[120] To reinsure against a possible Anglo-German deal and to cover war in Spain, Mussolini also revived the nostrum with which he had attempted to blunt British disapproval in the autumn of 1935: protestations of desire for a Mediterranean settlement with London.

That diversionary tactic served briefly in 1937–38, with help from an increasingly terrified Grandi. It led first to the ironically misnamed "Gentlemen's Agreement" of January 1937, then to the abortive April 1938 treaty by which London recognized Italy's conquest of Ethiopia, and finally to a minor historical industry built around the assertion that Mussolini continued to seek balance between Berlin and London.[121] That claim ignores Mussolini's insistence from 1937 on that an Italian war of aggression against Britain was "inevitable," his predictions to the Hungarians that his September 1937 visit to Germany would "lead to the full realization of the Rome-Berlin axis" as a "*blocco formidabile*," his subsequent revelling in the Rome-Berlin-Tokyo alignment that allegedly placed Italy "at the center of the most formidable military-political combine that has ever existed," and his

---

118. See, among much other evidence, DDI/8/2/738, 8/3/32, 115 (Eden); 8/3/91, 94 (Vansittart); 8/3/318, 326 (Blum).
119. Baleares and Ceuta: Ciano, in ADAP C/6/600; also Ciano, 9 November 1937 (Spain, "prolongation of the Axis into the Atlantic").
120. Hitler, in Ciano, *L'Europa verso la catastrofe* (Milan, 1948), p. 94; Ciano, in ADAP C/6/14, and Ciano, 2 November 1937 (the anti-British purpose of the Anti-Comintern Pact); for Mussolini's longstanding view of Soviet Russia as "a kind of Slavic Fascism," see Ciano, 16 October 1939.
121. For the most extreme version, see Rosaria Quartararo, *Roma tra Londra e Berlino* (Rome, 1980). In method and conclusions Quartararo rivals the notorious David L. Hoggan, whose *Der erzwungene Krieg* (Tübingen, 1961, 1964) Quartararo considers "perhaps still today . . . the best general account from the German side" of the Munich period (Quartararo, "Inghilterra e Italia. Dal Patto di Pasqua a Monaco," *Storia Contemporanea* 7:4 [1976], pp. 641–42 note). Her book claims that "if there nevertheless was an Ethiopian campaign, it was a consequence not of the will of Mussolini but of that of the English" (p. 93), that the war of 1939 was a British "preventive war" against Germany (pp. 490, 506, 516), and that British intransigence pushed into war in 1940 a Mussolini who sought compromise (pp. 610, 616–19).

inexorable movement toward economic and military alliance with Germany.[122]

Domestically, Mussolini intended that war without end should remold "the character of the Italians" through combat, while further sapping the resistance of the "useless superstructure" of monarchy and military to his "permanent revolution." He drove a reluctant public toward acceptance of the Axis, pledged loyalty to Berlin by imitating the Nuremberg Laws, and risked in the 1938 Czech crisis a war that he claimed to believe would have "liquidate[d] forever France and Great Britain."[123] Establishment pressure, along with Italian military weakness and strategically misguided help from London, nevertheless held him back in 1939. But in 1940, as Mussolini had always hoped, the Germans turned western Europe upside down, and freed him to drive generals and king into war by telling them they need not fight. He himself sought by force of arms to make Italy a world power with an empire from Gibraltar to the Persian Gulf. Only war, he told Italy and the world on 10 June 1940, would "resolve . . . the problem of our maritime frontiers" and "break the military and territorial chains that suffocate us in our sea, for a people of forty-five million souls is not truly free unless it has free access to the ocean."[124]

From the vantage point of 1940, it is worth looking back at the questions with which this essay began: the nature and distinctiveness of Fascist foreign policy, the constraints on its implementation, and the causes of the radicalization that led to war at Hitler's side. Broad elements of continuity inevitably linked Mussolini's foreign policy – as they did Hitler's – with what had come before. Mussolini shared with predecessors and flankers the Adriatic, Mediterranean, and African

---

122. Quotations: Mussolini in Ciano, 12 December, 6 November 1937, and Szabó to Honvéd chief of staff, 7 September 1937, papers of László Szabó, 1937, K100, Foreign Ministry Archive, Hungarian National Archives, Budapest. War with Britain: Ciano, 21 December 1937, 2 January 1938, 3 February 1938; Bottai, 31 October 1937; German alliance: Bottai, 4 September, 31 October 1937; Ciano, 29 September 1937, 5, 20 May, 27 June 1938, 1 January, 8 February, 3, 5, 16, 18, 21 March, 6–7 May 1939; for delay due to the public's aversion to Germany, 11, 12 July, 28 October, 15 December 1938, 19 March 1939. In spring 1937 Italy took the initiative toward military-economic coordination with Germany for the coming war: see Fortunato Minniti, "Le materie prime nella preparazione bellica dell'Italia (1935–1943)," *Storia contemporanea* 17:1,2 (1986), pp. 26–28.
123. "Carattere": Ciano, 13 November 1937; also Bottai, 26 October 1937. "Rivoluzione permanente": Ciano, 23 September 1937; similarly OO 26:192 (1934); "superstructure": Ciano, 7 January 1938; racial laws: Meir Michaelis, *Mussolini and the Jews* (Oxford, 1978); Munich: Ciano, 25, 28 September 1938.
124. Knox, *Mussolini*, Chapters 1–4; idem, "L'ultima guerra dell'Italia fascista," pp. 24–27; OO 29:403–05.

ambitions and the search for economic independence that marked Italy's claim to great-power status.

But Mussolini's foreign policy was also new in three decisive ways. First, it was blindly and dogmatically geopolitical. Mussolini defined great power status and true independence monocausally, by geography. His theory dictated that Italy "march to the ocean" against Britain and France. Second, Mussolini's policy was overtly and insistently ideological. He saw himself as the "Pope of Fascism" and considered ideological affinity the guarantee of the common revolutionary goals that made allies useful and reliable.[125] Third and most important, Mussolini's foreign policy was – in a way unique to his regime and that of his German ally – not simply *foreign* policy. Its internal revolutionary purpose made it domestic policy as well. Unlike Liberals, Nationalists, or Fascism's successors, Mussolini aimed to destroy rather than consolidate the Italian establishment. Fascist wars and Fascist revolution were dialectically intertwined in an upward spiral of violence.

The constraints upon Mussolini's policy and the sources of its radicalization are clear. After 1922 he faced a usually cohesive establishment that typically vetoed risk. The foot-dragging of diplomats, generals, and admirals under the ultimate protection of the king repeatedly thwarted and enraged him. Even that secret *bienpensant*, Galeazzo Ciano, railed that "to conquer Palazzo Chigi fifteen years were needed; and I alone know the travail I must endure to make these goats move at a Fascist quick-march."[126] Worse still, Italy's economy depended upon foreign capital and raw materials. And worst of all, Mussolini faced an international order that until 1933 did not permit

125. Grandi and other despairing Duce subordinates argued that Mussolini departed from the stern path of Cavour and di San Giuliano by placing ideological affinities ahead of the "permanent national interests" (see Grandi diary, and Guariglia, *Ricordi*, especially pp. 9, 25, 39, 48, 63, 66). Mussolini himself thought it realistic to despise Stresemann, "masonic social democracy," and the French republic, and to look to the German Right and ultimately to the Hitler movement for allies. Only a Germany set upon the destruction of the 1919 order could serve as ally in the great war for Italian empire in which the dictator saw the *true* national interest. Given that "permanent national interests" are not objective truths but rather depend on values and aims, it would be unwise to describe the Duce's policy as *more* ideological than that of his diplomats and flankers. But as Grandi bitterly recognized in his diary musings, Mussolini's policy was certainly the consequence of a new – party – ideology, and in this way also broke with Italy's foreign policy traditions.
126. For Mussolini and diplomats, see especially Grandi diary, 12 September 1930, 6 January 1931; also Aloisi, 25 July 1932, and Ciano, 16 November 1937; Ciano remark: 21 November 1937; see also 21 October, 26 December 1937.

the expansion by force that he had sought from the beginning.

Once the Great Depression had loosened the West's financial grip on Italy and had helped Hitler into the saddle, Mussolini was increasingly able to translate dogma into warfare. When monarch, flankers, and French placed Yugoslavia off-limits in early 1933, he turned to Ethiopia. Enough flankers helped; this was not the enterprise of "one man alone." Some hoped for Franco-Italian agreement against Germany, almost all aspired to "avenge Adua" and secure the nineteenth-century African empire missed in 1896 and 1919. Despite trepidations and doubts, they made Mussolini "founder of the Empire" and gave him the ascendancy he needed to almost destroy Italy in 1940–45.

The breakthrough of 1936 at last freed the dictator to translate into practice the militant fanaticism he had hitherto poorly concealed. Revolution and geopolitics in command, along with the German victories of May 1940, launched the last Fascist war. Establishment and public momentarily suspended disbelief; perhaps Mussolini *was* right. Perhaps Italy could at one blow achieve the Mediterranean domination that more prudent heads thought was at best its due over the next several generations.[127] Only the ensuing catastrophe impelled moderate Fascists, flankers, and monarchy to repentance and ultimately to hesitant revolt. At the close of the humiliating 1940–41 campaign against Greece that broke the regime's morale and reduced it to dependence on Germany, Grandi ruefully summed up the essential difference between establishment and Fascist foreign policy. The officer corps had finally taken the measure of Mussolini's war aims: "We are fighting for purposes declaredly hostile to our own class."[128] That proved a belated and dearly bought insight.

---

127. See Knox, *Mussolini*, pp. 110–12, and Piero Calamandrei, *Diario 1939–1945* (Florence, 1982), vol. 1, pp. 168, 172, 178–79, 194–95, 200, 207, 214–15.
128. Quoted in Pirelli, *Taccuini*, p. 296.

4

THE ITALIAN ARMY AT WAR, 1940–1943:
A STUDY IN COMBAT EFFECTIVENESS

The maxim that victory has many fathers but defeat is an orphan applies only imperfectly to the fate of the Fascist movement and regime – even if all concerned hastened to deny responsibility. Italy's catastrophic defeat in the great war that Mussolini sought for twenty years and finally found had many fathers. Society, industrial establishment, regime, and armed forces all contributed in vital ways.

The regime inherited a society poor both in relative terms and in the aggregate. By the late 1930s Italy was thirty to fifty years behind its German ally in becoming an industrial society, a gap overcome only during the long peace after 1945. Virtually all adult Germans were literate by 1900; illiteracy and a semiliteracy that entailed mutually opaque dialects embraced perhaps a third of Italy's population in 1940. The Italian economy by 1938 had a total industrial potential slightly over a fifth of Germany's and half of Japan's. Italian society's peasant base, an industrial sector employing less than a third of the workforce, and a narrowly selective educational system (85,535 university students, of whom only 13.6 percent were studying engineering, out of a total population of just under 44 million in 1939–40) meant a pervasive shortage of technical talent.[1] And a parochial, cartelized, and in some cases corrupt industrial establishment was incapable of design-

1. Literacy, semiliteracy: SVIMEZ, *Un secolo di statistiche italiane*, p. 795; Daniele Marchesini, "Città e campagna nello specchio dell'alfabetismo (1921–1951)," in Simonetta Soldani and Gabriele Turi, eds., *Fare gli italiani: Scuola e cultura nell'Italia contemporanea* (Bologna, 1993), vol. 2, pp. 9–10; total industrial potential: Paul Bairoch, "International Industrialization Levels from 1750 to 1980," *Journal of European Economic History* 11:2 (1982), p. 299; industrial workforce: B. R. Mitchell, *European Historical Statistics, 1750–1975* (2nd rev. ed., New York, 1981), pp. 164, 166; university population: Lucio Ceva, "Italy," in I. C. B. Dear and M. R. D. Foot, eds., *The Oxford Companion to the Second World War* (Oxford, 1995), p. 582.

ing, much less mass-producing, effective armored fighting vehicles. Fighter aircraft fully competitive with those of Italy's enemies and ally appeared in small numbers only in 1943.[2]

Fear of offending constituted interests was characteristic of the war effort. The regime failed to decree general mobilization in 1940 as its Liberal predecessor had unhesitatingly done in 1915. Mussolini's flankers and Italian opinion had already ruled out in the 1920s the terror that made sacrifice palatable in Soviet Russia and Nazi Germany. A series of attempts on Mussolini's life in 1925–26 gave pretext for creation of a "Special Tribunal for the Defense of the State." But that institution put to death only nine men in peacetime, and twenty-two, mostly Slavs from the eastern borderlands, in war. Persistent political opponents risked mortal beatings or internal exile in the desolate South, but repression remained sporadic and selective. And despite Hitlerian exhortations in winter 1940–41 to use "barbaric methods such as shooting generals and colonels . . . and decimating units," the armed forces apparently condemned to death fewer than 150 men between June 1940 and September 1943 – a record that contrasted sharply with the 4,000 or more death sentences, 750 executions, and numerous shootings without trial with which Cadorna and Diaz had held Italy's peasant infantry in line in 1915–18. Ribbentrop's alleged advice of March 1943 that the regime bolster the collapsing war effort by shooting 100 prominent Italians was not practical politics.[3]

The regime scarcely even dared to tax its subjects: overall tax receipts, despite wartime increases and surcharges, *decreased* by 20 percent between 1939–40 and 1942–1943. Wealthy and powerful interests with friends in high places such as Count Galeazzo Ciano,

---

2. For carefully documented and sometimes lurid descriptions of industry's failings, see Lucio Ceva and Andrea Curami, *La meccanizzazione dell'esercito italiano dalle origini al 1943* (Rome, 1989), and *Industria bellica anni trenta* (Milan, 1992); also Ceva, "Grande industria e guerra," and Curami, "Commesse belliche e approvvigionamenti di materie prime," in Romain H. Rainero and Antonello Biagini, eds., *L'Italia in guerra: il primo anno – 1940* (Rome, 1991), pp. 33–53 and 55–66; Curami, "Piani e progetti dell'aeronautica italiana, 1939–1943. Stato maggiore e industrie," *Italia contemporanea* 187 (1992), pp. 243–61.

3. Special tribunal: Aquarone, *L'organizzazione dello Stato totalitario*, p. 103 and note; Hitler (to Ciano, 8 December 1940), ADAP D/9/477, p. 685; ninety-two army death sentences 1940–43 (partial data, estimated at 65 percent of the overall total, for the army alone; evidence on how many were actually carried out is lacking): Rochat, "La giustizia militare nella guerra italiana 1940–43," *Rivista di Storia Contemporanea* 1991:4, pp. 536–37. For 1915–18, Enzo Forcella and Alberto Monticone, *Plotone d'esecuzione: I processi della prima guerra mondiale* (Bari, 1968), especially pp. 433–512; Ribbentrop: Ernst von Weizsäcker, *Die Weizsäcker-Papiere 1933–1950*, ed. Leonidas E. Hill (Frankfurt a. M., 1974), p. 334 (perhaps reflecting ADAP E/5/184).

Mussolini's putative successor until 1943, successfully asserted free-dom from taxation – or outright evasion – as their immemorial right.[4] Mussolini, his generals, and his admirals showed slavish deference to the large industrial combines that produced the least effective, most expensive, and least numerous armaments of any major combatant in the Second World War. They tolerated the erection of the FIAT-Ansaldo joint monopoly on armored vehicles, its almost endless delays, exactions, and inefficiencies, and the artisanal production habits and sometimes unflyable wares of Italy's oligopolistic aircraft firms. The organization of war production was even more chaotic than in Germany; the dictator's refusal to permit centralization outside his own person, and pervasive bureaucratic dysfunctions in both military and civilian ministries, ensured that the armed forces would fail to exploit fully even industry's meager capabilities.[5]

Nor did Italy have access to the external inputs that helped push the war production of other powers sharply upward. Britain's choke points at Gibraltar and Suez barred a projected two-fifths of the imports needed in wartime. Dependence on outside sources of energy other than hydroelectric power was almost total. Steel production was at best a tenth of Germany's. The foreign loans that had provided over 13 percent of the Italian government's receipts in 1915–18 were absent. And unlike his German and Japanese allies in 1940–41, Mus-solini proved unable to fuel his war economy with loot. By an author-itative recent estimate, Italian military expenditure peaked in 1941 at the paltry level of 23 percent of gross domestic product, compared to Germany's 70 percent in 1943.[6]

Perhaps the most telling indicators of Fascist Italy's inadequacy – in

---

4.   Massimo Legnani, "Sul finanziamento della guerra fascista," in Gaetano Grassi and Legnani, eds., *L'Italia nella seconda guerra mondiale e nella Resistenza* (Milan, 1988), pp. 302–06 and, in general, Giuseppe Maione, *L'imperialismo straccione: classi sociali e finan-za di guerra dall'impresa etiopica al conflitto mondiale (1935–1943)* (Bologna, 1979), which rests largely on the rich personal papers of the finance minister, Paolo Thaon di Revel. For Ciano's role, see especially Bottai, 6 June 1942; Ciano, 5, 6 June 1942; Giuseppe Gorla, *L'Italia nella seconda guerra mondiale: Diario di un milanese, ministro del re nel gov-erno di Mussolini* (Milan, 1959), pp. 243–44.
5.   See especially Ceva and Curami, *Meccanizzazione*; their "Industria bellica e stato nel-l'imperialismo fascista degli anni '30," *Nuova antologia* 2167 (1988), pp. 321–28, and Minniti, "Aspetti organizzativi del controllo sulla produzione bellica in Italia," *Clio*, 1977:4, pp. 305–40.
6.   Mark Harrison, "The Economics of World War II: An Overview," in Harrison, ed. *The Economics of World War II* (Cambridge, 1998), Table 1.8, p. 21; also Zamagni, "Italy: How to Lose the War and Win the Peace," ibid., pp. 177–222; import projections: Umberto Spigo, *Premesse tecniche della disfatta* (Rome, 1945), p. 84; allied loans, 1915–18: Legnani, "Finanziamento della guerra fascista," p. 304.

a global war shaped and decided by the internal combustion engine – were those relating to its stock of vehicles. In 1939 the nation possessed only 469,000, against 1.99 million in Germany, 2.25 million in France, and 2.42 million in Britain. That amounted to 11 motor vehicles for each thousand population, against 25 per thousand in Germany (proportionately more than twice as numerous), 54 and 51 per thousand in Britain and France (almost five times more numerous), and 227 per thousand in the United States (over twenty times more numerous). The Italian armed forces could not take for granted even competent drivers, much less mechanics.[7]

Mussolini's choice of an ally with too weak a resource base to seize the world domination that it claimed was the ultimate cause of defeat. Italy's economic and organizational weakness helped make defeat, when it came, uniquely humiliating. What passed for Italian strategy also contributed mightily to that outcome, first in Mussolini's 1940 war "parallel to that of Germany to reach our [own] objectives," then in the *guerra subalterna* under the tutelage of Hitler, General Erwin Rommel, and lesser Germans that resulted from Italy's defeats at Greek and British hands between November 1940 and February 1941.

Culturally determined strategic myopia rendered both dictator and associates incapable of understanding their enemies or their ally. Frenetic dissipation of resources on theaters other than North Africa was primarily the dictator's own doing, but he had much help. Strategic passivity bordering on autism, both before and after the dictator's removal in July 1943, characterized the *Comando Supremo* under its three successive chiefs, Marshal Pietro Badoglio, Marshal Ugo Cavallero, and General Vittorio Ambrosio.[8] Logistical incapacity at the theater level multiplied the effects of industrial failure in depriving Italian strategy of a material base.[9] And an ever-greater dependence on the

7. Table: DRZW 5/1:651; drivers: see for instance *Africa*, vol. 1, p. 117, and the AAR from November 1942 printed in Ceva, "4a armata e occupazione italiana della Francia. Problemi militari," in *8 settembre: lo sfacelo della quarta armata* (Turin, 1979), p. 98.
8. See especially the remarks of Ceva, *Africa settentrionale*, pp. 166–67, and *La condotta italiana della guerra: Cavallero e il Comando Supremo 1941/1941* (Milan, 1975), pp. 121–22, on the "resigned but farsighted passivity" of the high command in 1940, and Elena Aga Rossi, *Una nazione allo sbando: l'armistizio italiano del settembre 1943* (Bologna, 1993), pp. 45–46, 66–73, 79–124.
9. See Ferruccio Botti, "La logistica dei poveri: organizzazione dei rifornimenti e amministrazione dell'Esercito nel 1940," *Memorie storiche militari 1992* (Rome, 1994), pp. 407–43; "Problemi logistici del secondo anno di guerra – aspetti interforze," in Rainero and Biagini, eds., *L'Italia in guerra: Il secondo anno – 1941* (Gaeta, 1992), pp. 291–327; "Strategia e logistica in un'ottica interforze," in idem, eds., *L'Italia in guerra: Il terzo anno – 1942* (Gaeta, 1993), pp. 225–72; and Botti, *La logistica dell'esercito italiano, 1831–1981*, vols. 3 and 4 (Rome, 1994–95).

German Reich yielded only to even greater dependence on the Western powers after the armistice of 8 September 1943 and the concurrent collapse of the armed forces. Finally, the absence – as in previous Italian wars – of an effective high command, as well as the lack of even a rudimentary conceptual or organizational framework for interservice cooperation until 1941–42, also contributed mightily to a uniquely dispiriting outcome.[10]

Yet from the beginning the performance of the armed forces at the operational and tactical levels was the chief determinant of whether Italy would retain a measure of dignity in defeat. The army's performance was most decisive of all: the senior service absorbed almost two-thirds of the wartime armed forces budget, dominated the high command, and alone held the power to destroy the regime. But of the three armed forces it was also least capable, whether conceptually, operationally, or tactically, of fighting the war of 1940–43.

MEN AND MACHINES: THE ARMY AND MODERN WAR

"Men, our indisputable resource" – as Mussolini's first minister of war, General Diaz, put it in 1923 – and mind over matter were the *Regio Esercito*'s twin credos. That cultural limitation long antedated Fascism, and proved almost impervious to experience in 1940–43.[11] Numerical superiority in infantry was in the army view the decisive factor in war, a view supposedly confirmed by the experience of 1915–18. The *Regio Esercito* had acquired numerous machines by that war's end, but its leaders never accepted what the German high command had recognized as early as mid-1916: warfare had become "machine warfare."[12] Belief in the human will paralleled faith in numbers. Both together perhaps contributed to the army's tolerance as its main battle tank throughout the late 1930s of FIAT-Ansaldo's 3.5-ton L3 tankette, a vehicle easily perforated by machine-gun fire that had on occasion succumbed to Ethiopians wielding stones. Reverence for the human spirit and a culturally determined faith in genial improvisation may

10. Ceva, *La condotta italiana*, provides masterful treatment of the high command.
11. For the quotation (General Armando Diaz, 1923) and an excellent introduction to interwar army thought, see Antonio Sema, "La cultura dell'esercito," pp. 91–116 in *Cultura e società negli anni del fascismo* (Milan, 1987). For the very slow assimilation after 1940, especially at the highest levels, of the principles of machine warfare, see Ceva and Curami, *Meccanizzazione*, vol. 1, pp. 310–14.
12. Geyer, "German Strategy in the Age of Machine Warfare, 1914–1945," in Peter Paret, ed., *Makers of Modern Strategy* (Princeton, 1988), pp. 537–54.

also have helped to cause the army's universally attested disdain for cadre and unit training.

Like its German counterpart between 1933 and 1941, the army made its doctrinal and force structure decisions under the Fascist regime with considerable freedom, subject only to the dictator's demands for fighting power. But the structure the *Regio Esercito* chose for itself, unlike that erected by its German counterpart and eventual ally, perpetuated the "atavistic intellectual narrowness" later detected and analyzed in detail, after several false starts, by the army's postwar official historians.[13]

Reverence for numbers dictated as many divisions as the army budget permitted. Corporate self-interest powerfully reinforced doctrinal choice: the higher officer corps had grown disproportionately during the First World War and had subsequently exploited its bargain with Fascism to reestablish its numbers after forced personnel cuts in 1918–22. The more divisions, the more command positions for its members. That logic culminated in 1937–38 with the decision of the chief of staff and undersecretary of the army, General Alberto Pariani, to increase the army from forty-odd to seventy-odd divisions by decreeing that each would have two infantry regiments – the "*divisione binaria*" – instead of the usual three.

Regardless of the structure of its divisions, the army leadership's insistence on maintaining as large a force as budgetarily feasible condemned the service to intellectual torpor and physical immobility. Nondiscretionary expenses consumed all available funds: regular officer pay; enormous static bureaucracies dictated by the need to employ as many regular officers as possible; and the numerous installations and immense stocks of basic equipment – rifles, mess kits, canteens, rucksacks, uniforms, and blankets – that the inflated force structure required. Combat units consequently remained at less than half-strength throughout most of the year during peacetime, suffered massive shortages of crew-served weapons, vehicles, horses, and mules, and were rarely able to train companies or even platoons as units. The army leadership also economized on its junior cadres, with disastrous consequences for tactical expertise and unit solidity to be described later.

Machines were low on the army's scale of priorities, and the

---

13. For this courageous phrase, accompanied by much astute analysis, see Mario Montanari, *L'esercito italiano alla vigilia della seconda guerra mondiale* (Rome, 1982), especially p. 251; likewise his *La campagna di Grecia* (Rome, 1980) and *Africa*, works in the best traditions of Clausewitzian *Kritik*.

machines it commissioned were correspondingly inadequate. The war ministry's bureaucratic "labyrinths" alone – even discounting industry's manifest inadequacies – made failure almost inevitable. Each new equipment item or weapon required approval of the artillery (or engineer, or motorization) technical office, the appropriate department of the ministry itself, the inspectorate of the branch concerned, the training section of the army staff, and finally the ministry secretariat. If even one of these organizations proposed a minor modification, the entire process had to begin once more. It required six months to approve a Molotov cocktail anti-tank weapon that the technical staff had put together and successfully tested in less than a week in July 1940. This system, and the ministry's return in July 1940 to its traditional daily closing hour of 2 P.M., so compounded the dysfunctions of industry that it is surprising that the army received any new equipment at all before 1943.[14]

The army's highest priority was artillery, a weapon that did not challenge its 1915–18 conceptual framework. But inexplicably in view of its straightened circumstances, the service demanded as early as 1929 a total renewal of all artillery, a course upon which Germany only embarked because forced disarmament after 1918 had left it no alternative. As a senior artillery officer pointed out in 1933, Italy could simply refurbish, with immediate effect and at considerable savings, many of the excellent weapons produced before 1915 on German and French licenses or captured thereafter from Austria-Hungary. New shells and propellant charges giving longer ranges were feasible, and modern gun carriages, off-road tractors, and half-track carriers would have worked wonders. But the half-track only came to Italy in wartime as a belated means of saving rubber, and the sometimes excellent new cannon the army finally ordered in 1938 reached the troops in small numbers only in 1941–42.[15] In the event, the immense bulk of the army's artillery in 1940–43 remained that of 1915–18, but without the improvements that would have given it a mobility and range closer to the weapons of Italy's ally and adversaries.

Conceptual blinkers narrowed further by penury also slowed the army's fitful attempts to acquire an effective medium tank. Pariani cor-

14. Labyrinths: Cavallero, *Diario 1940–1943*, ed. Giovanni Bucciante (Rome, 1984), p. 582; Mario Caracciolo, *E poi? La tragedia dell'esercito italiano* (Rome, 1946), pp. 58–60; closing time: Soddu to subordinates, 61920, 27 August 1940, ACS, Primo Aiutante di Campo, Sezione Speciale, bundle 67, folder "Circolari Varie 1940."
15. Refurbishment of artillery: Ceva and Curami, "Industria bellica e stato," pp. 326–29 and note 24; Ceva, "Rapporti fra industria bellica ed esercito," pp. 220–21; half-tracks: Ceva and Curami, *Meccanizzazione*, vol. 1, p. 411.

rectly foresaw as early as 1936–37 that a drive on Suez would be the strategic center of gravity of Italy's coming war. But he planned to fight that war primarily with truck-borne infantry. Italy's first medium tank, the failed M11/39, had its main gun rendered almost useless by its placement in the hull rather than in a turret, a solution apparently dictated by the inability to design turret mechanisms, or the alleged need to reduce vehicle width to fit Italian mountain roads. And one of Italy's few generals with experience commanding mobile units in combat, General Ettore Bastico, was apparently so intimidated by his colleagues' opposition to the new weapon that at a meeting of senior generals called to discuss the future of armor in November 1937 he conceded that "the tank is a powerful tool [*mezzo*] but let us not idolize it [*non gridiamogli osanna*]; let us reserve our reverence for the infantryman and the mule."[16] Innovation was and remained suspect, because it meant scrapping a force structure that derived from the army's deeply felt conception of war, and directly served the interests of the officer corps.

What was truly remarkable was how little, and how slowly, the shock of war affected the army's reverence for infantry and mules. After the *Wehrmacht*'s destruction of Poland and the penury and confusion revealed by the Italian army's own partial mobilization that autumn, the army staff began to have second thoughts about its 120- to 126-division target figure for the war army. Despite an attempt by Pariani's successor as chief of staff, Marshal Rodolfo Graziani, to hold the line at 100 divisions, the final figure selected for activation in spring 1940 was 73.[17] The 73 divisions of June 1940 grew to a nominal 91 by mid-1943, despite catastrophic defeats in North Africa (December 1940–February 1941), Russia (November 1942–February 1943), and Tunisia (January–May 1943) that eliminated 34 divisions. Cavallero – who had won his spurs in 1915–18 in the operations section of the high command and had subsequently served a scandal-ridden term as managing director of Ansaldo – claimed to perceive as early as 1941 that "the general experience of the war . . . has emphasized the importance of quality rather than numbers." A few officers at the *Comando Supremo* recognized by July 1941 that "a single motorized division, EVEN FOR DEFENSE AND OCCUPATION MISSIONS, has the capability of four infantry divisions, while it eats only

16. Botti, "I generali italiani e il problema dei corazzati: la riunione tenuta dal Generale Pariani il 23 e 24 novembre 1937 sul carro armato e i suoi riflessi," *Studi storico-militari 1993* (Rome, 1996), pp. 211–14, 241.
17. Figures: Montanari, *Alla vigilia*, pp. 280–81, 305–06 note 35; Carlo Favagrossa, *Perché perdemmo la guerra: Mussolini e la produzione bellica* (Milan, 1946), p. 115.

a fourth as much and requires only a fourth as much transport from Italy."[18]

Yet Cavallero failed to fully motorize a few picked divisions while eliminating the many useless mouths that were in part responsible for the armed forces' North African logistical nightmare. Mussolini's own rage for numbers and the political imperative of outnumbering the Germans in that vital theater were doubtless partly responsible.[19] But the root cause was the army hierarchy's own continuing faith in numbers. Cavallero sought to bring Italian forces in North Africa up to sixteen divisions, of which all except two or three would of necessity be foot infantry.[20] In the event, he maintained the equivalent of at least eight foot infantry divisions in North Africa until the destruction of much of the North African army at El Alamein in October–November 1942. As late as July 1942 the *Comando Supremo* proposed to add a further 67,000 troops to the mostly immobile 150,000 already overseas.[21]

At the army's high point in April 1943 it thus numbered almost 3.7 million officers and men. Its combat units were as underequipped, undermanned, inadequately officered, and poorly supported as they had been at the outset. Its bloated and static rear area commands had absorbed 500,000 men, a full third of the personnel stationed in Italy and the islands. The gigantic Roman bureaucracies possessed one officer for every thirteen enlisted men, and a largely superfluous entity such as the horse cavalry school at Pinerolo employed 3,650 officers and men.[22]

As in the interwar period, the technological poverty that accompanied the army's numerical hypertrophy was self-inflicted. Badoglio was so uninterested in mechanized warfare that his only recorded comment on a perceptive army intelligence analysis of German methods in

18. On Cavallero's strange career at and sudden dismissal from Ansaldo (as well as his apparent role as patron of the FIAT-Ansaldo armor monopoly), see Ceva and Curami, *Industria bellica anni trenta* and *Meccanizzazione*; quotations: Cavallero to Roatta, 8 June 1941, and *Comando Supremo* office note, July 1941, in Ceva, *La condotta italiana*, pp. 151, 110 (emphasis in original). The author of the note was probably Colonel Giuseppe Cordero Lanza di Montezemolo, chief of the operations section for Africa.
19. The latter is the thesis of Ceva, *La condotta italiana*, pp. 76, 109–110.
20. Cavallero to Roatta, 8 June 1941, in Ceva, *La condotta italiana*, p. 151; Cavallero diary, 20 July 1941, ibid., p. 77; similarly, army staff memorandum on reinforcement of North Africa, 23 May 1941 (110,000 additional men, but only 14,000 vehicles and tanks), in Ceva, *Le forze armate*, pp. 582–87.
21. *Comando Supremo* memorandum, "Ripartizione tonnellaggio negli avviamenti in A.S.," 22 July 1942, NARA T-821/144/000486–91.
22. Rochat, "Gli uomini alle armi 1940–1943," in his *L'esercito italiano in pace e in guerra* (Milan, 1991), pp. 271, 278–80, 290 (Table H); for the army's size over the course of the war, Tables A, B, C, pp. 284–86, and Ceva, "Italy," Dear and Foot, eds., *Oxford Companion*, p. 592 (graph).

July 1940 was "we'll study it when the war is over." It apparently required Mussolini's intervention that same month to compel the war ministry bureaucracy to begin work on specifications for a 75mm-gun tank – which in the event FIAT-Ansaldo failed to produce before collapse in 1943 rendered it useless.[23] The army's wartime record on motor transport was only slightly less disastrous. The war ministry had failed to anticipate before June 1940, or to recognize thereafter, the sheer numbers of vehicles required and the fact that fighting might not be confined to hard-surface roads; for off-road mobility Italian units in North Africa had to rely largely on captured British equipment.

And in areas such as communications, where relatively small investment could have produced dramatic results, the army failed dismally. Italian tank crews suffered without voice radios until 1941. Even after that, no long-distance radio that could operate on the move existed. Nor did anyone in Rome think to provide inexpensive items such as the compensated vehicle compasses essential in the desert – this despite thirty years of Italian military experience in Libya. When the reconnaissance units of the Italian mobile divisions fighting alongside Rommel's *Afrika Korps* belatedly received their first armored cars in 1942, vehicle commanders had to stop and walk away from their vehicles to take bearings with hand compasses. Even basic infantry weapons such as the excellent and inexpensive 81mm mortar were in short supply and scantily provided with ammunition until 1941. By then Italy had long since lost the initiative to enemies and ally.

OPERATIONS

"*Operation* is movement" was the principle on which General Hans von Seeckt refounded the post-1919 German armed forces. They in turn imposed that principle on the armed forces of Germany's main adversaries. The purpose of movement was the surprise concentration in time and/or space of strength against enemy weakness within a theater of war, in execution of a campaign plan designed to achieve the strategic objectives of the state. The conduct of operations required a doctrine that fostered the combined employment of the three services and the combination of arms – their coordinated use – within the ground forces. Operations, the Germans discerned, also required a

---

23. Ceva and Curami, *Meccanizzazione*, vol. 1, pp. 297–301, 360, 393–95, 481, 484; vol. 2, pp. 532–33.

particular command structure and style. Unity of command was highly desirable; creative freedom for subordinates within the framework
of their superiors' intent was vital; and commanders capable of exploiting that freedom were indispensable. Operational success also
required a force structure that combined foresight, coordination,
movement, and striking power: intelligence and reconnaissance,
supremely effective communications, mechanization to the greatest
extent possible, massive firepower, and lavish logistical support to sustain both fire and movement. A further prerequisite was constant
training exercises to test and refine the ability of both leaders and large
units to frame and execute campaign plans.

The Italian army in 1940 recognized virtually none of these principles except in a purely verbal sense. Its inability to plan campaigns had
been the root cause of the great defeats of 1848–49 and 1866. The
Great War had taught little; tactical stalemate had so crippled movement that only the Germans and the British in Palestine and in the
West after July 1918 learned much about the conduct of operations.
The *Regio Esercito* simply threw away the experience gained in its one
major operational success, the Vittorio Veneto offensive of October
1918, despite the vital role of Cavallero himself in its planning and
execution.

Ethiopia was the unique exception. On the eve of war, Mussolini
and his army chief of staff promulgated a new *Directives for the
Employment of Major Units* premised on the notion that Italy's resource
dependence ruled out wars of attrition: "Ours must be a war of movement."[24] To that end, Mussolini insisted on pressing upon the army
leadership unprecedented numbers of men and machines. Ultimately,
a coherent and moderately effective campaign plan took shape, based
on successive bounds forward and extravagant logistical support.[25]
Technological superiority, from Caterpillar tractors imported from the
United States to mustard gas to truck columns supplied on occasion by
air, assured the swift victory needed to end the campaign before Italy
succumbed to economic and diplomatic pressure.[26] Yet the army came
to regard many of these innovations – and especially their coordinated use – as somehow inapplicable to other theaters. In 1940–43 nei-

---

24. Quoted in Montanari, *Alla vigilia*, p. 256.
25. For the planning, see Rochat, *Militari e politici*.
26. On the massive use of gas, which representatives of the Italian state denied for decades
    after 1945, see Rochat, *Guerre italiane in Libia e in Etiopia* (Padua, 1991), Chapter 4.

ther the army, nor the other service staffs, nor the *Comando Supremo* ever *planned* a campaign, in the sense of defining a set of coherent operational steps designed to lead to the achievement of a strategic objective.

The authors of the *Directives* and of subsequent army doctrine implementing Pariani's vision of a "war of rapid decision" (*guerra di rapido corso*) also paid lip service to the concept known in German doctrine and practice as the creation of a *Schwerpunkt*, of "massing where one wishes to create superiority of forces."[27] Yet in 1940–43, the armed forces typically despaired of achieving surprise – through concentration at unexpected times or places – and made virtually no use of deception, the systematic control of enemy expectations. Not concentration but dissipation of effort – the uniform distribution of weakness and failure – was as characteristic of Italian operations as of strategy. In the French Alps in June 1940 and in Greece that October, the army advanced on broad fronts in pursuit of Mussolini's megalomaniacal objectives, and suffered defeat in detail. In the defense, the desire to be strong everywhere usually precluded the accumulation of mobile reserves; the December 1940 débâcle in North Africa under Graziani's command and the rapid collapse in East Africa in winter–spring 1941 bore witness to that vice. Thereafter, at least in North Africa, the Germans selected the *Schwerpunkt*. But they also imposed on the Italian army in Russia an overstretched cordon deployment that Russian armor ripped to shreds after the Stalingrad battle had consumed the German mobile reserves that might have plugged gaps in the Italian front.

The army repeatedly demonstrated its structural and intellectual incapacity in mobile warfare. Staffs such as that of the Italian expeditionary force in the Ukraine were immobile, weighed down with as many as 150 officers, compared to 66 in a German corps staff.[28] In the judgment of a German staff officer with long experience with the Italian army,

> The command apparatus is ... pedantic and slow. The absence of sufficient communications equipment renders the links to the subordinate units pre-

---

27. See the lengthy analysis of the *Directives* in Filippo Stefani, *La storia della dottrina e degli ordinamenti dell'esercito italiano* (Rome, 1984–86), vol. 2, part 1, pp. 345–65.
28. Italian corps: Deutsches Verbindungskommando b. ital. Expeditionskorps in Russland to DVst.b.it.AOK 8., 7.8.1942, NARA T-501/326/000149–50; German corps: Martin van Creveld, *Fighting Power* (Westport, CT, 1982), p. 50.

carious. The consequence is that the leadership is poorly informed about the friendly situation and has no capacity to redeploy swiftly. The working style of the staff is schematic, static [*unbeweglich*], and in some cases lacking in precision.[29]

The army's performance on all fronts and much Italian testimony confirms this picture. The only exceptions were the few Italian mobile units, such as the *Ariete* armored and *Trieste* motorized infantry divisions, that operated with the Afrika Korps. Those units also suffered from inadequate communications and vehicles. But by dint of practice alongside the Germans, their staffs acquired the experience and some of the habits of mind needed to cope with rapidly changing situations in a war without fixed fronts, under the leadership of the most volcanically unpredictable of Germany's generals. The commander of the *Ariete* at El Alamein, General Francesco Arena, found Rommel's tendency to give operation orders over the radio rather than in writing a shade eccentric, but nevertheless attempted to educate the *Comando Supremo* about "the advantages of a morale and operational nature" of the German practice of commanding from well forward.[30] Not everyone learned. Rommel's titular superior throughout most of the North African campaign, Bastico, continued to regard German scurrying about the battlefield as undignified, bizarre, and productive of "excesses the consequences of which I believe [Rommel] himself does not understand."[31]

The army's command structures fit poorly with operations. Its command style was flatly incompatible with their effective conduct. Mutual mistrust, clique rivalries, and personal feuds divided the higher officer corps. In Rome, General Ubaldo Soddu, undersecretary for war and deputy chief of Badoglio's *Comando Supremo*, feuded with the equally unprincipled and inept Giacomo Carboni of military intelligence, while intriguing to supplant first Badoglio and then the com-

---

29. Gyldenfeldt report, 8 August 1942, NARA T-501/320/000289–95; for corroboration see Becker, "Erfahrungsbericht als Verb. Offz. bei der Ital. mot. Div. 'Pasubio,'" 15 August 1941, NARA T-312/360/7934956–57; Giuseppe Mancinelli, *Dal fronte dell'Africa settentrionale (1942–43)* (Milan, 1970), pp. 15, 175, who points out that poor communications helped engender the schematism the Germans lamented; and (among much evidence in army files) Caracciolo to Corpo d'Armata Celere, 22 February 1942, NARA T-821/86/001024. For more on the German view of the Italians in Russia, see Jürgen Förster, "Il ruolo della 8a armata italiana dal punto di vista tedesco," in *Gli italiani sul fronte russo* (Bari, 1982).
30. Arena AAR, 13 December 1942, NARA T-821/31/000018–20.
31. Bastico on Rommel: *Africa*, vol. 3, p. 117; Rommel on Bastico: "fondamentalmente una brava persona, di ponderata intelligenza militare e considerevole dirittura morale" (vol. 4, p. 190).

mander of Italian forces in Albania, Sebastiano Visconti Prasca. Badoglio sought to undermine Graziani and was the sworn enemy of Cavallero from the mid-1920s. Cavallero removed Alfredo Guzzoni, who had attempted to loosen FIAT-Ansaldo's grip on armored vehicle production while minding the *Comando Supremo* as Cavallero staved off collapse in Albania in winter 1940–41. He destroyed Gastone Gàmbara of the mobile corps in North Africa for communicating with Ciano behind Cavallero's back and for "intellectual indiscipline" in a dispute between Rommel and Cavallero. He prevailed on Mussolini to retire Francesco Pricolo of the air force for failing to jump at Cavallero's word of command. And he sent General Mario Roatta, Graziani's deputy and successor as chief of the army staff, off to command the Italian army in Yugoslavia in early 1942, perhaps because Roatta had supported Guzzoni on the tank issue against Ansaldo.[32] At a less exalted level, the East African command had unwisely attempted to turn personal rivalries to operational advantage in the attack on British Somaliland in summer 1940: "We . . . placed at the head of the [attacking] echelons officers whom we knew to be hostile to one another, hoping that this would put wings on their feet." The unexpected result was that "both of them concentrated essentially on preventing the other from getting there."[33]

Commanders habitually oversupervised their subordinates in obsessive detail. Graziani found it necessary to emphasize in 1940 to his chief subordinate, Mario Berti, the need for "*absolute precision*" and "a complete and absolutely *true* outline" of the motor transport requirements of one of Berti's divisions – an astonishing commentary on the ethos of the higher officer corps.[34] The marshal also invaded Berti's field of responsibility by dictating in detail the operational plan (which in any event miscarried chaotically) for the advance into Egypt in September 1940.[35] A complement to mistrust and oversupervision was the sport of "*palleggiamento delle responsabilità*," or the passing of decisions to subordinates or superiors, while storing up evidence with which to damn them in case of disaster.[36] Graziani bitterly resented his transfer to North Africa in June 1940, and sought to minimize his own responsibility for immobility by sending Rome the minutes of councils

32. Guzzoni and Roatta: Ceva, "Industria bellica ed esercito," pp. 227–29; Gàmbara: *Africa*, vol. 3, pp. 74, 104–05.
33. Trezzani to Badoglio, 25 August 1940, quoted in Knox, *Mussolini*, p. 154.
34. Graziani to Berti, 26 August 1940, ACS, Carte Graziani, bundle 42 (emphasis in original).
35. See the critical analysis in *Africa*, vol. 1, pp. 103, 119.
36. That is the origin of Graziani's wonderful collection of papers at the ACS.

of war with his subordinates. Cavallero's frequent envoy to North Africa and the *Comando Supremo*'s sharpest brain, Colonel Giuseppe Cordero Lanza di Montezemolo, reported in December 1941 the persistence of a

> command style [*modo di comandare*] . . . not suited to this kind of war: commanders show little initiative, [and] ask for orders on matters within their own sphere, as if to place the responsibility [for decision] on their superiors. These in turn contribute to this situation by tying their subordinates down and checking over in advance the orders [the subordinates] issue.

In no aspect of war were the differences between Italian and German practice greater, for in Germany a century's traditions and the *Reichswehr*'s meditations on the First World War dictated parsimonious orders, creative freedom, and thirst for responsibility at all levels.[37]

The vicious circle of mistrust and oversupervision stemmed in part from the very nature of the army's higher officer corps. The commander of one of the Italy's two armies in Albania in winter 1940–41 described the general level of his division and corps commanders in merciless language:

> Some did not show sufficient strength of character, physical robustness, professional competence and initiative together with love of responsibility. Too many have presumably arrived at high rank by virtue of administrative drudgery, and without having well understood the meaning of the leadership of men and the active employment of units on the battlefield.

Corporate self-defense and barracks army routine had also produced a sedentary and overage higher officer corps: colonels of fifty, division commanders in their late fifties, and corps and army commanders of sixty or more.[38] Symptomatically, some of the paratroops who trained in 1941–42 for the planned Axis air-sea assault on Malta appear to have believed that their division commander, General Enrico Frattini, had been the only general officer in the entire army willing to accept a command that involved jumping from aircraft in flight.[39]

---

37. Cavallero, *Diario 1940–1943*, p. 279. On German traditions, see Chapter 5 of this volume. An outstanding example of Royal Navy practice is Admiral Andrew Cunningham's masterful restraint – despite excellent communications between his operations room in Alexandria and the forces in contact – during Admiral Philip Vian's brilliant convoy defense against the *Littorio* in March 1942 (see John Winton, *Cunningham* [London, 1998], p. 262).
38. Geloso AAR, quoted in Montanari, *Grecia*, vol. 1, p. 907; age: ibid., 905.
39. Marco Di Giovanni, *I paracadutisti italiani: Volontari, miti e memoria della seconda guerra mondiale* (Gorizia, 1991), p. 132.

Catastrophic failure in the Albanian mountains in 1940–41 offered an unused occasion for wholesale housecleaning of the army's operational leadership. But both then and later, inhibitions against washing dirty linen in front of the Germans and of the Italian public, the absence of long-lasting ground combat involving most of the army, and the army's sclerotic promotion system combined to block renewal. During the first eleven battles of the Isonzo in 1915–17, Cadorna had "torpedoed" unsuccessful or suspect subordinates with savage abandon. Commanders who survived Cadorna had in many cases fallen ill or died in battle. By 1916–17 a crude and often counterproductive process of selection had rejuvenated and notably improved the army's operational leadership. The ductile Cavallero had served in Cadorna's operations section, but did not in this respect acquire the master's touch. The chief of general staff was delighted to eliminate actual or potential rivals, but treated indulgently those who failed as combat leaders, clearing for future reemployment as a division or corps commander a former Badoglio aide who had fled to the rear while his division disintegrated in the face of Greek probing attacks.[40]

Other than Badoglio, whom Mussolini designated as scapegoat for the Greek fiasco, the only prominent army victims of battlefield defeat were Graziani, who suffered a nervous breakdown and pleaded piteously for his own relief, and Soddu, who panicked during the Greek counteroffensive of November–December 1940. Mussolini had Graziani investigated with a view to court-martial; nothing came of it. The marshal's immediate successor in North Africa, Italo Gariboldi, showed little energy or aptitude, but nevertheless went on to preside inertly over the disintegration of 8th Army in Russia in 1942–43.[41] Division and corps commanders showed similar stability, except for Sebastiano Visconti Prasca, who commanded the failed invasion of Greece at the outset, and those killed or captured in Africa and Russia. In North Africa, war, fatigue, and disease took their toll, but Cavallero was hard-pressed to ensure – as he felt compelled to direct the army staff explicitly as late as September 1942 – that general officer replace-

---

40. Ceva, *Le forze armate*, 357–58; for Cavallero, General Ottavio Bollea, and the collapse of the "Wolves of Tuscany" (January 1941) see Knox, *Mussolini*, pp. 258–59 and notes.
41. The official historians, after heaping deserved praise on his predecessor in Russia, Giovanni Messe, say of Gariboldi only that his command activity "had without doubt very narrow limits" due to German interference (Stato Maggiore dell'Esercito, Ufficio Storico, *Le operazioni delle unità italiane al fronte russo* [Rome, 1977], pp. 507–08, 510); on Gariboldi's inertia in North Africa, see Roatta to Cavallero, 10 July 1941, in *Africa*, vol. 2, pp. 279–80.

ments be "up to operational requirements, not [simply] chosen from the seniority list."[42]

The promotion system, in sharp contrast to its German counterpart – analyzed in the next chapter – added a further layer of resistance to any renewal of the higher officer corps. In theory the *Regio Esercito* promised swift promotion to "merit in war." In practice, seniority and connections counted heavily, and Mussolini unlike Hitler never took a grip on officer policy. Cavallero's reaction to Hitler's decrees of fall–winter 1942 promoting all combat commanders – without regard for age, seniority, education, or social distinction – to the substantive rank appropriate to their battlefield duties was a dismayed "for us this would be a bit excessive [*un pò forte*]," and a listing of the bureaucratic obstacles facing general officer promotions. What little selectivity the *Regio Esercito*'s system possessed appears to have operated perversely: Italy's finest theater commander of the war, General Giovanni Messe, complained fiercely from Tunisia that desk warriors in Rome were receiving promotion ahead of his battle-tested division commanders.[43]

Severe and interlocking defects of force structure and performance that derived primarily from the army's already-described vision of war further compounded its operational inadequacies. Operational knowledge and foresight about the enemy through intelligence were not a high priority of the army's staffs, although they were not entirely lacking. The army's *Servizio Informazioni Militare*, rechristened *Servizio Informazioni dell'Esercito* in a 1941 reorganization of intelligence by Cavallero, achieved two major operational coups. In April 1941 it used its expertise with cyphers to disorganize with bogus orders a dangerous Yugoslav advance against the poorly defended rear of the Italian forces in Albania. And throughout the first half of 1942 Italian decrypts of U.S. Army messages from Cairo gave Rommel and Cavallero vital information about British 8th Army's forces and intentions.[44] Signals intelligence units specializing in traffic analysis and

---

42. The division, corps, and army commanders of June 1941 show remarkable continuity with those of June 1940 (order of battle lists, Ceva, *Le forze armate*, pp. 492–95, 501–05); Cavallero, *Diario 1940–1943*, pp. 489–90.

43. The exemplary analysis of Montanari, *Africa*, vol. 4, pp. 574–76, suggests that close study of the army's interwar and wartime promotion policies is overdue; Messe: ibid., vol. 4, pp. 636, 661.

44. See "The Contribution of 'S.I.M.' to the Second Counteroffensive of [sic] Cyrenaica (21 January–5 February 1942)," and "The Contribution of the Information [sic] Service to the May–June 1942 Offensive in North Africa," NARA RG 457/1035 (records of the National Security Agency; my warmest thanks to Brian R. Sullivan for copies of these documents); also Carlo De Risio, *Generali, servizi segreti, e fascismo* (Milan, 1978), pp. 111–12, and F. H. Hinsley et al., *British Intelligence in the Second World War* (London, 1979–90), vol. 2, p. 389.

low-level British army and RAF cyphers also provided valuable operational and tactical intelligence throughout the North African campaign.

Air reconnaissance was as vital as signals intelligence to the planning and conduct of army operations, but the air reconnaissance units assigned to the army were initially equipped with biplanes proven in Ethiopia but unable to coexist in the same sky with modern fighters. Strategic reconnaissance was almost nonexistent at the outset, a situation the air commander in North Africa rightly viewed as "an unpardonable error." Aging medium bombers and twin-engined monoplanes of less than stunning performance replaced the biplanes. But not until December 1941 did the first fast monoplanes with Kodak automatic cameras provide the constantly updated photo mosaics needed to plan the Malta landing.[45] In joint theaters such as North Africa, the Luftwaffe inevitably carried the weight of the air reconnaissance effort.

Intelligence and reconnaissance can only find the enemy and estimate his strength and intentions. The operations that follow require coordinated movement to ensure surprise and thus depend absolutely upon swift and secure communications. The *Reichswehr* leadership had therefore decided in the late 1920s that it would develop the best operational and tactical communications systems in the world.[46] The Italian army did not follow suit, and entered and fought the conflict of 1940–43 with communications inadequate for static warfare; shortages of telephone wire crippled even its 1915–18 land-line systems in the final defensive battles in Tunisia.[47] Radio communications between divisions, corps, and higher headquarters depended upon equipment that functioned only when stationary and after a lengthy set-up process, and proved largely useless in the Russian winter. Army communications security was relatively weak. Especially after October 1940, Cairo read much of the army's lower-grade operational traffic and an increasing amount of higher-level material, including information that allowed General Richard O'Connor to cut off the remnants of Graziani's 10th Army at Beda Fomm in early February 1941. Cairo likewise read virtually all high-level army traffic from East Africa in winter–spring 1941, including the viceroy's daily situation reports to Rome,

45. Felice Porro, "La Quinta Squadra Aerea in Libia (10 giugno 1940–5 febbraio 1941)," *Rivista aeronautica*, 1948:8, p. 487; Nino Arena, *La Regia Aeronautica 1940–1943* (Rome, 1982–94), vol. 1, pp. 93, 581–82; vol. 3, pp. 366, 392.
46. See James S. Corum, *The Roots of Blitzkrieg: Hans von Seeckt and German Military Reform* (Lawrence, Kansas, 1992), pp. 107–08.
47. *Africa*, vol. 4, p. 453.

Table 4.1. *Italian and British infantry divisions, North Africa (table of organization strength; actual combat strength was invariably lower)*

Italian infantry division type A.S.42		British infantry division, 1941
7,000	Officers and men	17,300
72	Anti-tank rifles	444
146	Automatic rifles	819
92	Machine guns	48
–	Light mortars	162
18	81mm mortars	56
60	Field guns	72
72	Anti-tank guns	136
16	Light anti-aircraft guns	48
142	Trucks	1,999
35	Other vehicles	268
–	Trailers	197
72	Artillery tractors	159
147	Motorcycles	1,064
–	Tracked ammunition carriers	256
–	Armored cars	6

a circumstance that speeded markedly the dismantling of Mussolini's empire. Communications security improved thereafter, but the army's adoption of German ENIGMA cypher machines, which British intelligence had broken, rendered high-level Italian communications in Tunisia largely transparent to the Western powers.[48]

The army's operational concepts and structure were unserviceable at the outset, and scarcely improved thereafter. In North Africa, the theater in which (as an eloquent *Comando Supremo* memorandum put it in early 1941) "our flag is committed before all the world," Italian forces enjoyed a ratio of motor vehicles to men of about 1:20 on 1 June 1940. By early 1942 that ratio had dropped only insignificantly, to 1:19, while Rommel's forces enjoyed a ratio of 3.6 men to each vehicle. Infantry divisions and corps, the *Regio Esercito*'s basic operational

48. Bastico AAR, February 1943, NARA T-821/9/000232; Alessandro Massignani, *Alpini e tedeschi sul Don* (Novale di Valdagno, 1991), pp. 114–119; security: Hinsley et al., *Intelligence*, vol. 1, pp. 378–81; vol. 2, pp. 294, 588–89, 599.

Table 4.2: *Italian and British armored divisions, North Africa*[49] *(table of organization strength; actual combat strength was invariably lower)*

Italian armored division (*Ariete*)		British armored division, 1942
8,600	Officers and men	13,235
18	Anti-tank rifles	348
900	Machine guns	868
–	Light mortars	60
9	81mm mortars	18
70	Field guns	64
61	Anti-tank guns	219
34	Light anti-aircraft guns	88
918	Trucks	1,415
205	Other vehicles	374
–	Trailers	134
54	Artillery tractors	53
504	Motorcycles	956
–	Tracked ammunition carriers	151
–	Other armored vehicles	37
40	Armored cars	60
189	Tanks	280

units, could neither move at more than walking pace nor hope realistically to attack their British counterparts, even after discounting the 2.5:1 manpower advantage of the British three-brigade division over the Italian *divisione binaria* (see Table 4.1).[50]

The Italian motorized infantry division was similarly ill-equipped; Gàmbara had to explain patiently to the Germans that the *Trieste*, unlike a German light division, could only fight on foot and was at the mercy of "any idiot armored car" when mounted in its defenseless trucks.[51] The virtual absence of effective anti-aircraft defense except for a few modern 20mm cannon meant that occasional flights of

49. Tables 4.1 and 4.2 adapted from *Africa*, vol. 3, pp. 707, 710 (the source's implausible figure of 250 anti-tank guns has been adjusted downward by subtracting the 47mm main guns of the division's tanks).
50. Base figures for ratios: *Africa*, vol. 1, pp. 463; vol. 3, p. 104; quotation: Montezemolo memorandum, 5 July 1941, Ceva, *Le forze armate*, p. 591.
51. *Africa*, vol. 2, p. 628.

British fighter bombers could paralyze whole Italian divisions; RAF attacks reduced Graziani himself to the verge of a nervous breakdown in August 1940.[52]

The Italian armored division was similarly uncompetitive, especially considering that the Italian M13 and M14 main battle tanks had half the weight and a fraction of the firepower and off-road speed of the Grant and Sherman tanks from the United States that British units in the desert received in increasing numbers in 1942 (Table 4.2). The *Ariete* as originally deployed to North Africa in February–March 1941 had been even more deficient; initially its only tanks had been a doomed regiment of 3.5-ton L3 tankettes, and it received no armored cars until spring 1942. Yet Graziani's successor, Gariboldi, had indignantly rejected Rommel's well-meant March 1941 suggestion that the North African command attach additional vehicles, artillery, and support units to the division to give it the mobility and firepower needed to fight alongside German units. The army staff had established the division's table of organization and equipment, and that – except for the addition of M13 medium tank battalions to supplement the useless L3s – was that.[53]

Not even the airborne operations that became possible by 1942 – despite a perceptible lack of enthusiasm in the army leadership – offered much prospect of operational movement. The *Comando Supremo* estimated in 1941 that dropping the entire paratroop division (then being formed, and soon to be baptized *Folgore*) in a single lift would require sixteen months' production of transport aircraft, not including predictable aircraft losses in the meantime.[54]

Much of the penury that hampered Italian operations was deliberate: in an effort to render the *divisione binaria* "nimble" and "agile," Pariani and his successors had invented and implemented a theory of theater logistics found in no other army. A centralized *Intendenza*, equipped with the lion's share of the few trucks the army staff saw fit to provide, would replenish corps, divisions, and even regiments *from the rear forward* on a daily basis. In 1940-43 fear of logistical abandonment consequently rooted to the spot all division and corps commanders facing the enemy. Even immobility might not ensure the uninterrupted resupply without which their units, lacking organic transport

52. Knox, *Mussolini*, p. 163 (Graziani diary, ACS).
53. Gariboldi letter, printed in *Africa*, vol. 2, pp. 29–30.
54. Di Giovanni, *Paracadutisti italiani*, p. 94.

and reserves of food, ammunition, and water, would disintegrate. The slightest movement might, and usually did, disrupt the supply chain. Nor did the highly effective German system of replenishment from the front back with divisional truck columns inspire emulation.[55] Cavallero was not even content with an *Intendenza* centralized dysfunctionally under the theater commander: he inexplicably placed supply of forward units in North Africa under his own immediate authority in August 1942.[56]

The army's logistical system frequently failed even on its own terms. Central vehicle maintenance depots in North Africa and elsewhere often functioned barely or not at all, and restricted further what little operational reach Italian ground forces might have possessed. As late as spring 1942 neither armored units nor *Intendenza* possessed trailers or specialized vehicles for the recovery and forward repair of immobilized armored vehicles. Unserviceable rates for trucks and other vehicles in North Africa approached 40 percent for much of the campaign. The multiplicity of types issued to units – in the forces sent to Russia alone, seventeen different species of light truck and thirty of heavy – taxed drivers and technicians, and made it almost impossible to ensure an adequate flow of replacement parts.[57] The war ministry also failed inexplicably to provide the units in Russia with low-temperature lubricants, necessary even in north Italian winters, for vehicles and weapons. The army's physical immobility and operational paralysis were powerfully overdetermined.

TACTICS

Tactics is the art of battlefield destruction of the enemy; its essence is the concentration of strength against enemy weakness. Tactical suc-

---

55. See Montanari's ironic comments on the army's quest for "*snello*" and "*agile*" units (*Africa*, vol. 3, p. 709), and the devastating analysis of Botti, "Logistica dei poveri," pp. 425–32, and "Problemi logistici," pp. 301–03; for the contrast with the German system, Mancinelli, *Dal fronte dell'Africa settentrionale*, pp. 46–47.
56. *Africa*, vol. 3, pp. 537–41.
57. See the sad tale of bureaucratic dysfunction in 1941–42 with regard to vehicle maintenance at all levels from the army staff downward, in *Africa*, vol. 3, pp. 864–65; vehicle totals/unserviceable, vol. 1, p. 170, note 185 (8 November 1940); vol. 2, pp. 17–19 (20 February 1941: 26 percent of 5,000); vol. 2, p. 440 (15 November 1941: 38.8 percent unserviceable); vol. 3, pp. 104, 106; Ceva, *La condotta italiana*, p. 71 (17 July 1941: 36 percent of the entire army's 47,500 motor vehicles unserviceable); types in Russia: Ceva, "Industria bellica ed esercito," p. 247.

cess, like that at the operational level, requires seasoned and daring leadership, creative freedom for subordinates, foresight, coordination, movement and surprise, firepower, and support. The *Regio Esercito*'s recruitment, training, and promotion policies; tactical intelligence and reconnaissance; tactical communications; ability to engage the enemy in a coordinated manner; and support of its combat units were all moderately to severely deficient.

Part of the inheritance of the *Regio Esercito* hierarchy was a congenital inability to create cohesive fighting units. Fear of regional mutinies and the Liberal state's hope that military service would "make Italians" had from the mid-1870s dictated the recruitment of each regiment from several different regions, and its stationing in yet another region.[58] Only the Alpine divisions, in which each battalion derived from the close-knit mountain communities of a particular valley, were exempt. Neither the battlefield disadvantages of national recruitment in a society fractured by dialects, nor the enormously slow and cumbersome mobilization system that resulted, nor the obvious success of the German and British armies in creating strikingly cohesive regiments and battalions through regional recruitment led to revision of what by the 1940s had become time-hallowed dogma.

Relentless individual and unit training might have redeemed the performance of units thrown together from disparate human materials. The obvious alternatives or complements to such training were ideological fanaticism on the one hand, and the disciplinary terror that Cadorna had practiced enthusiastically in 1915–18. Perhaps the *Regio Esercito* did modernize sufficiently after 1919 to see Cadorna's tactical moralism, his ascription of failure solely to cowardice or treason and his savage demands for ever more executions, as militarily unproductive. The army's initial catastrophes in 1940 and persistent visible inferiority to enemies and ally thereafter in any event ruled out the conjoined use of ideology and terror as practiced by Nazis and Soviets. That solution was not merely wholly outside the royal officer corps' mental world; it also required for its application leaders consecrated by success – even Cadorna had his victories – within military institutions that retained some shreds of professional self-respect.

The army's higher leadership did not discover the connection between training and military performance until 1941. Pariani sent a senior commander off to Libya as late as 1937 with the remarkable

---

58. See Rochat, "Strutture dell'esercito dell'Italia liberale: i reggimenti di fanteria e bersaglieri," in his *L'esercito italiano in pace e in guerra*, pp. 41–73.

injunction not to do "too much training." An eminent staff officer, in a well-known postwar work otherwise devoted to defending the wartime record of the armed forces, wrote of "the widespread assumption that in battle, intuition and individual valor counted for more than training."[59] With the unique exception of the paratroops of the *Folgore* division, whose brief but supremely professional resistance at El Alamein testified to the wisdom of their commanders and the effects of a year and a half of often imaginative training, no Italian ground unit in the Second World War entered combat as well prepared as corresponding units of the British or U.S. armies, much less those of Italy's German ally. On-the-job training was the norm, and even elite units did not escape: tank battalions of the *Ariete* division routinely received drivers and gunners who had never driven a tank, or had fired at most three rounds with the 47mm main gun.[60] Even commanders who understood the imperative necessity of training were helpless in the face of the army's force structure megalomania, which so diluted the officer corps' store of experience and talent that much training was of little use.[61]

The same combination of megalomania and neglect presided over the army's training of its junior leaders. Throughout the interwar period the hierarchy had deliberately limited the intake of regulars in order to provide the privileged few with decorous careers. In wartime, as in other armies, the immense majority of junior officers were reservists: 90 percent of all lieutenants and two-thirds of all captains as of March 1942.[62] But unlike other armies, the *Regio Esercito* made virtually no attempt to select its reserve officers for military aptitude or to train them to recognizable standards of tactical or technical competence. Well over 90 percent of officer candidates normally received commissions after courses that the school authorities themselves recognized as wholly inadequate. University officer training courses employed instructors who – in the words of a senior commander – were on occasion "so incompetent as to give rise to criticism and comments among the officer candidates." Selection, insofar as it existed, merely

59. Mario Caracciolo, *La tragedia dell'esercito italiano*, p. 43; Faldella, *L'Italia e la seconda guerra mondiale*, p. 114; on pre-war training see also Roatta, *Otto milioni di baionette* (Verona, 1946), pp. 37–41.
60. Enrico Serra, *Tempi duri: Guerra e Resistenza* (Bologna, 1996), p. 122; also *Africa*, vol. 2, pp. 792–93; Ceva and Curami, *Meccanizzazione*, vol. 1, p. 309.
61. See particularly almost despairing circulars on unit training and readiness issued in 1942–43 by the commander of 5th Army (garrison units in central Italy and Sardinia), Caracciolo di Feroleto: NARA T-821/86/000872ff.
62. Figures: Rochat, "Uomini alle armi," Table E.4, p. 287.

eliminated those who were physically unfit. Overage retreads from earlier wars, the army's principal source of captains and majors, had even less training in modern warfare than the green lieutenants, and often collapsed in the face of the physical and psychological rigors of combat. Worse still, according to one retired general whose opinion the *Comando Supremo* found worthy of respect, junior regular officers in too many cases "allowed themselves to be attracted by choice to the quietism of sedentary functions" in the army's immense bureaucracies.[63]

The army hierarchy's deliberate stunting of its NCOs deprived combat units of the experienced leaders that might have compensated for the inadequacies of the army's junior officers. The NCO corps was calculatedly small (only 41,200 NCOs and technical specialists to 56,500 officers in June 1940) and long-service NCOs served primarily in unit administration.[64] The army's promotion system, although less static at the lower ranks – due to greater battlefield attrition – than for general officers, also offered little motivation to the competent. NCOs, in particular, could not aspire to become officers, as in the *Wehrmacht* or even the U.S. Army; battlefield commissions were apparently unknown to the *Regio Esercito*.

These forces were not the only impediments to the creation and maintenance of well-led and cohesive units. Strategic improvisation in attacking Greece begot organizational improvisation. Less than a month before the attack, with Badoglio's eager assent, Mussolini had ordered the demobilization of 600,000 men – half the army stationed in Italy. The army staff consequently found itself by November 1940 shipping to Albania units hastily filled out with partially trained reservists and untrained recruits; the regime and perhaps the army staff as well had apparently lacked the moral courage to recall the trained reservists the army had just released. The Albanian command threw these units into line a battalion at a time, as they disembarked,

---

63. Rochat, "Qualche dato sugli ufficiali di complemento dell'esercito nel 1940," *Ricerche Storiche* 18:3 (1993), pp. 616, 621–23 (data for 1940, with excerpts from the school commanders' reports); Roatta, *Otto milioni di baionette*, pp. 32–33; OTC instructors: Caracciolo (5th Army) to subordinate commands, 19 January 1942, NARA T-821/86/001029; *"funzioni sedentarie"*: Bongiovanni to Mussolini, "Vincere la guerra," 15 March 1941, p. 32, NARA T-821/249/000412; *Africa*, vol. 3, pp. 876–77 (retreads: vol. 2, p. 812); and in general, Sullivan, "The Primacy of Politics: The Influence of Civil-Military Relations on Italian Army and Fascist Militia Junior Officer Selection and Training, 1918–1940," in Elliott V. Converse III, ed., *Forging the Sword: Selecting, Educating, and Training Cadets and Junior Officers in the Modern World* (Chicago, 1998), pp. 65–81.
64. Montanari, *Alla vigilia*, p. 220.

often without their supporting weapons, communications, or supply echelons. Cavallero, who was ultimately responsible as theater commander, put it unhappily as late as March 1941: "we are making a tossed salad!" Under these conditions, units blessed with particularly inept commanders collapsed; the cases of the "Wolves of Tuscany" and Bari divisions were especially conspicuous.[65]

In addition – and throughout the war – the caste mentality of the officer corps itself precluded a relationship of trust with the lower orders. Officers had by right personal servants, better uniforms and equipment, more leave, and above all more and better food and drink than their enlisted men. General officers often viewed the troops with a patronizing self-sufficiency that sometimes cost lives – including their own, as in the case of General Federico Ferrari Orsi, who walked into a minefield at El Alamein after apparently ignoring an enlisted man's warning.[66] The exceptions were above all the officers of the Alpine troops and of elite units such as the *Folgore*, where common danger, specialization, and esprit de corps created a bond between ranks that overcame the officer corps' hierarchical mentality. One *Folgore* recruit noted almost with wonder: "if we have to jump off a four meter wall, the senior ranks jump first, and then we jump." The usual sort of junior officers, "full of exaggerated dignity and bluster," did not survive in such an atmosphere.[67]

After the initial defeats, and at the urging of Mussolini himself, the army staff polled subordinate units for their views on adopting the German system of common rations and food distribution for officers and men, at least in the field.[68] The replies received at 2nd Army, at that point occupying Yugoslavia, have survived. Most corps commanders took a favorable view for logistical rather than leadership reasons, but "the mass of the officers" was apparently far from delighted.[69] One commander insisted that officers were simply not capable of functioning on the normal enlisted ration of a mess tin slopped full of pasta or

65. Roatta, *Otto milioni di baionette*, p. 131, and the more nuanced Roatta to *Comando Supremo*, 13 November 1940, in Biagini and Ferdinando Frattolillo, eds., *Diario Storico del Comando Supremo* (Rome, 1986–), vol. 2, part 2, pp. 161–62; "Stiamo facendo un'insalata!" and Bari: Montanari, *Grecia*, vol. 1, pp. 724, 282, 293–94, 308; "Wolves of Tuscany": Knox, *Mussolini*, pp. 258–59, and the Albanian Command file, NARA T-821/210/000080ff.
66. See Raffaele Doronzo, *Folgore! . . . e si moriva: Diario di un paracadutista* (Milan, 1978), pp. 93–94, and Cavallero, *Comando Supremo* (Bologna, 1948), pp. 346, 333.
67. Doronzo, *Folgore!*, pp. 12, 33.
68. Cavallero, *Diario 1940–1943*, p. 211; Scuero (War Ministry) to major commands; Scuero to Ambrosio (2nd Army), 26 July 1941, NARA T-821/395/000034–36, 000041.
69. Corpo d'Armata Celere (Ferrari Orsi) to 2nd Army, 28 August 1941, ibid., 000014–17

crude minestrone: "the officers' mess relaxes [*ristora*] and puts the officer in the physical and psychological conditions necessary for the
accomplishment of his far from easy task . . . there must be some dif-
ferentiation – for the purposes of the officers' morale."[70] The suppression of officers' field messes might also produce "excessive famil-
iarity [*domestichezza*] and consequent loss of prestige," as well as a loss
of "collaboration and comradeship" among unit officers.[71] Finally, the
new system, if extended to garrison, might lead to "diminution of the
already tenuous authority of the young subalterns, as a consequence of
the suppression of formal distinctions."[72] The fierceness of the officer
corps' defense of "formal distinctions" suggests the extent of its doubts
about its own ability to lead.

The disasters of winter 1940–41 led the staff to diagnose belatedly
the army's vices in leadership and training. In an emphatic circular that
made no reference to his own heavy responsibility for the deficiencies
revealed in recent disasters, Roatta listed yawning gaps in the professional accomplishments of Italy's junior leaders and troops. Junior officers suffered from:

1. insufficient capacity for command (lack of authority, timidity in ordering
   and demanding, uncertainty in addressing troops),
2. inadequate knowledge of the mechanical side of weapons,
3. limited knowledge of small-unit tactics,
4. rudimentary knowledge of communications equipment and organization,
5. insufficient knowledge of how to read topographic maps, and little understanding of the compass,
6. insufficient knowledge of field fortification,
7. inadequate conditioning for long marches, [and]
8. total administrative ignorance.

NCOs were correspondingly deficient, and showed an "almost total
absence of initiative." The troops themselves tended to act only in
response to direct orders, were poorly acquainted with their individual weapons and with siting and digging foxholes, and were prone to
"extreme emotional reactions to threats, real or assumed, to their
flanks or rear." Roatta closed with an astonishing exhortation that documents – by the fact that he felt the need to utter it – the army's professional destitution: "Instructors must keep in mind that battles are

70. XI Corps (Robotti) to 2nd Army, 26 August 1941, ibid., 000018–20.
71. VI Corps (Dalmazzo) to 2nd Army, 24 August 1941, ibid., 000023–25.
72. V Corps (Balocco) to 2nd Army, 24 August 1941, ibid., 000026–27.

not only won on the battlefield, in the face of the enemy, but also in the barracks, on the firing ranges, and in field exercises."[73]

Roatta's remedies were reasonable ones, given competent instructors: much practice in platoon and company tactics "using a variety of simple tactical situations, close to the real thing." Cavallero, evidently converted to the necessity for training by his hard winter in command in Albania, took a hand in June 1941, and personally ordered the creation of training battalions for the junior leaders of units destined for early combat. Roatta's implementing order was a compound of common sense (as much live-fire and anti-tank training as possible) and bluster: "education [*la cultura*] counts for nothing." *La cultura* might indeed count for nothing until it was time to navigate in the desert or adjust mortar fire. Italian units in North Africa prized enemy vehicle compasses, but even in *Ariete* their effective use was a skill that few tank commanders possessed.[74]

The consequences of the army's discovery of training in spring-summer 1941 are hard to establish with precision. But with the conspicuous exception of the armored or motorized units and the *Folgore*, which attracted large numbers of career officers, some of them of distinguished lineage, the average infantry battalion in North Africa in 1942 still had one or two regular officers at best, with corresponding shortages of experienced NCOs. The reserve officers, in the words of a division commander at El Alamein, were willing to learn but suffered from "notable deficiencies in professional preparation." The result was inevitably the overtaxing of the few regulars, and repeated crises that a corps commander in that same theater summed up scathingly to his division commanders in July 1942: "the lack of will to defend to the end, if attacked, is widespread among our soldiers, and is beyond doubt a result of the faults of our cadres."[75]

A final built-in deficiency in training that the army never even attempted to remedy was what the very perceptive military attaché in Berlin, in reporting the disintegration of 8th Army in Russia, des-

---

73. All from Annex 2 to Roatta circular, 4100, 15 March 1941, NARA T-821/-130/000870–72 (emphasis in original).
74. Cavallero to Roatta, 8 June 1941; Roatta to major commands, 15 June 1941, in Ceva, *La condotta italiana*, pp. 151–52, 161–64; Bizzi report, March 1942, in Ceva and Curami, *Meccanizzazione*, vol. 2, p. 340 (also NARA T-821/250/000100ff.); Serra, *Tempi duri*, p. 139.
75. Fabris AAR, April 1943, NARA T-821/355/000644–55; Bastico AAR, February 1943, T-821/9/000226–27; Gioda to division commanders, 18 July 1942, *Africa*, vol. 3, p. 950.

cribed scornfully as "the principle that service support personnel do not fight." Italian support and headquarters units, unlike German ones, did not train as infantry and normally made no attempt to establish all-around defensive perimeters to ward off enemy raids. In North Africa that principle proved dangerous. In Russia it proved fatal: during the retreat from the Don, Soviet armor patrols attacked the main Italian logistical base at Kantemirovka and routed both service troops and thousands of infantry undergoing reorganization.[76]

A further limit on the army's tactical effectiveness was its inability to avoid surprise and to inflict it on the enemy through intelligence and reconnaissance. Even the *Ariete* was short of two-way voice radios for its tanks until spring 1942. The equipment it did eventually receive broke down at intervals from the shaking received during movement and battle. The continuing weakness of communications at regimental level and above deprived signals intelligence and air reconnaissance of much of their timeliness. An on-the-spot investigation into armored vehicles and tactics in North Africa made at *Comando Supremo* request in winter–spring 1941–42, at the height of the *Ariete*'s relative success, gives the measure of the tactical blindness (in the literal sense) that attended the most effective Italian offensive actions of the war:

> our troops . . . lacking both speedy armored cars with which to locate the enemy and air reconnaissance . . . end up steering [toward the enemy] more or less randomly, using above all what evidence there is of the direction of incoming artillery fire, which however emanates from extremely mobile [British] batteries spread over a wide front.

Not until late spring 1942 did *Ariete* finally receive a short-lived reconnaissance battalion with forty radio-equipped armored cars.[77] Italian infantry divisions had to rely on foot patrols for direct information about the enemy. But no activity in war requires more of the junior leaders whose selection and training the army had so neglected; the paratroops of the *Folgore* and some Alpine divisions were the only units consistently capable of effective patrolling.

The overall key to the army's offensive tactics in 1940–43 was neither movement nor surprise but the *Regio Esercito*'s time-honored faith in numbers. A British analyst writing in late 1940 or early 1941 noted:

---

76. Ceva, *Le forze armate*, p. 564 note; Mancinelli, *Dal fronte dell'Africa settentrionale*, p. 65.
77. Bizzi report, March 1942, in Ceva and Curami, *Meccanizzazione*, vol. 2, p. 344 (see also vol. 1, p. 310); *Africa*, vol. 3, pp. 198–99.

The principal characteristic of Italian tactics in both theaters, Libya and East Africa, has been rigidity. They have remained attached to one principle, the concentration of the greatest possible mass for every task that faces them. In the attack they deploy this mass in line and rely solely on weight of numbers to clear the way.[78]

If stalled, Italian commanders attempted to regain momentum by committing their reserves frontally to reinforce failure.

Tactical rigidity stemmed in part from the already described deficiencies in junior leadership and unit training that rendered Italian infantry incapable of infiltrating enemy positions in small semi-independent groups – the German method of 1917–18 that became the basis of small-unit tactics for the remainder of the century.[79] But in a larger sense rigidity was the consequence of the deliberate choice of numbers over machines that persisted to the bitter end in 1943.

Only in North Africa did a new tactical style, improvised and poorly understood by the hierarchy, emerge. Despite what Bastico rightly described as the "brutal qualitative and quantitative inferiority" of its equipment, *Ariete* developed some limited ability to move at night, to find and attack enemy flanks and rear, to use deception by feinting withdrawal or creating clouds of dust to bluff the superior British into pulling back. The effective range of the 47mm main tank gun against British armor of around 600 meters severely constrained its commanders. *Ariete* armored battalions in the attack tended to make mad dashes toward the enemy at the M13's lamentable cross-country top speed of roughly 13 kilometers per hour, to bring the range down to 400 meters or less before British artillery and tank guns could perforate too many Italian tanks. Closer ranges also made best use of the M13's limited ammunition supply; as in other forms of firefight, the side that ran out first suffered deep embarrassment.[80] The arrival in spring 1942 of FIAT-Ansaldo 75mm assault guns on an M14 chassis allowed the *Ariete* and the newly arrived *Littorio* division a somewhat wider tactical repertoire, until British deployment of U.S. medium tanks eventually negated that small advantage.

In the desert, even the best Italian infantry was capable only of stat-

78. Ceva, *La condotta italiana*, pp. 190–92 (my retranslation).
79. See the lament of Cavallero after the failed March 1941 counteroffensive in Albania: Knox, *Mussolini*, p. 260, and Montanari, *Grecia*, vol. 1, pp. 656–57, 664, 667–69, 680–83.
80. Quotation: Bastico AAR, February 1943, NARA T-821/9/000226; on *Ariete* tactics, see particularly Oderisio Piscicelli-Taeggi, *Diario di un combattente in Africa settentrionale* (Bari, 1946), pp. 34–42, and Bizzi report, March 1942, in Ceva and Curami, *Meccanizzazione*, vol. 2, pp. 344–45.

ic defense and was poorly equipped even for that. But in hilly or mountainous terrain, and despite all their deficiencies in cadres and armament, Italian infantry units often fought remarkably well, as demonstrated by their dogged stand at Keren in East Africa throughout February and March 1941, Cavallero's laboriously constructed but ultimately impenetrable "wall" against the Greeks in Albania, and the often excellent performance of improvised Italian units in the final battles in Tunisia. Even in the desert, infantry units such as the paratroops of the *Folgore* and the improvised unit of volunteers that became the *"Giovani Fascisti"* division fought in a manner that inspired German respect.

And the army – for all its manifold faults – at least had a conception of the integration of arms denied to some its British adversaries, who as late as El Alamein attempted to funnel two corps – one infantry, one armored – simultaneously through a narrow attack corridor without effective coordination between them.[81] The Italian mobile units that accompanied Rommel in his desert peregrinations learned far more quickly than the British the lesson that armor, artillery, and infantry must function as a team. The German example was decisive, but Italian doctrine, precisely because its authors had never heard of the work of the British all-tank theorists, was already predisposed toward integration. Army doctrine inevitably proclaimed the absolute primacy of the infantry, "the decisive element of combat; if it advances, all advance, if it gives way, all give way," But it also stressed the obvious necessity for infantry-artillery cooperation. Armor, which the army saw as a supporting weapon until 1941 and even thereafter, was similarly linked to the infantry.[82] Weak communications, inadequate training, and the army's 1914–18 artillery limited the effectiveness of all-arms cooperation. On the offensive, Italian artillery frequently could not cover or talk to its infantry. But on the defensive, artillery support was generally more effective. The commander of the *Ariete* in its final desperate stand at El Alamein could plausibly claim that Italian artillery, with its emphasis on centralized direction, had in Montgomery's set-piece 1918 battle cooperated with other arms more effectively than had the decentralized German gunners.[83]

The army would also have gladly used close air support: in

---

81. On this well-known episode, which reflects so poorly on Montgomery, see the balanced comments of Montanari (*Africa*, vol. 3, pp. 832–33).
82. See especially the survey of army doctrine in Montanari, *Alla vigilia*, pp. 252–74.
83. Arena AAR, 13 December 1942, NARA T-821/31/000011–12; also (rhetorically) Messe AAR on Enfidaville, 30 April 1943, *Africa*, vol. 4, pp. 760, 765.

June–July 1940 its forward units in Libya had frantically demanded medium bomber sorties to ward off British armored cars. But the failure of the air force and of Italian industry to develop effective ground attack aircraft until 1942 and the absence throughout of voice radio and effective smoke grenade signals linking Italian (but apparently not German) ground units with Italian aircraft overhead made close support of the kind practiced by the RAF and British 8th Army a utopian aspiration.[84]

Finally, the logistical support the army provided to its line units was as inconsistent with tactical success as were its training and tactical methods. Combat units in all theaters, once committed, were perpetually short of fuel, ammunition, water, food, vehicles, weapons, and even manpower. But the army hierarchy was not finished. The troops' rations, even when they arrived, were by universal testimony execrable in quality and notably inferior in quantity to the rations of enemy or ally; they contained even fewer calories than the already barely adequate Italian rations of the First World War. The army's mobile kitchens consisted of primitive woodburning devices dating from 1907–09 that were as useless in treeless North Africa as they were difficult to load and transport. Armored and motorized units might improvise mess vehicles in imitation of the motorized field kitchens and portable gasoline stoves of their German allies. But Italian infantrymen in their holes in the desert, when they ate at all, ate cold canned goods and hardtack.[85]

The services most vital to troop morale after food – medical care and evacuation, mail delivery, home leave, and rotation out of combat – were likewise frighteningly deficient. The army began the Greek campaign with two ambulance platoons in all Albania, although improvised air evacuation did good service thereafter for those wounded lucky enough to reach the airfields alive. Field medical services were ineffectual throughout the war; Italian units in North Africa were perhaps better at field sanitation than their German allies, but both lived amid clouds of flies and suffered inordinately from dysentery and hepatitis. The army's mail service was from the outset wholly inadequate, despite a stream of complaints from combat units and frequent mention in the morale reports that the military police drafted for the hierarchy. Leave was infrequent, and until autumn 1942, despite the

84. See especially *Africa*, vol. 3, p. 613 (July 1942).
85. Rations: Ceva, *Le forze armate*, p. 269; Botti, "Logistica dei poveri," pp. 432–33; Serra, *Tempi duri*, p. 122; Cavallero, *Diario 1940–1943*, p. 448.

German example of tours of duty of twelve months or less, the *Regio Esercito* required that its enlisted men serve a full thirty-four months in North Africa before rotation. The troops inevitably came to regard themselves, as Bastico put it in early 1943, as "sentenced to remain 'until consumed.'" They were not wrong.

Issue clothing and personal equipment ranged from the inferior to the unusable: enlisted uniforms came unsewed and the famous "cardboard" boots disintegrated in the snow and mud of Albania. The war ministry gratuitously rejected requests from the units in Russia for felt *valenki* to replace the hobnailed alpine boots that invariably caused frostbite. The troops were also perpetually short of small items that made the difference between discomfort and despair: buttons, thread, needles, razor blades, envelopes, writing paper, postcards, pencils, and rank and unit badges. Finally, the self-contradictory and almost unimaginably complex regulations governing unit administration and finance, which the Italian state and its army had evolved as an ineffectual barrier to corruption, exacted an enormous cost in wasted energy at company and battalion level.[86]

These dysfunctions for the most part derived neither from penury nor from technological backwardness, but rather from the attitudes of the higher officer corps. Roatta, for instance, made light of the accumulation of sixty tons of undelivered troop mail at Bologna in July 1940, ascribing complaints to the "pathological Italian characteristic of insisting on daily news of relatives about whom the average soldier, in normal circumstances, is merrily unconcerned."[87] Mail service did not improve thereafter because the hierarchy was unable to understand that caring for the troops might lead the troops to reciprocate – a concept Roatta might have absorbed during his pre-war duty as attaché in Berlin, but had not.[88] The army's lack of cohesion was mysterious primarily to its higher leadership.

The troops themselves in any event did not necessarily show in 1940–43 the readiness to surrender of popular legend. Units in North

---

86. Medical service, sanitation: De Risio, *Servizi segreti*, p. 84; *Africa*, vol. 2, pp. 794–95; David Hunt, *A Don at War* (London, 1966), p. 135; for graphic description, Doronzo, *Folgore!*; mail: *Africa*, vol. 1, pp. 96, 433; vol. 3, p. 996; leave and rotation: *Africa*, vol. 1, p. 433; vol., 3, pp. 98, 339–40, 995; vol. 4, p. 574; Bastico AAR, February 1943, NARA T-821/9/000233; sundries: *Africa*, vol. 4, p. 576; administrative burdens: Botti, "Logistica dei poveri," pp. 425–26.
87. 4 July entry, Roatta to Graziani, 140, 9 July 1940, ACS, Carte Graziani, bundle 42.
88. See Oberkommando des Heeres, H.Dv. 300/1, *Truppenführung*, I. Teil (Berlin, 1936), paragraph 8: "[The leader] must . . . find the way to the hearts of his subordinates and earn their trust through . . . tireless attention to their welfare."

Africa, Albania, and Russia held together in conditions deriving from the army's logistical inadequacies that would have caused soldiers of the industrial democracies to quail.[89] With the exception of the Albanian retreat of 1940–41, where the disorganization resulting from hasty remobilization and chaotic shipment overseas was decisive, Italian collapse, like that of the French in 1940, tended to stem from surprise envelopment by enemy mobile forces. Graziani's desert débâcle of December 1940–February 1941, with its 130,000 prisoners out of a total force of 140,000 to 150,000, was nevertheless unique until the 600,000 prisoners that fell into German hands in September 1943.[90] In Albania, the casualty figures from the doomed March 1941 offensive that Mussolini ordered and Cavallero planned without regard for the deficiencies of his units and of their logistical support suggest that Italian troops were at least as willing to die in fruitless frontal assaults as they had been in 1915–18: almost 25,000 casualties from two corps in six days, including 29 per cent of the infantry and artillery strength of the lead corps.[91] In their ratio of dead and wounded to prisoners of war – a key indicator of commitment to the fight – Italian forces in North Africa rivaled their German allies from the beginning of the British offensive at El Alamein to the final collapse at Tunis: 3 dead or wounded to every 7 prisoners, against 3.4 dead or wounded to every 6.6 prisoners for the Germans.[92] That record also suggests the extent to which the troops, even after a long string of defeats, responded to capable commanders – for Messe's last fight in Tunisia was the best-led Italian campaign of the war.

CONCLUSION: THE WEIGHT OF THE PAST

The army's lamentable performance in 1940–43 derived in part from factors other than institutional failure. The backwardness of Italian society compared to those of ally and enemies, the failure of dictator and regime to prepare and mobilize Italy effectively for war, concep-

---

89. For life in North Africa with the *Ariete* armored division, see the diary of Serra, *Tempi duri*; for the Russian front, especially Nuto Revelli, *Mai tardi: Diario di un alpino in Russia* (Turin, 1989).
90. Numbers: *Africa*, vol. 1, p. 443 note 5; Schreiber, "Gli internati militari in Germania," in Rainero, ed., *L'Italia in guerra: Il quarto anno – 1943* (Gaeta, 1994), p. 531.
91. Montanari, *Grecia*, vol. 1, pp. 667, 669–70; see also 661 (also Chapter 9, for Italian failure even to assure numerical superiority).
92. Calculated from *Africa*, vol. 4, p. 550; it seems unlikely that the difference between allies is statistically significant.

tual and organizational dysfunctions common to all three armed forces, and "Duce strategy," the dictator's insistence on scattering Italy's meager resources from the Channel coast to Ethiopia and from southern France to the Balkans and the Don, all contributed power-fully to defeat and humiliation.

Yet the final indignity of Italy's war, the delivery of 600,000 of its soldiers as slave laborers to the German Reich in September 1943, was the doing of the generals and king, who after removing Mussolini on 25 July 1943 made the worst of the desperate situation he had created. They and the aged and passive Badoglio, the king's choice as Mus-solini's successor, so feared the Germans that they deliberately and consciously refrained from preparing the armed forces to implement the approaching armistice with the Western powers and to resist the savage German reaction it would provoke. The disorderly flight of Badoglio, Ambrosio, and the king from Rome at the announcement of the armistice on 8–9 September 1943 intentionally left the army with-out orders, and ensured that what little resistance it offered was disor-ganized and brief.[93]

The army was a decisive factor in Fascism's seizure of power in 1922–25 and an inescapable part of its inheritance. The *Regio Esercito*'s very autonomy after 1922 refutes the often-made claim that Mussolini, by suppressing public debate on military affairs and by selecting his chief subordinates with an eye to his own power rather than to mili-tary effectiveness, precluded military modernization.[94] Neither a con-trolled press nor a high degree of professional autonomy inhibited the modernization of the German army in the 1930s. Conversely, the open societies of interwar France and Britain tolerated armies striking in their backwardness. The Regio Esercito's failure to modernize result-ed above all from the attitudes of its leaders, with Diaz at their head.[95] They destroyed Di Giorgio, the reforming minister of war of 1924–25, and with him the best chance for some small degree of renewal. Mussolini bore formal responsibility for that step, but it was the generals who decided. The revolt of Italy's admirals against the air-

93. An immense polemical literature exists; see above all Aga Rossi, *Una nazione allo sban-do*, pp. 45–46, 66–73, 79–124, and her *L'inganno reciproco: l'armistizio tra l'Italia e gli angloamericani del settembre 1943* (Rome, 1993)

94. For this thesis, see the works of Rochat since the 1960s and his recent restatement, with references to earlier work: "Il fascismo e la preparazione militare al conflitto mondi-ale," pp. 151–65 in Angelo Del Boca et al., eds., *Il regime fascista: Storia e storiografia* (Bari, 1995).

95. Sema, "La cultura dell'esercito," explains in detail the inherited *mentalité* of the officer corps.

craft carrier, which they damned almost unanimously in solemn conclave and in Mussolini's presence in 1925 and publicly anathematized thereafter, suggests that the perverse use the army made of its autonomy was not unique in the Italian armed forces.[96]

The army's institutional character and officer corps – its inheritance from its own past – was the chief determinant of its trajectory through Fascism to disintegration in 1943. That officer corps had shown in the Great War many of the characteristics that distinguished it under Fascism. As during the nine months' grace period of 1939–40, when the army staff learned virtually nothing from Germany's destruction of Poland, the army had failed between autumn 1914 and May 1915 to draw useful operational or even tactical lessons from the trench fighting on the western front that its attachés closely observed.[97] Hostility to imagination and initiative were pervasive among its commanders. Cadorna's staff historical officer lamented to his diary in June 1917 that

> We have to confess that the Austrian [tactical system] is a great deal more nimble, more elastic than ours . . . the Austrian in his entire conception of warfare is less rigid than we are. It's odd, it may seem impossible, given our constant boasts about Latin geniality, but that's the way it is. [The Austrians] prove it every day . . .[98]

Italy's line units performed to their full potential only once, in the chaotic defensive battles on the Mt. Grappa massif in late 1917, when communications breakdown freed the army's by-then experienced division, regimental, and battalion commanders to fight an elastic defense without constant interference from above.[99]

---

96. For this episode, Alberto Santoni, "La mancata risposta della Regia Marina alle teorie del Douhet. Analisi storica del problema della portaerei in Italia," in *La figura e l'opera di Giulio Douhet* (Caserta, 1988), pp. 257–69 (Cavagnari's veto, p. 262); also Giorgio Giorgerini, *Da Matapan al Golfo Persico: La Marina militare italiana dal fascismo alla Repubblica* (Milan, 1989), pp. 420–445.

97. Compare Rochat, "La preparazione dell'esercito italiano nell'inverno 1914–15 in relazione alle informazioni disponibili sulla guerra di posizione," *Il Risorgimento* 13 (February 1961), pp. 10–32, with Roatta to Servizio Informazioni Militare, 16 September, 8, 19 October 1939, NARA T-821/108/000006–76; the army in 1939 concluded that the Germans had "pushed motorization to excess" (Servizio Informazioni Militare, *L'occupazione della Polonia* [Rome, 1939], p. 16).

98. Angelo Gatti, *Caporetto: Dal diario di guerra inedito (maggio–dicembre 1917)*, ed. Alberto Monticone (Bologna, 1964), p. 140; similarly, pp. 154–56.

99. See the detailed comparison between Italian and German doctrine and training in 1914–17 in Mario Silvestri, *Caporetto* (Milan, 1984), pp. 38–111, and Silvestri's analysis of the Grappa fighting, Chapter 23.

Care for the troops had been as lamentable in 1915–18 as in 1940–43. Units had languished for months in the mud and excrement of the trenches without rotation. Illness killed almost 30 percent of the roughly 500,000 dead of the *Regio Esercito*'s line units in 1915–18, whereas the German army, despite the privations inflicted by the Allied blockade, held its death rate from illness to under 10 percent. In the view from the trenches, the army hierarchy valued its troops less than its pack animals. Dead mules, noted a junior officer, cost money and therefore required "forms on top of forms, committees of inquiry. When a soldier dies, it's much simpler: a stroke through his name on the roster and a number on the morning report."[100]

As for training, Italy's company commanders, platoon leaders, squad leaders, and riflemen had in 1915–18 learned on the job and perished in the attempt, as in 1940–43. The Germans and to some extent the Austro-Hungarians had used their specialized assault units as a pattern on which to train the rest of the army, with spectacular results seen in Ludendorff's spring 1918 offensives. The *Regio Esercito* had designed its *Arditi*, its only units to receive regular live-fire tactical training, solely for swift raids, without the German emphasis on deep penetration as part of an operational design. The Italian high command employed them not as a model but as a substitute for a line infantry always clumsy in the attack and by 1917 too beaten down to show much offensive willpower. And after 1918, the army hierarchy hastily abolished the *Arditi* and ignored the tactical lessons the assault units had learned.[101]

Even the proclivity of some regular officers for the "quietism of sedentary functions" detected in 1940–43 was not new; the regular officer corps had also been missing in relative terms from the 1915–18 battlefield. Its *effort du sang* (only the French "blood effort" will serve) had registered as an overall 1915–18 death rate of 7.7 percent, hardly more than half that of the general run of Italians mobilized, and less than a third that of Germany's regular officers, of whom a staggering 24.8 percent had died in 1914–18.[102]

100. Paolo Caccia-Dominioni, quoted in Piero Melograni, *Storia politica della grande guerra 1915/1918* (Bari, 1969), p. 122 note 116; illness deaths: Ilari, *Storia del servizio militare*, vol. 2, p. 444, and F. Bumm, ed., *Deutschlands Gesundheitsverhältnisse unter dem Einfluss des Weltkrieges* (Stuttgart, 1928), p. 166.
101. Compare the story told in Bruce I. Gudmundsson, *Stormtroop Tactics: Innovation in the German Army, 1914–1918* (Westport, CT, 1989), with Rochat, *Gli arditi della Grande Guerra: Origini, battaglie e miti* (Gorizia, rev. ed., 1997), especially pp. 31–32, 131.
102. Figures: Ilari, *Storia del servizio militare*, vol. 2, pp. 443, 446, and Constantin von Altrock, *Vom Sterben des deutschen Offizierkorps* (Berlin, 2nd rev. ed., 1922), pp. 64, 69.

Finally, as in 1940–43, the pre-1922 officer corps had faced perennial difficulties in recruiting from the nation's limited pool of educated talent. Giolitti had cruelly remarked during the Great War that Italy's generals had emerged from a society that consigned to army careers the "stupidest sons of the family," the "black sheep and half-wits."[103] The same generals Giolitti had encountered as prime minister recruited and trained the men who became the generals of Mussolini. Fascism exacerbated an already pervasive reverence for numbers and for the power of the human spirit. The dictator's geopolitical fantasies and Hitler's failure in global war helped create a strategic situation that even far better trained and equipped armies could not have mastered. But the inherited and entrenched attitudes and habits of the military caste share responsibility with the regime for the uniquely demoralizing character of Italy's defeat.

Altrock's numbers cover a somewhat longer period (2 August 1914 to 10 January 1919) than Ilari's, but it is noteworthy that German regular officers far outdistanced in death not merely their Italian counterparts, but also their own troops, of whom only 15.4 percent died.

103. Malagodi, *Conversazioni della guerra*, vol. 1, pp. 58, 199–200 ("i discoli e i deficienti").

5

THE "PRUSSIAN IDEA OF FREEDOM" AND THE CAREER OPEN TO TALENT:

Battlefield Initiative and Social Ascent from Prussian Reform to Nazi Revolution, 1807–1944

> . . . the change in men weighs more heavily than that in technology. The French we met in battle were no longer those of 14/18. The relationship was like that between the revolutionary armies of 1796 and those of the [First] Coalition – only this time *we* are the revolutionaries and Sans-Culottes.
>
> – *Generalmajor Erich Marcks, 19 June 1940[1]*

Erich Marcks, soldier son of an eminent neo-Rankean, saw more clearly than he knew. In July 1940, a few weeks after he had written these lines, the German army staff gave him the intriguing task of drafting Germany's preliminary plan for an attack on Soviet Russia. That attempt at global Blitzkrieg, in both aims and consequences, was National Socialism's most revolutionary deed. Limitless military violence and pitiless racial-ideological genocide, conquest both external and internal, fused in the "East" into the consummation of the German Revolution.[2]

Like the Paris revolutions of 1789–94 and unlike the German "military strike" of 1918, the German Revolution of 1933–45 transformed politics and society at home while generating unprecedented external destruction. Yet except in the air, German technological or numerical superiority was either absent or contributed relatively little to the ruin of France and the humiliation of Britain in April–June 1940.[3] In the attack on Soviet Russia, as Omer Bartov has shown, most German units found themselves by winter 1941–42 reduced almost to the technological levels of the First World War against an increasingly mechanized and motorized enemy.[4] Yet Hitler's army fought on for a further three and a half years against ever-increasing odds.

---

1. Letter of 19 June 1940, quoted in Otto Jacobsen, *Erich Marcks: Soldat und Gelehrter* (Göttingen, 1971), pp. 87–8 (emphasis in original).
2. "Weltblitzkrieg": Hillgruber, *Hitlers Strategie*, p. 16.
3. See especially R. H. S. Stolfi, "Equipment for Victory in France in 1940," *History* 55 (1970), pp. 1–20.
4. Bartov, *Hitler's Army: Soldiers, Nazis, and War in the Third Reich* (Oxford, 1992), Chapter 1.

Operations research in the 1960s and 1970s suggested that the German army and Waffen-SS, whether in attack or defense, in favorable or unfavorable terrain and weather, with air cover or without it, enjoyed in 1943–44 an edge in combat effectiveness of roughly 1.2 to 1 against British and U.S. ground troops, and of up to 3 to 1 against the Soviets. Those figures were not news to surviving veterans of combat against the *Wehrmacht*. And in terms of casualty-inflicting power per man, the gap between the Germans and their adversaries was even greater: 1.55 to 1 against the Western powers and almost 6 to 1 against the Red Army.[5] In April 1945, Hitler repudiated his people as unworthy of world mastery, but to the bitter end his soldiers enjoyed world primacy in *Kampfkraft* – man-for-man tactical fighting power.[6]

Explanations for this excellence in the service and pursuit of evil have varied. The unfailing professionalism of Prusso-German forces from the Great Elector onward has long been an obvious and persuasive answer, although recent pioneering work has only partially charted the exact nature and extent of German professional military superiority in the twentieth century.[7] Scholarship on German battlefield performance in 1939–45 has also begun to pay ideology and terror a due long denied them. The German soldier in the "East," as Bartov has shown, could not always have conformed to the supposedly universal "primary group" model of combat motivation developed by American sociologists in and after the Second World War. Individual loyalty to comrades and leaders could not necessarily sustain the Germans in an environment so lethal that the life of new arrivals and of the eastern army's primary groups themselves was often measured

---

5. Trevor N. Dupuy, *Numbers, Predictions, and War: Using History to Evaluate Combat Factors and Predict the Outcome of Battles* (Indianapolis, 1979), pp. 86–97, 104, 108–110; for criticisms of Dupuy's method, and his defense, see John S. Brown, "Colonel Trevor N. Dupuy and the Mythos of *Wehrmacht* Superiority: A Reconsideration," *Military Affairs* 50/1 (1986), pp. 16–20; Dupuy, "Mythos or Verity? The Quantified Judgment Model and German Combat Effectiveness," *Military Affairs* 50/4 (1986), pp. 204–10.
6. For a definition of the concept, see Creveld, *Fighting Power*, p. 3.
7. See especially Martin Samuels, *Command or Control? Command, Training and Tactics in the British and German Armies, 1888-1918* (London, 1995), and *Doctrine and Dogma: German and British Infantry Tactics in the First World War* (Westport, CT, 1992); Williamson Murray, "The German Response to Victory in Poland: A Case Study in Professionalism," pp. 229–243 in his *German Military Effectiveness* (Baltimore, 1992); Creveld, *Fighting Power*; and the brilliant surveys by Michael Geyer, "The Past as Future: The German Officer Corps as Profession," in Geoffrey Cocks and Konrad H. Jarausch, eds., *German Professions, 1850-1950* (New York, 1990), pp. 183–212, and "Professionals and Junkers: German Rearmament and Politics in the Weimar Republic," in Richard Bessel and E. J. Feuchtwanger, eds., *Social Change and Political Development in Weimar Germany* (London, 1981), pp. 77–133.

in days or weeks.[8] Instead ideology forged a fictitious primary group, the *Kampfgemeinschaft* or German *Volk*-community embodied in its soldiery, that fought to the end because it *believed* in its own collective racial superiority, had faith in the Führer's word, and placed its hopes in the regime's promised new weapons of staggering power. Terror in a measure unprecedented in any modern army except Stalin's also punished with swift death all forms of "undermining the will to fight," from jokes about the leader's moustache to desertion in the face of the enemy. And criminal solidarity and fear of retribution – "blood cement," in a phrase that Hitler and Heinrich Himmler apparently derived from a popular biography of Genghis Khan – powerfully inhibited any impulse to surrender.[9]

Yet the precise balance and mix of the sources of German battlefield performance remain puzzling. Although ideology was in principle most in play in the cosmic struggle against the "Judeo-Bolshevik subhumans" of the Red Army, German forces fought with equal bitterness and effectiveness against Americans, British, and Canadians in the defensive attritional battles in Normandy, Aachen, and the Huertgen forest or in the offensive lunacy of the Ardennes. And professionalism is itself an elusive notion: in what sense were the fanatical boys, weary middle-aged men, and much-diluted cadres of the battered German army of 1944 more "professional" than their English, American, or Soviet counterparts?

It is at this point that the concept of revolution, and in particular the prototype offered by the social and military history of the French Revolution, may prove useful. That upheaval, propelled by ideologies unleashed through the political collapse of a highly stratified society, sent Europe to war for twenty-three years. The principal ingredients that combined to give France unparalleled external power were four: its tradition of operational, tactical, and military-technical innovation in the three decades preceding 1789; the desertion of much of the pre-1789 officer corps, the revolutionary purge of the remainder, and the consequent exuberant "career open to talent" for professional and

---

8. See especially E. A. Shils and Morris Janowitz, "Cohesion and Disintegration in the *Wehrmacht* in World War II," *Public Opinion Quarterly* 12 (1948), pp. 280–315, and (more recently, in the context of an overall assessment of German unit organization and performance), Creveld, *Fighting Power*, p. 45. For Bartov's evidence on life expectancy in the German infantry in Russia, see *Hitler's Army*, Chapter 2.

9. See Messerschmidt, "German Military Law in the Second World War," in Deist, ed., *The German Military in the Age of Total War* (Leamington Spa, 1985); for "Blutkitt," Richard Breitman, "Hitler and Genghis Khan," *Journal of Contemporary History* 25 (1990), pp. 345–47.

social ascent; the battlefield power of nationalist ideology; and (at least through 1794–95) the generous application of terror. The result was modern warfare: war between armed nations, or armed doctrines, in Edmund Burke's famous phrase, rather than princes and standing armies. Even before the advent of Napoleon, French battlefield superiority rested on the motivation, the tactical initiative and flexibility, and the logistical adaptability of France's soldiers and their junior leaders. The new tactical regulations of 1791 and the *amalgame* of line units and conscripts in 1793–94 gave France an army that was a unique synthesis of professionalism and revolution. It swept its enemies before it for twenty years.[10]

Just as French nationalism compelled the peoples of Europe to follow, the French military revolution forced the great powers to adapt or perish. Prussia learned most, and most swiftly. Crushing defeat at Jena-Auerstädt in 1806 forced on it military reforms that founded the leadership tradition that ultimately merged – in a later revolutionary era – with a new career open to talent, with a nationalist ideology that left Robespierre and Saint-Just in the shade, and with a terror far surpassing the puny efforts of the men of blood of 1793–94. The National Socialist *amalgame*, like its French predecessor, was a unique compound of tradition and revolution. And of its four principal elements, the contributions of tradition and those of careerism remain as yet relatively unexplored.

Neither element can be understood without analysis of the pivotal event in Prussian history, Prussia's response to defeat in 1806–07. From its beginnings as a major state, Prussia's existence had rested on battlefield success. At Jena and Auerstädt Napoleon had made brutally clear the direct connection between military prowess and France's newly transformed political and social order. Prussia therefore had to change, despite the timidity of its king, Frederick William III, and the recalcitrance of many in Prussia's almost exclusively noble officer corps. Defeat offered a brief opportunity to a unique group of reformers, mostly non-Prussian and in many cases non-noble. The most radical of them sought to unleash the same energies that powered revolutionary and imperial France by remaking Prussia as an economically advanced, self-governing, and intellectually free civil society. For Gerhard von Scharnhorst, son of a Hanoverian master sergeant and

---

10. The often-heard claim that the soldiers of 1793 were ideologically motivated amateurs while Napoleon's army was "professional" rests in part on the misconception, common in the Western democracies among both academics and soldiers, that fanaticism and professionalism are incompatible.

greatest of the military reformers, the foremost task was to "infuse the nation with the notion of self-reliance [*Selbständigkeit*]." Only *thinking combatants* could match the French in tactical initiative, flexibility, and willingness to die.[11]

The military reformers thus inaugurated a radical change in Prussian doctrine made feasible in turn by equally radical changes in troop recruitment, discipline, and motivation. The basis of the new system was individual initiative; recruitment, discipline, and motivation of officers and men rested on initiative's precondition, education, and its reward, the career open to talent within the framework of an explicit and unprecedented "alliance between government and nation." That alliance proved short-lived: with Napoleon caged, the Prussian state and its military-bureaucratic nobility refused to wither away. And the reformers themselves shared what Leonard Krieger has described as the "German idea of freedom," the conspicuously un-Lockean notion that freedom, both political and economic, is defined *by* rather than *against* the state. That notion left them powerless when the state turned on them after 1815.[12] Their legacies were a modern and supremely efficient bureaucratic absolutism that endured to 1918 and beyond, and a peculiarly Prussian freedom: a creativity on the battlefield increasingly divorced from the reforming politics from which it had sprung.

PRUSSIAN FREEDOM TO 1933

Selbständigkeit was not entirely unknown in Prussia before 1806. Frederick the Great had struggled with the problem that Prussia's mechanistic tactical system and his own artistry had in part created: a paucity of subordinates who could act intelligently on their own.[13] Reforming officers subsequently sought to loosen the rigid linear tactics inherited from Frederick even before their first encounter with the

---

11. Quoted in Rainer Wohlfeil, *Vom stehenden Heer des Absolutismus zur allgemeinen Wehrpflicht* (1789-1814), HDMG 2:105.
12. See Krieger, *The German Idea of Freedom*, especially pp. 30, 36; Hans Rosenberg, *Bureaucracy, Aristocracy, and Autocracy: The Prussian Experience, 1660-1815* (Cambridge, MA, 1958), especially pp. 206–210, and for general context, Reinhard Koselleck, *Preussen zwischen Reform und Revolution* (Stuttgart, 1967).
13. Dennis Showalter, *The Wars of Frederick the Great*, p. 109, argues that "the antecedents of the Prussian/German army's historic emphasis on *Auftragstaktik* had one of its taproots in Frederick's oblique order," but Showalter also suggests the narrow character of the initiative the king sought to foster, and its concentration at regimental or battalion level.

clouds of skirmishers of the French revolutionary armies in 1792–95.[14]

Catastrophe at Jena wrought almost instant change. At the operational level, the king issued instructions that gave higher commanders wide responsibility for deployment and movement to contact within the limits of the commander-in-chief's "overall concept."[15] At the tactical level, skirmishing, of which the essence was individual initiative, gained swift acceptance: defeating the French required it. The infantry *Reglement* of January 1812, the principal distillation of five years of doctrinal effort, was noteworthy for its parsimony: a slim pocket-sized volume a third the length of contemporary French, British, and Russian regulations. The authors of the *Reglement*, in contrast to the drillmasters of the pre-1806 era, accepted the disorder and confusion of the battlefield as given. They sought to limit that disorder less through detailed prescription than through general tactical principles whose application depended on the "sound common sense" of the commander and the "exceptional ability in the use of his weapon, physical agility, sound judgment, cunning, boldness at the right moment, and self-confidence" of the individual soldier.[16]

The 1812 *Reglement* proved a notable success in the wars of 1812–15. Its successors, although with gradually increasing emphasis on open-order combat, retained its basic features until well after the Franco-Prussian War.[17] Nor did the inevitable peacetime resurgence of the reformers' antagonists, the Prussian noble conservatives who had accepted reform in 1806–14 either grudgingly or not at all, lessen the army's insistence on battlefield creativity. By 1860, the most talented soldier among the royal princes, Frederick Charles, could write that

> in the Prussian corps of officers nowadays *there is a stronger desire for independence from above and for taking responsibility upon one's self than in any other army.* . . . *This habit of thought has undeniably had an influence on our battle-tac-*

14. See especially Peter Paret, *Yorck and the Era of Prussian Reform* (Princeton, 1966), and Charles Edward White, *The Enlightened Soldier: Scharnhorst and the Militärische Gesellschaft in Berlin, 1801-1805* (New York, 1989).

15. Frederick William III instruction to higher commanders, 18 November 1806, quoted in *Das preussische Heer der Befreiungskriege* (Berlin, 1914; Wiesbaden, 1982) vol. 1, pp. 246–47; also Dieter Ose, "Der 'Auftrag': eine deutsche militärische Tradition," *Europäische Wehrkunde* 31:6 (1982), pp. 264–65.

16. See in general Paret, *Yorck*, Chapter 5 (quotations, pp. 182, 185), and *Exerzir-Reglement für die Infanterie der königlich preussischen Armee* (Berlin, 1812), p. 103.

17. See the major revision of 1847, *Exerzir-Reglement für die Infanterie der Königlich Preussischen Armee* (Berlin, 1847), especially pp. 154–55, 162; the 1847 regulations reappeared with minor changes in 1870 and 1876 (Eugen von Frauenholz, *Das Gesicht der Schlacht: Taktik und Technik in der deutschen Kriegsgeschichte* [Stuttgart, 1937], p. 156).

tics. Prussian officers object to being hemmed in by rules and regulations, like officers in Russia, Austria and England. . . . We look at the way things tend to go and leave the individual more freedom to use initiative; we ride him on a looser rein, back up each separate success even if it had run counter to the intentions of a commander-in-chief such as Wellington, who used to insist on having full control over every unit at all times. But that you cannot have if subordinate commanders, without the knowledge or instructions of their seniors, go off into action on their own, exploiting each and every advantage, as they do with us.[18]

Battlefield conditions increasingly favored this leadership style; a new challenge – the Industrial Revolution – demanded a degree of *Selbständigkeit* far greater than anything required to defeat Napoleon. By 1870–71 the transformation of metallurgy and weapons design had multiplied the infantry's speed of fire up to five times compared to the Napoleonic period, and had increased effective combat range from the 50–100 meters of the musket to the 300 meters or more of the rifled breechloader. Firepower was swiftly eliminating movement and combat in closed and ordered bodies, the essence of warfare since the ancient world; in August 1870 at St. Privat the Prussian Guards made at a cost of over 8,000 casualties the same discovery that Lee and Pickett had made seven years earlier at Gettysburg. And although telegraph, railroad, and universal military service allowed the assembly of ever-larger armies, technology had yet to provide any means of tactical and operational field communication more advanced or effective than the battalion runner or the horse-borne staff officer.

The army's leaders, and especially the general staff of Helmuth von Moltke the elder that led the great victories of 1866–71, countered by accentuating the army's already marked emphasis on initiative. Moltke's "Instructions for Higher Commanders of 24 June 1869" sought to grapple with the central paradox resulting from the army's now-ingrained insistence on "independence from above and . . . taking responsibility upon one's self." Not only the "fog of uncertainty" shrouding the battlefield but also the very exercise of initiative by subordinates made it difficult for higher commanders to coordinate units in contact with the enemy. "The will of the superior" therefore had to guide "the intelligence that is widespread in the officer corps" and upon which the army depended. But except in rare emergencies, superiors conversely had a duty to respect the chain of command and to

---

18. "On the Origins and Development of the Spirit of the Prussian Officer, Its Manifestations and Its Effects" (January 1860), in Karl Demeter, *The German Officer-Corps in Society and State 1650–1945* (London, 1965), pp. 260–61 (emphasis in original).

refrain from giving direct orders to units far below them; the task of maintaining control consisted above all in restraining where necessary "the impulse to advance that by experience inspires our troops and their officers."[19]

Moltke's parting gift to the army was the infantry regulations of 1888, the field manual that finally superseded the principles of the 1812 *Reglement*. The 1888 manual was yet another slim volume in which training and tactics occupied only slightly more than 140 pages of text. It insisted that infantry combat was now "*as a rule decided by fire action*," and that consequently "*the swarm of skirmishers has become the chief combat technique [Hauptkampfform] of the infantry*." In deference to the effects of fire on communications as well as movement, the army now explicitly urged extreme parsimony in giving orders, for "orders from the rear were easily overtaken by events." The consequent un-ambiguous demand that subordinates act on their own initiative with-in the intent of the commander was the culmination of the army's doc-trinal development since 1806: "*Independence [Selbstthätigkeit] exercised within such boundaries is the foundation of great results in war*." Those subordinates now included the leaders of sections of twenty-five or so men, who were expected to "find on their own [*selbständig*] the means to carry out the tasks that have been set them or arising out of the combat situation". As had Moltke's "Instructions" of 1869, the 1888 regulations spelled out the narrow line that both superiors and subor-dinates must walk if initiative from below was not to lead to chaos, or supervision from above to paralysis.[20]

A further technological leap to the smokeless-powder small-bore magazine rifle, the machine gun, and the long-range shell-firing artillery piece was in progress as the regulations of 1888 were pub-lished. The result by 1900 was a battlefield so dominated by firepow-er that assault in closed ranks was suicidal and communication with higher commanders was broken; once in contact with the enemy, a leader's span of control extended no further than the men visible from ground level. The German infantry regulations of 1906 and field ser-

19. Daniel J. Hughes, *Moltke on the Art of War: Selected Writings* (Novato, CA, 1993), pp. 173, 177, 205, 216.
20. *Exerzir-Reglement für die Infanterie* (Berlin, 1889)(promulgated 1 September 1888), pp. 93, 94, 109, 126 (emphasis in original), and pp. 141–2; see also the index entries for "Selbständigkeit," index p. 19. For the drafting of the *Reglement*, see E. Freiherr von Gayl, *General von Schlichting und sein Lebenswerk* (Berlin, 1913), pp. 120, 125, 271-72. Its text (see especially pp. 93–94, paragraphs 13, 14, 19) does not bear out the claim of Gudmundsson, *Stormtroop Tactics*, p. 8, that the *Reglement* "recommended" close order as "the best means of gaining fire superiority."

vice regulations of 1908, although they shared with their French and British counterparts an attempt to counter the vast and continuing increase in firepower by ever-greater stress on the spirit of the bayonet, nevertheless maintained the now traditional Prusso-German emphasis on decentralized decision making for "thinking [junior] leaders trained in *Selbständigkeit* and riflemen who act without requiring orders."[21]

So intense was the Prussian cult of battlefield freedom, and so at variance with most other features of Prussia-Germany's startlingly authoritarian society, that even observers deeply familiar with the Prussian army could profess shock at the consequences. Ludwig von Gebsattel, Bavarian military representative in Berlin, reported to his superiors in Munich in 1905 that a striking difference between the Bavarian army and that of its Prussian ally was

> the appreciation and promotion accorded [in Prussia] to officers, who, while efficient and thoroughly expert, are individuals who, as result of a self-will [*Eigenwille*] that sometimes crosses the bounds of normal self-reliance [*Selbständigkeit*], are difficult to control, equally brutal and ruthless toward subordinates and superiors, and inclined to usurpations of authority . . .

This passionately competitive leadership style was no accident, Gebsattel insisted, but "a well-thought-out and implemented system."[22] It even extended to toleration – almost unheard-of in other armies of this era – of public criticism by serving officers of the army's doctrine and approach to war.[23]

The Great War completed the democratization of the battlefield freedom initiated in 1806–08. An unprecedented intensity of fire swiftly checkmated movement. The French and especially the British sought above all technological answers that ranged from the crude and disastrous – the six-day British preparatory bombardment on the Somme in 1916 – to the technologically sophisticated but as yet

21. *Exerzier-Reglement für die Infanterie* (Berlin, 1906), quoted in Heinz-Ludger Borgert, "Grundzüge der Landkriegführung von Schlieffen bis Guderian," HDMG 9:486; also Samuels, *Command or Control?*, pp. 76–77; for the army's internal debates, Antulio J. Echevarria II, "A Crisis in Warfighting: German Tactical Discussions in the Late Nineteenth Century," MGM 55 (1966), pp. 51–68.
22. Gebsattel to Bavarian minister of war, 23 November 1905, in Hermann Rumschöttel, "Bildung und Herkunft der bayerischen Offiziere 1866 bis 1914," MGM 2 (1970), p. 123.
23. See Showalter, "Goltz and Bernhardi: The Institutionalization of Originality in the Imperial German Army," *Defense Analysis* 3 (1987), pp. 305–18; the army was less tolerant of criticism by civilians, especially those on the Left.

imperfect – the tank. In both cases the higher officer corps sought to maintain control of battle by rigid timetables and stern restrictions that actively prevented junior leaders from exploiting success.

The Germans responded as they had to past challenges, by accentuating *Selbständigkeit* and combining it with the new weapons of industrial warfare. Tactics now at last became, in the words of Colonel Max Bauer, the Great General Staff's chief technical, tactical, and political brain, "the rational and appropriate application of technical means to both attack and defense."[24] In 1915 and 1916 German experimental units under Bauer's aegis pioneered the specialized weapons and methods required to give the infantry the ability once more to move under fire: hand grenades specifically designed for the attack, small portable cannon, light machine guns, grenade launchers, flamethrowers, and eventually submachine guns. The primary tactical unit of these *Stosstruppen* became the infantry squad – eight men and an NCO – the largest organization a single individual could reliably control in person on the modern battlefield.[25]

That radical solution to the paralysis created by firepower proved itself in the trench raids and counterattacks mounted by German picked units, in combination with the army's increasingly sophisticated use of indirect artillery fire in support. Then the swift and seemingly inexorable increase in the weight of British and French shellfire in 1916–17 forced the new techniques on the entire German army. The obliteration of communications, trench lines, and bunkers by enemy bombardment, and the twin imperatives of dispersion – to cause the enemy to "scatter his fire both in time and space," and immediate response to throw back attackers before they could consolidate gains – persuaded even extreme authoritarians such as Bauer and his chief after 1916, Erich Ludendorff, to democratize battlefield decision making as in no other army. Even squad leaders were now to counterattack without specific orders, in accordance with the intent of their superiors and the standard operating procedures of the moment. The same insistence on individual initiative within the framework of higher intent and guided by a combined arms doctrine validated by experiment was the mainspring of the terrifying "infiltration tactics" of the German offensives of 1918. Battlefield *Selbständigkeit*, the

24. Bauer, *Der Grosse Krieg in Feld und Heimat: Erinnerungen und Betrachtungen* (Tübingen, 1921), p. 70; see in general Geyer, "German Strategy in the Age of Machine Warfare."
25. See Samuels, *Command or Control?*, p. 93; also Gudmundsson, *Stormtroop Tactics*, pp. 49–50, 101–02, 171–92.

"Prussian idea of freedom," became the essence of tactics in the age of industrial firepower.[26]

The shock of defeat in November 1918 intensified rather than diminished the army's emphasis on initiative. General Hans von Seeckt, the greatest operational artist of the lost war, imbued the 100,000-man Versailles Treaty army with the uncompromising aim of "making of each individual member of the army a soldier who, in character, capability, and knowledge, is self-reliant, self-confident, dedicated, and joyful in taking responsibility [*verantwortungsfreudig*] as a man and as a military leader."[27] The army's summation of the wisdom acquired painfully in the Great War, "Leadership and Combat of Combined Arms Forces" of 1921, placed an even higher value than had pre-war doctrine on individual initiative within the framework of assigned tasks and the intentions of superiors. And *Truppenführung*, the field manual of 1933 under which the army fought the Second World War, was categorical: "The emptiness of the battlefield demands fighters [*Kämpfer*] who think and act on their own [*selbstständig*], and can analyze any situation and exploit it decisively and boldly." The manual's authors, of whom the most prominent was the later chief of staff Ludwig Beck, sternly enjoined all combat leaders in now-canonical fashion to "allow their subordinates freedom of action, insofar as this does not endanger [their] own intent."[28] A conception originally sprung from the encounter of the Prussian absolutist state with the armies of the French Revolution had become the key element in the tradition on which the armies of a new revolutionary state were about to be built.

26. Quotation: "Allgemeines über Stellungsbau" (1917/18) in Erich Ludendorff, *Urkunden der Obersten Heeresleitung über ihre Tätigkeit* (Berlin, 1920), p. 595; see also Ludendorff, *Meine Kriegserinnerungen 1914-1918* (Berlin, 1919), pp. 307–07, 460–61, 493–94. The best overviews of the development of German doctrine in 1915–18 are Samuels's brilliant comparative treatment; Timothy T. Lupfer, "The Dynamics of Doctrine: The Changes in German Tactical Doctrine during the First World War," *Leavenworth Papers*, vol. 4 (1981); and C. G. Wynne, *If Germany Attacks: The Battle in Depth in the West* (London, 1940).
27. The final, virtually untranslatable sentence of Seeckt's famous order of the day of 1 January 1921, in Manfred Messerschmidt and Ursula von Gersdorff, eds., *Offiziere im Bild von Dokumenten aus drei Jahrhunderten* (Stuttgart, 1964), pp. 224–26.
28. *Führung und Gefecht der verbundenen Waffen* (1921), in Ose, "Der 'Auftrag,'" p. 264; Oberkommando des Heeres, *Truppenführung*, I. Teil, paragraphs 10, 37.

THE CAREER OPEN TO TALENT PROMISED AND DENIED, 1808-1933

The military reformers had insisted that the thinking combatants that the new warfare demanded were only conceivable within the framework of universal service by free citizens that the French had pioneered. The ideal of *Selbständigkeit* at all levels required an end to the barbaric system of corporal punishments designed for an army of automatons recruited from non-Prussians and bond peasants, the abolition of serfdom itself, and the creation of a new kind of officer. The army enacted in 1808 the "freedom from the lash" and from the corporal's stick emphatically demanded by the most radical of the reformers, Neithardt von Gneisenau. Serfdom, if not peasant dependence on the nobility, duly ceased in 1810. And within the officer corps itself the reformers sought a noteworthy break with tradition in the two most decisive areas: recruitment and advancement. They demanded the fullest possible opening of the officer corps to non-nobles, and an end to the tradition of promotion by seniority rather than merit on which the pre-1806 officer corps, as a closed corporation or *Stand* of noble social equals, had rested.[29]

Defeat had discredited the old system and temporarily disarmed its partisans. The reformers and Napoleon's strict treaty limits on Prussia's forces between them removed virtually all of the generals of 1806 and over three-quarters of the pre-Jena officer corps. Courts-martial of those who had failed or fled and peer review of each member of the 1806–07 officer corps were the principal mechanisms of a massive purge. This unique episode of corporate self-cleansing disposed for good of almost half of the officer corps of 1806.[30]

The reformers simultaneously redefined the basis of officer status: "Birth confers no monopoly of merit," proclaimed Gneisenau. Achievement and effectiveness – *Leistung* – must have its due. The new Articles of War of August 1808 that abolished the old punishments also contained a promise that the king would promote noncommis-

---

29. Gneisenau newspaper article, 9 July 1808, in Georg Eckert, *Von Valmy bis Leipzig* (Hannover, 1955), pp. 135–36, and the new articles of war and implementing instructions of 3 August 1808, in Eugen von Frauenholz, *Entwicklungsgeschichte des deutschen Heerwesens*, vol. 5, *Das Heerwesen des XIX. Jahrhunderts* (Berlin, 1941), pp. 101-16.

30. Wohlfeil, *Vom stehenden Heer*, HDMG 2:141, gives the most balanced of the many accounts of the purge: 1,791 (or 23 percent) of the 7,096 officers of 1806 remained active by September 1808, and only 3,898 (or 54 percent) of the officer corps of 1806 took part in the wars of 1813–15.

sioned officers and common soldiers "to even the highest officer ranks" for exceptional performance, "taking into account their capabilities and knowledge, and without regard for their birth." The new regulation on officer candidacy, issued a few days later, began with proud words:

> From now on knowledge and education [*Bildung*] shall give claim to officer positions in peacetime, and in war outstanding bravery and presence of mind. Therefore all individuals from the entire nation who possess these qualities may lay claim to the highest posts of honor in the army. All previously exercised precedence based on social status [*Vorzug des Standes*] in the army ceases utterly herewith, and all have equal duties and equal rights.[31]

The Prussian monarchy appeared to have adopted the revolutionary career open to talent, but one that unlike its French counterpart rested on intellectual cultivation as well as on battlefield *Leistung*.

Appearances were deceptive. After 1815, the same absolutist mechanisms through which the reformers had transformed Prussia allowed monarch, bureaucracy, and nobility to slow dramatically the pace of further transformation. Non-nobles and outsiders who entered the officer corps in 1813–15 tended to languish in the lower officer ranks, despite important exceptions such as the chief of general staff from 1848 to 1857, General Carl von Reyher, who had begun his career as an NCO. The unique privilege – accorded to Prussia's regimental officers in 1808 – of choosing all entrants into the officer corps by election evolved by midcentury into a discriminating social as well as professional filter that confirmed rather than weakened the corporate and noble character of Prussia's military elite. An 1844 reform raised educational requirements for officer candidacy, but also implicitly legitimated the blackballing of candidates on grounds of "unworthiness."[32] Seniority still provided the framework for promotion, although its operation was now "conditional" upon satisfactory annual efficiency reports and upon passage through successively finer sieves above the rank of captain; a reform of 1867 also conceded some degree of accelerated promotion based on merit to junior officers.[33]

31. Article 2 of "Krieges-Artikel für die Unter-Offiziere und gemeinen Soldaten," 3 August 1808, printed in Frauenholz, *Entwicklungsgeschichte des deutschen Heerwesens*, vol. 5, pp. 101–13; regulation on officer recruitment issued by Frederick William III, 6 August 1808, in Messerschmidt and von Gersdorff, eds., *Offiziere*, p. 171.
32. Messerschmidt, "Das Preussisch-deutsche Offizierkorps 1850–1890," in Hanns Hubert Hofmann, ed., *Das deutsche Offizierkorps, 1860-1960* (Boppard, 1980), p. 26.
33. On "conditional seniority," see Wohlfeil, "Die Beförderungsgrundsätze," pp. 48–52, 56–57 in Gerhard Papke et al., *Untersuchungen zur Geschichte des Offizierkorps: Ancien-*

The reformers' educational requirement, although intended to open the road to talent, was under the conditions existing in nineteenth- and even early twentieth-century Germany a further barrier to the vast majority of the population too poor to send its sons to the elite classical secondary school (the *Gymnasium*) that led by stages to the *Abitur*, the college-entrance qualification that certified the definitive possession of *Bildung*. Nor could the lower orders hope to meet the private income requirements, ever more stringent after midcentury, imposed by regimental commanders on their officers, or the armywide standing orders, in place since 1798/1802, that officers' brides pass muster with both regimental commander and king, and that young officers intending to marry prove that they or their prospective brides possessed the funds needed to support households "commensurate with their *Stand*."[34]

Yet by separating, even notionally, noble from officer status in 1808, the state had in fact imposed a new social cleavage potentially more incisive – because of the officer corps' preeminent position in the state from which its social prestige now derived – than the noble-commoner line inherited from the old regime. The Prussian state created a society, unique in Europe, cloven deeply in two by *military* function. On one side stood all those, noble or commoner, who were capable of passing through the twin filters of birth and "character" on the one hand and of *Bildung* on the other.[35] On the other side stood the rest, including sons of the nobility unable to meet the slowly increasing educational requirements for officer candidacy.

Several forces propelled both this rise in standards and the limited social opening of the officer corps to the upper middle classes over the long century from 1808 to 1914. First in its impact, and operative throughout the century, was the need to preserve the officer corps' status as "first *Stand*" in an era of ever-increasing educational attainment.[36] As early as 1828, as a senior officer later recalled, it "appeared

nität und Beförderung nach Leistung (Stuttgart, 1962); Hughes, *The King's Finest: A Social and Bureaucratic Profile of Prussia's General Officers, 1871-1914* (New York, 1987), p. 82.

34. Hughes, *The King's Finest*, pp. 68–74, 99; Messerschmidt and von Gersdorff, eds., *Offiziere*, pp. 158–61.

35. For the underlying conception, see Ernst Rudolf Huber, *Deutsche Verfassungsgeschichte seit 1789* (Stuttgart, 1957–), vol. 1, pp. 232–38; for the contrary view that the new arrangements were by themselves not sufficient to create a new *Stand*, and that the victories of 1866 and 1870–71 and the rise of Socialism were needed to combine military nobility and middle-class elite, Messerschmidt, "Die Preussische Armee," HDMG 4/2:63.

36. Karl A. Schleunes, "Enlightenment, Reform, Reaction: The Schooling Revolution in Prussia," *Central European History* 12:4 (1979), pp. 315–42, offers a useful introduction.

necessary to raise the requirements for the ensign's examination in order to maintain the social standing of the corps of officers; and the main reason for this was that a higher general education was becoming necessary in the other branches of the civil service."[37] The officer likewise had to be seen as not too far inferior in *Bildung* to the liberal professions. And perhaps most threatening of all, Bavaria imposed the *Abitur* in 1872 as a requirement for officer candidacy, with the apparent aim of equalling or surpassing the Prussians.[38] Official pronouncements on officer recruitment and successive officer candidacy regulations consequently acknowledged the ever-rising "degree of learning" of the German people and the necessity of safeguarding the Prussian officer's prestige by keeping pace.[39] Despite tenacious rearguard struggle by officers to whom tradition meant recruitment by birth alone, a series of piecemeal reforms from the late 1820s to 1900 ultimately made the step below the *Abitur*, the *Primareife*, the usual minimum qualification for officer entry in the Prussian army. By 1912, 65 percent of Prussian officer candidates possessed the *Abitur* itself.[40]

The second major pressure acting on the social composition of the officer corps was likewise a constantly operating one, above all after midcentury. Improbably – to an age inclined to ascribe *all* features of military institutions to socioeconomic or cultural causes – that factor was the demands of war and of preparation for war, the ostensible reason for being of all military institutions. The reformers' universal service *Wehrgesetz* of September 1814 carried into peacetime – as the French army did not – the revolutionary concept of universal service and the resulting revolution in the size of armies. Until the mid-1850s, however, Prussia's limited ambitions in Germany and Europe, fears of social revolt, and a narrow economic base dictated that the army train less than half its available manpower.

Then the army's success in crushing revolution from the Left in 1848, the Prussian state's historic rivalry with Austria, and the professional ambitions of the soldier king, William I, made possible and

---

37. Quoted in Demeter, *The German Officer-Corps*, p. 285.
38. See Rumschöttel, "Bildung und Herkunft der bayerischen Offiziere," pp. 87, 90–91.
39. See the preamble of Hermann von Boyen's reforming regulation of 1844, in Messerschmidt, "Die preussische Armee," HDMG 4/2:100, and Wilhelm II's famous speech of 1890 calling for the recruitment of all those possessing "nobility of spirit" (ibid., 4/2:18). For similar motivations in the Bavarian army's insistence on the *Abitur*, Rumschöttel, "Bildung und Herkunft der bayerischen Offiziere," pp. 109–110, 111, 117, 118.
40. Wilhelm II made numerous exceptions to the rule requiring the *Primareife*, but the percentage of officer candidates so favored declined from 18 in 1895 to 3.7 in 1912 (Demeter, *The German Officer-Corps*, pp. 88–89).

demanded an army both larger and better-trained than that of 1815–48, just as rapid economic growth gave the Prussian state new sinews of war. The consequent expansion of the line army by forty percent in 1859–61 and the ensuing wars of 1864, 1866, and 1870–71 required noteworthy expansion of the officer corps. The other powers inevitably reacted to Prussia-Germany's triumph by likewise adopting near-universal service. The resulting further increase from the 1870s in the size of European armies, the concurrent arrival of smokeless powder weapons, the consequent decline of the most aristocratic and least intellectually demanding arm, the cavalry, and the increasing likelihood even before the Franco-Russian alliance of 1891–93 that Germany's next war would be fought on two fronts, ultimately forced an unprecedented degree of change. The nobility, almost static in numbers at perhaps 45,000 adult males at mid-century, simply could not provide enough officer candidates to lead the vast infantry armies that Germany's swelling population and expanding economy made possible and Germany's deteriorating strategic situation seemed to demand. Nor were young nobles usually inclined toward or educated for the increasingly vital technical branches, from artillery and engineers to logistics and communications. Slowly, grudgingly, and partially, the noble conservatives in the Prussian war ministry and the emperor's officer personnel department, the Military Cabinet, yielded to the logic of war. The share of nobles in the Prussian officer corps dropped from 65 percent in 1865 to 30 percent in 1914, as the strength of the regular officer corps rose from 7,907 (1866) to 22,112.[41]

As early as 1902, in the judgment of the Military Cabinet, more than half of new officers came from "occupational circles from which the officer corps had earlier only seldom recruited." A thirty- to forty-year interval inevitably intervened before the higher ranks reflected the gradual changes that had occurred from 1860 onward within the lower officer corps. By 1914 the continuing appearance of noble domination even of the corps of general officers was deceptive: the proportion of nobles among newly promoted brigadier generals had fallen from almost 82 percent in 1871–81 to slightly less than 58 percent in 1904–14, of whom fewer than half possessed titles dating from before 1400. A century after 1808, the most salient feature of the

---

41. Figures: Hughes, *The King's Finest*, p. 15; Messerschmidt, "Das preussisch-deutsche Offizierkorps 1850–1890," p. 31, and Deist, "Zur Geschichte des preussischen Offizierkorps 1890–1918," in Hofmann, ed., *Offizierkorps*, p. 54.

Offizierstand that the reformers had created was an occupational, political, regional, and religious exclusiveness, rather than one defined by
the line between noble and commoner. Roughly two-thirds of the generals of 1871–1914 had fathers (and many also had grandfathers) who
had served the Prussian state as officers or higher bureaucrats. Almost
two-thirds had been born in the eastern provinces (including Berlin).
And only 5 percent of all generals of 1871–1914 whose religion is
known were Catholics, although 35 percent or more of Prussia's population was Catholic.[42]

At the summit of the army, a far narrower new elite based on both
Bildung and birth emerged. Scharnhorst had sought to make the general staff corps that he in essence had founded into a group of "aides
to the commander" imbued with a common understanding of doctrine, capable of independent decision, and co-responsible with division, corps, and army commanders for the outcome. This system was
unique to Prussia; along with the army's very demanding staff and
command school, founded in 1810 and known as the *Kriegsakademie*
after 1859, it survived the lean years after 1815. It also retained the
preemptive claim that Scharnhorst had made on the services of the
very brightest junior officers, chosen by competitive examination.

Moltke the elder's victories and doctrinal writings between 1866
and 1871 consolidated the staff's position as a sort of central nervous
system for an army whose higher commanders had by now been sys-
tematically schooled in competitive and often headstrong self-assertion. All units down to divisional level had general staff officers whose
career paths also required serving tours of duty both with the Great
General Staff in Berlin and as unit commanders. The resulting blend
of *Bildung* – which under Moltke took on a narrowly professional cast
– and practical military experience proved startlingly effective in hon-
ing the army's tactical, operational, and organizational skills. Despite
the overwhelming preponderance (an aggregate 83 percent) of nobles
among the general officers appointed to staff positions between 1871
and 1914, *Leistung* was the organization's central value, and non-noble
experts increasingly flourished. Ludendorff, Bauer, and Wilhelm
Groener, determined at all costs to enlarge the army to meet the Fran-

---

42. Daniel J. Hughes, "Occupational Origins of Prussia's Generals, 1871–1914," *Central
European History* 13:1 (1980), pp. 5 (quotation), 15–17, 32; figures: Hughes, *The King's
Finest*, pp. 12, 29, 42; Lamar Cecil, "The Creation of Nobles in Prussia," *American
Historical Review* 75:2 (1969), pp. 784, 795; see also Ulrich Trumpener, "Junkers and
Others: The Rise of Commoners in the Prussian Army 1871–1914," *Canadian Journal
of History* 14 (1979), pp. 32–33.

co-Russian challenge, were their prototypes. Their attributes (in the eyes of a hostile critic) were "bomb-like energy and the crassest *Unbildung*" in the word's original sense of upper-middle-class self-cultivation: "in the end an Americanized type – narrow."[43]

The resultant of social forces, military requirements, and the example and leadership of the general staff corps was an army more learned (however narrowly), more intellectually flexible, and more efficient than any rival within the bounds of tactics and operations that was the domain of "Prussian freedom." At entry level, the requirement that candidates pass competitive examinations before being considered for election by the officers of the regiment tended to weed out the least intelligent. Even the Prussian cadet school system, which had originated in the mid seventeenth century to prepare needy noble sons for entry into the officer corps, came to provide its graduates with a degree theoretically equivalent to the *Abitur*; the later performance of cadet school "old boys" in high command and staff positions in the twentieth century does not suggest a lack of either brains or *Bildung*.[44] And above the rank of captain, an increasingly searching selection process and the related custom requiring officers passed over for promotion to resign provided exits for those found wanting.[45]

Scharnhorst had once complained that the stupidest sons of noble families went into the army; his reforms and those of his successors ultimately ensured that only those who were reasonably bright or served in the cavalry could expect long military careers. Yet in the last decades before 1914, as the barrier between noble and commoner within the *Offizierstand* lost its salience as commoners achieved numerical dominance as company and battalion officers, the gulf between the officer corps as a whole and the rest of the army deepened. The long-promised ascent from the ranks through outstanding *Bildung* and competence was in essence closed off even more tightly than in the past. The steadily rising educational qualifications demanded of candidates reinforced the continuing resistance of regimental officers, Prussian war ministry, and Military Cabinet to officer candidates lacking the requisite noble or upper-middle-class back-

---

43. Kurt Riezler, *Tagebücher, Aufsätze, Dokumente*, ed. Karl Dietrich Erdmann (Göttingen, 1972), pp. 401–02.
44. See John Moncure, *Forging the King's Sword: Military Education Between Tradition and Modernization: The Case of the Royal Prussian Cadet Corps, 1871-1918* (New York, 1993), especially pp. 140, 174–75, 208–09.
45. On the "up or out" policy applied in promotion to major and above, see Wiegand Schmidt-Richberg, "Die Regierungszeit Wilhelms II," HDMG 5:88–89, and Hughes, *The King's Finest*, pp. 81–82.

ground. Concurrently, the Prusso-German noncommissioned officer evolved, as the demands of the battlefield required and the population's improvement in educational levels permitted, into an increasingly expert and authoritative figure. Technical branches such as ordnance, communications, and the construction engineers offered NCO careers that culminated in a status resembling that of the modern warrant officer.[46] But the NCOs of the combat arms, however secure in their experience of soldiering, in general lacked the opportunity, once in service, to acquire the *Bildung* needed for the officer candidacy examination.

Nor did the immense cataclysm of the World War ensure that the sons of the German lower middle and lower classes could aspire in a lasting way to officer status. War ultimately destroyed whatever homogeneity the regular officer corps still possessed. Almost a quarter of the roughly 51,000 regular army officers and officer candidates (*Fähnriche*) who served in 1914–18 died, and wounds incapacitated many others.[47] Industrial warfare divided even the regulars into those who had fought at the front, and the rest. Those who had fought came to share in many cases the attitudes as well as the risks, wounds, and privations of the army's almost 230,000 reserve officers. Firepower erased social distinctions along with men and trench lines; those who had passed through the "storm of steel" tended to view battlefield effectiveness as the only test of the officer.[48] Within the general staff corps, the "Americanized types" who supervised the "rational and appropriate application of technical means to both attack and defense" gained the absolute advantage. They owed their status to professional *Leistung* rather than birth, and as they established their ascendancy within the staff, the staff itself further strengthened its grip on the conduct of the war.[49]

Yet in 1914–18 *Leistung* alone was insufficient to break down the long-established barrier between the "first *Stand*" and the rest of society. To avoid admitting combat NCOs of unsuitable background into the reserve officer corps, the army bureaucracy expanded or created two demeaning intermediate ranks: the sergeant-lieutenant [*Feld-*

---

46. See especially Werner Lahne, *Unteroffiziere Gestern-Heute-Morgen* (Herford, 1974), pp. 238, 289–301, 343–47; and pp. 381–89 for similar developments in the navy.
47. Percentages calculated from Altrock, *Vom Sterben des deutschen Offizierkorps*, pp. 54, 64: German regular officers, 24.8 percent dead; Prussian regular officers, 24.9 percent dead.
48. See the pointed remarks of Ernst Jünger, *Copse 125: A Chronicle from the Trench Warfare of 1918* (New York, 1988), pp. 82–83.
49. Deist, "Preussischen Offizierkorps," p. 57.

webelleutnant] and the officer substitute [*Offizierstellvertreter*]. The Prussian army had created 21,607 of the former by July 1918, and despite widespread demands from front commanders for the promotion of combat-proven NCOs, the Kaiser's Military Cabinet prevented all but 300-odd sergeants from crossing the line to regular officer status in 1914–18. The sense of injustice thereby generated among both long-service and wartime enlisted men was a powerful corrosive of unit morale and performance, and a major factor in final collapse.[50]

Nor did the army offer much of a wartime career open to talent to those already admitted to the *Offizierstand*. As in its policy toward outsiders, the Military Cabinet placed the internal solidarity and social homogeneity of the corps before the demands of military effectiveness. It resolutely refused after 1914 to loosen appreciably the rule of promotion by seniority for company officers. The result was that infantry officers promoted to first lieutenant in 1918 had entered service on average in 1913, and those promoted to major in 1918 had entered service on average in 1896.[51]

Even defeat and the decapitation of the state in 1918 failed to abolish the barrier between the *Offizierstand* and the rest of society. The army's collapse in 1918 had a far more purgative effect than the catastrophe of 1806 to which contemporaries frequently compared it: fewer than 4,000 of the 34,000 regular officers in service in late 1918 found places in the Versailles Treaty *Reichswehr* of 100,000 men formed in 1919–20. Groener and Seeckt, the preeminent architects of the new army, pressed Reich President Friedrich Ebert to retain as many general staff officers from the old army as possible, and successfully urged the centralized control of operations, doctrine, and force structure under the camouflaged successor to the outlawed Great General Staff. Seeckt, whose influence on officer selection was decisive from 1920 to 1926, rightly insisted that "the level of intellectual development of the officer is decisive for the quality of the army as a whole."[52]

---

50. Ibid., p. 54; Rudolf Absolon, *Die Wehrmacht im Dritten Reich* (Boppard, 1969-95), vol. 2, pp. 94-97, 175-79; Heinz Hürten, "Das Offizierkorps des Reichsheeres," in Hofmann, ed., *Offizierkorps*, p. 235; for the view of one of the chosen few, Hermann Ramcke, *Vom Schiffjungen zum Fallschirmjäger-General* (preface by Hermann Göring) (Berlin, 1943), pp. 99–101. Erich Otto Volkmann, *Soziale Heeresmissstände als Mitursache des deutschen Zusammenbruchs von 1918* (Berlin 1929), pp. 33–46 (protests by front commanders, pp. 38–42), and Martin Hobohm, *Soziale Heeresmissstände als Teilursache des deutschen Zusammenbruchs von 1918* (Berlin, 1931), pp. 105–10, address some of the consequences for the army's effectiveness and cohesion.
51. Figures derived from Edgar Graf von Matuschka, "Die Beförderung in der Praxis," in Papke et al., *Anciennität*, pp. 168–69.
52. Hürten, "Offizierkorps des Reichsheeres," pp. 234–35; Seeckt order of 5 November 1919, in Messerschmidt and von Gersdorff, eds., *Offiziere*, p. 222.

The *Abitur* or its equivalent consequently became the general prerequisite for officer candidacy, although several hundred long-service NCOs with exceptional war records were guardedly admitted to the corps in the early 1920s, and a few each year thereafter. Rigorous preinduction psychological testing and unit service as a private soldier and as a squad leader imposed filters that were primarily professional rather than social. Regimental commanders could no longer require that their officers give evidence of independent means. Yet the *Reichswehr* retained the old army's regimental election procedure, stressed the need for social graces as well as professional skill, and continued to insist that officers seeking to marry must clear their prospective bride with their superior; only "the genuinely cultivated [*gebildeten*] spouse from a good family" (as Seeckt put it in a 1924 directive) would do.[53] The officer corps, at least in the eyes of its supreme leadership, remained a *Stand* rather than a profession.[54]

Nor did promotion policy offer the career open to talent ("*Freie Bahn dem Tüchtigen*") that Groener for one had vehemently urged in 1919. The drastic Versailles-dictated shrinkage of 1919–20, not the army's own advancement mechanism, was the decisive force in placing what Groener described as "young, energetic, and modern officers into leading positions."[55] *Leistung* as judged by one's superiors now determined who was promoted among those whom seniority placed within the zone of consideration; those not promoted ultimately resigned. But ascent in a corps static in size and unbalanced in age structure nevertheless remained excruciatingly slow. No officer who had entered the *Reichswehr* as an officer candidate reached the rank of captain before 1935.[56]

---

53. Hürten, "Offizierkorps des Reichsheeres," pp. 240–41; Seeckt on "Erziehung des Offizierkorps und des Offiziernachwuchses," 30 August 1924, in Messerschmidt and von Gersdorff, eds., *Offiziere*, p. 240.
54. See the use of the word *Stand* in the army's 1923 guidelines on officer candidate training in Hans Meier-Welcker, "Der Weg zum Offizier im Reichsheer der Weimarer Republik," MGM 1976/1, p. 169 (see also p. 167). The essay also contains much intriguing autobiographical detail on the extent to which the officer candidate, as his seniority increased, was expected to play a role in polite society befitting his status.
55. Quotations from Groener memorandum for Ebert, 17 September 1919, in Dieter Dreetz, "Denkschrift der deutschen Obersten Heeresleitung vom 17. September 1919 über die Reichswehr und deren Rolle bei Schaffung einer imperialistischen deutschen Grossmacht," *Militärgeschichte* 21 (1982), pp. 603, 607–08.
56. Wohlfeil, "Heer und Republik (1918–1933)," HDMG 6:179; Hürten, "Offizierkorps des Reichsheeres," p. 231; Matuschka, "Die Beförderung in der Praxis," pp. 173–75. Deichmann, *Der Chef im Hintergrund* (Oldenburg, 1979), p. 46, notes that the sluggish pace of *Reichswehr* promotions made the pre-1914 era seem a time of "lightning careers."

The social profile – if no longer necessarily the attitudes – of the *Reichswehr* officer corps thus resembled that of the pre-1914 army. Roughly a fifth of the army officer corps was noble in 1926, and almost 24 percent in 1932; the percentage of nobles in the officer candidate classes of 1929 through 1932, for which figures exist, revolved around 26 percent. Perhaps more significantly, the proportion of sons of officers among the *Reichswehr*'s officer candidates ran at perhaps a third of the total until 1926, and then rose steadily – as did the proportion of nobles – as the military profession's stock began to rise from defeat. In the 1930 officer candidate class the proportion of officers' sons was 55.4 percent: in 1933, 51 percent. Correspondingly, after the mid-1920s markedly fewer candidates than in the decade before 1914 came from middle- and lower-middle-class backgrounds.[57] Given the army's small annual intake and the consequent overabundance after 1924 of promising candidates, the system's educational and social filters in conjunction almost totally barred *both* dull-witted or slothful noblemen *and* intelligent and dedicated social outsiders. The broadly accessible career open to talent in warfare that Scharnhorst and Gneisenau had promised seemed more distant than ever before.

THE NATIONAL SOCIALIST REVOLUTIONARY SYNTHESIS

The *Reichswehr*'s relentless tactical-operational debate, technical experiment, and study and training at all levels duly produced the "army of leaders" that Seeckt had sought. Its members were the embodiment of *Selbständigkeit* and joy in responsibility. But until 1933 their responsibilities were small and their potential recompense uncertain and far distant. That was a contradiction that Adolf Hitler was happy to resolve – at a price.

Defeat in 1918 had decapitated the state, stunted the army, and opened the road for Hitler by rendering the old elites incapable of ruling in their own right; hence the ill-conceived attempt of some of their members to bend him to their service in 1932–33. The post-1919 army's dwarf existence had also diverted into paramilitary organizations and militant nationalist parties, of which the SA and NSDAP were by far the most mighty, many young Germans who knew only the

---

57. Figures: Friedrich Doepner, "Zur Auswahl der Offizieranwärter im 100,000-Mann-Heer," *Wehrkunde* 22 (1973), p. 202; Detlev Bald, *Sozialgeschichte der Rekrutierung des deutschen Offizierkorps vom Reichsgründungszeit bis zum Gegenwart* (Munich, 1977), p. 45; also Wohlfeil, "Heer und Republik," HDMG 6:177.

career of arms or – conditioned by a hundred years of quasi-universal service and the myths of the lost war – aspired to it. And after 1933 those persisting aspirations and the existing army's diminutive size offered Hitler a further unique opportunity that he was swift to seize.

War and conquest on the one hand and the career open to talent on the other were fundamental to Hitler's world view. Races or states that failed to select "their best talents" as leaders in the struggle for existence were doomed. In the German case, the nationalist upper middle class and the nobility had jealously kept *Bildung*, wealth, and titles for themselves and their children, but had then failed lamentably in the one test that might have justified their privileges, the Great War. Only the primordial brutality and undaunted willpower of the lower orders (exemplified, in all modesty, by himself) could now save Germany, and then only if new mechanisms of selection brought "to the top the most capable heads from below." The essence of the socialism in National Socialism, Hitler proclaimed throughout his long political career, was unconditional equality of opportunity for all racially sound German males.[58]

In civil society this "National Socialist principle of achievement [*Leistungsprinzip*]" required massive state intervention to provide equal access to education for talented children of workers and peasants – a goal that the regime sought persistently if imperfectly to realize.[59] War, Hitler's chosen instrument of social transformation, ultimately required a revolutionary army recruited according to *Leistung*. But the SA, led by the disreputable Captain (Ret.) Ernst Röhm, could not be that army, although it claimed to embrace the élan and careers of 1793 and the spirit of 1807–13; only the professionals of the *Reichswehr* offered assured success in rearmament. Hitler had the self-proclaimed "Scharnhorst of the new army" and his entourage shot in June 1934, but sought thereafter to realize their aims through the very expansion of the armed forces for conquest for which the generals were indispensable. As he prophesied resentfully in 1938 to his army adjutant, the admission of former Hitler Youths to the officer corps would ultimately expunge the "spirit of the 100,000-man army."[60]

---

58. See the exhaustive discussion, with extensive quotation of both public and private utterances, of the central place of "equality of opportunity" in Hitler's world view in Zitelmann, *Hitler: Selbstverständnis eines Revolutionärs*, pp. 93–115; for the quotations, pp. 99–100.

59. For the phrase, Schmundt diary, p. 8 (9 October 1942); for National Socialist educational policy, see especially Karl Christoph Lingelbach, *Erziehung und Erziehungstheorien im nationalsozialistischen Deutschland* (Berlin, 1970), and Harald Scholtz, *Erziehung und Unterricht unterm Hakenkreuz* (Göttingen, 1985).

60. Engel, *Heeresadjutant*, p. 61 (10 September 1939).

The new universal-service army founded between 1933 and 1936 had the staggering projected wartime strength of 4.6 million men, to be operationally ready by October 1940. *All* its officers beyond the roughly 3,200 carried over from the 1932 army owed their officer status to National Socialism, and the vast majority had served only in an army openly professing loyalty to the "national revolution" of 1933. The rise in numbers was gradual in the regime's first years, but the implementation of universal service in 1935–36 more than doubled the army officer corps to roughly 8,400 men; by 1938 it had multiplied almost seven times to 21,700. The renewed creation of reserve officers – forbidden to the *Reichswehr* – from 1936 further increased the speed of the influx. The army mobilized by 1 September 1939 had 89,075 regular and reserve officers. By its wartime high point of 1 September 1943 it had attained a total of 243,453 officers of whom roughly 40,000 were regulars. That represented a thirteen-fold increase in regular officers in the decade since 1932, and a seventy-two-fold multiplication of the army officer corps as a whole.[61] The other three services – of which two owed their entire existence to the regime – likewise expanded massively. The *Führerkorps* of what became the Waffen-SS increased thirteen-fold, from 1,203 at the end of 1938 to 15,777 in June 1944; the naval officer corps multiplied itself by 25, from 1,100 men in 1932 to almost 28,000 in 1944; and the Luftwaffe's officers swelled from 900 (mostly transferred from the army) at the service's official founding in March 1935 to 80,688 in December 1944. At almost ninety times original officer strength, that was the greatest proportional increase of all the services. By war's end, perhaps half a million Germans had served as officers in the ground forces (army, Waffen-SS, and Luftwaffe ground combat units) alone.[62]

This gigantic influx had many sources. Army and navy increased their intake of officer candidates swiftly from 1933–34 on, and the army achieved by 1938 a tenfold increase (to 2,000 a year) over its

---

61. Figures: Deist et al., *German Aggression*, p. 446; Rudolf Absolon, "Das Offizierkorps des deutschen Heeres 1935–1945," in Hofmann, ed., *Offizierkorps*, p. 250; Herbert Schottelius and Gustav-Adolf Caspar, "Die Organisation des Heeres 1933–1939," HDMG 7:373.

62. Data: Bernd Wegner, "Das Führerkorps der Waffen-SS im Kriege," p. 329, and Horst Boog, "Das Offizierkorps der Luftwaffe 1935–1945," pp. 288–89, both in Hofmann, *Offizierkorps*; Charles S. Thomas, *The German Navy in the Nazi Era* (London, 1990), pp. 116, 236; navy monthly strength returns for 1944 in BA-MA RW6/535; Bernhard R. Kroener, "Auf dem Weg zu einer 'nationalsozialistischen Volksarmee.' Die soziale Öffnung des Heeresoffizierkorps im Zweiten Weltkrieg," in Martin Broszat et al., *Von Stalingrad zur Währungsreform: Zur Sozialgeschichte des Umbruchs in Deutschland* (Munich, 1988), pp. 652–53.

annual intake under Weimar.[63] In 1935–36 the army absorbed 2,500 officers – many of whom had begun their service as NCOs – from the militarized police units, which had become superfluous when their internal security tasks passed to the SS. By 1935 the army had also promoted to lieutenant some 1,200 *Reichswehr* NCOs – with preference for unmarried men unencumbered by spouses lacking the still indicated "genuine cultivation." It reinstated as regular officers some 800 carefully selected former officers and reserve officers lost in 1918–20 or retired thereafter. It freed most regular officers for troop commands by filling administrative and logistical positions with some 5,000 (through 1938) less capable Great War retreads designated as "augmentation officers." Finally, the Anschluss in March 1938 brought a windfall of roughly 1,600 Austrian officers judged suitable for retraining. The Luftwaffe for its part started with around 500 of the 3,724 army officers of 1932 and added almost another 400 such transfers by 1938; it also received a few officers from the navy, and otherwise made do with a bizarre assortment of ex-police officers, resurrected 1914–18 combat pilots, civilian fliers, and youthful recipients of clandestine flight training.[64]

Entry to the officer corps thus became radically easier even before Hitler's war; by 1939 the *Abitur* and upper-middle-class provenance were still helpful, but were no longer indispensable even for officer candidates. And to the "immense jubilation" of the *Reichswehr*'s officers and men, the need for commanders for the army's seemingly ever-expanding numbers of companies, battalions, regiments, and divisions also speeded promotion after 1935 to an extent undreamed-of in the 1920s, although the army retained the time-honored principle of conditional seniority.[65] The NCO corps prospered even more notably. The peacetime army of 1938–39 was roughly the same size as its 1913–14 counterpart but the size of its regular officer corps was only three-quarters of that of 1914, whereas the NCO corps was 40 percent larger than in 1914. The regime's enthusiastic efforts to inculcate the will to arms in the young and the overt espousal of the "marshal's baton in the knapsack" by both Hitler and his chief military subordinate, Field Marshal von Blomberg, made military careers increasingly attractive to enterprising youths who lacked sufficient education for officer candidacy. As a result, "[i]f the intelligent NCO [*Unterführer*]

63. Burckhardt Müller-Hillebrand, *Das Heer 1933-1945: Entwicklung des organisatorischen Aufbaues*, vol. 1, *Das Heer bis zum Kriegsbeginn* (Darmstadt, 1954), p. 29.
64. Absolon, "Offizierkorps," pp. 248–49; Boog, "Das Offizierkorps der Luftwaffe," p. 270.
65. "Ungeheurer Jubel": Ramcke, *Fallschirmjäger-General*, p. 196.

was more the exception than the rule before 1914, he now became a type."[66]

The joint efforts of National Socialism and of the army leadership made war possible. War in turn required further radical expansion of the army and of its cadres. And its culmination in *Barbarossa* provoked and made possible the final decisive changes in the system of officer recruitment and promotion. When Hitler dismissed Field Marshal Walther von Brauchitsch as commander-in-chief of the army on 19 December 1941 and wrathfully assumed the position himself, his immediate purpose was to master the catastrophe that threatened the German army in Russia. But his unbounded fury at what he took to be the inadequacies of the higher officer corps and general staff revealed by the failure of *Barbarossa*, and the confidence in his own military talents generated by the success of his stand-fast order in the East, led him to turn increasingly to the creation of the "National Socialist revolutionary army" to which he had aspired since 1933. In that task he had powerful assistance from middle-level figures in the hierarchy – above all from his devoted *Wehrmacht* adjutant, Generalmajor Rudolf Schmundt – who had shared with Hitler the "front experience" of 1914–18.[67]

Ideology, since 1933–34 an aid to German commanders in assuring fighting power, now assumed, between 1941 and 1945, a place coequal to tactics. The day he dismissed Brauchitsch, Hitler informed the army chief of staff, General Franz Halder, that National Socialist *"Erziehung"* – indoctrination – of the *Wehrmacht* was the decisive task in the face of Russian numerical and material superiority, a task only the dictator in person could accomplish. And as he fired Halder himself in September 1942, Hitler insisted on the necessity for *"Erziehung"* of the general staff itself "in fanatical belief in the Idea."[68]

The National Socialist career open to talent thus came finally into its own. Hitler had as early as winter 1939 expressed the wish that officers who performed well in combat, especially lieutenants serving as company commanders, be immediately promoted. The army's refusal

---

66. Blomberg speech excerpts, 27 April 1937, in Messerschmidt and von Gersdorff, eds., *Offiziere*, p. 269; intelligent NCOs: Schottelius and Caspar, "Organisation des Heeres," HDMG 7:378.

67. See the astute generational analysis of the 1941–45 officer corps and its attitudes in Kroener, "Strukturelle Veränderungen in der militärischen Gesellschaft des Dritten Reiches," pp. 267–296 in Michael Prinz and Rainer Zitelmann, eds., *Nationalsozialismus und Modernisierung* (Darmstadt, 1991), pp. 272–79; for the 1914–18 *Frontoffiziere*, pp. 274–76.

68. Franz Halder, *Hitler als Feldherr* (Munich, 1949), p. 45; Halder diary, 3:528 (24 September 1942).

in 1914–18 to promote outstanding junior officers and the preferential treatment it had accorded regulars over reserve officers had "decisively affected the relationship between commanders and troops, especially in the final years of the war"; the dictator had insisted that these errors must not recur.[69] Yet little action by the army bureaucracy had followed, even after Hitler had insisted in late 1940 and spring 1941 that this war was "a unique opportunity" for the selection of the fittest, and had pressed for the accelerated promotion of "Blücher types," commanders distinguished by combativeness rather than operational intellect.[70]

At the end of December 1941, after assuming command in person over the army, Hitler confided to Mussolini his renewed intention to reward with promotion all who had proven themselves at the front. He passed word through army channels to the eastern front that officers who had distinguished themselves as combat leaders should be promoted to the next higher rank, and ordered in his capacity as commander-in-chief of the *Wehrmacht* that reserve officers as well as regulars receive accelerated promotion for "outstanding deeds performed in combat units." A further order demanding accelerated promotion was issued in his name in mid-January, and in mid-February he "once again" commanded that capable officers be promoted swiftly to the rank appropriate to the command they currently held. He pressed repeatedly throughout winter–spring 1942 for the "rejuvenation" of the officer corps through battlefield selection.[71] And on 7 June 1942 the bureaucracy decreed that *Leistung*, without regard for age or

69. "Bemerkungen des Führers über Offizierbeförderungen im Kriege," Engel memorandum, 3 December 1939, copy in BA-ZNS Offizierbeförderungs-Bestimmungen I.
70. Unsigned draft headed "Chef des Heeres-Personamtes," 28 November 1940, responding to criticism from Hitler that the *Leistungsprinzip* was being insufficiently observed; Engel to von Gyldenfeldt, Br.B.Nr. 197/41 geh., 6 April 1941; and Hitler's views as reported by Schmundt, in the immediately following unsigned memorandum, "Bevorzugte Beförderungen," probably by *Generalleutnant* Bodewin Keitel (chief, army personnel office), undated (but April–May 1941), NARA T-78/40/6002480–84, 6002491–92, 6002493–97.
71. Hitler to Mussolini, 29 December 1941, ADAP E/1/62, pp. 108–09; similarly, *Hitler's Secret Conversations, 1941-1944* (New York, 1961), pp. 231–32 (20 January 1942); Heeresgruppenkommando Nord to AOK 16, AOK 18, Bef.r.H.G. Nord, Ia Nr. 10500/41 geh., 2 January 1942, BA-MA RH 19 III/772; "Richtlinien für die Beförderung von Offizieren d. B.," OKW Nr. 21p 4602/41 WZ (II), December 1941, *Luftwaffen-Verordnungsblatt*, 1942, p. 164 (Nr. 286); Army personnel office circular 750/42 Ag P1/11, 17 February 1942, in Papke et al., *Anciennität*, p. 303 ("Der Führer hat *erneut* befohlen . . . " (my emphasis); "Vorläufige Wertung der Auswirkungen der für die Verjüngung und Führerauslese gegebenen Weisungen," Chef HPA Nr. 1/42 pers., 16 April 1942, BA-MA RH2/156.

seniority, would henceforth determine promotion for outstanding regular officers, if not yet for reservists.[72]

Yet Hitler was far from satisfied. The June directive was optional and discretionary: it failed to confer the unconditional right to promotion through battlefield performance that he demanded. In the upheaval surrounding his dismissal of Halder in late September 1942 the dictator therefore imposed Schmundt – who had originally pressed upon Hitler the idea of succeeding Brauchitsch in person at the head of the army – as chief of army officer personnel. Schmundt remained the Führer's chief adjutant and had direct access to Hitler in his new capacity as well. He also received control, at Hitler's direct order, over general staff appointments: a power that Halder had jealously guarded, but which his hapless successor, Kurt Zeitzler, was unable to retain.[73]

Schmundt's new role as ultimate successor to the chiefs of the Kaiser's Military Cabinet had an immediate and explicit purpose. As Schmundt noted in his official diary under the date of 2 October 1942, "the Führer had ordered a fundamental change in the conduct of personnel policy." Or as Schmundt put it the following month before an audience of future high personnel officers, his appointment meant the "direct influence of the Führer on the framing [*Gestaltung*] of the Führerkorps of the *Wehrmacht*. The supreme commander [*Feldherr*] shapes his officer corps in the manner required by the assigned tasks."[74]

What that *Feldherr* decreed was the supremacy of the "National Socialist *Leistungsprinzip*." Promotion for all categories of officers would follow function rather than seniority. The "one-sided qualification" of *Bildung* would no longer in any way restrict access to officer candidacy. NCOs promoted to officer rank since September 1939 (who, in an echo of the "officer substitutes" of 1914–18, had been carried on a separate and implicitly second-class seniority list) would

72. [Field Marshal Wilhelm] Keitel to major commands, OKH Chef. PA Nr. 4300/42 g., 7 June 1942, "Grundsätze für die Beförderung von aktiven Offizieren," BA-MA RH 2/156.

73. See the embarrassed account of Schmundt's takeover of general staff personnel matters given by the losing side in "Die Personelle Entwicklung des Generalstabes des Heeres während des Krieges 1939-194 . . . ," November 1942, p. 53, BA-MA RH2/238; for Schmundt's appointment as Chef HPA, Schmundt diary, p. 4 (3 October 1942); Schmundt, Brauchitsch, and Hitler: Engel, *Heeresadjutant*, p. 117 (7 December 1941).

74. "Vortrag v. 17.11.42 des Herrn Generalmajor Schmundt, Chef PA und Chefadjutant, vor einer Lehrgang für höhere Adjutanten in der Kriegsakademie," BA-MA RH12–1/75, pp. 140–43.

merge fully with the officer corps. Even the army's intellectual elite, the general staff corps, would henceforth receive promotion only after successful combat command. The final goal, as Hitler announced in January 1943 in a famous order on "Führer-selection through battle [*Führerauslese durch den Kampf*]" communicated to every officer in the army and extended at Hitler's request to the other services, was to recognize and to use "extraordinary and utterly unflappable [*krisenfesten*] personalities from rifleman to general" in the highest commands for which they were suited. Only the ability to "master critical situations" would henceforth decide who filled Germany's "Führer-positions in the face of the enemy."[75] Hitler's order did not use the word *Offizier*; the Prusso-German officer corps had ceased to exist.

The foremost student of German wartime manpower policy, Bernhard R. Kroener, has argued against the view that National Socialist "elite manipulation" was at the core of the new system of officer entry and promotion, and has insisted that "ideological motives manifestly [*offenkundig*] played no role" in the decision to introduce unrestricted promotion according to *Leistung* in 1942. It was rather the massive losses in Russia, along with the perpetual shortage of middle-level officers that had resulted from the Versailles limits on the *Reichswehr*'s size, that had led inexorably to the new system, which was the only possible response to "the implacable demands of modern technological mass warfare."[76] This is a view that dovetails neatly with the "structuralist" or "functionalist" interpretation of the Third Reich, which condemns references to individual will and design as outmoded "methodological individualism" and invokes impersonal social forces or bureaucratic rivalries to explain events.[77] Kroener's view also supports and perhaps derives from the parallel and widely shared contention that any "modernization" of German society after 1933 was an

---

75. Schmundt diary, pp. 7, 8 (9 October 1942); Schmundt Vortragsnotiz, "Fortfall des Dienstaltersliste C," 9 October 1942, NARA T-78/40/6002477–79; Hitler decree, 19 January 1943, in Papke et al., *Anciennität*, p. 276, and cover letter, Schmundt to Göring, 20 January 1943, BA-ZNS Offizier-Beförderungsbestimmungen I.

76. Kroener, "Nationalsozialistische Volksarmee," pp. 673–674; see also pp. 654, 655, 659; DRZW 5/1:897, 902, 906; his "Strukturelle Veränderungen," p. 285; and DRZW 5/2:878 (but see also pp. 856-57); similarly if less emphatically Jürgen Förster, "Vom Führerheer der Republik zur nationalsozialistischen Volksarmee," pp. 311–28 in Jost Dülffer, Bernd Martin, and Günter Wollstein, eds., *Deutschland in Europa: Kontinuität und Bruch, Gedenkschrift für Andreas Hillgruber* (Frankfurt a. M., 1990), p. 317–18; for additional evidence on Hitler's intentions, see Reinhard Stumpf, *Die Wehrmacht-Elite: Rang- und Herkunftsstruktur der deutschen Generale und Admirale 1933-1945* (Boppard, 1982), pp. 303-48.

77. The most eloquent statement of this approach remains Tim Mason, "Intention and Explanation," in his *Nazism, Fascism and the Working Class*, pp. 212-30.

unintended consequence of Nazi policy, and stemmed above all from total war.[78]

But such views appear to rest on the bizarre assumption that the European war of 1939 and the global war of 1941 – and at least some of their consequences – were *unintended*. They also fail to fit the evidence surrounding the decisions that destroyed the officer corps as a *corps*. Why did "modern technological mass warfare" produce its allegedly inevitable result only after Hitler appointed Schmundt as personnel chief, and stripped the army general staff of control even over general staff promotions? Hitler himself thought – as he told Joseph Goebbels in May and October 1942 – that he was imposing with some difficulty "an entirely new principle of leadership" against obstinate resistance from "reactionary forces" and "the calcified *Wehrmacht* old gang."[79] And Schmundt's own diary account, the wording and content of the relevant directives, and comparison of German officer losses through mid-1942 and after with those of the Great War make clear the central role of Hitler's revolutionary ideology. As in other areas, Hitler indeed could not act freely until circumstances and "structures" permitted. But when he did act, his role was decisive.

Schmundt ascribed the revolution in officer policy to the issue's "fundamental importance" in Hitler's eyes – although he noted retrospectively that "a contributing factor was that according to our statistical data the [numbers of new regular] officers required could not be even approximately covered from graduates with the *Abitur* alone."[80] Yet tension between battlefield demand and home-front supply could scarcely by itself have produced an officer recruitment and promotion policy that celebrated "brutal energy" and disparaged *Bildung*, that sought pitilessly to eliminate even effective older officers, and that tenaciously sought to substitute function for rank.

The language of the implementing orders likewise demonstrates both the primacy of Hitler's will and ideology, and the relentlessness of his repeated demands for results. "According to the will of the Führer and Commander-in-chief of the *Wehrmacht* . . . The Führer has once more ordered . . . The Führer takes the view . . . The Führer

78. Unintended consequence: Ralf Dahrendorf, *Society and Democracy in Germany* (New York, 1967), p. 382; see, in general, the survey of Michael Prinz, "Die soziale Funktion moderner Elemente in der Gesellschaftspolitik des Nationalsozialismus," pp. 297–327 in Prinz and Zitelmann, eds., *Nationalsozialismus und Modernisierung*.
79. Hitler, in Joseph Goebbels, *Die Tagebücher von Joseph Goebbels: Sämtliche Fragmente*, ed. Elke Fröhlich et al. (Munich, 1987–96), Teil 2, *Diktate*, vol. 4, p. 358 (24 May 1942) and vol. 6, pp. 51–52 (2 October 1942).
80. Schmundt diary, p. 8 (9 October 1942).

wishes . . . The Führer has established . . ." and the like are the operative words in *all* key directives on officer policy in 1942–43. Was this
bureaucratic ventriloquism or cleverly disguised obeisance to "the
implacable demands of modern technological mass warfare"?[81] It
seems unlikely. The army personnel office, in an exhaustive forty-four-
page study on the structure of the officer corps presented to Halder in
July 1942, had pronounced itself satisfied that the qualified acceleration of promotion for outstanding regular (but not reserve) officers
ordered in winter, spring, and summer 1941–42 would solve the temporary shortage of battalion, regimental, and division commanders
that derived from the 100,000-man army's age structure. It also recommended only modest improvements in recruiting procedures to
make up a growing shortfall in regular lieutenants. These evolutionary
measures were clearly not what Hitler had repeatedly demanded: the
bureaucracy planned to retain the *Abitur* as the usual precondition for
regular officer candidacy, and had stopped far short of unrestricted
promotion to the rank appropriate to the command position held. On
the eve of Schmundt's advent, the personnel office still reportedly
thought it "scarcely tolerable . . . to promote to colonel – for example
– a major who was leading a regiment."[82]

Nor was the pressure of losses uppermost in the minds of the
bureaucrats; the July 1942 personnel office study suggests that its chief
concern – and probably Halder's as well – was less to cope with losses
than to ensure a balanced age pyramid and career structure for the
future peacetime regular officer corps.[83] And so far officer losses (both
army and *Wehrmacht*) were in any case lower, on a daily basis, as a proportion of those serving, and in proportion to population, than the
losses of the Great War that had signally failed to transform the officer corps. Over the 36 months from 1 September 1939 to 31 August
1942, the daily average of dead and missing German officers was 30.6
– against 33.3 for the much longer 1914–1918 period. Schmundt's
office calculated that as late as 30 September 1943 German army offi-

---

81. See the orders of 17 February, 4/5 November 1942, 19 January, 11 and 14 May 1943,
     in Papke et al., *Anciennität*, pp. 303, 286–92, 276, 295, 311, and the archival documents
     cited in notes 71 and 72 above.
82. [General Bodewin] Keitel to Halder, Chef HPA Nr. 549/42 g. Kdos., 6 July 1942,
     "Übersicht über die Zusammensetzung und Schichtung des Offizierkorps und die
     daraus sich ergebenden Folgen," p. 11; Anlage 7 ("Offiziernachwuchslage"), p. 1;
     Anlage 9 ("Gedanken über den künftigen Beförderungsablauf: Offizier-
     beförderungskegel"), p. 3, BA-MA RH 2/156; Albrecht (Reich Air Ministry) Akten-
     vermerk, "Beförderungen von Offiziere ausser der Reihe . . . ," 9 October 1942, copy
     in BA-ZNS, "Führerbefehle" III.
83. Keitel, Chef HPA Nr. 549/42 g. Kdos, 6 July 1942, Anlage 9.

cer dead totalled only 14.7 percent of those who had served, compared to 18.2 percent for the Great War. In proportion to population, dead and missing German officers through August 1942 amounted to roughly 47 per 100,000, compared to 79 for 1914-18. Finally, the 180,765 regular and reserve army officers of 1 October 1942 constituted roughly 3.1 percent of total army strength, up from the 2.4 percent of total strength represented by the 89,000 officers of September 1939.[84] No immediate crisis demanded the forceful measures of October–November 1942.

The implacable demands of Verdun, of the Somme, of Passchendaele, and of Ludendorff's murderous 1918 offensives had failed to break the mold of the Prusso-German *Offizier* because the officer corps had been embedded in a political system that refused change, and because the corps' preeminent link to that system, the Kaiser's Military Cabinet, had been socially and ideologically impervious to the demands of military effectiveness. The lesser – although still enormous – losses of 1941–42, by contrast, led to decisive results because the head of state had chosen war as his instrument of domestic conquest. Military crisis both impelled and legitimated his seizure of personal control over officer recruitment and promotion. Hitler himself viewed the change as a long overdue introduction into the army of the Party's principles of Führer-selection, which in turn derived from the notions of charismatic personal leadership pioneered by the front officers of 1914–18. The new system, as Schmundt proudly proclaimed, answered at last the widespread expectations and hopes thwarted in the Great War: "[The] needs and wishes of the Front of [19]14–18 are the same as those of today."[85]

Even the post-1806 tradition of the election of officer candidates by their future regimental officers fell victim in December 1942 to the necessities of mobile warfare and the seemingly endless campaign in Russia; its irrelevance was already manifest.[86] The line between offi-

---

84. Figures derived or calculated from "Gesamtausfälle der Wehrmacht (nach dem Stand von 31.12.44)," IWM MI 14/147; Linnarz memorandum, 33416/44 geh., 18 May 1944, "Vergleich der Offiziersverluste in den Jahren 1914–1918 und 1939–30.4.1944," annex 2 (table), IWM AL 2507; Altrock, *Vom Sterben des deutschen Offizierkorps*, p. 64; Schmundt diary, pp. 3–4 (1 October 1942); army size from DRZW 5/1:731 and Burckhart Müller-Hillebrand, "Personnel and Administration," Monograph P-005, U.S. Army, HQ European Command, Historical Division (1949), p. 90, IWM AL 1361.

85. See Hitler, in *Die Tagebücher von Joseph Goebbels, Diktate*, vol. 6, p. 51 (2 October 1942), and "Vortrag v. 17.11.42 des Herrn Generalmajor Schmundt," BA-MA RH12–1/75.

86. OKH 2118/42 P4 (1b), 24 December 1942, HVBl 1943, B, p. 6; Friedrich-Wilhelm von Seydlitz, "Der Offiziernachwuchs des deutschen Heeres im 2. Weltkriege," p. 31,

cers and NCOs, almost inviolable in 1914–18, eroded swiftly; the latter, Schmundt noted in late 1943, "formed in large part the preliminary step from which the huge gaps in the officer corps could be filled." Only the Luftwaffe and above all the navy, which continued to privilege seniority, resisted the promotion of qualified NCOs to officer rank in order – as Schmundt described it – to "prevent undesirable social mobility [*Umschichtung*]."[87] The army, for its part, no longer judged prospective marriages of officers and officer candidates by social criteria, but by racial ones – a development that had been gathering force since early 1940, when Hitler had damned the existing officer marriage regulations to his army adjutant as antieugenic, "reactionary, an encouragement to celibacy, and hidebound."[88] Soon, as in the SS, even a child out of wedlock by a mother of suitable pedigree was transmuted from fatal career impediment to a sign of healthy *Volk*-consciousness.

The predominance of function over status and of battlefield Darwinism over formal *Bildung* was the central feature of the revolutionary shift from *Offizier* to battlefield Führer from October 1942 onward. The *Offizierstand*, already radically diluted by the widespread admission even before 1939 of former NCOs and other previously unacceptable elements, now dissolved into a larger *Führerkorps* – a concept pioneered by the Waffen-SS – that also included the army's NCOs.[89] Symptomatic of the growing supremacy of function over status was the gradual advance, at Hitler's repeated insistence and despite tenacious resistance from the units, of proposals for *demoting* to positions appropriate to their level of competence officers who had failed in combat commands. Nor could disabled or forcibly retired older officers, whatever their former rank, now lay the customary claim to a civilian wartime employment commensurate with their earlier status.[90]

Anlage 4 to Helmuth Reinhardt, "Ersatz, Ausbildung und Verwendungskontrolle der Offiziere im deutschen Heere," Monograph P-021, U.S. Army, HQ European Command, Historical Division (1949), BA-MA F2/2.

87. Schmundt diary, pp. 101, 71.
88. Schmundt diary, p. 32 (12 December 1942); Hitler, in Engel, *Heeresadjutant*, p. 72. The evolution of the *Wehrmacht*'s marriage regulations toward eugenic correctness is instructive: see HVBl 1936, p. 121 (Nr. 364); 1937, p. 482 (Nr. 1317); 1940 C, pp. 55–56 (Nr. 188) and pp. 108–109 (Nr. 324); 1941 C, pp. 396–401 (Nr. 581).
89. "Sammelbegriff: Führerkorps des Heeres": Schmundt diary, p. 298: see also pp. 20, 40, 90.
90. Schmundt diary, pp. 46, 57, 67, 69, 73–75, 153–54, 157, 185–86, 202. Schmundt's entries make clear that the demotion proposal was not simply a corrective measure, necessitated by inevitable combat failure of those promoted beyond their level of competence, or of the unlucky; it was also an expression of Hitler's insistence on the primacy of function over status.

The new system also bore the marks of Hitler's own peculiar attitude toward risk and reward. Since the Party's early days, and in accordance with the myth of charismatic Germanic tribal leadership on which he modelled his own power, membership in the Führer's *Gefolgschaft* had by his frequently expressed wish been rewarded by spoils. Promotion for battlefield performance was in his view thus not merely a Darwinian selection device in the interests of the *Volk*. It was also part of the individual's just reward and a vital measure for cementing the Führer's following, analogous to the lavish cash gifts used to increase the malleability of figures such as Brauchitsch, and thereafter spread liberally throughout the higher officer corps. War, as Hitler had intended, made the whole nation his *Gefolgschaft* in this as in other ways.[91]

By late 1944, the National Socialist breakthrough within the army was almost complete in both social and institutional terms. Socially, the "armed brotherhood" of the front exemplified the National Socialist ideal of *Volk*-community to an extent unparalleled in any other sphere of German life. Command authority in combat units now rested in large part on charisma – which is established and demonstrated by success. Superior and subordinate had became "Führer and follower in the sense of the National Socialist community." And total war was unthinkable without military leaders capable of inoculating their "followership" with an "ungovernable will to annihilation" of the enemy.[92]

The Waffen-SS *Führerkorps* was one prototype for this development. By mid-1944 over half of the higher ranks of its line officers from major upward had no more than a middle-school education without the *Abitur*, and 21.3 percent had only an elementary education. In general, the lower the rank and the younger the officer, the lower the average educational level. And roughly a third of the extremely het-

---

91. On Hitler's bribery of his chief military subordinates, see Engel, *Heeresadjutant*, pp. 85–86; Weinberg, *The Foreign Policy of Hitler's Germany*, vol. 2, pp. 384–85; *A World at Arms* (Cambridge, 1994), pp. 305 and 1015 note 156; and "Zur Dotation Hitlers an Generalfeldmarschall Ritter von Leeb," MGM 2/1979, pp. 97–99; also the well-documented and wittily illustrated article of Peter Meroth, "Vorschuss auf den Endsieg," *Stern* 25/1980, 12 June 1980, pp. 86–92.

92. Charisma: Max Weber, *Economy and Society* (Berkeley, 1978), vol. 1, p. 242; "Führer and follower": Ruder speech, 23 February 1944, in Waldemar Besson, "Zur Geschichte des nationalsozialistischen Führungsoffiziers (NSFO)," VfZG 9 (1961), p. 111; "Vernichtungswille": speech by General Ritter von Hengl, chief of NS-Führungsstab OKH, summer 1944, quoted in Messerschmidt, "Der Reflex der Volksgemeinschaftsidee in der Wehrmacht," in his *Militärgeschichtliche Aspekte der Entwicklung des deutschen Nationalstaates* (Düsseldorf, 1988), p. 212.

erogeneous Waffen-SS general officer corps consisted of men from working-class, peasant, or lower-middle-class backgrounds, while only 8 percent were noble. The highest ranking Waffen-SS officer – and highest-ranking former NCO in the armed forces – was *Oberstgruppenführer* and (four-star) general of the Waffen-SS Sepp Dietrich, a former shop assistant, 1914–18 sergeant, and chauffeur to Hitler whose battlefield energy and brutality made up for his legendary lack of *Bildung* and subtlety.[93]

The army, especially at the higher ranks, was inevitably slower to change than the Waffen-SS. By May 1944, 21.5 percent of the army's 1,246 generals were still noble – but at the other end of the social scale, the number of generals from lower-middle-class backgrounds had increased markedly as a result of the numerous casualties and dismissals since the winter crisis of 1941–42.[94] At intake level, the nobility and upper middle classes already provided only a quarter of officer candidates in 1939–41, while candidates from working-class backgrounds increased from none in 1936 to 9 percent of the total by the end of 1942. As late as 1941, 90 percent of all candidates possessed *Abitur* or *Primareife*; by end 1942, only 78 percent did, while the proportion of candidates with primary education alone rose from 4.1 to 11.8 percent. Only 44 percent of officers commissioned in the second half of the war had an *Abitur* or equivalent, and by 1 May 1943 a mere 3.9 percent of the army's 22,535 regular lieutenants were nobles.[95] In the middle of the age and rank pyramid, former sergeants from the *Reichswehr* or police found the road open to the highest ranks to which

---

93. Bernd Wegner, *The Waffen-SS: Organization, Ideology and Function* (Oxford, 1988), p. 248; Wegner, "Das Führerkorps der Waffen-SS," pp. 338–39; Nicolaus von Preradovich, *Die Generale der Waffen-SS* (Berg am See, 1985), pp. 10–11.
94. Nicolaus von Preradovich, *Die militärische und soziale Herkunft der Generalität des deutschen Heeres, 1. Mai 1944* (Osnabrück, 1978), p. 80; Stumpf, *Wehrmacht-Elite*, pp. 298–302. Stumpf's figures are unfortunately an aggregate, for each rank, covering the entire 1933–45 period, and thus not directly comparable with those of Preradovich: they do nevertheless suggest a decreasing proportion of nobles and rapid increase in generals from previously unacceptable backgrounds by war's end.
95. Kroener, "Volksarmee," pp. 679–80; "Strukturelle Veränderungen," p. 295; and DRZW 5/2:865-67 (centerpiece of an exemplary statistical analysis of officer candidate intake from 1928/30 to end 1942). *Leutnante* and *Oberleutnante*, 1 May 1943: table in Rudolf Absolon, *Sammlung wehrrechtlicher Gutachten und Vorschriften* (Aachen-Kornelimünster, 1963–85), vol. 12, p. 8. These figures, and much other evidence, undermine the apparent suggestion of David Schoenbaum, *Hitler's Social Revolution* (New York, 1966), pp. 285–86, that the Nazi revolution existed primarily in "*interpreted* social reality" (my emphasis); for more on the issue, see William Jannen, Jr., "National Socialists and Social Mobility," *Journal of Social History* 9 (1976), pp. 339–66.

battlefield performance could carry them; by 1945 at least eighteen former NCOs had reached the rank of general or admiral.[96]

Politically and institutionally, defeat on all fronts, the public apostasy of high officers captured by the Soviets, and the abortive 20 July 1944 bomb plot accelerated and vindicated the final stage of the Party's "seizure of power" in the military sphere: the takeover of the army's central machinery and many of its duties by Himmler and Martin Bormann.[97] Himmler had secured permission from Hitler even before 20 July to establish "*Volksgrenadier*" divisions under his own control but using army personnel, and a vengeful dictator subsequently gave him command of all army rear services and units within Germany. In the autumn, Bormann and Himmler set up yet another party-army, the *Volkssturm*, for last-ditch defense of German soil by the very young and very old. And Himmler argued semipublicly that the critical opportunity to Nazify the army had been missed in 1934 as a result of contingent factors: Röhm's "unholy proclivities, unholy activities, unholy disloyalty." Himmler explicitly misappropriated for National Socialism the example of the reformers of 1807–08: a new band of "outsiders" would once again pitilessly purge an "army eaten through by treason." Germany's "holy peoples' war" would and must be won by a "National Socialist People's Army."[98]

The response of the individual officer or aspirant to this revolutionary breakthrough is poorly documented. The swift collapse, between 1935 and 1942, of rigid barriers to entry and ascent in a calling that had traditionally constituted the first *Stand* in German society clearly generated heartfelt enthusiasm. But even the intensely ambitious usually refrain from confessing their ambitions on paper – and army regulations damned as a "character defect" all "ambition solely for personal gain, [and] striving that degenerates into unscrupulous hustling [*Streberei*]."[99] Surviving letters from the front appear to emphasize the collective rather than individual satisfactions of war and conquest as well as the fears and hardships it entailed.[100]

---

96. Career summaries in Lahne, *Unteroffiziere*, pp. 479–82.
97. For Himmler, see the useful summary by Stumpf, *Wehrmacht-Elite*, pp. 345–47 note 177; for Bormann, see Besson, "NSFO," especially pp. 94, 98–113.
98. Theodor Eschenburg, ed., "Die Rede Himmlers vor den Gauleitern am 3. August 1944," VfZG 1 (1953), pp. 366, 384, 392.
99. HDv 291 (1936), quoted in Schmundt diary, p. xv.
100. See especially the effusions printed in Ortwin Buchbender and Reinhold Stertz, eds., *Das andere Gesicht des Krieges: Deutsche Feldpostbriefe 1939-1945* (Munich, 1982), nos. 21, 40, 41, 44, 82, 98, 99, 131, 157, 174.

But deeds also speak. Combat leadership cannot be coerced; only those willing to raise their heads when sane men hug the ground in terror will do. The numbers of Germans who accepted the measurably greater risks and vastly greater pressures of service as officers makes the extent of the response clear enough. In 1938–39 one fifth of all German students receiving the *Abitur* sought careers in the *Wehrmacht*, a figure unthinkable in Italy, Britain, or the United States.[101] And between June 1942 and April 1944, 90,718 officer candidates – a figure corresponding to almost 40 percent of the spring 1944 officer corps – received commissions as lieutenants.[102] The proportion of officer candidates volunteering to serve as regular rather than reserve officers concurrently rose from 1 in 7 of the October 1942 intake to 1 in 3.5 for 1943 – testimony to the intensity of the militant ambition that pervaded German society. The catastrophes of 1944 in East and West had only a slight damping effect: 1 in 4.5 of the roughly 54,000 lieutenants commissioned from January through November 1944 were regulars. The ambition to serve in the most lethal arm – infantry – held up well (1:4.5) and 1944 vocations for the *Panzertruppen* ran at the striking rate of 1 regular to every 2.1 reservists. Even reserve officers made increasingly noteworthy careers after 1942: freed from the custom that had restricted them to the rank of major or below, they ascended to lieutenant colonel and colonel in increasing numbers, and ultimately in a few cases reached general officer rank. Schmundt noted proudly in early 1944 that hitherto "men of ability had been suppressed, and that the new promotion system has given greater satisfaction to [the reserve] officer corps."[103]

An enormous expansion of NCO recruitment was similarly successful. Army "NCO preparatory schools" for likely youths below military age were oversubscribed, and the graduates of the Hitler Youth military training camps [*Wehrertüchtigungslager*] organized from 1942 onward became the armed forces' most reliable source of enthusiastic NCO and officer candidates. The regime was immensely successful in harnessing adolescent revolt to its own militant purposes; it indeed "won the loyalty of Germany's children and youths by entrusting them

101. Memorandum of the Reich education ministry, September 1939, in Herbert Michaelis and Ernst Schraepler, eds., *Ursachen und Folgen* (Berlin, 1958–64), vol. 13, p. 654.
102. Figures: Schmundt diary, pp. 34, 123, 132.
103. Schmundt memorandum, 23 January 1944, "Auswertung der Übersicht über die Entwicklung des Offizierkorps in der Zeit v. 26.8.39–1.10.43," pp. 3, 5; 1944 ratios calculated from Ag P.1/1.(Zentral-)Abt. (IIIa), 23 February 1945, "Beförderung zum Offizier im Jahre 1944 aufgeschlüsselt nach Waffengattungen und Wehrverhältnissen," both in IWM AL 2507; reserve general officers: Stumpf, *Wehrmacht-Elite*, p. 63.

with tremendous destructive powers."[104] The NCO corps also gave up its best men on an accelerated basis, especially after officer losses reached the staggering average of 317.5 casualties a day in September 1944. From that point on, NCOs who led platoons or companies adequately for even brief periods could expect promotion to lieutenant after one-month courses.[105]

The battlefield consequences of the new system are neither directly measurable nor easily separable from the effects of other influences on German combat performance such as ideology and terror. But the new selection criteria and the available information on those actually recruited make persuasive conjecture possible. The efforts of Hitler, Schmundt, and Schmundt's deputy and successor, Wilhelm Burgdorf, to rejuvenate the army officer corps were successful. As Burgdorf noted after the change was already largely accomplished, "the type of the future division commander should be a young, combat-experienced and combat-proven officer, who can carry the troops with him through his élan and willpower, and has already demonstrated this in leadership positions as battalion and regimental commander."[106]

By 1944–45, men best able to bear the extraordinary physical and psychological strains of combat had reached midlevel positions in large numbers, with the youngest receiving promotion to captain at twenty-two, to major at twenty-five, and to lieutenant colonel at twenty-seven. By late 1944 the youngest sometimes lacked the experience, training, and maturity necessary to command battalions and regiments well – but they proved good enough to maintain the army's leadership superiority over its opponents.[107] The change in age structure also assisted mightily in the penetration of ideology: from midwar onward the immense majority of company officers had passed through the Hitler Youth. Finally, the new policy guaranteed the solidarity of leaders and led. It ensured that those who served with luck and credit in combat as enlisted men could expect swift promotion into the Führerkorps. The perceived justice of their rise to leadership cemented the *Kampfgemeinschaft* against any repetition of 1918, and their

---

104. Lahne, *Unteroffiziere*, p. 468; Gerhard Rempel, *Hitler's Children: The Hitler Youth and the SS* (Chapel Hill, 1989), Chapter 7; quotation from Bartov, *Hitler's Army*, p. 110.
105. Schmundt diary, pp. 238, 250, 284.
106. Schmundt diary, p. 213 (18 August 1944).
107. "Lebensalter der jüngsten und ältesten am 1.1.1945 planmässig *und* vorzugsweise beförderten Offiziere . . . ," IWM AL 2507. For analysis of the dysfunctions of the new system brought out by the genuinely immense losses of mid-1944, see unsigned Vortragsnotiz (typed on a "Führer-Schreibmaschine"), apparently by Burgdorf, 22 November 1944, BA-MA H 4/5.

often unassuming origins gave them decisive advantages in establishing and maintaining rapport with their troops. Above all else, the post-1942 entry and promotion process rested on an objective professional test that dispensed entirely with social privilege, and even preceded ideology. Victory and defeat, mission success and failure, unit collapse and unit survival are stark and easily measurable alternatives.

Battlefield selection and National Socialist fanaticism were not exclusively responsible for the desperate fighting power of the Third Reich's final phases. At the tactical level they complemented – and fostered – the individual creativity in combat that the Prussian reformers had championed. The Nazi regime's "political free enterprise" found its battlefield counterpart in intensely competitive displays of "self-will that sometimes crosses the bounds of normal self-reliance." In the period of lightning campaigns up to November–December 1941, *Eigenwille* was most conspicuous in the operational leadership, especially among the intensely competitive commanders of the large armored units. Yet the 1940 fighting in Norway, the Low Countries, and France showed that the army had succeeded at all levels: it possessed "*Kämpfer* who think and act on their own" to a degree that surpassed all opponents.

The next year, the immense initial successes against the Red Army bore out the optimism of the army's leaders about their subordinates. The chief of staff of one of the lead armies in the East summed up before the campaign in remarks characterized by hubris in most respects – but not in this: "The [Russian] *junior* leadership is by-the-book [*schematisch*], without self-reliance [*Selbständigkeit*] and lacking in flexibility. We are in this area *far* superior! *Our* junior leaders boldly attack, without fear of 'responsibility.'"[108] The forty-six months of war in the East that followed accentuated beyond all previous measure the requirement for self-reliance and fearlessness in taking responsibility, on a battlefield of unparalleled vastness and emptiness, against an enemy almost as merciless if not as skilled as the Germans themselves. From the camps of the Hitler Jugend onward, Hitler's regime, his army, and his Waffen-SS inculcated brilliantly all the skills of modern tactical leadership: command of map and compass, inconspicuous movement and swift grasp of terrain, mastery of weapons and of communications techniques, swift judgment of situations and framing of

---

108. Günther Blumentritt, chief of staff of 4th Army (and later operations chief of the army general staff), 8 May 1941 (emphasis in original), quoted in Hillgruber, "Das Russland-Bild der führenden deutschen Militärs vor Beginn des Angriffs auf die Sowjetunion," Bernd Wegner, ed., *Zwei Wege nach Moskau* (Munich, 1991), pp. 178–79.

orders, the gift for inspiring others, and above all else the ability to react in a practiced way to the unexpected.[109] Those skills, energized by the "National Socialist Idea" and the regime's revolution of individual ambition, so helped to prolong Hitler's war that by its bitter end in 1945 it had killed three times as many Germans as had died in 1914–18.

CONCLUSION

It was both ironic and characteristic that the regime squandered much of the power generated through military-social revolution. The very force that had unleashed it – Hitler's will and Hitler's ideology – increasingly deprived the German armed forces after 1941 of the *operational* creativity required to put *tactical* brilliance and individual ambition to best use. Hitler had taunted Halder in 1941 that "anyone can handle this little matter of operational command." But the dictator's insistence after 1941 on holding every square meter of conquered *Lebensraum* and his daily niggling interference to division level and below was so contrary to Prussian tradition and so obviously counterproductive that in later decades the Führer's surviving generals dined out on tales of the victories of which he had allegedly deprived them.[110] Rage against the constraints of military and economic reality, a deep mistrust of the officer corps that surfaced once more as failure in Russia became manifest, and boundless contempt for formal education led Hitler increasingly to target his own general staff corps as the enemy. As a four years' *Frontkämpfer* he was confident that he knew infinitely better than men – as he mocked Halder to his face in September 1942 – who had allegedly sat out the Great War on their swivel-stools.[111] In the end, the ideology of will overcame the profes-

---

109. For an exemplary snapshot of the concepts and techniques involved, see "Ausbildungsplan für Unteroffizieranwärter (6 Wochen-Lehrgang)(Ausbildung zum Gruppenführer und als Ausbilder)," Anlage zu OKH/GenStdH/Ausb.Abt.(Ia) Nr. 340/44 g., 23 January 1944, BA-MA RH 2/78.
110. Halder, *Hitler als Feldherr*, p. 45. The generals' tales lost nothing in the telling: see especially Erich von Manstein, *Verlorene Siege* (Bonn, 1955); Basil H. Liddell Hart, *The German Generals Talk* (New York, 1948); and Bernd Wegner, "Erschriebene Siege: Franz Halder, die 'Historical Division' und die Rekonstruktion des Zweiten Weltkrieges im Geiste des deutschen Generalstabes," in Ernst Willi Hansen et al., eds., *Politischer Wandel, organisierte Gewalt und nationale Sicherheit* (Munich 1995), pp. 287–302.
111. Engel, *Heeresadjutant*, p. 125 (4 September 1942); see also Hitler's increasingly fierce denunciations of his generals, general staff corps, and officer corps, ibid., pp. 124, 127, 128, 129.

sional rationality that the Prussian reformers had sought to guarantee through *Bildung*.[112]

Yet the strategic intransigence and operational rigidity that radiated outward from Führer-headquarters should not obscure the extent to which Hitler realized key aims of the reformers and belatedly redeemed promises they had made. The young *Kämpfer* and battlefield Führer of 1944 might well have made Scharnhorst and Gneisenau quail. The racist fanaticism, pitiless and sometimes gleeful reprisals against noncombatants, and lack of educational polish of the German junior leaders in the war's final phases would presumably have seemed alien even to combat soldiers steeped in German romanticism's bloodthirsty response to Napoleonic France.[113] National Socialism nevertheless succeeded conspicuously in fusing the Prussian military reformers' central concepts – battlefield *Selbständigkeit* and careers open to "outstanding bravery and presence of mind" without regard for social origin. The result by 1944 was far more that the mere "alliance of government and nation" that the reformers had sought. The Nazi regime, even as it went down in ruin, came close to achieving the *identity* of army and society and of officers and men: a murderous racist *Kampfgemeinschaft* molded by "selection through battle" and united unto death by its ideals and its crimes. That community was the living essence of the German Revolution.

<hr />

112. As also arguably occurred in other fields: see Klaus Hildebrand, *The Foreign Policy of the Third Reich* (Berkeley, 1973), especially pp. 121–22, 140–41.

113. See for instance Clausewitz's passionate – and chaotic – "Profession of Faith [*Bekenntnisdenkschrift*]" of February 1812, in Carl von Clausewitz, *Schriften-Aufsätze-Studien-Briefe*, ed. Werner Hahlweg (Göttingen, 1966), especially Clausewitz's almost Fichtean disparagement of the French, pp. 735–36.

Conclusion

EXPANSIONIST ZEAL, FIGHTING POWER, AND STAYING POWER IN THE ITALIAN AND GERMAN DICTATORSHIPS

The similarities in structures and dynamics between Fascist Italy and Nazi Germany provide few clues to help explain the enormous disparities between them in expansionist zeal, fighting power, and staying power. Both regimes arose from compromises between militant nationalist mass parties born of the Great War an⎯ ⎯tablishments that same war had shaken and humiliated. For both, waɪ was an instrument not merely of external conquest but also for the barbarization of their societies and the final taming or destruction of all institutions, from churches to officer corps to the Italian monarchy, that blocked their paths to total power at home. Fascist and Nazi expansion was the polar opposite of "social imperialism," the preservation or restoration of the political and social order at home through success abroad. The wars of Fascism and Nazism, far from aiming to avert revolution, were designed to make it.[1]

Yet one dictatorship crumbled almost apologetically. The other defended to the last cartridge an empire that at its height stretched from the North Cape to the Western Desert and from the Pyrenees to the Caucasus. Understanding that difference in outcome requires an attempt to separate the layers of causation involved. The most important factors appear to fall into three roughly chronological categories: underlying or inherited structures and forces, structures and forces connected with the regimes themselves, and events and their sequence.

---

1. See especially Tim Mason's suggestion that "National Socialism appears as a *radically new* variant of the social imperialism of Bismarck and Wilhelm II. . . . successful foreign expansion would legitimize not an inherited political and social system but an entirely new one" ("The Legacy of 1918 for National Socialism," in A. J. Nicholls and E. Matthias, eds., *German Democracy and the Triumph of Hitler* [London, 1971], p. 218 [my emphasis]).

I

The regimes inherited from their respective national pasts wide differences in socioeconomic conditions, political institutions, military-economic potential, military expertise and traditions, and ideological climate. Italy was in the aggregate thirty to fifty years behind Germany in becoming an industrial society, and deeply split between city and country, North and South. Germany's deepest cleavages were of an entirely different character. Deep regional economic disparities and sociocultural divides existed – East Elbia was in some respects a far more literate Italian South. Religion and political religion divided the Catholic and Socialist subcultures from the dominant Protestant Prussian culture. But regional and confessional divides were ultimately of less consequence than the rigid horizontal segmentation between *Stände* inherited from the old regime.

Despite industrialization and the lifting in 1918 of the last laws that enshrined social distinctions, the divisions between *Stände* – especially those frozen into the educational system – retained much of their force. And Germany's higher level of industrialization and literacy made these inherited distinctions more galling to those they held down than any social barriers in Italy. Most galling of all was the cleavage the Prussian military state had erected between the *Offizierstand* and all other Germans. The collapse of the monarchy in November 1918 largely failed to throw open new paths of social ascent, and the ensuing economic roller-coaster ride through inflation, uneven and uneasy prosperity, and deepening slump after 1927–28 further constricted opportunity.

The political structures that the Fascist and Nazi regimes inherited were almost equally disparate. Liberal Italy was not quite as unlike Imperial Germany as often thought: foreign and military policy formed a preserve of royal and ministerial quasi-absolutism. Parliaments in both countries before 1918/19 were either unrepresentative of the electorate and/or could block but not initiate policy. But Italy's ruling groups, bound together by Masonry and Catholicism as well as by monarchism, nevertheless formed a far more cohesive whole than Germany's.

The Great War, bitterly lost or barely won, ended some crucial similarities. War and its aftereffects did paralyze and destroy parliamentary institutions in both countries: almost immediately in the Italian case and in the German case by delayed action. But the Italian monarchy and its officer corps nevertheless survived the war and the postwar crisis. And the social conservatism of the Vatican and the deep roots of the Italian Church made them tenacious forces against change that were lacking north of the Alps. In Germany the war, with its interminable quarrels between generals and civilians, interest groups and bureaucrats, industry and labor, further intensified the polycratic character of the state. Defeat and the 1918 revolution left a vacuum at the top that Weimar, even after Hindenburg became its president, could not fill. The army and navy, cut loose from the monarchy, were now answerable to no one but themselves. And religion, far more than in Italy, was a source of conflict rather than of cohesion within the establishment. The Nazi movement faced far less tenacious establishment opposition after 1933 than did its Italian counterpart after 1922; Germany's preexisting "polycracy" contributed mightily to Hitler's success.

The Nazi movement also inherited a military-economic potential that by 1938 was almost five times that of Italy, although the ratio between the two populations was only 5:3. And in most areas of military and production technology, Germany's scientists, engineers, and industrialists were level with or ahead of those of Britain and the United States.

The two nations' disparity in military traditions and expertise was almost equally great. Conscription, and the training in national loyalty, sense of duty, obedience, punctuality, and precision that went with it, dated from the early eighteenth century for Prussia's agricultural population. In theory military service had become universal in 1814, in practice from the 1860s onward. In Italy universal service had taken hold only in the 1870s. Nor did the *Regio Esercito* ever enjoy anything remotely resembling the social distinction conferred by Prussia's long if not unbroken run of victories from 1740 to 1871. After 1871, the Prussian lieutenant – but not his Italian counterpart – had "made his way through the world as a young god and the civilian reserve lieutenant at least as a demigod."[2]

Correspondingly, the Prusso-German army had a genuine mass following utterly without counterpart in Italy. The *Kriegervereine* ("warrior clubs") of veterans formed Imperial Germany's largest mass organization, encompassing in 1913 better than one in every seven adult male Germans.[3] As a result, the German army could take its pick of a

2. Friedrich Meinecke, *The German Catastrophe* (Boston, 1950), p. 12.
3. See Hansjoachim Henning, "Kriegervereine in den deutschen Westprovinzen," *Rheinische Vierteljahrsblätter* 32 (1963), pp. 430–58, and Klaus Saul, "Der 'Deutsche Kriegerbund.' Zur innenpolitischen Funktion eines 'nationalen' Verbandes in kaiserlichen Deutschland," MGM 6 (1969), pp. 95–130 (2,837,944 members, against the 2,483,661 members of the SPD trade unions); Gerd Hohorst et al., *Sozialgeschichtliches Arbeitsbuch II: Materialen zur Statistik des Kaiserreiches 1870–1914* (Munich, 1975), p. 23, gives the male population 20 or older as 17,757,000 (1911).

large pool of eager well-trained talent. The Italian army had no such good fortune, nor did anything in its barrack-square leadership tradition equip it to cope with the emptiness of the modern battlefield on which Prussian *Selbständigkeit* found its true home.

Last but not least, the ideological climates that the two regimes inherited were markedly different. Neither Rome, which over a millennium of history condemned Italian nationalism to share with the papacy, nor the *Risorgimento* that in Gramsci's despairing words "produced a bastard," nor the almost-lost Great War had produced myths easily bent to the service of nationalist dictatorship. German myths were of sterner stuff, and near-universal literacy and the relative absence of countervailing forces gave them a far deeper grip on the population than their Italian counterparts. The *Bildungsbürgertum*'s national mythology combined cults of the national Führer and of Germany's world mission with the Protestant Apocalypse and a supreme Hegelian confidence that spirit ruled over matter.

The apocalypse of the Great War reinforced and further spread the most radical elements in Germany's national myths, but had if anything a chastening effect on Italy. The enthusiasm of August 1914 gave way to a grimmer myth of German sacrifice and embittered endurance. The western front's "storm of steel" transformed Germany's infantrymen into *Frontkämpfer*, faces shadowed after fall 1916 by their medieval-modern "Siegfried-helmets," prototypes of the anti-Semitic "political soldiers" of the postwar and Nazi eras.[4] Italy's closest counterpart to that myth was far more exclusive; the epic of the *Arditi*, a myth for and in part about the supermen of urban, literate, literary Italy, rather than of the whole nation.[5] The momentary flush of national unity that helped ward off the Germans and Austro-Hungarians after Caporetto was short-lived.

Finally, the German and Italian myths of war's end were unequal in their virulence and appeal. In Germany the stab-in-the-back legend emerged effortlessly from the officer corps' hatred for civilians in general and Socialists and Jews in particular, from the agitations of the anti-Semites, from Protestant war theology (since God could not have

4.   For the origins of the myth in summer–fall 1916, see Gerd Krumeich, "Le soldat allemand sur la Somme," in Jean-Jacques Becker and Stéphane Audoin-Rouzeau eds., *Les Sociétés européennes et la guerre de 1914–1918* (Nanterre, 1990), pp. 367–74; for its later development, Volker R. Berghahn, *Der Stahlhelm: Bund der Frontsoldaten 1918–1935* (Düsseldorf, 1966), pp. 91–101 (but see also Jünger, *In Stahlgewittern* [Berlin, 1920]).
5.   See Rochat, *Arditi*.

failed the German people, the German home front must have failed God), and from the way in which the *Bildungsbürgertum* had cast the war as a struggle between spirit and matter in which matter was doomed to defeat – unless dark forces first blunted the edge of German *Geist*.[6] The legend's Italian counterpart was the myth of the "mutilated victory" (D'Annunzio's phrase), the thwarting of Italy's far-reaching war aims in 1918–19. Caporetto had allegedly been the work of Socialists and of other representatives of that "cowardly, ignorant, and corrupt little Italy that stabbed us in the back as we fought."[7] Then that "internal enemy" had combined with Italy's faithless allies to undo the final victory it had failed to prevent. But that myth, although a powerful force in middle-class opinion, failed to command the widespread assent that many elements of the *Dolchstosslegende* enjoyed in Germany. To the level-headed upon mature reflection, Austria-Hungary's disintegration in 1918 and the achievement of Italy's natural frontiers were already immense victories – whereas even moderate Germans utterly rejected the Reich's territorial mutilation in favor of the hated and despised Poles.

II

The two regimes built upon their inheritances edifices of markedly different shapes and sizes. The principal factors within the regimes that affected their expansionist zeal, fighting power, and staying power were three. First came their depth of ideological conviction, then the scope they gave to individual initiative and the extent to which they rewarded that initiative with "careers open to talent," and finally their ability and willingness to use terror.

Depth of conviction was in part a function of the convictions and personal qualities of the leaders themselves. Mussolini's ideology indeed celebrated force: "machine guns are adorable devices, especially when they serve an idea."[8] But Fascism, unlike Nazism or Marxism,

---

6. For the last two points, Arlie J. Hoover, "God and Germany in the Great War: The View of Protestant Pastors," *Canadian Review of Studies in Nationalism* 14:1 (1987), pp. 65–81.
7. Piero Jahier (a democratic *interventista* and later opponent of Fascism), September 1919 (". . . quella Italiuccia vigliacca, ignorante e corrotta che ci pugnalava alle spalle mentre combattevamo"), in Mario Isnenghi, *I vinti di Caporetto nella letteratura di guerra* (Padua, 1967), pp. 258–59; similarly OO 11:402.
8. OO 24:125.

lacked a teleological mechanism that rooted the dictator's geopolitical and domestic goals in the historical process. The "Fascist idea" also had to compete with the monarchy, the focus of loyalties for the officer corps and the pre-Fascist notables. From the Church it faced – behind a façade of astute collaboration with the regime – a hostility to Mussolini's neopaganism and total claims that markedly increased as the Fascist regime drew closer to its even more neopagan and totalitarian German counterpart after 1935. "Fascist faith" failed to inspire the working classes of north Italy and scarcely reached the peasantry of the South and islands. And Mussolini himself, while ever more impressed with German power, regarded his German partner as something of a freak – testimony to his own more skeptical nature.

Hitler by contrast genuinely believed that history was biology and that the Germans under his "unique" and "indispensable" leadership were bound for world mastery. His force of conviction and the comparative clarity and consistency of his ideology were a major source of the tighter grip of his personal cult and of the "National Socialist idea" upon the German people.[9] His ideology derived from and resonated with the ideas of nationalist-racist movement that had taken off in the 1890s and achieved a mass following in 1914–23. His cult of the will, of the primacy of spirit over matter, had even older and deeper roots. His promise to reverse the internal and external verdict of 1918 – peacefully or otherwise – evoked widespread enthusiasm. And thanks to the decapitation of the state in November 1918 and the mutual rivalry and weakness of the German churches, he faced far less competition for popular loyalties than did Mussolini.

At least as important as ideology in propelling the regimes' expansion was the scope that they gave, or could afford to give, to individual initiative and the extent to which they could reward their followers with careers and booty. Mussolini – unfortunately for his prospects but fortunately for Italy – took power *after* Socialist ineptitude, the recession of 1920-21, and the bludgeons of his movement had ended Italy's "two red years" of strikes and Socialist agitation. The indispensability of Fascist violence and disorder was no longer apparent to his conservative allies. And Mussolini's perpetual skepticism about his sometimes rebellious Party subordinates' abilities and loyalties, the myth of the

---

9.   See especially Kershaw, *Hitler Myth*, Chapters 7 and 8, for the Führer-cult's strength even in adversity; for its Italian counterpart, see (with caution) Piero Melograni, "The Cult of the Duce in Mussolini's Italy," *Journal of Contemporary History* 11 (1976), pp. 221–237.

"new state" that Fascism and its nationalist and bureaucratic allies claimed to incarnate, and the watchfulness of the monarchy, its military, and those same allies led him to demand subordination and order rather than decentralization and movement. Not for nothing did the regime's ideological journal bear the title *Gerarchia* – hierarchy. Inconvenient subordinates and potential rivals he curbed by sudden and repeated "changes of the guard" among his ministers. His aim was not the primacy of the *Partito Nazionale Fascista* over the state but a gradual fusion of the two that would stealthily unseat both Party rivals and conservative allies.

In the short term, Mussolini demanded the Party's subordination to the state, confident that that meant subordination to himself. In 1926-28 he publicly placed the PNF under the authority of the prefects at the periphery and of the determined and loyal Augusto Turati at the center. The Party provided candidates for leadership positions in the state and eventually pressed Party cards on the civil service. But the static and inefficient state bureaucracy, whether in the traditional ministries or in the quasi-governmental organizations that sprouted like mushrooms in the 1920s and 1930s, ultimately owed its loyalty to Mussolini only as chief of government, a position the king had given and the king might yet take away.[10] The Party retained freedom for bureaucratic expansion; by 1939 it was about the same size in relative terms as its German counterpart, encompassing roughly 6 percent of Italy's population to the NSDAP's 7 percent of the Germans in pre-war "Greater Germany." But the expansion of the PNF was a tightly controlled top-down exercise aimed less at power in the present than at gaining commanding positions for the inevitable succession struggle.[11] The PNF and its offshoots provided static jobs – *il posto* or *la sistemazione* – not the frenetic careers in domination and violence of their German counterparts. Even the Fascist Militia, the regime's "armed guard of the revolution" or SA and SS – failed to take wing; its ostensibly voluntary recruitment and its residue of old *squadristi* was not enough to make its members fanatical "political soldiers." Despite Mussolini's care to give the MVSN prominent combat roles in Libya,

---

10. For the bureaucracies and the regime, see especially Mariuccia Salvati, *Il Regime e gli impiegati: La nazionalizzazione piccolo-borghese nel ventennio fascista* (Bari, 1992).
11. Numbers and PNF policy: Emilio Gentile, *La via italiana al totalitarismo: Il partito e lo Stato nel regime fascista* (Rome, 1995), pp. 195–96 (2.63 million members, end 1939) and Chapter 5; for the NSDAP (5.3 million members in 1939), Michael Kater, *The Nazi Party: A Social Profile of Members and Leaders, 1919–1945* (Cambridge, 1983), Figure 1.

Ethiopia, and Spain, it remained a black-shirted and subordinate copy of the army, whose low level of fighting power it shared.[12] Nor did the army itself offer scope for initiative or reward effectiveness in battle, and the vast majority of the overage figures of doubtful leadership qualities with whom Fascist Italy began its last war remained firmly in place.

Germany was very different. Hitler became chancellor in an atmosphere of apocalyptic crisis. The deepest depression yet to strike industrial societies, the paralysis of the hated parliamentary state, the apparent Communist threat, and their own thirst for revenge upon the Left made his conservative allies willing to overlook until too late the violence and disorder of his *Machtergreifung*. Germany's preexisting polycratic structure and the decapitation of the state in 1918 helped create the weaknesses and divisions among the conservatives that Hitler exploited. And on top of their rivalries he imposed, even before Hindenburg's death in 1934, his own social Darwinist style. Whereas Mussolini merely preserved his personal authority by the "changes of the guard" that devoured the PNF's leaders, Hitler fostered a war of all against all for missions, authority, and booty that encompassed both Nazi Party and state, and progressively increased both his own power and his subordinates' loyalty to him personally. The winners were not merely the fittest, but the fittest as defined by Hitler, those whose aims and deeds coincided most closely with the Führer's wish.[13] Political free enterprise was the political mainspring of the regime, the complement from below of the Führer's foreign and internal policy program above. It was integrally connected to the regime's social mainspring and chief legacy: the career open to talent in bureaucratic piracy, warfare, and mass murder.[14]

The far greater relative strength of Hitler and his movement compared to their conservative allies and – paradoxically – the efforts of the victors to disarm Germany after 1918 combined to offer immense opportunities for ambition. Rearmament brought full employment, and lavishly rewarded the technically inclined. The expanding Party

---

12. Ceva, "Fascismo e ufficiali di professione," in *Ufficiali e società: Interpretazioni e modelli* (Milan, 1988), pp. 387–95.
13. For a good description of the technique, and Himmler's imitation of it, see Shlomo Aronson, *Reinhard Heydrich und die Frühgeschichte von Gestapo und SD* (Stuttgart, 1971), p. 112.
14. See Smelser, "Nazi Dynamics"; Martin Broszat, "Soziale Motivation und Führerbindung des Nationalsozialismus," VfZG 18:4 (1970), pp. 392–409; and, for a bold and influential statement of the long-term impact of Nazi careerism on German society, Dahrendorf, *Society and Democracy in Germany*, especially Chapter 25.

organizations offered astonishing careers to figures such as Reinhard Heydrich and Theodor Eicke, who rose – respectively – from disgraced ex-naval officer and police informer to "Himmler's Himmler" and highly decorated Waffen-SS division commander. And the armed forces, from the first round of breakneck expansion in 1934-36 to the full impact of the Nazi career open to *Leistung* in 1942-43, offered the greatest opportunities of all.

Last but decidedly not least of the features of the regimes that contributed to fighting power and staying power came the use of terror. Thanks to the circumstances under which he took power and the continuing resistance of the monarchy, of the officer corps, of upper-middle-class opinion, and of the Church, Mussolini's dictatorship was unable to wield terror in either peace or war. The German record was utterly different. Hitler, his Party, and the leaders of Germany's armed forces were determined to repair what they took to be the criminal weakness of their predecessors in 1917-18. And although the initial compromise between Hitler movement and German establishment did not allow him to dispense entirely with legality, SA, SS, and Gestapo terror was outside or above the law from the beginning. The judiciary, despite Hitler's frequent private attacks on its alleged "otherworldliness" and lack of "healthy *Volk*-consciousness," followed its Führer. By August 1944 the civilian courts alone had condemned to death at least 12,000 Germans and inhabitants of areas annexed to Germany. The *Wehrmacht*, not to be outdone, made up for the Imperial German Army's execution of a mere forty-eight men in 1914-18. By 1945 *Wehrmacht* courts had condemned at least 35,000 military personnel to death and had executed up to 22,000 of them for offenses ranging from desertion and theft to newly minted ideological crimes such as *Wehrkraftzersetzung*, "subversion of the will to fight."[15]

III

Finally, events and their sequence had striking effects on the two regimes' fighting power and staying power. Fascist Italy began its supreme military test, the war of 1940-43, with a string of catastrophic failures. Defeats inflicted not merely by the British but also by the

15. Civilian death sentences (1938 to August 1944): Martin Broszat, *The Hitler State* (London, 1981), pp. 340–41; military death sentences: Manfred Messerschmidt and Fritz Wüllner, *Die Wehrmachtjustiz im Dienst des Nationalsozialismus* (Baden-Baden, 1987), p. 87.

unwisely despised Greeks destroyed for good the prestige of dictator and regime. Italians thenceforth might fight for Italy, but with an enthusiasm sapped by the sensation that Italy's real enemy was its over-mighty Nazi ally and by the likelihood of good treatment on surrender by British and Americans. But willingness to die for the Duce sharply diminished, while war and blockade demoralized the home front, cutting food consumption by a quarter or more between 1939 and 1943. Hitler by contrast became Führer indeed – for his generals, his junior officers, his troops, and his people – by defeating France in 1940 where William II had failed. Victory seized the food, goods, and slave and conscript labor that kept the German people from feeling the full weight of the war until 1943–44. And with the launching of his racial-ideological war of annihilation in the East, Hitler locked in loyalty through forced complicity. The immensity of German crimes against POWs and civilians left the Soviet peoples little alternative but to fight for Stalin; those same crimes also left the Germans little alternative but to fight for Hitler.

Between 1922/33 and 1943/45 these three layers of factors and forces combined to produce the wide difference in lust for expansion and in *Leistung* that distinguished the two regimes. Fascist Italy lacked the ideological coherence and conviction needed to generate fanaticism. It lacked the courage to delegate authority and the political freedom of action to exploit the population's thirst for careers. Italy's lower levels of literacy, economic development, and national integration, its less virulent national mythology, and the pervasive influence of the Church also meant a shortage of talent for many such careers, a lowered receptiveness to Fascist appeals, and a wide gulf in most Italian units between officers and men. In Germany, racist fanaticism, "political free enterprise," and careers for masses eager to trample flat the remaining barriers of *Stand* drove Nazism forward against both internal and external foes. Germany's traditional military and economic prowess gave assurance of success. The dictator took the key decisions in foreign policy and war, but the pace and success of expansion also depended on the enthusiasm, ambition, and initiative of his subordinates at all levels.

In war the disparities in equipment, doctrine, training, and leadership between the German and Italian armed forces became immediately obvious. Ever-growing dismay at the inadequacy of the military preparations of armed forces and Fascist regime undermined what fighting spirit Italy possessed. Victory rarely came, and when it did rarely brought accelerated promotion – and defeat or dereliction of duty little punishment. In North Africa, Italy's longest campaign, only picked ground units such as *Ariete*, *Folgore*, and the youthful volunteers of the *Giovani Fascisti* emerged as equals to the Germans after making allowance for disparities in equipment. The case of the *Giovani Fascisti* is particularly instructive as an example of the regime's failure or inability to mobilize the fighting power of its strongest potential supporters. The unit originated in 1940 in a sort of conspiracy – against the army hierarchy – by enterprising junior officers and enthusiastic Fascist youth volunteers. Its members secured passage to North Africa in mid-1941 by luck and influence, and achieved divisional status and an enviable combat record with little encouragement from the regime. Only after 1943, under Mussolini's puppet "Italian Social Republic," did a Fascist regime shorn of most of its conservative allies override the continuing opposition of the military professionals and acquire, with German help, volunteer forces glued together by ideology.[16]

The German case, especially after 1942, was the epic of the *Giovani Fascisti* writ very large indeed. The perpetual emergency, appalling conditions, and immense casualties on the eastern front demanded in fullest measure the initiative from below that German tactical traditions encouraged. Ideological indoctrination – which troops in the East themselves eagerly and repeatedly demanded – taught that final victory was certain and surrender to the "Judeo-Bolshevik subhumans" unthinkable.[17] The career open to talent *in killing* of the "National Socialist people's army" and the Waffen-SS brought talent to the fore and fostered deep commitment born of gratitude to the regime. And terror of the regime's drumhead courts-martial and of Stalin's tender mercies concentrated the minds of all concerned on resistance to the last cartridge. Even in the West, against enemies who threatened their prisoners with Canada and Arizona rather than Siberia, the Germans fought with dogged inspiration. It was no accident that the unit that gave the Allies the greatest difficulty in the Normandy campaign was the 12th SS *Panzerdivision* "Hitler Jugend," formed from young enthusiasts under the leadership of eastern front veterans. So powerful was the force of belief that wounded "Hitler Jugend" prisoners refused medical care, preferring to "die for the Führer" until quelled by the

---

16. On the origins of the *Giovani Fascisti*, see particularly Alpheo Pagin, *Mussolini's Boys: La battaglia di Bir el Gobi* (Milan, 1976); on the RSI, Virgilio Ilari, "Il ruolo istituzionale delle forze armate della RSI e il problema della loro 'apoliticità,'" in Ilari and Antonio Sema, *Marte in orbace. Guerra, esercito e milizia nella concezione fascista della nazione* (Ancona, 1988), pp. 415–54.

17. Omer Bartov, *Hitler's Army* and *The Eastern Front, 1941–1945: German Troops and the Barbarization of Warfare* (London, 1985).

threat of transfusions with Jewish blood.[18] Nor did the end come easily in 1945; German forces were so reluctant to give in – even to the
Americans – that they killed 9,373 U.S. ground troops and aircrew in
April 1945, only slightly below the monthly average for the entire U.S.
advance from Normandy to the Elbe.[19]

The home fronts showed much the same pattern. In Italy, thanks to
early defeats, the public turned – "in the name of the best kind of
Italian nationalism" – *against* the regime that had brought Italy so
low.[20] The Church's semipublic rejection of the regime's efforts to
instill hatred of the enemy, the regime's own inner lack of conviction,
the growing inefficiency, corruption, and disloyalty of its organizations
and leaders, the steady decline in rations and living standards, and the
impossibility of using terror meant swift and bloodless collapse once
the king at last determined on Mussolini's removal.[21] The Fascist
regime's foremost legacy to its successor was a tradition of bureaucratic elephantiasis, inept or corrupt intervention in the economy, and
static mass-party patronage machines.

The German regime after 1938 was by contrast irreversible from
within short of a successful assassination of Hitler. The German home
front held on thanks to memory of the benefits the regime had
brought, to the relatively high standard of living enjoyed until
1943–44, to the satisfactions of dominating the Reich's millions of foreign and slave laborers, to conviction of racial superiority and devotion
to Hitler, to fear of both Himmler and Stalin, and to anger and thirst
for vengeance through the new V-weapons.[22] Only in the last months,
and then above all in the West, did the loyalty of key subordinates, of

18. John Colville, *The Fringes of Power: 10 Downing Street Diaries, 1939–1945* (New York,
    1985), pp. 497–98; for 12th SS *Panzerdivision* military performance, Max Hastings,
    Overlord: D-Day and the Battle for Normandy (New York, 1984), pp. 127–28, 317.
19. U.S. Army battle dead, European Theater: June 1944, 10,539; December 1944, 14,675;
    March 1945, 12,077; April 1945, 9,373; monthly average, June 1944–April 1945,
    10,972 (data: Department of the Army, *Army Battle Casualties and Non-Battle Deaths in
    World War II: Final Report*, 7 December 1941–31 December 1946 [Washington, D.C.,
    n.d.], p. 106).
20. Knox, *Mussolini*, pp. 268–72, 289 (quotation: *Questore* of Venice to Senise, 11 February
    1941).
21. For Church opposition at all levels to Mussolini's repeated exhortations to hate the
    enemy, Franco Malgeri, *La chiesa italiana e la guerra (1940–1945)* (Rome, 1985), espe-
    cially pp. 34–40; on corruption and disorganization, De Felice, *Mussolini l'alleato*
    (Turin, 1990–96), vol. 1, part 2, Chapter 5.
22. German workers, slave labor, and the war: Gillingham, "Ruhr Coal Miners and Hitler's
    War," and Lüdke, "German Workers and the Limits of Resistance"; on the V-weapons,
    Gerald Kirwin, "Waiting for Retaliation: A Study in Nazi Propaganda Behavior and
    German Civilian Morale," *Journal of Contemporary History* 16 (1981), pp. 565–83.

some combat units, and of the population begin to crumble under intolerable strain. Yet in essence the Nazi regime made good its promise that Germany would never suffer another November 1918. And along with the ruins it bequeathed to its successor, the shining new steel-and-glass *Leistungsgesellschaft* of the postwar era, came a society leveled and fierce individual expectations raised through the National Socialist career open to talent in war and mass murder. In that disquieting sense, if hardly in the way he had intended, Hitler indeed consummated the German Revolution.

FREQUENTLY CITED WORKS

An exhaustive account of sources consulted would be very long and serve little purpose. What follows is a listing of all works cited in the notes more than once, for use in conjunction with the list of abbreviations.

Absolon, Rudolf, "Das Offizierkorps des deutschen Heeres 1935–1945," pp. 247–68 in Hanns Hubert Hofmann, ed., *Das deutsche Offizierkorps, 1860–1960* (Boppard, 1980).

Aga Rossi, Elena, *Una nazione allo sbando: l'armistizio italiano del settembre 1943* (Bologna, 1993).

Allen, William S., *The Nazi Seizure of Power* (New York, 2nd ed., 1973).

Altrock, Constantin von, *Vom Sterben des deutschen Offizierkorps* (Berlin, 1922).

Aquarone, Alberto, *L'organizzazione dello Stato totalitario* (Turin, 1965).

Archives Parlementaires de 1787 à 1860, première série (Paris, 1867–1980).

Barberis, Walter, *Le armi del principe: La tradizione militare sabauda* (Turin, 1988).

Bartov, Omer, *Hitler's Army: Soldiers, Nazis, and War in the Third Reich* (Oxford, 1992).

Bernardi, Giovanni, *Il disarmo navale fra le due guerre mondiali (1919–1939)* (Rome, 1975).

Besson, Waldemar, "Zur Geschichte des nationalsozialistischen Führungsoffiziers (NSFO)," VfZG 9 (1961), pp. 76–116.

Biagini, Antonello, and Alessandro Gionfrida, eds., *Lo Stato Maggiore Generale tra le due guerre (verbali delle riunioni presiedute da Badoglio dal 1925 al 1937)* (Rome, 1997).

Boog, Horst, "Das Offizierkorps der Luftwaffe 1935–1945," pp. 269–325 in Hanns Hubert Hofmann, ed., *Das deutsche Offizierkorps, 1860–1960* (Boppard, 1980).

Borgert, Heinz-Ludger, "Grundzüge der Landkriegführung von Schlieffen bis Guderian," HDMG 9:427–584.

Bosworth, R. J. B., *Italy, the Least of the Great Powers* (Cambridge, 1979).

Botti, Ferruccio, *La logistica dell'esercito italiano, 1831–1981*, vols. 3, 4 (Rome, 1994–95).

"La logistica dei poveri: organizzazione dei rifornimenti e amministrazione dell'Esercito nel 1940," in *Memorie storiche militari 1992* (Rome, 1994), pp. 407–43.

"Problemi logistici del secondo anno di guerra – aspetti interforze," pp. 291–327 in Romain H. Rainero and Antonello Biagini, eds., *L'Italia in guerra: Il secondo anno – 1941* (Gaeta, 1992).

Bracher, Karl Dietrich, *Die Auflösung der Weimarer Republik* (Düsseldorf, 5th ed., 1984).

Bracher, Karl Dietrich, Wolfgang Sauer, and Gerhard Schulz, *Die nationalsozialistische Machtergreifung* (Cologne, 2nd rev. ed., 1962).

Broszat, Martin, *The Hitler State* (London, 1981)

Buccianti, Giovanni, *Verso gli accordi Mussolini-Laval* (Milan, 1984).

Cafagna, Luciano, *Dualismo e sviluppo nella storia d'Italia* (Padua, 1989).

Canevari, Emilio, *La guerra italiana* (Rome, 1948–49).

Carocci, Giampiero, *La politica estera dell'Italia fascista 1925–1928* (Bari, 1969).

Cavallero, Ugo, *Diario 1940–1943*, ed. Giuseppe Bucciante (Rome, 1984).

Ceva, Lucio, *Africa settentrionale 1940–1943* (Rome, 1982).

La condotta italiana della guerra: Cavallero e il Comando Supremo 1941/1942 (Milan, 1975).

"Fascismo e militari di professione," pp. 379–436 in Giuseppe Caforio and Piero Del Negro, eds., *Ufficiali e società: Interpretazioni e modelli* (Milan, 1988).

Le forze armate (Turin, 1981).

"Grande industria e guerra," pp. 33–53 in Romain H. Rainero and Antonello Biagini, eds., *L'Italia in guerra: il primo anno – 1940* (Rome, 1991).

"Rapporti fra industria bellica ed esercito," pp. 215–47 in Romain H. Rainero and Antonello Biagini, eds., *L'Italia in guerra: Il secondo anno – 1941* (Gaeta, 1992).

Ceva, Lucio, and Andrea Curami, *Industria bellica anni trenta* (Milan, 1992).

"Industria bellica e stato nell'imperialismo fascista degli anni '30," *Nuova Antologia* 2167 (1988), pp. 316–38.

La meccanizzazione dell'esercito italiano dalle origini al 1943, 2 vols. (Rome, 1989).

Chabod, Federico, *Storia della politica estera italiana dal 1870 al 1896*, vol. 1, *Le premesse* (Bari, paperback ed., 1971).

Class, Heinrich (pseud. Daniel Frymann), *Wenn ich der Kaiser wär'* (Leipzig, 5th exp. ed., 1914).

Cora, Giuliano, "Un diplomatico durante l'era fascista," *Storia e politica* 5:1 (1966), pp. 88–98.

Creveld, Martin van, *Fighting Power* (Westport, Connecticut, 1982).

Curami, Andrea, "Commesse belliche e approvvigionamenti di materie prime," pp. 55–66 in Romain H. Rainero and Antonello Biagini, eds., *L'Italia in guerra: il primo anno – 1940* (Rome, 1991).

"Piani e progetti dell'aeronautica italiana, 1939–1943: Stato maggiore e industrie," *Italia contemporanea* 187 (1992), pp. 243–61.

"I riflessi delle operazioni nello sviluppo della Regia Aeronautica," pp. 493–518 in Romain H. Rainero and Antonello Biagini, eds., *L'Italia in guerra: Il secondo anno – 1941* (Gaeta, 1992).

Dear, I. C. B. and M. R. D. Foot, eds., *The Oxford Companion to the Second World War* (Oxford, 1995).

De Felice, Renzo, ed., *Mussolini e Hitler* (Florence, 1983).
De Felice, Renzo, *Mussolini il duce*, 2 vols. (Turin, 1974–78).
  Mussolini il fascista, 2 vols. (Turin, 1966–68).
  Mussolini il rivoluzionario (Turin, 1965).
  Mussolini l'alleato, 2 vols. (Turin, 1990–96).
De Risio, Carlo, *Generali, servizi segreti e fascismo* (Milan, 1978).
Di Giovanni, Marco, *I paracadutisti italiani: Volontari, miti e memoria della seconda guerra mondiale* (Gorizia, 1991).
Di Nolfo, Ennio, *Mussolini e la politica estera italiana 1922–1933* (Padua, 1960).
Deist, Wilhelm, "Zur Geschichte des preussischen Offizierkorps 1890–1918," pp. 39–57 in Hanns Hubert Hofmann, ed., *Das deutsche Offizierkorps, 1860–1960* (Boppard, 1980).
Deist, Wilhelm, Manfred Messerschmidt, Hans–Erich Volkmann, and Wolfram Wette, *Germany and the Second World War*, vol. 1, *The Build–Up of German Aggression* (London, 1990).
Demeter, Karl, *The German Officer–Corps in Society and State 1650–1945* (London, 1965).
Domarus, Max, ed., *Hitler: Reden und Proklamationen* (Munich, 1965).
Doronzo, Raffaele, *Folgore! . . . e si moriva: Diario di un paracadutista* (Milan, 1978).
Dülffer, Jost, *Weimar, Hitler und die Marine* (Düsseldorf, 1973).
Engel, Gerhard, *Heeresadjutant bei Hitler* (Stuttgart, 1974).
Faldella, Emilio, *L'Italia e la seconda guerra mondiale* (Bologna, 1960).
Falter, Jürgen W., *Hitlers Wähler* (Munich, 1991).
Farneti, Paolo, "Social Conflict, Parliamentary Fragmentation, Institutional Shift, and the Rise of Fascism: Italy," in Juan J. Linz and Alfred Stepan, eds., *The Breakdown of Democratic Regimes* (Baltimore, 1978).
Fischer, Fritz, *Germany's Aims in the First World War* (New York, 1967).
Frauenholz, Eugen von, *Entwicklungsgeschichte des deutschen Heerwesens*, vol. 5, *Das Heerwesen des XIX. Jahrhunderts* (Berlin, 1941).
Gallarati Scotti, Tommaso, "Idee e orientamenti politici e religiosi al Comando Supremo: appunti e ricordi," pp. 509–15 in Giuseppe Rossini, ed., *Benedetto XV, i cattolici e la prima guerra mondiale* (Rome, 1963).
Gentile, Emilio, *Le origini dell'ideologia fascista (1918–1925)* (Bari, 1975).
  Storia del partito fascista 1919–1922: Movimento e milizia (Bari, 1989).
Geyer, Michael, *Deutsche Rüstungspolitik 1860–1980* (Frankfurt a. M., 1984).
Geyer, "German Strategy in the Age of Machine Warfare, 1914–1945," pp. 527–97 in Peter Paret, ed., *Makers of Modern Strategy* (Princeton, 1988).
Gillingham, John, "Ruhr Coal Miners and Hitler's War," *Journal of Social History*, Summer 1982, pp. 637–53.
Goebbels, Joseph, *Die Tagebücher von Joseph Goebbels: Sämtliche Fragmente*, eds. Elke Fröhlich and Jana Richter (Munich, 1987–96).
Gramsci, Antonio, *Il Risorgimento* (*Quaderni del carcere*, vol. 3)(Turin, 1974).
Griffin, Roger, *The Nature of Fascism* (London, 1993).
Guariglia, Raffaele, *Ricordi* (Naples, 1949).
Gudmundsson, Bruce I., *Stormtroop Tactics: Innovation in the German Army, 1914–1918* (Westport, Connecticut, 1989).
Halder, Franz, *Hitler als Feldherr* (Munich, 1949).

Hamilton, Richard F., *Who Voted for Hitler?* (Princeton, 1982).

Hildebrand, Klaus, *The Foreign Policy of the Third Reich* (Berkeley, 1973).

Hanlon, Gregory, *The Twilight of a Military Tradition: Italian Aristocrats and European Conflicts, 1560–1800* (London, 1998).

Hillgruber, Andreas, "The German Military Leaders' View of Russia Prior to the Attack on the Soviet Union," pp. 169–85 in Bernd Wegner, ed., *From Peace to War: Germany, Soviet Russia and the World, 1939–1941* (Providence, 1997).

Hitlers Strategie (Frankfurt, 1965).

Hitler, Adolf, *Monologe im Führerhauptquartier 1941–1944* (Hamburg, 1980).

Hofmann, Hanns Hubert, ed., *Das deutsche Offizierkorps, 1860–1960* (Boppard, 1980).

Horn, Wolfgang, *Führerideologie und Parteiorganization in der NSDAP (1919–1933)* (Düsseldorf, 1972).

Hughes, Daniel J., *The King's Finest: A Social and Bureaucratic Profile of Prussia's General Officers, 1871–1914* (New York, 1987).

Hürten, Heinz, "Das Offizierkorps des Reichsheeres," pp. 231–45 in Hanns Hubert Hofmann, ed., *Das deutsche Offizierkorps, 1860–1960* (Boppard, 1980).

Ilari, Virgilio, *Storia del servizio militare in Italia* (Rome, 1989–).

Kerekes, Lajos, *Abendämmerung einer Demokratie* (Vienna, 1966).

Kershaw, Ian, *Hitler, 1889–1936: Hubris* (London, 1998).

Kotze, Hildegard von, and Helmut Krausnick, eds., *"Es spricht der Führer"* (Gütersloh, 1966).

Knox, MacGregor, "The Fascist Regime, Its Foreign Policy and Its Wars: An 'Anti-Anti-Fascist' Orthodoxy?," *Contemporary European History* 4:3 (1995), pp. 347–65.

Mussolini Unleashed, 1939–1941: Politics and Strategy in Fascist Italy's Last War (Cambridge, 1982).

"L'ultima guerra dell'Italia fascista," in Bruna Micheletti and Pier Paolo Poggio, eds., *L'Italia in guerra 1940–43* (Brescia, 1991), pp. 17–32.

Krieger, Leonard, *The German Idea of Freedom* (Chicago, 1972).

Kroener, Bernhard R., "Auf dem Weg zu einer 'nationalsozialistischen Volksarmee.' Die soziale Öffnung des Heeresoffizierkorps im Zweiten Weltkrieg," pp. 651–82 in Martin Broszat, Klaus-Dietmar Henke, and Hans Woller, eds., *Von Stalingrad zur Währungsreform.: Zur Sozialgeschichte des Umbruchs in Deutschland* (Munich, 1988).

"Strukturelle Veränderungen in der militärischen Gesellschaft des Dritten Reiches," pp. 267–296 in Michael Prinz and Rainer Zitelmann, eds., *Nationalsozialismus und Modernisierung* (Darmstadt, 1991)

Lahne, Werner, *Unteroffiziere Gestern-Heute-Morgen* (Herford, 1975).

Lüdke, Alf, "The Appeal of Exterminating 'Others': German Workers and the Limits of Resistance," *Journal of Modern History* 64 (supplement)(1992), pp. 46–67.

Lyttelton, Adrian, *The Seizure of Power* (Boston, 1973).

Malagodi, Olindo, *Conversazioni della guerra (1914–1919)*, 2 vols. (Milan, 1960).

Mancinelli, Giuseppe, *Dal fronte dell'Africa settentrionale (1942–43)* (Milan, 1970).

Mason, Tim, *Arbeiterklasse und Volksgemeinschaft* (Opladen, 1975)

"Innere Krise und Angriffskrieg 1938/1939," pp. 158–88 in Friedrich

Forstmaier and Hans-Erich Volkmann, eds., *Wirtschaft und Rüstung am Vorabend des Zweiten Weltkrieges* (Düsseldorf, 1975).

Nazism, Fascism and the Working Class (Cambridge, 1995).

"The Primacy of Politics: Politics and Economics in National Socialist Germany," pp. 53–76 in his *Nazism, Fascism and the Working Class* (Cambridge, 1995).

Matuschka, Edgar Graf von, "Die Beförderung in der Praxis," pp. 153–76 in Gerhard Papke, Hans Black, Edgar Graf von Matuschka, and Rainer Wohlfeil, *Untersuchungen zur Geschichte des Offizierkorps: Anciennität und Beförderung nach Leistung* (Stuttgart, 1962).

Messerschmidt, Manfred, "Das Preussisch-deutsche Offizierkorps 1850–1890," pp. 21–37 in Hanns Hubert Hofmann, ed., *Das deutsche Offizierkorps, 1860–1960* (Boppard, 1980).

Messerschmidt, Manfred, and Ursula von Gersdorff, eds., *Offiziere im Bild von Dokumenten aus drei Jahrhunderten* (Stuttgart, 1964).

Minniti, Fortunato, "Aspetti organizzativi del controllo sulla produzione bellica in Italia," *Clio*, 4/1977, pp. 305–40.

Montanari, Mario, *La campagna di Grecia* (Rome, 1980).

L'esercito italiano alla vigilia della seconda guerra mondiale (Rome, 1982).

Moore, Barrington, Jr., *Social Origins of Dictatorship and Democracy: Lord and Peasant in the Making of the Modern World* (Boston, 1966).

Mori, Renato, "Verso il riavvicinamento fra Hitler e Mussolini," *Storia e politica* 15:1 (1976), pp. 70–120.

Mosse, George L., *The Nationalization of the Masses* (New York, 1975).

Müller, Klaus-Jürgen, *Das Heer und Hitler* (Stuttgart, 1969).

Oberkommando des Heeres, H.Dv. 300/1, *Truppenführung* (Berlin, 1936).

Orlow, Dietrich, *The History of the Nazi Party*, 2 vols. (Pittsburgh, 1969–73).

Ormos, Maria, "Sur les causes de l'échec du pacte danubien," *Acta Historica* 14:1–2 (1968), pp. 21–83.

Papke, Gerhard, Hans Black, Edgar Graf von Matuschka, and Rainer Wohlfeil, *Untersuchungen zur Geschichte des Offizierkorps: Anciennität und Beförderung nach Leistung* (Stuttgart, 1962).

Paret, Peter, *Yorck and the Era of Prussian Reform* (Princeton, 1966).

Petersen, Jens, *Hitler-Mussolini* (Tübingen, 1973).

Peukert, Detlev J. K., *The Weimar Republic: The Crisis of Classical Modernity* (New York, 1992).

Pirelli, Alberto, *Taccuini 1922/1943* (Bologna, 1984).

Prinz, Michael, and Rainer Zitelmann, eds., *Nationalsozialismus und Modernisierung* (Darmstadt, 1991).

Ramcke, Hermann, *Vom Schiffjungen zum Fallschirmjäger-General* (preface by Hermann Göring)(Berlin, 1943).

Répaci, Antonino, *La marcia su Roma* (Milan, rev. ed., 1972).

Roatta, Mario, *Otto milioni di baionette* (Verona, 1946).

Rochat, Giorgio, *Gli arditi della Grande Guerra: Origini, battaglie e miti* (Gorizia, rev. ed., 1997).

L'esercito italiano da Vittorio Veneto a Mussolini (1919–1925) (Bari, 1967).

Militari e politici nella preparazione della campagna d'Etiopia (Milan, 1971).

Rosenberg, Alfred, *Das politische Tagebuch Alfred Rosenbergs aus den Jahren 1934/35 und 1939/40*, ed. H.-G. Seraphim (Göttingen, 1956).

Rumschöttel, Hermann, "Bildung und Herkunft der bayerischen Offiziere 1866 bis 1914," MGM 2 (1970), pp. 81–131.

Samuels, Martin, *Command or Control? Command, Training and Tactics in the British and German Armies, 1888–1918* (London, 1995).

Schottelius, Herbert, and Gustav-Adolf Caspar, "Die Organisation des Heeres 1933–1939," HDMG 7:289–399.

Schulz, Gerhard, *Aufstieg des Nationalsozialismus* (Frankfurt, 1975).

Sema, Antonio, "La cultura dell'esercito," pp. 91–116 in *Cultura e società negli anni del fascismo* (Milan, 1987).

Serra, Enrico, *Tempi duri: Guerra e Resistenza* (Bologna, 1996).

Smelser, Ronald, "Nazi Dynamics, German Foreign Policy, and Appeasement," pp. 31–47 in Wolfgang J. Mommsen and Lothar Kettenacker, eds., *The Fascist Challenge and the Policy of Appeasement* (London, 1983).

Stumpf, Reinhard, *Die Wehrmacht-Elite: Rang- und Herkunftsstruktur der deutschen Generale und Admirale 1933–1945* (Boppard, 1982).

Sullivan, Brian R., "A Thirst for Glory: Mussolini, the Italian Military, and the Fascist Regime, 1922–1936" (Ph.D. dissertation, Columbia University, 1984).

Thies, Jochen, *Architekt der Weltherrschaft* (Düsseldorf, 1976).

Turner, Henry Ashby, Jr., *Hitler's Thirty Days to Power: January 1933* (London, 1996).

Veneruso, Danilo, *La vigilia del fascismo: Il primo ministero Facta nella crisi dello stato liberale in Italia* (Bologna, 1968).

Vigezzi, Brunello, *L'Italia neutrale* (Milan, 1966).

Vivarelli, Roberto, *Storia delle origini del fascismo* (Bologna, 1991).

Vogelsang, Thilo, "Neue Dokumente zur Geschichte der Reichswehr 1930–1933," VfZG 2:4 (1954), pp. 397–436.

Wegner, Bernd, "Das Führerkorps der Waffen-SS im Kriege," pp. 327–50 in Hanns Hubert Hofmann, ed., *Das deutsche Offizierkorps, 1860–1960* (Boppard, 1980).

Wehler, Hans-Ulrich, *Deutsche Gesellschaftsgeschichte* (Munich, 1989–).

Winkler, Heinrich August and Elizabeth Müller-Luckner, eds., *Die deutsche Staatskrise 1930–1933: Handlungsspielräume und Alternativen* (Munich, 1992).

Wohlfeil, Rainer, "Heer und Republik (1918–1933)," HDMG 6:11–303.

—*Vom stehenden Heer des Absolutismus zur allgemeinen Wehrpflicht (1789–1814)*, HDMG, vol. 2.

Wollstein, Günter, Das *"Grossdeutschland" der Paulskirche: Nationale Ziele in der bürgerlichen Revolution 1848–49* (Düsseldorf, 1977).

Zitelmann, Rainer, *Hitler: Selbstverständnis eines Revolutionärs* (Hamburg, 1987).

INDEX

The purpose of the index is analytical and comparative; matters not directly related to the argument do not appear.